ALCATRAZ JUSTICE

The Cell House

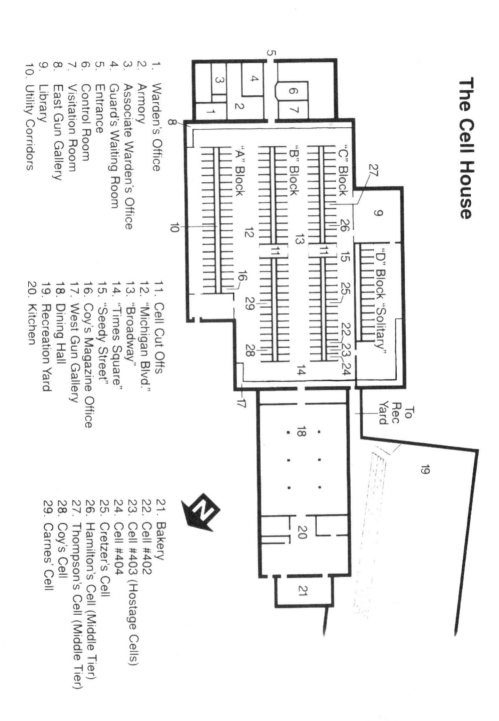

1. Warden's Office
2. Armory
3. Associate Warden's Office
4. Guard's Waiting Room
5. Entrance
6. Control Room
7. Visitation Room
8. East Gun Gallery
9. Library
10. Utility Corridors

11. Cell Cut Offs
12. "Michigan Blvd."
13. "Broadway"
14. "Times Square"
15. "Seedy Street"
16. Coy's Magazine Office
17. West Gun Gallery
18. Dining Hall
19. Recreation Yard
20. Kitchen

21. Bakery
22. Cell #402
23. Cell #403 (Hostage Cells)
24. Cell #404
25. Cretzer's Cell
26. Hamilton's Cell (Middle Tier)
27. Thompson's Cell (Middle Tier)
28. Coy's Cell
29. Carnes' Cell

ALCATRAZ JUSTICE

The Rock's Most Famous Murder Trial

Ernest B. Lageson

CREATIVE ARTS BOOK COMPANY
Berkeley ∾ California

Grateful acknowledgment is made to the following organizations
for permission to publish photographs: San Francisco History Center;
San Francisco Public Library for the photos on pages 151, 152, 153 (Dan
Deasey), 162, and 166; Golden Gate NRA for the photos on pages 159, 160,
161, 163, 164, and 165 (top); UPI/Corbis-Bettman for the photos of Warden
Johnston on pages 165 and 166.

For information contact:
Creative Arts Book Company
833 Bancroft Way
Berkeley, California 94710
www.creativeartsbooks.com

ISBN 088739-408-6

Library of Congress Catalog Number 2002101342

Printed in the United States of America

To Douglas Quinlan, Lawrason Driscoll, and James E. Martin, outstanding trial lawyers, men of integrity, and mentors of mine

ACKNOWLEDGMENTS

I received help from a number of people in the preparation of this book, and I am sincerely grateful to them all.

First, I wish to recognize the contribution of my father, who provided a great deal of first hand information regarding both the escape attempt and the trial. I am also grateful for the help of other members of my family. My daughter Kristine Cardall provided invaluable aid as my editor and collaborator. My son Ernie designed the cover and assisted with the technical and artistic aspects of the work. Finally, my wife Jeanne contributed her thoughts, time, and encouragement to help make the whole thing happen.

I also wish to acknowledge and pay tribute to the many outstanding trial lawyers with whom and against whom I tried cases throughout my career. Much of what I learned from those fine practitioners prepared me to write this book.

I am particularly appreciative of the research support I received from the staff at the National Archives in San Bruno, California, especially from Lisa Miller, Neil Thomsen, and Claude Hopkins. I also wish to thank Michael Griffith, Archivist for the U.S. District Court, and Irene Stachura, librarian, and Bill Kooiman of the staff at the National Maritime Museum. Thanks too, to the staffs of the San Francisco, Berkeley, Oakland, University of California, and Boalt Hall School of Law libraries for facilitating my research. I want to specially acknowledge the help of Patricia Akre, Photograph Curator of the San Francisco Public Library History Center for her invaluable help in providing historical photographs. Chuck Stucker, a former resident of the island, deserves enormous thanks for all his help with photographs as well as his general support and encouragement. Thanks to Jennie Peuron for sharing with me her research concerning Sam Shockley, part of her work in writing the play *Crazy Sam*.

The Park Rangers of the Golden Gate National Recreation Area, particularly John Cantwell, were extraordinarily cooperative, and allowed me unlimited access to various Alcatraz venues. They are a dedicated group of professionals who do a wonderful job.

Special thanks go to a number of individuals who gave freely of their time and recollection. The following persons greatly assisted my research: The late Jim Quillan, an author and former inmate, who was confined in

D block at the time of the riot; Mrs. Kay Sullivan, the widow of attorney William Sullivan, who defended Sam Shockley; Mrs. Annette Newmark, the widow of Aaron Vinkler, one of the attorneys for Miran Thompson; Lois Vinkler and Hermine Simon, the daughters of Aaron Vinkler; Elisabeth Burch, the daughter of Dr. John Alden; Archer Zamloch, the attorney who defended Clarence Carnes; attorney George Finnigan, former law partner of Aaron Vinkler and long-time San Francisco practitioner; the late Judge Joseph Karesh, former assistant U. S. attorney and counsel for the Alcatraz prison administration; and Donald Martin, a close friend of my father and former Alcatraz custodial officer.

Author's Note

In May of 1946 Alcatraz Island Prison experienced the bloodiest and most violent escape attempt in its history. Six inmates invaded a gun gallery and obtained the weapons stored there. They captured the cell house and took nine custodial officers, one of whom was my father, as hostages. During the uprising three of the prisoners and one of the hostages, Officer William Miller, were killed. Five other hostages, including my father, were wounded. The three surviving inmates, Sam Shockley, Miran Thompson, and Clarence Carnes were charged with the murder of Officer Miller.

In *Alcatraz Justice* I have presented an historical account of the trial of those three defendants. It is based on personal knowledge of the case, extensive research, and my thirty-five years experience as a trial lawyer. Where necessary, I have contributed my own interpretation and portrayal of events when the precise facts are unknown.

I learned a great deal about the events from my father, who survived the terrifying experience and was a key witness at the trial. My independent research included review of hundreds of newspaper accounts of the escape attempt and the trial, the FBI investigation report of more than 1100 pages; the trial transcript which exceeded 2500 pages; and hundreds of pages of court files, court opinions, appellate briefs, and related documents. Among those I interviewed during my research were the late Jim Quillen and attorney Archer Zamloch. Quillen was an Alcatraz inmate at the time of the uprising and and was a witness on behalf of Shockley at the trial. Zamloch was Carnes's defense attorney. *Alcatraz Justice* is the most accurate and authoritative account of one of the landmark trials of the Federal District Court for Northern California.

ALCATRAZ JUSTICE

1
—

The sound of a special boat run was always of particular interest to those who lived on Alcatraz. Off duty officers, wives, and children starting their summer vacation all turned a curious eye to the dock on the morning of Tuesday, June 25, 1946 when Miran Thompson, Sam Shockley and Clarence Carnes arrived to board the island launch. The scene on the dock was tense. In addition to several uniformed guards, three of whom would accompany the prisoners, Warden James A. Johnston was present. Johnston had chosen to deliver the three defendants to court personally, and his presence heightened the curiosity of the spectators. All that the children knew was that some prisoners were being taken off the island. The adult observers, however, realized that the survivors of the bloodiest escape attempt in the history of Alcatraz were on their way to face murder charges arising from the death of Officer William Miller. Most hoped it would be the first step toward their conviction and execution.

The bay was calm and the weather warm for June. The prop-wash of the launch idling in its slip created enough disturbance in the water to interest a few sea gulls in the possibility of an early morning snack. The two sea lions seen regularly off the island's northwest corner made a disinterested pass by the dock, as they headed for their fishing grounds below the Power House Tower. The waves splashed quietly over the rocks at the water's edge.

Miran Thompson, his felt hat at a rakish angle, looked boldly from side to side as he boarded the boat, smiling at his companions and clearly enjoying the stares of the onlookers. The three, wearing handcuffs and shackled to one another, were placed on one of the forward benches in the main cabin, surrounded by their escort of custodial officers. As the launch pulled away from the dock, nineteen year old Clarence "Joe" Carnes looked across the calm water to Marin County and the northern shore of the San Francisco Bay. He studied the coastline and thought about what it would have been like if they had succeeded in getting off the island. Armed with guns from the guard towers and gun gallery, they would have herded their hostages ashore, commandeered automobiles, and eventually made their way to freedom.

Turning his gaze from the Marin hills, the young man recalled with regret the ill-fated escape attempt of two months earlier. Things had happened so fast that day that he had been swept along on a wave of incredible excitement. Given the wisdom and courage of the participants, and the meticulous planning of the leader, Bernard Coy, Carnes had been convinced that the escape would succeed. Now he was being arraigned on a charge of first degree murder and faced the death penalty. The youngster was frightened.

Carnes was a relative newcomer to Alcatraz, having been transferred from Leavenworth on July 6, 1945. When he arrived at the island prison, the full-blooded Choctaw Indian was the youngest inmate ever to serve time on the Rock. On the morning of May 2, 1946, Carnes had not yet been assigned to a permanent work detail and was lounging in his cell. Coy, who worked as a cell house orderly, approached the young inmate with the startling news that an escape was coming down that afternoon, and an invitation to join if he wished. Carnes had been flattered and excited that Coy included him, and readily agreed to join. Coy assured him that the plan was flawless. They would first capture the cell house, then the prison launch, and escape to the Marin shore. Coy claimed things were so well planned that they would be able to get off the island without having to injure any guards. They would take several hostages with them to aid in their flight to freedom once they were on the mainland.

But the attempt had failed. At no time during the escape had Carnes ever considered the possibility that the adventure might cost him his life. But now, that likelihood loomed large.

2
—

Born in McAlester, Oklahoma in 1927, Carnes had grown up among the rolling hills of the eastern part of the state along the banks of Eufala Lake. His father, Jimmy, had no regular occupation and the family moved a great deal as he sought employment. It was an unhappy childhood for Clarence, for no matter how hard his father tried, there was never enough food, money, or love.

The elder Carnes believed strongly in education and enrolled his son in Jones Academy, a nearby boarding school. Although Jones was a private institution, tuition was waived for Native Americans. While it was a fine school, unfortunately for Carnes, Jones Academy became his criminal training ground. Seeking the camaraderie and affection he never had at home, he became the youngest member of a school gang. His criminal career began with petty thievery and minor school infractions. Clarence was a small boy, but made up for what he lacked in size with aggressiveness and fearlessness. His need for acceptance led him to solve problems and settle disputes with his fists. When the fifteen-year-old gang leader was jailed for armed robbery in the fall of 1937, Carnes at the tender age of ten emerged as the gang leader.

In the summer of 1943 Carnes and a friend, Cecil Berry, attempted to rob a service station using a .22 pistol they had stolen in a residential burglary. It was a hot, July day and the service station attendant, twenty-two-year-old W. M. Weyland, was sitting in the station office drinking an orange soda. When Carnes demanded money, Weyland, both amused and annoyed, leapt to his feet and hurled the half full bottle at Carnes, sneering "Get outta here you fuckin' half breed and take Tonto there with you." Carnes fired in anger, killing Weyland instantly. The two teenagers fled in panic without touching the cash drawer. They were captured a few hours later as they headed for the safety of the Atoka Indian Reservation. The next day, while being fed the noon meal, the two boys overpowered the jailers on duty and escaped. Captured in a matter of hours, Carnes pleaded guilty to murder, assault, and escape and received a life sentence.

After serving a year and a half as a model prisoner in the McAlester State Prison, Carnes was transferred to the Granite State Reformatory. One afternoon in the spring of 1945, he and two fellow prisoners slipped away from the rock quarry to which they were assigned. They kidnapped farmer, Charlie Nance, working in a nearby field, stole his truck, and headed for Texas.

The trio was soon captured by the FBI and taken to Oklahoma City to face federal charges. Carnes pleaded nolo contendere to kidnapping and escape and was sentenced to ninety-nine years for violation of the Lindbergh Act and five years for escape. At the age of eighteen, therefore, he was facing a life sentence in the state prison of Oklahoma plus 99 years in the federal prison system. After a brief confinement at Leavenworth Federal Prison, he was transferred to Alcatraz.

Following the indoctrination procedures and interviews every new Alcatraz prisoner undergoes, Carnes requested a work assignment in the prison kitchen. No jobs were available so he opted for idle status, which involved spending most of the time in his cell. Coy, the library orderly, maintained a small work space in one of the empty cells across the corridor from Carnes's cell, and the two men were in daily contact. They became friends and talked frequently. Coy, several years older than the youngster, adopted a paternal relationship toward him, in part because of the enormous sentences Carnes had to serve.

At forty-six years of age, Bernie Coy was one of the elder statesmen of the Alcatraz convict population. Raised in the backwoods of Kentucky, he had suffered through an unhappy and violent childhood. His father was an unsuccessful dirt farmer, who drank heavily and frequently beat his wife and seven children. Driven from home in his early teens by the conditions that existed there, Coy joined the Army and served with distinction during World War I. After he married, he deserted from the military and attempted to make a living as a painter and decorator. Unable to support his family, he drifted into a life of crime. After various arrests and convictions, he was sentenced to the federal penitentiary in Atlanta for bank robbery. His love of the outdoors and the inability to roam the hills he so loved made prison life unbearable. He became involved in numerous violent assaults with other prisoners, often using weapons, and in a short time was looked upon as an incorrigible. In July of 1937 he was transferred to Alcatraz.

There he became a model prisoner. He read extensively, and refined his skill as an artist, even teaching the art of oil painting to his fellow prisoners. He also became an accomplished "cell house lawyer," filing writs and briefs of his own and on behalf of fellow prisoners.

In November of 1940, he filed what he believed to be a winning brief to vacate his sentence based on a violation of his right against double jeopardy. After reviewing his in pro per filing, the federal court appointed legal counsel to assist him, which convinced Coy that his claim was meritorious. After a four year legal battle, however, his arguments were rejected, leaving him a bitter man. From that time on he dedicated himself to finding a way of escaping from the impregnable island penitentiary.

Coy concluded that a successful escape had to originate from within the cell house. He determined that any escape had to be supported by firearms to match the heavy armament maintained in the various guard towers. A rifle and pistol were part of the equipment of the officer in the west gun gallery of the cell house, and this was where Coy felt a break should start. Another reason that the break had to start with an invasion of the west gun gallery was that all the cell house keys were stored there. Included among those keys was #107, which opened the rear cell house door, the only realistic escape route from the building. He also believed that a breakout had to be by boat, namely the prison launch. Swimming the mile-and-a-half to the mainland through the chill water and treacherous tides was impossible. Several escape attempts in the past had involved men going into the water, and none of them had succeeded. Finally, he decided that hostages would be needed, again to equalize the overwhelming advantage maintained by the custodial force.

Coy volunteered for duty as a cell house orderly and in time received two such assignments. In the morning he worked as the library orderly, delivering books, magazines, and other reading material from the library to the various cells. In the afternoon he was a clean-up orderly, sweeping, mopping, waxing, and dusting the cell house. With these jobs he had unlimited access to the cell house to study the physical structures of the building, and observe the activities of the custodial force.

The main cell house contained three cellblocks oriented east and west. Along the north side was A block, which had never been remodeled from the days when Alcatraz had been an Army installation. It was used for storage and housed no inmates. B and C blocks consisted of two rows of cells, three tiers high, each block containing 174 cells. A utility corridor ran down the center of each block containing the water, sewer and electrical lines, which led to the rear wall of each cell. D block, which contained the isolation and solitary cells, was a separate enclosure on the south side of the building, connected to the main cell house by a single door at the west end. The general prison population was housed in B and C blocks. The inmates in D block were those who could not be trusted in the general population, either because they constituted a threat to themselves or others, were escape threats, or were being disciplined. The D block inmates spent virtually all their time in their cells. They only left their six by nine-foot cubicles for a weekly shower and an hour in the recreation yard once every week or two.

Across the east and west ends of the main cell house were the east and west gun galleries. Each was a two-tiered, barred cage at approximately the same height above the cell house floor as the two upper tiers of cells in B and C blocks. The galleries were four feet wide, with vertical bars across the front. These bars were approximately 5 inches apart and were reinforced by horizontal bars at one and a half foot intervals. Ladders connected the levels of the gallery and a sheet of steel 39 inches high protected the lower portion of each tier. The west gun gallery projected into D block with soundproof doors between the D block and main cell house portions of the gallery. The gallery ran along the west wall of D block and approximately forty feet along the south wall. The west gallery was manned at all times, but the east gallery was only occupied when all the inmates were in the cell house.

The breakthrough in Coy's planning came when he discovered a defect in the bar structure of the west gun gallery. He noted that where the vertical bars curved at the top of the gallery and angled back to the west wall, there was no crossbar reinforcement. He correctly concluded that was the weakest point, and the bars there could be spread sufficiently to allow him to enter the gallery. He designed a simple, yet powerful bar spreader, employing the screw jack principle. He also calculated that he would only have to move two adjacent bars one inch each to create a large enough opening for him to enter.

The preparation involved months of work. The bar spreader was fabricated surreptitiously in the prison machine shop and smuggled into the cell house. It came into the kitchen in the false bottom of a garbage can and was then hidden with the plumbing equipment stored in the utility corridor of C block.

Coy observed that each day between 1:00 and 2:00 P.M. the officer on duty in the west gun gallery, Bert Burch, would retire to the D block side of the gallery. This was a quiet time in the cell house and Burch would sit reading or dozing in the afternoon sun. To perpetuate this habit, Coy supplied the guard with the latest edition of all the popular magazines as soon as they were received in the library.

The plan of escape required the assistance of several other inmates and Coy was extremely careful in his selection of personnel. Joseph Cretzer was one of Coy's first choices. Courageous and fearless, Cretzer had attempted escapes from both the federal penitentiary at McNeil Island and Alcatraz. He had even attempted to escape from the federal court in Tacoma while he was on trial for escaping from McNeil Island. Having lived in the Bay Area, Cretzer had numerous local underworld contacts, including his wife Edna. Coy believed many of these, would be of assistance once they made it to the mainland. Cretzer was also familiar with guns, having led one of the most feared and violent bank robbery gangs in the country.

In 1939, after a reign of bank robbery terror from Seattle to San Diego, Cretzer and his brother-in-law, Arnold Kyle, were arrested in Chicago. At the time of his arrest, Cretzer was listed by the FBI as Public Enemy #5, a status in which he took great pride. The two were tried in Los Angeles on charges stemming from a bloody Pasadena bank holdup. Convicted and sentenced to McNeil Island, they were soon transferred to Alcatraz as escape risks.

Marvin Hubbard was another of Coy's choices. He was a quiet man, who read a great deal, and, although he kept to himself, was well thought of by his convict contemporaries. His criminal activity had been primarily armed robbery, which included several shoot-outs with the police. In August of 1942, Hubbard and two others overpowered a jailer in Walker County, Alabama and escaped with a machine gun and three handguns. They were captured following a spectacular gun battle involving more than two hundred FBI agents, State Troopers, local police, and outraged citizens. Following his capture, Hubbard claimed he was beaten by the FBI and forced to sign a false confession. He also contended he was lied to by the FBI and tricked into pleading guilty based on the forced confession. At the time of the 1946 escape attempt, Hubbard was pursuing a writ of habeas corpus that even the U. S. Attorney handling the case admitted would probably be successful. Although he would likely have received a new trial and been transferred away from Alcatraz, Hubbard so distrusted the judicial system that he ignored the pending court proceeding and joined Coy in the escape attempt.

Miran "Buddy" Thompson was another southern holdup man selected by Coy to become part of the blastout team. The youngest of six children, Thompson had chafed under the yoke of parental control. He left home as a teenager expressing a desire to be on his own and learn a trade. He immediately turned to crime and supported himself for many years as a lone wolf bandit. During the 1930s and early 1940s, he operated throughout Alabama and Mississippi robbing stores, bars, and service stations. He was repeatedly arrested, and became an accomplished escape artist, fleeing police custody on eight occasions. By 1944, his reputation was such that he was an immediate suspect in nearly any armed robbery committed in the Alabama-Mississippi area. As a result he moved his base of operation to Texas.

On March 12, 1945 he and a friend, Elbert Day, were arrested by Amarillo police detective Lem Savage. While being transported to jail without handcuffs in the front seat of Savage's unmarked police car, Thompson drew a small revolver he had hidden in his sock. A struggle ensued during which the gun fired five times wounding both Thompson and Day and killing Savage. Eventually captured by the FBI, Thompson received a ninety-nine year sentence. Viewed by authorities as a high-risk inmate, Thompson was initially confined at the federal penitentiary at Leavenworth and transferred almost immediately to Alcatraz.

The final participant was Sam Shockley, a mentally retarded, paranoid schizophrenic, known to officers and inmates alike as "Crazy Sam." He was not part of the plan, and it was never considered by the leaders that he be included. Once the escape was underway, however, and his D block cell was opened, Shockley simply tagged along. Already mentally unbalanced, Shockley was driven over the edge by the excitement of the events. There was serious question as to whether he ever really knew what was going on or appreciated the magnitude of the unfolding events.

The son of an Oklahoma sharecropper, Shockley left school as soon as he was able to work in the fields. His formal education ended at the third grade and by the age of thirteen he exhibited signs of serious instability. He repeatedly ran away from home and his work habits became erratic and unpredictable. His relationships with his parents and siblings were strained. He left home for good at the age of eighteen and within a year was confined in the Granite State Reformatory. While in prison he was savagely beaten by a fellow inmate, suffering demonstrable brain damage. Within a year of his release from Granite, he sustained a second brutal beating, which inflicted further major head trauma.

His life of crime peaked and ended on March 15, 1938, when he and a confederate robbed a bank in Paoli, Oklahoma. As part of their escape, they kidnapped the bank president and his wife after collecting $947.38 from the cash drawer. He was arrested ten days later at the nearby home of his brother.

Shockley was initially incarcerated in Leavenworth. There it was determined that he had an IQ of 68, suffered episodes of hallucination, and demonstrated serious emotional instability. Rather than confine the obviously mentally deranged prisoner in the Medical Center for Federal Prisoners at Springfield, Missouri, the authorities sent him to Alcatraz.

At Alcatraz Shockley's mental condition worsened. His IQ dropped to 54, indicating a mental age of an eight-year-old. He was unable to hold a steady work assignment and exhibited classic schizophrenic symptoms. In 1942 the Alcatraz prison physician described Shockley as "...emotionally very unstable with episodes of hallucination. His conduct has been erratic and unpredictable. He would likely break down again under the confusion and tension of a disaster and be dangerous to those about him. His transfer is suggested on that ground." But he was not transferred or treated. Instead he was placed in D block, the isolation section, where for more than three years he sat alone with his hallucinations.

After years of careful planning and meticulous preparation, Coy had put together an escape plan that he and his fellow conspirators were convinced could not fail.

The precise time of the breakout was set for May 2 at 1:30 P.M. That day was to be Cecil Corwin's first day back from two weeks of annual leave, and he was scheduled to start as the day watch officer in charge of D block. Corwin, in his fifties, was one of the gentlest and least aggressive officers on the staff. Coy believed Corwin could be easily intimidated and therefore would be the best officer to have on duty in D block. Coy thought Corwin might be the one guard who would panic and not turn in the alarm if he heard the attack on Burch in the gun gallery. In addition, Ernie Lageson, the officer in charge of the cell house, took his lunch break at 1:30 and would be in the administrative offices from 1:30 to 2:00. Coy's plan contemplated attacking the cell house officer while he conducted a routine search of Hubbard when he returned to the cell house from his duties in the kitchen. Coy did not want to risk such an attack with Lageson on duty. "We gotta' wait till Lageson goes to lunch," he had told Cretzer. "He's a tough little bastard and he'll set up his shakedown of

Marv in such a way that I won't be able to get behind him. Besides, he knows judo from being in the Navy and it's just not worth it try'n to screw around with him."

So on May 2, 1946, while Lageson was at lunch and his assistant William Miller was the only officer on duty on the cell house floor, Coy put his plan into effect. Along with Marv Hubbard, who was returning to the cell house from his work station in the kitchen, he overpowered Miller. They knocked him unconscious, tied him up, and placed him in cell #404 at the west end of C block. Next they released Carnes, Cretzer, and Thompson from their cells. Using the bar spreader, Coy gained access to the west gun gallery while Burch was lounging in the D block portion of the gallery. When Burch returned to the cell house side of the gallery, Coy knocked him unconscious, and tied him up. From the gallery he obtained a .45 automatic pistol, a Springfield 30.06 rifle, and more than seventy rounds of ammunition. He also collected all the cell house keys stored there, along with several standard billy clubs, gas dispensing billy clubs, gas masks, and Burch's uniform. The convicts intended to wear guard's uniforms as they made their way out the rear door of the cell house and down to the dock in order to confuse any of the tower guards who might be in a position to fire at them and their hostages. Coy passed all these items down to the excited prisoners below and, after returning to the cell house floor, moved on to the next phase of the blastout.

3
—

Cretzer and Hubbard invaded D block, captured Cecil Corwin and released most of the prisoners confined there including Shockley. Their purpose in entering D block was to free inmate Rufus "Whitey" Franklin, an expert in both locks and guns, so he could join them. Unaware of the escape plans, Franklin was in solitary confinement for his participation in a riot just three days earlier. Unable to open the solitary cells, they proceeded without Franklin. Coy also opened a number of cells in the main cell house and released not only those involved in the escape, but many of the convicts who were in their cells on idle status.

After taking control of D block, they captured the kitchen officer Joe Burdett when he made a routine check of the cell house. When inmates Joe Moyle and "Lefty" Egan wandered onto the scene from their work assignments they were hustled into cell 404 with the hostages. They were later released and allowed to wait out the events in another cell. Next, the chief steward Robert Bristow and cell house officer Lageson returned from lunch and were taken prisoner. When the cell house duty stations did not make their periodic reports to the armory, Cliff Fish, the officer on duty there, expressed concern to the captain of the guard. In rapid succession, four more officers, Captain Henry Weinhold, Lieutenant Joseph Simpson, mail censor Robert Baker, and records clerk Carl Sundstrom rushed into the cell house and were all taken prisoner. The hostages were initially confined in cell 404. This cell was used as the officer's toilet and the door had been adjusted so it wouldn't lock. Wanting the captives locked in the cells, Coy ordered that they be moved into the next two adjacent cells. Lageson, Corwin, Bristow, Miller, Weinhold, and Burdett were placed in cell 403 and Simpson, Baker, and Sundstrom were confined in 402. As the hostages were being captured, the crazed Shockley ran back and forth cursing at the officers. At one point he charged at Captain Wein-hold, swinging wildly at him with his fists, and had to be restrained by Cretzer. Later, as Sundstrom was being herded into cell 402, Shockley ran up behind him, striking him twice in the back of the head.

Soon after Burdett was captured and placed in 404 with Miller, he asked if Miller's hands could be untied. Carnes, his ego inflated by the inquiry, acceded to the request and Burdett untied his fellow officer. The insurgents had collected all the keys from the gallery, and had confiscated Miller's key ring as well as his uniform trousers and jacket. They believed they possessed all the cell house keys. What they didn't know was that Miller had retained key #107 in his shirt pocket. This key opened the rear door of the cell house, which led to the recreation yard. It was through this door that the convicts intended to leave the cell house. Without key #107 the escape could not succeed. Knowing he would have to open and close the rear door several times that afternoon, Miller had kept the key in his pocket rather than follow prison regulations and pass it up and down between him and the gallery. As soon as his hands were untied, Miller handed the key to Burdett, who hid it under the wall seat in cell 404.

At the start, the spirits of the insurgents were high and they were excited. Cretzer carried the .45 like it was a work of art, strutting back and forth in front of the hostage cells. Hubbard had the rifle and the others carried billy clubs or the large butcher knife taken by Hubbard from the kitchen. The convicts not involved in the escape stood at a safe distance and watched in awe as their fellow prisoners prepared to blast out of the seemingly impregnable cell house. Shockley ran up and down the corridors carrying a large wrench and wearing an officer's uniform jacket several sizes too large for him. He looked like a clown, which amused the onlookers. He repeatedly swore at the hostages and announced repeatedly "…me and my buddy Joe Cretzer are bust'n outta' here." Seeing Shockley for the first time, Carnes asked Hubbard who he was and what was wrong with him. "That's Crazy Sam," was Hubbard's response, "he's been in solitary and isolation too long. He's crazy."

Although it appeared to the inmates that they had all the cell house keys, none of them fit the lock in the rear door. Cretzer and Coy had been calm and calculating at the beginning, but when none of the keys would open the door to the outside they both became agitated and jumpy. Cretzer paced back and forth in front of the hostage cells and hissed under his breath to Coy, "Goddammit Bernie, Frisco's as far away as ever."

Confusion reigned in the prison administration offices, and armory officer Cliff Fish was becoming concerned. He has seen six officers enter the cell house over a twenty-minute period and none of them had reported back to him. In addition, none of the phones in the cell house, gun gallery, or D block were being answered. He had received a cryptic call from Officer Ed Stucker in the basement work area that there appeared to be some kind of serious trouble in the cell house, but because of the proximity of several inmates, Stucker could not explain what the problem was. Associate Warden E. J. Miller was somewhere at the north end of the island, and could not be located. When Fish telephoned the warden his wife responded that her husband was taking a nap. When the warden finally was roused and came to the phone, he did little to alleviate Fish's dilemma. "Well Mr. Fish, keep trying to find the associate warden. If you think the situation is serious enough, sound the alarm. I'll be coming over to my office in about fifteen minutes." Eventually Fish reached Lieutenant Ike Faulk, the officer in charge of the dock, and the decision was made to sound the escape alarm. This brought all off duty officers on the island running to the cell house and alerted the entire Bay Area to the emergency on Alcatraz. But confusion and indecision prevailed.

Unable to open the rear door, Coy ordered Carnes and Thompson to go down by the library and move the large rolling scaffold that was used to change light bulbs in the ceiling to the west end of the corridor between C and D blocks. Frustrated in his plan to exit the cell house through the door to the recreation yard, Coy intended to explore the possibility of breaking through a skylight or vent onto the roof. The two men responded immediately, and without knowing Coy's purpose, began moving the huge structure down the aisle. As they did, the escape siren sounded prompting both men to abandon the task and run to the west end of the cell house. Panic swept over young Carnes as he realized that the escape was over and they would never get out of the building.

The situation had become desperate. Sick that he had allowed himself to become involved in such a fiasco, Carnes started for his cell. But Coy called to the youngster, "Come on kid, let's go into the kitchen and get us some screws." Coy had earlier boasted to Carnes about an old tunnel that led to the dock from the kitchen. Thinking this might be what Coy had in mind, the youngster followed, joined by Hubbard. But there was no talk of a tunnel, and once in the kitchen, Coy methodically gunned down the three officers standing watch in the Dock, Hill, and Road Towers. Carnes watched in stunned disbelief as Coy fired twice at the Dock Tower and Officer Jim Comerford fell as if dead onto the walkway of the tower. Carnes protested, "What good is that gonna do, Bernie?" But Coy ignored him and moved to one of the windows in the bakery shop. From there he fired twice at Elmus Besk in the Hill Tower. The officer spun around from the force of the bullets and lay motionless on the floor of the tower. As Coy repeated his deadly performance, shooting twice at guard Irving Levinson in the Road Tower, Carnes quietly retreated to the dining hall and sat at one of the tables, his head in his hands. As he stared blankly through the glass panel in the door to the cell house, he heard two volleys of pistol shots from the direction of the hostage cells.

Immediately thereafter, Coy and Hubbard came out of the kitchen in animated conversation. "Nice goin' Bernie," congratulated Hubbard. You nailed all three of them screws. Just like shootin' squirrels."

"Yeah, guess I ain't lost the touch," Coy responded. As they headed for the cell house Carnes followed behind in confusion.

At the cell house door the trio saw Associate Warden Miller running toward them down "Broadway," the corridor between B and C blocks. Hubbard took the rifle from Coy announcing, "Gimme the gun, Bernie. I want to blow old 'Jughead' away." Coy relinquished the weapon and pulled the door open, giving Hubbard an unobstructed shot at the heavy-set man as he lumbered close to them. Hubbard took careful aim at the startled Miller, who struggled to reverse his direction and run back to the main gate at the east end of the cell house. Hubbard fired point blank at his target so he could not miss. It seemed Miller was a dead man.

Realizing the escape was over and Miller was about to die for nothing, Carnes continued walking and bumped Hubbard as he fired. This jostled the rifle, and the bullet fired harmlessly into the ceiling. Miller spun around and ran back down Broadway to the main gate. As he retreated, he threw an activated gas billy over his shoulder at his assailants. It struck the underside of the tier above and exploded in his face, inflicting a serious burn. He was, nevertheless, able to escape from the cell house before the infuriated Hubbard could get off another shot.

Carnes followed the others back to the hostage cells. The pungent smell of gunpowder hung heavily in the air. Cretzer, along with Shockley and Thompson stood silently in front of the two cubicles. "Where's the screws?" Coy inquired.

"They're all dead," Cretzer responded calmly. Looking through the bars,

Carnes saw the guards sprawled lifeless on the floors of the two cells. The carnage shocked him. Killing the hostages had been a senseless act, but now it was done, and whether he liked it or not, Carnes was a part of it.

Suddenly Shockley cried out, "Hey, Joe, there's a son of a bitch in the corner there that's still alive. Kill him."

"Yeah Joe, kill him, we don't want to leave no witnesses." It was the voice of Thompson.

Cretzer studied the back of the cell and saw Lageson sitting calmly in the left rear corner. Cretzer hesitated, then protested, "Naw, that's Mr. Lageson. He's my friend. He's a good screw."

"Friend hell!" Thompson shot back, he'll testify against us. He'll go to court and fuck us all. Kill him! We don't want no live witnesses." Carnes protested meekly, but his words were ignored.

Cretzer raised the .45 automatic and rested the barrel on the cross bar. He paused, then addressed the unflinching officer. "I'm sorry Mr. Lageson," and pulled the trigger. The hammer clicked harmlessly. The gun was empty. Cretzer removed the spent clip and rammed in a full one. As Cretzer was reloading, Carnes, standing behind the gunman, motioned to Lageson to duck. When the gun went off, Lageson lurched forward and his head pitched down between his legs.

The rioters gathered at the west end of C block where they made a few more futile efforts to open the rear cell house door. The excitement over, Shockley drifted back into D block and returned to his cell. Thompson was restless and appeared ready to walk away from the entire mess. Carnes was ready to call it off, but was afraid to be the first to give up. He feared the stigma of being a quitter. Coy, Cretzer, and Hubbard made it clear they would never surrender, but would "…go the hard way." They laid out the weapons and counted their bullets, preparing for the final battle when the guards invaded the cell house.

When Coy announced that he was going to check the hostage cells to be sure the guards were all dead, Carnes volunteered. "I'll go Bernie, I'll go see."

As Carnes turned to leave, Hubbard handed him the butcher knife and instructed, "Here kid, if any of 'em's still alive use this."

Carnes returned to the hostage cells and peered in. He could see that Weinhold and Miller, though wounded and unconscious, were still breathing. He heard someone groan, but could not determine which officer made the sound. In the next cell, Baker and Simpson were breathing and the lieutenant moved slightly. Carnes couldn't tell about the others, but whatever their condition, he had no intention of being a part of any more blood-shed. He returned to the west end of the cell house and handed the knife to Hubbard. "The cocksuckers are all dead. They're just the way we left them." The disconsolate mutineers accepted his report without question.

The breakout was over. The key to the outside door could not be located. Even though they had guns, ammunition and hostages, they weren't going anywhere. While Hubbard and Coy climbed to the top of C block to position themselves for the final gun battle, Carnes quietly re-turned to his cell. A shoot-out to the death was not what he wanted and the time had come to accept whatever consequences the system had in store for him. Thompson too, returned to his cell.

Associate Warden Miller and the senior officers all urged the warden to send an armed party into the cell house to rescue the hostages, but he refused. He cited various reasons for his refusal, including a shortage of personnel, risk that more weapons would fall into the hands of the insur-gents, and lack of information as to where the holdouts were located. None of these excuses satisfied his officers, most of whom attributed his inaction to fear and indecision. Even after all off duty officers returned, bringing the custodial staff to full complement, Johnston denied Miller's request to storm the cell house. When the officers manning the east gun gallery reported that no more than three prisoners appeared to be out of their cells, the warden still refused to permit an assault.

At approximately 7:00 P.M., more than five hours after the uprising began, Johnston authorized the associate warden to send an armed party to occupy the west gun gallery. The only entry into the west gun gallery was through an outside door into D block. This door was reached from a cat-walk along the south side of the cell house. A party of more than a dozen heavily armed men under the command of Lieutenant Phillip Bergen stormed into the D block side of the gallery firing rifles, pistols, machine guns, and shotguns. They rescued Burch and secured the gallery. During the assault, inmate fire and ricocheting bullets from friendly gunfire wounded several guards. One officer, Harold Stites, was killed, shot in the back by an unknown fellow officer firing into D block from the hill below. Stites had been facing into D block with his back to an outside window. The bullet entered his lower left flank, moving upward through his kidney and lung, killing him almost immediately. Although the prison administration strenuously urged that Stites had been killed by inmate fire, there was no doubt that his death was caused by custodial fire from outside the building.

At approximately 6:00 P.M., at Warden Johnston's request, a detachment of U.S. Marines arrived on Alcatraz. They were immediately assigned to sentry posts on the wall of the recreation yard to free the custodial officers for other duties. Throughout Thursday night, all the inmates who had been out of the cell house when the uprising began were confined in the recreation yard under the critical eyes of battle hardened Marine assault troops just back from the Pacific Theater of World War II.

Finally, at 10:30 P.M., more than eight hours after Joe Cretzer's maniacal shooting spree, Johnston allowed Associate Warden Miller to assemble a rescue party to enter the cell house to rescue the hostages. Despite the warden's fears and apprehensions, the rescue was effected in a matter of minutes with only a minor injury to one of the rescuers. Five of the hostages had been critically wounded. Officer William Miller died in the hospital six hours later.

With the hostages freed, Johnston became more adamant than ever against storming the cell house and capturing the holdout convicts. The rescue team reported that it appeared that all but three of the insurgents had returned to their cells. It was believed that Coy, Cretzer and Hubbard were holed up in the C block utility corridor. It was also known that between the three of them there were only two guns and limited ammunition. Despite the overwhelming superiority of the custodial force and their firepower, Johnston continued to reject the advice of his senior officers to enter the cell house and capture or kill the holdouts. Instead, he ordered a blistering bombardment of D block by his officers and a Marine special weapons unit. Thousands of rounds of mortar, rifle, pistol, grenade, and gas bomb fire poured into the confined area. Coast Guard vessels lying off the rocky beach of the island even fired their deck guns into the small cellblock. None of the holdouts were in D block and the rescue party had locked the door between D block and the main cell house. Despite the fact that no danger could come from D block, the merciless bombardment continued for nearly a day and a night, notwithstanding the pleas of the twenty-six inmates confined there.

While the shelling of D block went on unabated, a team of Marine weapons experts fired hundreds of grenades, gas bombs, and other explosives into the utility corridor of C block. They drilled holes in the roof above the corridor and blanketed the confined area with a lethal fusillade. The barrage went on from early Thursday evening until early Saturday morning. At approximately 10:00 A.M. Saturday, officers entered the south end of the utility corridor and removed the bodies of Coy, Cretzer, and Hubbard.

4
—

Once the boat was secured to the dock, the first to disembark was Warden Johnston, followed by officer Levinson, leading the three inmates. The convicts were chained to one another and to Levinson, and the four walked up the gangway in single file. Behind them came two more Alcatraz officers.

The transfer of the defendants from the boat to the U.S. Marshal's van was accomplished in less than a minute, much to the dismay of the newsmen and photographers covering the event. One of the photographers was able to snap a quick picture, which appeared prominently is the next day's San Francisco Examiner. It showed the three prisoners being led up the gangway beneath a length of rope on the boat coiled in such a way that it appeared to be a noose hanging over their heads. The headline over the photograph read, "ALCATRAZ KILLERS...AND THE SYMBOL." The photo caption noted "Noose hangs ominously over the heads of defendants Shockley, Thompson and Carnes." Although the case was only at the arraignment stage, all three were already labeled killers by the press.

The van pulled quickly off the dock and proceeded laboriously up the long Van Ness Avenue hill enroute to the Post Office Building at 7th and Mission Streets, which housed the federal courts. The traffic lights along Van Ness were not synchronized, and traffic was heavy. During the twenty-minute trip none of the prisoners spoke. The quiet of the darkened passenger compartment was broken only by the occasional whispered small talk of the guards and marshals. Transporting prisoners was a routine event for the marshals, but today there was an air of tension due to the notoriety of the crime and criminals involved. The van pulled up to the rear entrance of the building where it was met by several more marshals. At this point the Alcatraz officers relinquished legal and physical control of the inmates to the marshals, who hustled them through the back corridors of the building. Still wearing their handcuffs and leg irons, they were escorted to the holding cell adjacent to the courtroom of Judge Michael Roche.

Attorney Ernest Spagnoli sat at the counsel table in Roche's court awaiting the arrival of his clients. In his three-piece blue suit, crisply starched white shirt, and striped tie, he appeared to be a successful trial lawyer and could easily have been mistaken for a senior partner in one of the City's major law firms. Nothing could have been further from the truth. For the preceding few years the aging barrister's criminal practice had become a humdrum collection of misdemeanor and minor felony cases. The few civil cases he had were questionable personal injury claims rejected by more successful attorneys.

After thirty-eight years of patrolling the Bay Area courtrooms, Spagnoli was slowing down. He was unwilling to openly acknowledge it, but did occasionally consider the possibility of retiring. In fact, his retirement seemed to be happening naturally, whether he chose to admit it or not. His caseload was not nearly what it had been in past years.

Most of Spagnoli's cases came to him by referral from either a former client or through a network of underworld characters with whom he maintained contact. The defense of the accused Alcatraz murder defendants, however, did not come to the controversial litigator through any of his customary sources.

His first knowledge of the riot and the possibility of a murder case came on Friday morning, May 3, through the haze of a hangover. It was the morning after a long night of bourbon and waters at Cookie Piccetti's bar on Kearney Street, near the Hall of Justice. Cookie's was a favorite watering hole of San Francisco attorneys, police officers, and politicians, and was always busy after work in the evening. One of the customers was celebrating something and Spagnoli had joined in the festivities. He didn't know what was being celebrated, but woke the next morning with the inevitable parched lips, dry mouth, and pounding headache.

He shuffled into the kitchen, following the heady aroma of his wife Clare's coffee. He gingerly lowered himself into a chair at the table as Clare placed a steaming cup of black coffee and a large glass of chilled orange juice beside the folded copy of the morning *Examiner*. Clutching the glass with an unsteady hand, Spagnoli downed the juice. Unfolding the paper his gaze fixed upon the four-inch headlines shouting from the printed page:

ALCATRAZ RIOT STILL RAGES: 1 DEAD 14 SHOT

Below the banner headline, a huge picture covered nearly the entire front page showing a close-up of the cell house and members of the Alcatraz custodial force scrambling along the outside catwalk. The first few pages of the paper contained dramatic accounts of the battle underway at the island prison. Spagnoli's eyes raced from story to story, scanning the columns for familiar names. During his career, he had represented a handful of Alcatraz convicts and he wondered if any of them were involved. Having visited clients on the island and experienced the impervious security system, Spagnoli could not believe that the inmates had obtained guns and controlled the cell house as the paper described.

As he read about the events of the past several hours, another thought occurred to the attorney. It was almost certain that murder and assault charges would be filed against the participants. The possibility of defending such a case brought a rush of excitement to Spagnoli. There was currently nothing interesting scheduled on his trial calendar and his flagging practice could certainly benefit from an infusion of notoriety that an Alcatraz murder case would produce. He had a slight chance of being appointed to the defense team for the upcoming Japanese war crimes trial in Tokyo. His political allies at the Department of Justice indicated that his appointment was a possibility, but he looked upon the assignment as a long shot. The likelihood of being involved in the Alcatraz trial was far more realistic, and Spagnoli wanted to participate in the case. It being Friday with nothing on his trial calendar, Spagnoli had not planned to go to the office, which he maintained on the first floor of the flat he occupied at Mission and 20th Streets. The Alcatraz situation changed everything, and after a second cup of coffee, a shave, and a shower he was down the stairs to his office.

Spagnoli's father emigrated to Jackson, California from Italy at the age of fourteen, and within two years was appointed deputy county clerk of Amador County. The senior Spagnoli went on to build an enviable legal and public service career during the post-Gold Rush years. By the time Ernest was born, the elder Spagnoli was forty-five years of age and had significant political connections reaching all the way to Washington, D.C. In 1895, he was appointed by President Grover Cleveland as a U.S. Counsel to Italy and moved his family to Milan. When Republican William McKinley was elected President, Spagnoli's appointment was not renewed and the family returned to Jackson.

Ernest attended St. Mathews Military College in San Mateo and Hastings College of Law in San Francisco. After graduation, he returned to Jackson to practice law with his father in the firm of Spagnoli and Spagnoli. For the younger Spagnoli, however, the lure of the big city was great, and following his father's death he returned to San Francisco where he soon developed a flourishing and controversial practice. In time, he took his place in the long line of colorful and flamboyant San Francisco criminal defense lawyers, handling his share of notorious cases.

An early foe of capital punishment, in 1926, Spagnoli staged what was probably the first public demonstration against the death penalty. As his client's appeal worked its way through the appellate courts, Spagnoli demonstrated in front of San Quentin Prison, hoping to forestall the execution. The appeal failed, his demonstration was ignored, and his client was executed. In 1929, Spagnoli made legal history in his defense of Army Captain Jerome Merwin, an officer stationed at the Presideo, who was charged with the murder of his mother-in-law. Spagnoli was the first lawyer in California to plead the defense of not guilty by reason of temporary insanity, and he won a verdict of acquittal.

The polemic attorney's domestic life was as turbulent as his professional life. In the 1920s, he was married to Sally Stanford, San Francisco's most famous Madam and bordello operator. Their divorce was friendly and Miss Stanford proved to be a constant source of criminal defense cases for Spagnoli. He represented her for years, never charging a fee. In August of 1936, following a torrid courtship, Spagnoli, then fifty-one, married San Francisco model Muriel Rey in Reno. The following evening, on the return train trip the bride announced that not only was the honeymoon over, but so was the marriage. Once back in San Francisco, Spagnoli sought and was granted an annulment. Miss Stanford appeared as a corroborating witness. After the hearing, the barrister and his two ex-wives headed to Bardelli's restaurant to celebrate "the end of the adventure." For Spagnoli it was an embarrassing and degrading experience, but he put on a good front for the press and the public and went along with the burlesque. The next day, Miss Rey and Spagnoli were reunited, when Spagnoli posted bail to get her released from jail on a shoplifting charge for which he subsequently acted as her attorney.

But by May of 1946, such antics were behind him. At sixty-one, with his career winding down, Spagnoli had mellowed. He was happily married and lived a comfortable life. He would settle for the excitement provided by his career, and the kind of exhilaration that an Alcatraz murder trial would create.

During the next few days, Spagnoli read everything in all the papers about the riot, including detailed reviews of the Saturday night press conference given by Warden Johnston and Bureau of Prisons Director James Bennett. He then solicited the assistance of two of his old friends in the criminal bar and sent the following telegram to Miran Thompson:

> I am engaged to defend you in contemplated prosecutions impending against you and have engaged associate attorneys, Milton Dalo and Robert Boon. We are seeking consultations with you. Meanwhile advise you await our visit before making any statement. Answer collect.
>
> Attorney Ernest Spagnoli
> 3505 20th St. San Francisco

The telegram was delivered to Thompson early in the morning Tuesday May 7. Thompson denied any knowledge of Spagnoli and indicated to the FBI agents who were interrogating him that he did not want an attorney. "As I told you guys yesterday, I'm ready to make a deal and plead guilty to my part in this thing. Like I said, I'll testify against the others and tell things just the way they happened. I ain't interested in this Spagnoli guy. In fact, I'm not even gonna talk to him." Thompson went on to explain to the agents that he had not retained Spagnoli and had no knowledge of anyone who might have retained the attorney on his behalf. The investigators told Thompson that Spagnoli had alerted the newspapers of his involvement, crediting a "responsible man in Reno" as Thompson's mysterious benefactor. The inmate stressed his desire to make a deal and reiterated his lack of interest in Spagnoli's representation. He insisted he didn't even know anyone in Reno.

Later that same day, Spagnoli notified the press that he was filing a petition for habeas corpus in his capacity as attorney for the trio. He proclaimed that he had been retained by a friend of Thompson's to defend him and his co-defendants in the murder case the friend expected to be filed by the government. He claimed that his earlier requests to interview the three inmates had been denied by the warden, so he was seeking the aid of the court in obtaining a consultation with his clients. The matter was heard the next day by Judge Louis Goodman, and following Spagnoli's heated argument, Goodman denied the request. He ruled that no charges had been filed against the convicts, so there was no need for a defense and no need for an interview. With his efforts to obtain interviews blocked by both the warden and Judge Goodman, Spagnoli had no alternative but to wait for the next step in the process, the filing of formal charges by the Government.

Asked repeatedly by reporters to identify the alleged benefactor, Spagnoli evaded the issue, claiming it was a well-established, responsible individual in the Reno area who wished to remain anonymous. He also described the Good Samaritan as a "friend of Thompson," but never favored the press or the public with a name.

During the ensuing weeks, Thompson reconsidered his rejection of Spagnoli's legal representation. With the passage of time, it became clear that neither the Alcatraz administration nor the U.S. Attorney had any interest in making a deal. The story along the prison grapevine was that the three would be charged with murder and the prosecution would seek the death penalty. Faced with this realization, Thompson as well as Carnes wrote letters to Spagnoli requesting representation.

On June 19 the Grand Jury indicted the three inmates on first-degree murder charges and Spagnoli immediately renewed his petition for habeas corpus, citing the indictment and the correspondence from Carnes and Thompson. This time the hearing on the matter was a perfunctory one, with no opposition from the government. Following a brief statement by Spagnoli, Judge Michael Roche issued an order permitting the interview. Spagnoli now represented two of the Alcatraz murder defendants.

The three inmates remained in the holding cell until just before the judge left his chambers. They were then brought into the courtroom, seated at the counsel table, and unchained. It was obligatory within the federal courts that neither defendants nor witnesses were ever restrained while court was in session. Four armed marshals were stationed at various locations in the courtroom and the three Alcatraz officers sat in the rear of the courtroom in the spectator gallery. Warden Johnston sat inside the rail, directly behind Frank Hennessy, the United States attorney for the Northern District of California. Hennessy was a hands on prosecutor, and while he had a staff of highly competent trial attorneys, had chosen to try this case personally. He selected Dan Deasy, one of his staff attorneys, to assist him during the trial.

Roche's courtroom was large with a high ceiling. Above the elevated bench hung a replica of the great seal of the United States of America.

There were windows along one wall, but the mahogany wall panels gave the room a dark and somber air. Roche's court was a typical federal court of the 1940s. It was an austere, formal place, where the strictest of protocol was observed. Roche's manner was firm and formal. He maintained stern rules of conduct, and a spectator would be summarily ejected for chewing gum or reading a newspaper while court was in session. As the judge entered the courtroom and the bailiff called the court to order, the spectator section rose silently in unison as if rehearsed.

Word had spread throughout the building that the Alcatraz defendants were to be arraigned, and a large number of curious federal employees had stopped by to observe the proceedings. In addition, a couple dozen attorneys were in the audience waiting for their cases to be called on the criminal calendar. For security reasons, the Alcatraz defendants were first on the calendar. All eyes in the courtroom were riveted on the high visibility outlaws seated at the counsel table.

The case of *The United States of America vs. Samuel Richard Shockley, Miran Edgar Thompson and Clarence Victor Carnes* was called by the clerk, after which Hennessy rose and announced his appearance on behalf of the United States. Spagnoli, already on his feet, stated his appearance on behalf of Thompson and Carnes. Shockley was unrepresented, and Roche advised him of his constitutional right to representation by counsel. Roche explained that if Shockley had no means with which to procure counsel, the court would appoint an attorney to represent him free of charge. Shockley appeared meek and frightened as Judge Roche addressed him, but to the surprise of the courtroom observers, he responded in a firm, quiet, southern drawl.

"I ask that the court appoint me two lawyers." As he spoke he shifted slightly from one foot to the other.

Roche seemed annoyed by the request and asked brusquely, "Why do you want me to appoint two lawyers to defend you?" To the spectators it appeared to be a mismatch. The thin, docile Shockley, wearing an ill-fitting prison-made suit stood alone, staring blankly at the judge, who glared down at him from the bench. Roche was an imposing man, with a large head and a huge shock of gray hair, which gave him a larger than life appearance from his elevated position.

"Because, according to Title 18, Section 3005 of the United States Code I'm entitled to two lawyers and want the court to appoint me Mr. James Burns and Mr. Harold Faulkner."

Shockley's demand took Roche by surprise, but the mild-mannered convict was correct. By law he was entitled to two attorneys if charged with a capital crime, provided he made a specific request. Roche knew he had no choice but do as Shockley demanded.

"Suppose these attorneys are not available," snapped Roche, embarrassed at having the law publicly explained to him by a convict.

"Then I want the court to appoint me two more," responded Shockley.

The request was not well received by Roche, but he instructed his bailiff to contact Burns and Faulkner and ordered their appearance in his court at 2:00 P.M. that afternoon. The indictment was then read to the defendants and each of them was given a copy. Unable to proceed further with the arraignment, the judge announced that the matter would be put over until 2:00.

Without warning, Thompson stood and addressed the court directly, requesting that his case also be continued for arraignment so he could obtain the services of the attorney that had represented him in his Texas murder trial. A surprised and embarrassed Spagnoli slowly rose to face the judge, but said nothing. Roche, still rankled by his exchange with Shockley, was clearly annoyed at Thompson's impertinence.

"Mr. Thompson," he admonished, "you will please be seated and address this court through your attorney. Sir, you are no stranger to the protocol of the courtroom and I insist that you adhere to the rules of procedure. You are currently represented by Mr. Spagnoli and it is my understanding that you personally retained his services. If you wish to substitute in your Texas counsel you are free to do so, but that is a matter between you, the attorney in Texas, and Mr. Spagnoli. Such action does not require a continuance of the arraignment. Your motion is out of order and it is denied. The matter is set over until 2:00 P.M." Before they could rise from their chairs, the three defendants were surrounded by marshals and once again swathed in shackles and chains. With the restraints in place, the trio, locked to the wrist of one of the marshals, was hustled out the side door and back to the holding cell.

In the cell the handcuffs were removed, but the leg shackles remained in place. As he nibbled indifferently at the ham and cheese sandwich provided by the marshal's office, Thompson considered the question of his representation.

"Hey Sam," he inquired, "how'd you know all that shit about two lawyers?"

"Stroud told me to ask for 'em and he told me what law to say," Shockley responded proudly. "A lotta guys told me about Burns and Faulkner. They're sposta be real good lawyers. See, I got it all wrote down here." He pulled a scrap of paper from his pocket and self-approvingly displayed it to the others.

"Well," Thompson continued, "I ain't so sure about this old fart Spagnoli. I don't know where he come from in the first place, and there's somethin' about him that bites my ass. Maybe I'll take a look at these guys Burns and Faulkner."

The afternoon session brought the appearance of James E. "Ned" Burns and the answer to Thompson's problem. Burns was a prominent criminal defense attorney with significant federal court experience. He was also known for his frequent representation of indigent defendants. The attorney arrived half an hour prior to the 2:00 P.M. hearing, and was ushered into the holding cell to meet Shockley. Burns's demeanor and enthusiasm impressed Thompson as he listened to the handsome young lawyer interviewing Shockley. After about fifteen minutes, Burns and Shockley had completed their discussion and the attorney rose to leave. Thompson, who had not taken his eyes off Burns during the entire time, stood and faced him.

"How 'bout you be my lawyer too"? he proposed. "I don't know this guy Spagnoli." Thompson didn't know Burns either, but his first impressions strongly favored him over the older Spagnoli.

"Sure, if that's what you want and it's okay with the judge," Burns responded without emotion. "I'll talk to Ernie Spagnoli and see you in the courtroom."

The thirty-four old Burns was born and raised in San Francisco. He was the product of a strong Catholic family, and two of his siblings had followed religious callings. His brother Joseph served as assistant pastor of historic Old St. Mary's Church, and his sister Mary, a member of the Sisters of Mercy, was on the staff of St. Mary's Hospital. Burns was educated by the Jesuits, receiving his undergraduate and legal degrees from the University of San Francisco. He became a member of the bar in 1938.

Following the outbreak of World War II, he received an appointment as a special assistant U.S. attorney and was assigned to the Department of Justice, War Fraud Unit. It was during this time that his interest in criminal law developed.

After the war, Burns quickly established himself as an outstanding criminal defense attorney, specializing in federal cases. Despite the fact that he was a sole practitioner, Burns repeatedly accepted court appointments to represent indigent defendants without fee. He was also active in the movement to establish a federal public defender's office. Although a young man, he was a financial success. He resided with his wife Genevieve and infant daughters Bonnie and Terry on Greenwich Street in the upscale Cow Hollow district of the City.

The afternoon session was brief. The judge appointed Burns to represent Shockley and set July 9 as the date for plea and preliminary motions. Harold Faulkner had sent word to the court that he was ill, and unable to appear in court or represent any of the parties in the case. Burns also advised the court that following discussions between Spagnoli, Thompson, and himself it had been agreed that he would be representing both Thompson and Shockley. Additionally, he planned to file at least two if not three preliminary motions. The defendants acquiesced in this change in representation as did Spagnoli, and Burns filed his formal appearance with the clerk. Nothing more was said by Shockley about having two attorneys, but Burns was already contemplating bringing his colleague Wayne Collins into the case.

5
—

Even with the matter continued, Burns had only two weeks to prepare his preliminary motions and plan his defense. He immediately
began work on three motions, all of which he considered longshots. He
contacted Spagnoli, hoping to be able to divide the workload. Unfortunately, he found Spagnoli detached and preoccupied with the possibility of
becoming involved in the upcoming Japanese war crimes trial. Burns
explained his ideas to Spagnoli hoping to evoke a thoughtful response
from his more experienced co-counsel. But the more Burns talked about
the case, the less interested his co-counsel seemed to be. Finally Spagnoli
confessed, "You know Ned, with this Japanese thing coming to a head, I
may not be able to continue on with the Alcatraz case."

Burns realized he could not count on Spagnoli for any help, and proceeded immediately with the motions. He planned a motion to dismiss the
indictment, a motion seeking separate trials for each defendant, and a
motion to have the case transferred from San Francisco to another federal district or division. He made the motions on behalf of Thompson and
Shockley, and wondered what, if anything, Spagnoli would be doing for
Carnes. He had no intention of doing Spagnoli's work, yet was concerned
as to whether or not Carnes was receiving adequate representation.

The motion to dismiss proceeded on the theory that the indictment was
based on illegal and incompetent evidence that would not support a finding of guilt. Hennessy's opposition was simple and to the point. He argued
that there was no court reporter present during the grand jury proceedings and no transcript had been prepared. Burns had not been present so
he had no basis for the contention that the grand jury received illegal or
incompetent evidence.

The second motion sought separate trials as to each of the defendants
on the ground that they could not get fair trial if they were tried together.

Burns's contention was that because of the factual situation, the acts of each defendant would be considered by the jury to be the acts of all, and this would be unfair. Additionally, potential inconsistencies in the testimony of the three would make it impossible for them to cooperate. Again Hennessy's response was simple. In his written opposition he pointed out that as long as the defendants received a fair trial joinder was appropriate. The defense, he urged, had set forth no facts to support their request for severance and was only speculating that prejudice might result from the three being tried together. If any unfairness developed in the future, the court, in its discretion, could sever the case at that time.

Finally, Burns sought a transfer of the trial, arguing that widespread adverse publicity and press coverage prevented the defendants from obtaining a fair trial. During the riot, the San Francisco press carried in excess of fifty pages of news and photos of the events and related circumstances. Burns argued that the print reporting had not been objective, referring to the defendants in such prejudicial terms as "Killers," "Kidnappers," "Lifers," "Gangsters," and "Desperadoes." In many of the stories the defendants' guilt was accepted as fact and the discussion focused on whether the penalty would be death or another life sentence. The news accounts equated the conduct of Cretzer and Coy with that of the three survivors, linking them all to the killing and wounding of the Alcatraz officers.

The broadcast coverage was even more extensive, with all the major networks devoting many hours to what Burns described as "unfair and prejudicial coverage of the events." Most of the jurors would come from San Francisco, and since the press and broadcast coverage had been widespread and biased against the defendants, Burns argued that a fair trial there was not possible.

Hennessy responded by reminding the court that the defendants had the burden of proving that a fair trial was impossible. While the defense had addressed the vast scale of the publicity, some of which might have been interpreted as adverse, Hennessy stressed that nowhere in the motion or supporting documents was there any evidence that a fair trial was not possible or that the potential jurors could not be fair to the defendants. The defense, according to the prosecutor, had merely made an unsupported conclusion that because of the widespread publicity a fair trial was not possible.

In the absence of the vacationing Judge Roche, the July 9 hearing was set before Judge A. F. St. Sure. Before the judge could get to any of the pending legal issues, Spagnoli addressed the court with the request that he be permitted to withdraw as counsel for Carnes. Spagnoli explained that he expected to be departing in the near future for Tokyo, where he would assist in the defense of accused Japanese war criminals. He stated that he had discussed the matter with his client, who consented to the withdrawal. Burns then advised the court that Carnes had requested him to represent him as well as the other two defendants and that Burns had agreed to do so. Carnes verified this and St. Sure approved the change. The matter was continued another week to give the government more time to consider the motions and to allow Burns to make similar motions on behalf of Carnes, as Spagnoli had filed no preliminary motions.

At the hearing a week later, St. Sure exhibited outright disdain for the Motion to Dismiss and showed little inclination to rule favorably on either of the other two motions. Realizing that the judge's sympathies lay with the prosecution, Burns requested time to file additional written arguments and was granted one additional day. Although he combed the law books, Burns was unable to find any legal authorities that he felt would change St. Sure's thinking. Thoroughly discouraged with his efforts, Burns never filed a supplemental brief. The first legal volley fired by the defense had fallen well short of the mark, and one day after the oral argument, Judge St. Sure, without comment or explanation, denied all three motions and ordered the matter transferred to Judge Louis Goodman for trial.

Although he had expected to lose, Burns was moved by the profound disappointment the ruling brought to the three defendants. He delivered the news personally, and was distressed by the depression exhibited by all three. Even Thompson with his arrogant, nonchalant façade, seemed to view the ruling as carrying a sinister implication. Burns optimistically advised his clients that the court's ruling was without prejudice to making the motions again, although the attorney knew that the chances of Goodman overruling St. Sure and granting any of the motions was unlikely. His forced enthusiasm failed to convince his clients.

The first hearing before Judge Goodman was the entry of the defendants' pleas on July 23. Such a mundane appearance did not merit Hennessy's time, and one of his assistants appeared on behalf of the United States. Burns appeared as counsel for all three defendants, each of whom haltingly uttered the words, "Not guilty." Goodman ordered the matter set for trial on September 17th and remanded the three defendants into the custody of Warden Johnston, who sat quietly at the prosecution end of the counsel table.

Following the hearing, Burns told the press that Fred McDonald, an experienced and well respected trial attorney, formerly an assistant U.S. attorney in San Francisco, would be joining the defense team, working with him and Wayne Collins.

Throughout July and August, Burns devoted as much time as he could to trial preparation. The obstacles he faced in order to meet with a client or witness made the work arduous. A simple interview was a major undertaking, requiring advance arrangements with prison authorities and a trip to the island with its various check points and security procedures. Meetings at Alcatraz had to be scheduled well in advance and it was necessary for Burns to constantly reschedule his other activities around these island trips. The prison authorities never interfered with the attorneys, but neither were they particularly cooperative. Burns and Collins recognized, however, that there was no reason for the prison personnel to do anything more than they were required to for these inmates, whom they looked upon as murderers of their friends. Security took preference over everything on Alcatraz, and much of each visit was devoted to security matters, searches, and waiting.

It took a number of meetings with each of the defendants before Burns could assimilate and digest the facts and develop a defense theory. He had the transcript of the coroner's inquest, but the only meaningful testimony there was that of Burch and Lageson. Neither officer had been cross-examined, and Hennessy had carefully limited their testimony. They established little more than that Officer Miller had been shot by Cretzer. All the coroner's jury was required to determine was the cause of Miller's death, and Hennessy had been careful not to disclose any more of his case than necessary at the inquest.

Burns knew Hennessy to be a tough courtroom opponent. They had faced each other in trial before, and the win-loss score between them was about even. This was a big case for the U.S. Attorney's office and Burns knew that "the Boss," as he was referred to by his staff, would be meticulously prepared for such a high visibility trial. He also knew that Hennessy would use Warden Johnston as one of his key witnesses.

Hennessy and Warden Johnston were both integral parts of the San Francisco political and social life, and had known one another for more than forty years. The two men were at different ends of the political spectrum, but Hennessy had backed Johnston in his non-partisan, reform candidacy for the Board of Supervisors in 1907. At that time, Johnston was a clerk in a Fillmore Street department store, and the run for a Supervisor's seat was his first successful political endeavor.

Hennessy's father left his railroad job in Nebraska in 1884 and moved the family to San Jose, California, where he began work as a rancher. Young Frank's daily trip to school by horse and buggy was as much ranch life as he wished to experience. Matriculating at Santa Clara University as an undergraduate and later at Hastings College of Law, he was admitted to the practice of law in 1901. By the time of the 1906 earthquake and fire, he had a thriving law practice and impressive political contacts.

Hennessy was a dedicated Democrat, and by 1907 held offices in both the County Committee and the State Central Committee of the party. In 1917, he ran for City Attorney of San Francisco against the incumbent George Lull. It was Lull's first reelection campaign and the aggressive young Hennessy believed he had the political clout to unseat him.

The campaign soon turned into a battle over prohibition. Hennessy had previously taken a strong position against national prohibition. The temperance forces launched an all-out campaign against him, questioning his ethics and competence as an attorney and charging him with corruption. The San Francisco *Examiner* joined the fight, publishing scathing editorials opposing Hennessy and supporting the incumbent. Though he fought gamely, Hennessy could not overcome the crusade waged against him. Lull was returned to office with a sixty percent majority, receiving even the South of Market vote, always believed to belong to Hennessy.

Nevertheless, the young lawyer continued his involvement in state and national politics. In 1934 he was campaign manager for George Creel, a nationally known newspaperman and personal friend of Franklin D. Roosevelt, in his primary election campaign for the gubernatorial nomination against avowed Socialist Upton Sinclair. Although Creel lost the election, he developed great respect and admiration for Hennessy.

In 1937, Hennessy's three decades of devoted Democratic service proved to be the key that opened the door for him to the office of U.S. attorney. When the term of H. H. McPike, the Republican incumbent, expired, Hennessy's name rose to the top of the short list of possible replacements. While speculation persisted regarding other possible candidates, thirty years of tireless work in the Democratic vineyards made the job Hennessy's to accept or reject. Creel backed Hennessy, as did numerous Democratic leaders. Even the legendary Hiram Johnson, a Republican and one of the most powerful politicians in the state, urged Hennessy's appointment. With this overwhelming support, Hennessy was nominated by President Roosevelt on August 12, 1937 and confirmed by the Senate the following day.

The case at hand was not Hennessy's first experience with violent death on Alcatraz. Frequently during his trial preparation, he recalled the two previous capital cases he had tried, both of which had left him gravely disappointed.

In November of 1938 he prosecuted Rufus "Whitey" Franklin and James "Tex" Lucus for the murder of officer Royal Cline during an unsuccessful escape attempt. The evidence against the men was convincing, and Hennessy demanded the death penalty. The jury, however, sentenced the killers to life.

Hennessy's experience in 1941 was an even more painful wound to his ego. Henri Young had cold bloodedly stabbed inmate Rufus McCain to death with two homemade knives. Hennessy was convinced that the act was committed with deliberation, malice, and premeditation. The case was defended by renowned defense counsel Sol A. Abrams and his young associate James Martin MacInnis on the theory that the brutal treatment he received at Alcatraz had driven Young temporarily insane. MacInnis contended that Young did not know what he was doing when he killed McCain. This version, while vigorously challenged by Hennessy, was accepted by the jury. Young was convicted of the least serious crime permitted by law, involuntary manslaughter, which carried only a three-year sentence.

In addition to trivializing the crime, the jury had publicly attacked the Alcatraz prison administration as cruel and inhumane. Following the trial, the jurors sent telegrams to the United States Attorney General, national legislators, and other government leaders demanding that the island prison be closed and that the Alcatraz administration be investigated by federal authorities. To Hennessy it was a personal embarrassment as well as a slap in the face to Warden Johnston and his administration. That trial was an experience from which he never totally recovered.

Johnston had been the warden at Alcatraz since it opened as a federal prison in 1934. His career in penology prior to that had been legendary. Appointed by Governor Hiram Johnson as warden of California's Folsom Prison in 1912, he assumed leadership of that troubled institution with no prior experience in law enforcement. In a short time he converted the violence-torn, chaotic penitentiary into a model of penology. He accomplished a similar result a few years later at San Quentin. In 1933, while serving as the state director of penology, Johnston was contacted by United States Attorney General Homer Cummings with the request that he become the warden of the federal maximum security prison to be established on Alcatraz the following year. Without hesitation, Johnston accepted, and one of the nation's most liberal and progressive penologists became the head of the nation's maximum security prison.

6

___

Burns's initial interviews with Shockley were hampered by the lack of rapport between the two men. Shockley was in a world of his own, and much of the time was unable to communicate cogently. Thompson, on the other hand, had no difficulty focusing on trial preparation or defense theories. He constantly advised Burns how the case should be tried. Thompson's inflated opinion of his own legal abilities was a continuing irritant to Burns. Carnes was docile and quietly cooperative. Despite his youth and limited education, Burns felt he would be the most effective witness of the three.

The problems Burns faced in interviewing his clients were dwarfed by the difficulties confronting him in dealing with the other convict witnesses. He was forced to rely on his clients' recommendations as to who among the dozens of potential convict witnesses would be of assistance. Each of the defendants had his own ideas as to which fellow inmates would be able to assist in the defense. Burns interviewed every convict recommended by the defendants as a possible witness. He expended enormous amounts of time in these interviews and the analysis of the information he developed. Some of the witnesses were eager to talk and would say anything to help their fellow inmates. Others had their own agenda and hopes of personal gain or notoriety. Some refused to become involved, and Burns never knew if they had anything valuable to contribute. Still others volunteered, but had nothing worthwhile to provide or were obviously lying. The preparation seemed endless. Nevertheless, Burns forged ahead, ignoring the fact that his services were pro bono, and he would receive no compensation for his efforts.

Burns's first task was to develop one consistent factual scenario. The defendants' recollections differed; they had all become involved in the break at different times, and some of their observations were inconsistent. Carnes was a part of the escape attempt from the beginning and had been involved in the capture of Bristow and other hostages. Thompson joined the break later, and Shockley only became involved when the insurgents invaded D block. In Burns's opinion, Shockley was not a part of the plan at all, and merely tagged along because no one told him he couldn't.

Despite the inconsistencies, Burns felt he could persuade a jury that all three told basically the same story. All three denied any long-standing involvement in the escape. Thompson admitted knowledge of an escape, but claimed he learned of the actual attempt only the day before it occurred. Shockley's recollection was extremely limited. All contended that they became involved with the understanding that the escape would be carried out without violence, gunplay, or loss of life. When it became evident that escape from the cell house was impossible, all three abandoned the breakout attempt and returned to their cells. None of them did any of the shooting and all denied ever even handling a firearm. Carnes and Thompson contended that they counseled against the killings and attempted to prevent them. Finally, all of them emphatically denied that they aided or abetted in Miller's murder.

Initially, Burns had been concerned about a conflict of interest in representing all three defendants, and therefore made the motion to sever. With the passage of time, however, he became less concerned about a possible conflict. The more time he spent with the three, the more he was convinced that their stories meshed and a common defense was possible. He would stress Cretzer's role, arguing that he was the killer, and acted totally on his own. Burns also planned to argue that conditions on Alcatraz were so inhumane that the inmates were driven to desperate acts such as rebellion and attempted escape. This theory had been used successfully before, and presented no danger of conflict. So as the trial approached, Burns was comfortable that there would be no factual conflict.

By Thursday, September 5 Burns was devoting all his time to preparation for the trial. He traveled to the island daily, yet with the trial less than two weeks away he had not thoroughly interviewed every possible witness. His general theories were in place, but he still needed to flesh out many details. All three of the defendants would deny they were present when Miller was shot, having already abandoned their role in the escape. Burns knew this would be a difficult story to sell, based on what he knew the surviving hostages would say. On that bleak autumn day, Burns was in the prison visitors' room interrogating Thompson once more, reviewing in minute detail the events just prior to and contemporaneous with Cretzer's shooting orgy, hoping to uncover additional facts that would assist Thompson's defense.

"Okay, Buddy," the attorney probed, "tell me again exactly what Cretzer said just before he shot Captain Weinhold."

Wrinkling his brow as he struggled to recall as much of the critical information as he could, Thompson hesitated, then explained thoughtfully. "You know Mr. Burns, I've been thinking a lot about this and it would be easier for me to remember all these details if I could see that statement I signed for the FBI after the break. It was real long and it had a lotta' stuff in it. Is there any way I could see that statement?"

Instant fear and anxiety swept over Burns as he stared in disbelief at the man sitting on the other side of the table. Why hadn't this statement come to light before now? How could he have spent so much time working on the case without asking if Thompson had given a statement? Now, a scant seven court days before the trial, Thompson's already difficult defense was saddled with a new burden. Burns felt a sick feeling in his stomach. His mouth went dry.

"This could screw things up in a big way!" he thought. "A signed, written, statement taken just days, perhaps hours after the riot. What does it say? Does it differ from what he's told me up till now? How do we play it from here?" His mind was racing. He couldn't concentrate, and felt himself slipping into a state of panic. Little by little his intellect took control of his thoughts and he began to objectively review his options.

Burns was unable to disguise his concern as he pressed Thompson for details. When was the statement taken? Who took it? Who was present? What were the circumstances? Did he say anything different from what he is saying now? Burns silently wondered how someone so street smart and experienced with law enforcement procedures as Thompson could have signed a written statement, knowing he was certain to face murder charges. He concluded that it was an example of Thompson's ego and criminal machismo. Thompson believed that he was invincible in his dealings with the FBI investigators, and as a result had now greatly complicated his defense.

Immediately upon arriving back at his office, Burns phoned Collins with the news. Burns was angered by the turn of events and blamed himself for not uncovering the information sooner. With the defense planning in high gear and factual details still coming together, it was necessary to stop and reevaluate the state of trial preparation and determine what changes, if any, would be brought about by this new revelation.

"Wayne, we've got a serious problem in the Alcatraz case. I spent the day with Thompson and out of the blue he announced that he had given a statement to the FBI. I thought I had asked him about statements, but evidently I hadn't. I can't believe I didn't raise it with him. Apparently they interviewed him over a two or three day period right after the break. He told me the statement has several pages and he signed it. God only knows what's in it. The agents wrote it and he signed it. This really changes things. Are you able to meet me tonight for dinner?"

"Holy shit!" exclaimed Collins, "what a time for this to surface. But better now than during the trial. Don't blame yourself Ned, this kind of thing happens sometimes. We've got time to deal with it. I'll meet you at Hoffman's in an hour. We've got a lotta' work to do!"

Hoffman's Grill on Market Street was crowded. Tuxedo-clad waiters darted from table to table through the atmosphere of cigarette smoke and the din of chatter from the diners. A San Francisco landmark, the restaurant's clientcle was principally well-dressed business and professional men doing business or relaxing after a day of work. At an out of the way table, the two young barristers reviewed their problems and considered the possible courses of action.

"As I see it," Burns summarized, "this statement makes it impossible for us to represent all three defendants in the same trial. If there's anything in Thompson's statement adverse to the other two, that's a clear conflict. And the possibility of something adverse creates enough of a conflict that I believe we have to withdraw. Thompson claims there is nothing adverse, but he also doesn't recall what's in the statement. It's my guess that the FBI put plenty of bad shit in there and Buddy signed it. I called Hennessy when I got back to the office to get a copy of the statement, but he just laughed and said 'no way.' Obviously he's right; there is no authority to compel production, but we probably ought to make a motion to compel anyway."

"I agree, Ned, as long as we don't know what's in the statement, the potential for a conflict exists and we can't represent all three of them in the same trial. It's either a severance of Thompson or we've gotta get out of the whole damn case."

"We'll have to move fast," Burns continued. "Let's do a motion to sever Buddy out of the trial, a motion to produce the statement, and a motion to withdraw. The motion to produce will probably be denied and if Goodman denies us the severance, then each defendant has to have separate counsel, and it can't be you or me. We can stay in the case to help all the defendants as a group, like with instructions and legal stuff, but we can't represent any one of the defendants at trial."

As he enjoyed a bite of his rare roast beef, Collins nodded affirmatively, indicating his accord with Burns's analysis. It was a possibility they had recognized all along and had been the basis for the earlier motion to sever. Now, the conflict was real.

Time was critical, and Burns was in the office early Friday morning. He and Collins divided up the work, and both men worked feverishly. By Saturday morning all the moving papers were in the hands of the court clerk, setting the motions for hearing the following Wednesday, September 11. The formalities were concluded with such speed that the marshal's office had insufficient time to make arrangements for the defendants' transportation to court. The defendants were entitled to be present for all proceedings, and therefore the arguments could not proceed as scheduled. The judge continued the matter for one day.

On the morning of the 12th, Burns's first act was to explain to his clients what was taking place. They were able to understand the reasons for the motion to review Thompson's statement, but none of them understood Burns's explanation of the Motion to Withdraw or the possible conflict he faced in representing all three of them. Thompson steadfastly denied that anything he had said in his statement was inconsistent with what he had said later. If Burns could represent all of them before he knew about the statement, Thompson saw no reason why he couldn't continue to represent them after learning of it. They were all comfortable with Burns as their attorney, and with the trial only a week away, did not know why they should lose him over some technicality they didn't understand. It was not a happy scene at the defense counsel table when the case was called and Judge Goodman took the bench.

Hennessy was so confident that the request for production of the statement would be denied that he didn't even file written opposition to the motion. He did oppose the Motion to Sever, arguing that there was no showing that the defendants could not get a fair trial if tried together. Joint trials, he contended, were proper for the efficient administration of criminal justice and should be rejected only upon a showing by the defense of substantial injustice.

Goodman was unimpressed with Burns's arguments in support of the first two motions, and denied them both. "Counsel, I can sympathize with your desire to review Mr. Thompson's statement, but there is no judicial or statutory authority permitting me to make such a ruling in the face of the government's opposition. I will therefore deny your motion for discovery. On the question of severance, frankly I see no change in the case since Judge St. Sure considered this matter in July and denied the motion. I will deny the pending motion on the same grounds that the previous motion was denied."

While he was not surprised at the judge's rulings on severance and discovery, Burns was shocked when Goodman expressed doubts as to the existence of any conflict and addressed the defendants directly. "Mr. Burns has raised a question as to whether he can continue to represent all three of you in the trial because he feels it will present a conflict of interest for him to do so. Has he discussed this matter with you?"

The three defendants, surprised at being addressed personally by the judge nodded affirmatively.

"Before ruling on the motion to withdraw, I would like an expression from each of you as to your desire to have Mr. Burns and Mr. Collins continue to represent you. Mr. Carnes, is it your choice that these attorneys continue to represent you?"

"Yes Sir," Carnes quietly responded.

"How about you Mr. Shockley?"

Shockley glanced briefly at Burns, then nodded in the affirmative, but Goodman would not accept a nod of the head as a response. "You will have to answer audibly, Mr. Shockley, so the court reporter can record your response."

"Yes Sir," he responded, smiling broadly at Burns.

"Mr. Thompson?" Goodman continued.

Ever suspicious of the judicial system, Thompson was not ready to express his desires. "Your Honor, I'd like to talk to Mr. Spagnoli before I do anything." Turning around, Thompson acknowledged his former attorney who was seated behind him in the front row of the spectator section. Spagnoli, suddenly the center of attention rose and approached the bench.

"Your Honor," he began, "Mr. Collins called me over the weekend, and after explaining the conflict situation, asked me if I was available to once again participate in the case. I agreed to assist if my services were needed, now that I am no longer involved with the Japanese war crimes trial. I have not as yet had a chance to discuss the situation in detail with Mr. Thompson. It would be my suggestion that the court declare a brief recess so I may meet with Mr. Thompson and Messers Burns and Collins to discuss the best method of handling Mr. Thompson's representation."

Actually, Spagnoli had never been selected as part of the Japanese defense team, but he would never make such an admission. The investigation into his background conducted by Army Intelligence had produced an adverse recommendation. The conclusion from the final report of the investigation staff made it clear that Spagnoli was unfit for the job.

"...In view of the foregoing and in view of Spagnoli's general background and reputation as indicated in the testimony of responsible informants contained in the attached report, it is believed that he is entirely unsuitable for the contemplated assignment, particularly since there is every indication that he might attempt to use his position to further his own personal aggrandizement."

"Very well," Goodman agreed. "The Motion to Withdraw as it pertains to the defendants Shockley and Carnes is denied. I am not satisfied that a conflict exists and that Mr. Burns is unable to jointly represent these defendants. Additionally, both men are satisfied with Mr. Burns as their counsel and desire his continued representation. As to the defendant Thompson, the matter will stand in recess until 11:00 A.M."

As the judge disappeared into his chambers, his black robe billowing behind him, the marshals performed their solemn task of chaining the prisoners together for their short trek to the holding cell. The convicts were led down the corridor to the holding cell by the marshals, and the attorneys fell into line behind. Wedged into the crowded cubicle, Spagnoli was the first to speak.

"I don't understand Goodman's ruling on the conflict point and frankly I think he's wrong. It's my view that each defendant should be separately represented. There's bound to be inconsistencies in the testimony and it's just too risky for one lawyer to be representing all three parties. I agree with your motion to withdraw and it should be granted." He went on to point out that if Burns and Collins were permitted to withdraw the new attorneys would be granted a continuance of the trial and could still take advantage of all the preparation work done to date. Burns, who had been in the case from its inception, could help out in the background making a defense team of five or as many as seven attorneys. "Let's face it, we'll need all the help we can get to derail the Hennessy Express once it gets rolling."

"There's still a lot to do to get the case ready for trial," Burns admitted, "and we could sure use a continuance of a month or two. It's obvious to me that Wayne and I should withdraw and two new attorneys should be brought in to try the case for Clarence and Sam. That's the best thing for you guys," he recommended to the two confused defendants, "and keep in mind, I'll still be available to help."

The discussion went on for several minutes when Thompson, who had been strangely quiet, spoke up. "Well, I'd like to have you come back and be my lawyer, Mr. Spagnoli." Looking at his two co-defendants, he addressed them sagely, "I think you guys outta do what Mr. Burns says. It sounds right to me and let's face it, we ain't in no fuckin' hurry to go to trial here now are we? It was a bit of unintended humor, but it eased the tension and relaxed the other two convicts.

"Whatever you say Mr. Burns," Carnes quietly agreed. "It's okay with me and Sam. Right Sam?" Shockley nodded his affirmation, but did not speak.

When court resumed at 11:00 A.M., the defense team and all three defendants were in full agreement that Burns and Collins should withdraw and new counsel be appointed for each defendant. "Your Honor," Burns began, "during the recess the defendants decided that it would be in their best interests to each have independent representation. When the conflict point was thoroughly explained to them, they also agreed that it would be preferable for Mr. Collins and myself to withdraw and have new trial counsel appointed. We will still be associated in the defense, but will not participate in the trial. Additionally, Mr. Thompson requests that Mr. Spagnoli be re-appointed as his lead counsel and that Aaron Vinkler be associated with Mr. Spagnoli."

"Is that correct, Mr. Thompson?" Goodman interrupted.

"Yes, Your Honor," Thompson responded.

Vinkler was experienced, and had tried a number of capital cases. He was also a hard worker who could be counted on to attend to the details that Spagnoli would overlook. Goodman knew Vinkler both professionally and personally and held him in high regard.

Knowing that the granting of the motion would result in a continuance, Hennessy argued vigorously in opposition, but to no avail. Goodman was moved by the fact that all three defendants expressed a desire to have individual representation. He granted Burns' motion to withdraw, and rescheduled the trial for September 26. It was understood by all that before that date the new defense attorneys would move the court for a further continuance. Goodman terminated the hearing by announcing that he would appoint new trial counsel that afternoon.

7
—

Anticipating his return to the case, Spagnoli had contacted his friend, Aaron Vinkler requesting that he associate into the case. While not a specialist in criminal defense cases, Vinkler readily agreed. He liked Spagnoli and relished the challenge presented in defending the Alcatraz badmen. Vinkler's practice was principally in the business field, but he had tried a number of cases, both criminal and civil. There was no question in the minds of the other defense attorneys or the judge, that the handsome barrister would do an excellent job.

Vinkler was born in Scotland in 1900, the son of a successful shoe manufacturer, who gambled away most of his profits. As a youngster, Vinkler worked as a hospital clerk, and earned enough money to buy his passage to the United States at the age of sixteen. He settled in San Francisco, and lived with two of his older sisters in the Sunset District. He financed his own education, eventually receiving both undergraduate and law degrees from the University of San Francisco. During the course of his education he also managed to develop fluency in eight languages.

Admitted to the bar in 1925, he immediately entered private practice. Over the years he practiced with various attorneys in partnerships and cost sharing arrangements. As both a lawyer and a businessman, Vinkler developed an excellent professional reputation. His charming Scottish brogue was effective before a jury, and he was a worthy opponent in any piece of litigation in which he became involved. In 1929, he married eighteen-year-old Annett Freedman and they had two daughters. Vinkler's family soon became the center of his life. The debonair, pipe smoking attorney led a comfortable life, enjoying both professional and financial success. He also devoted a considerable amount of time to religious activities, acting as the Synagogue attorney without charge.

~

Back in his chambers the judge immediately began the task of naming attorneys for the two unrepresented defendants. After considering the Shockley matter for some time, Goodman decided to appoint William Sullivan to defend him. Sullivan had appeared several times in Goodman's court and the judge had been impressed with the young lawyer's ability and work ethic. Sullivan was an aggressive young litigator, and Goodman felt he would give Shockley a good defense. He had just returned from war service and was eager to re-establish his practice and return to trying cases. Goodman knew that the U.S. Attorney's Office would mount a powerful prosecution in the case, and he wanted a defense attorney that would fight just as hard to save Shockley's life. Bill Sullivan was that kind of a lawyer.

Weary from the rigors of a difficult trial and the jubilant late night that followed the favorable verdict, Sullivan had spent a leisurely morning. He called a number of the witnesses who had testified at the trial to advise them of the verdict. He took a couple of congratulatory calls from attorney friends who had learned of his victory. He then worked for a short time on a matter for a new client, Leon Uris. Uris, a former marine, had recently hired him to handle a contract dispute and the two had become friends. Sullivan found Uris to be an interesting individual and was impressed by the serious dedication he demonstrated about writing a book, chronicling his World War II experiences. The fledgling author even had a name for his yet unwritten historical novel, *Battle Cry*.

Sullivan was flattered by Goodman's call. "Mr. Sullivan, this is Louis Goodman at the District Court. I have a very serious case going to trial and the court needs your help." He went on to describe the details of the case, and requested that Sullivan undertake the pro bono defense of Shockley. The young attorney, like nearly everyone else in the Bay Area, was familiar with the facts of the riot, and had followed the press coverage of the resulting criminal charges.

"Yes, Your Honor," he responded, "I'd be more than willing to represent Mr. Shockley, provided I will have adequate time to prepare and can otherwise clear my calendar."

The judge assured him that scheduling would not be a problem suggesting, "Well Mr. Sullivan, the court will look favorably on a motion to continue the trial. I'm also sure that Mr. Hennessy will be cooperative regarding the trial date."

Sullivan was a native San Franciscan, and his maternal lineage was

"Old California." His mother, Laura, was born and raised in agricultural Yolo County near Sacramento. Her parents shocked the conservative rural society in the 1880s by divorcing, a disgrace she and her sister Vernetta found too painful to endure in the small farming community. To escape the stigma, the two girls moved to San Francisco. In the City, Laura met and married a brilliant young lawyer, William A. Sullivan, a partner in the law firm where she worked as a secretary. Sullivan's aspiring career, however, was cut short by his death from tuberculosis at the age of thirty-two. Life was not easy for the young widow, who was forced to go back to work to support and educate her two sons, William Jr., five, and Jack, three.

Young Bill Sullivan followed the typical San Francisco Catholic educational pattern, attending the parish elementary school, St. Ignatius High School and the University of San Francisco. After two years of undergraduate study he became disenchanted with the Jesuits and left USF in favor of Stanford. There he was an outstanding student, and enjoyed considerable success as a member of the boxing and tennis teams.

Although admitted to Stanford Law School, Sullivan chose instead to attend the tuition-free Hastings College of Law, part of the University of California. The Hastings campus was in San Francisco, enabling the young student to live at home. Throughout his formal education, his goal never wavered from the objective he had set for himself as a child, to become a trial lawyer. Not afraid to raise his voice to an opponent or a judge, the feisty litigator never backed down from a confrontation, even when it was appropriate to do so. Soon after his admission to the clubby San Francisco trial bar he became known among his colleagues as "Wild Bill" Sullivan.

Following his graduation from Hastings in 1939, Sullivan practiced law with the O'Gara brothers, Gerald and James until the outbreak of World War II. He enlisted in the Army early in 1942, and graduated from Officers Candidate School as a 2nd lieutenant. He requested immediate assignment to a combat unit, and saw considerable action in Europe, being awarded both the Distinguished Service Cross and the Silver Star. On one occasion, he single-handedly captured a German bunker and its eighty-one soldiers. He returned to civilian life a true war hero, but unlike a number of his contemporaries, chose not to trade on his war record. He simply resumed his San Francisco law practice and pursued his goal of attaining stature as a respected member of the trial bar.

Sullivan returned to the O'Gara law firm, renting space as a sole practitioner. It was a successful arrangement as neither of the O'Gara's had a fondness for the courtroom, and young Sullivan eagerly handled all of their trial work. He worked ceaselessly to develop his skills as a trial lawyer and accepted as many cases as he could, including pro bono criminal matters.

Goodman's choice for Carnes's attorney was Archer Zamloch, who had recently been impressive in a case he tried in the judge's court. Goodman assumed that the prosecution would be handled by Hennessy himself, and he believed that both Zamloch and Sullivan could hold their own against the experienced prosecutor.

Zamloch readily agreed to represent Carnes when Goodman called him. With two partners to whom he could turn for backup, Zamloch was unconcerned with scheduling. His first thoughts were of how he would get along with the other lawyers involved. He knew Sullivan from their undergraduate days at Stanford and thought highly of the wild young Irishman. "It'll be fun trying a case with Bill," he thought to himself, although he doubted that Sullivan had ever tried a capital case. He had seen Spagnoli in trial and was unimpressed with the older man's lawyering skills, but the two men got along well. "Spagnoli's good at getting his name in the paper," he mused, "so there'll probably be a good deal of publicity associated with the case."

As he hung up the phone, Zamloch looked up to see his partner Jim MacInnis returning from a long and somewhat liquid lunch with some of his detective friends in the police department. "That was Louie Goodman appointing me to defend Clarence Carnes in the Alcatraz murder case," he announced with pride. "Ernie Spagnoli and Ned Burns were handling the case, but apparently some kind of conflict developed and Burns had to bail out. Goodman appointed Bill Sullivan and me to defend two of 'em and Spagnoli will represent the third guy."

"Jesus Christ, what a cast of characters," quipped MacInnis in jest. "I'm sure Hennessy will try it for the government. With you four wild men in there anything can happen. You'll have your work cut out for you though, with Hennessy. He's a tough old son of a bitch and he's tried a ton of cases. There's nothing that guy doesn't know about the inside of a courtroom, but we stuck it up his ass in that Henri Young trial back in 1941, and he's never forgotten it. Hey! maybe I can be of some help to you in getting your case ready."

"That's right" Zamloch recalled, "you tried that case back when I was still with Hardware Mutual. And you got that guy off didn't you?"

"We sure as hell did. We got the jury so pissed off at Alcatraz that they brought in a verdict of involuntary manslaughter, then sent telegrams to congress, the attorney general and half the world demanding a federal investigation and closure of the prison. It was great! Sol Abrams co-defended with me. You may want to talk to Sol about the case. He played the 'good guy' and I was the asshole. I ripped and tore up the warden and his people on cross-examination. It was total 'pillage and plunder,' like you wouldn't believe. But it paid off. God, how it paid off! The jury foreman was the president of The City of Paris department store, a real law and order kinda guy. He was furious at the treatment Young got and really led the charge against the prosecution. He even called a press conference after the trial to blast Alcatraz and the conditions out there.

"You guys oughta think about using that approach, if it fits your case. I don't know anything about your guy, but they really beat the hell outta Young and treated him shitty. We got some good psychiatric testimony from Doctor Joe Catton and some of the guards were pretty poor witnesses.

"I may be able to help you with this thing, Archer. I'm happy to do anything I can. I'll have my secretary dig out the old file and you can take a look at it. It may help. Who knows? I'll agree though, that your case is a helluva lot different than ours. Young just killed another con. Out on the Rock they call that 'Misdemeanor Murder.' Your guy's charged with killing a guard. Big difference! But I'd still recommend that you look over the old file."

While not from a wealthy background, Zamloch had lived most of his life in upper-middle class surroundings. His father, Archer Sr., was a professional baseball player, playing in the Pacific Coast League for both the Sacramento Solons and the Oakland Oaks. The elder Zamloch was a swift centerfielder, acknowledged to be the fastest man in the league. Zamloch's uncle, Carl, also played professionally, and was able to advance to the major leagues. Zamloch's paternal grandfather had attained fame in another entertainment medium, as a highly successful magician. Antone Francis Zamloch was born in Austria, and was an exciting figure in his grandson's eyes. The youngster loved to watch his grandfather perform.

When he was twenty-eight and at the height of his career, the senior Zamloch's baseball career was cut short by a serious knee injury. Undaunted, he studied accounting and built a successful business career as an accountant and executive for Foster and Kleiser, the largest outdoor advertising company on the Pacific Coast.

Archer attended Lowell High School, San Francisco's college preparatory high school. He was a bright youngster, and did well academically. He was rarely challenged even by Lowell's advanced curriculum. Zamloch was a small boy, standing only 5'4" and weighing less than 150 pounds. He inherited his father's athletic genes, however, and enjoyed considerable success in both baseball and basketball.

With excellent grades, a full schedule of extra-curricular activities and family money, Zamloch was welcomed with open arms by Stanford University. There he was an excellent student and athlete, participating in baseball, basketball, and rugby until, like his father, he suffered a serious knee injury. He graduated in 1937, and was admitted to Stanford Law School that same year. Three years later he passed the bar examination.

Jobs for young lawyers were scarce, so Zamloch accepted employment with an accounting firm, but soon moved to Hardware Mutual Insurance Company as an insurance adjuster. This job brought him closer to the courtroom and realization of his dream of becoming a trial lawyer. He dealt frequently with trial attorneys, including the firm of Hallinan and MacInnis.

Vincent Hallinan was the senior partner in the firm and well on his way to becoming a San Francisco legend. A champion of unpopular and liberal causes, Hallinan maintained a busy criminal defense trial schedule. The civil cases he accepted were generally on behalf of individuals, and the tireless warrior took pride in his frequent battles with the establishment and corporate communities.

The junior partner in the firm, James Martin MacInnis, graduated from Stanford Law School the year Zamloch began there. Personable and well liked, MacInnis was a terror in the courtroom, and was widely regarded as one of the top litigators in the City. His remarkable success in the celebrated Henri Young murder case was only one example of MacInnis's many courtroom triumphs as both a civil and criminal litigator.

It was with excited anticipation, therefore, that Zamloch accepted employment with the firm when offered a job by MacInnis in 1942. Zamloch was permitted to share in the fees from the cases on which he worked, and those he brought in. There was plenty of work and he did well financially. He worked hard, learned fast, and tried cases every opportunity he was given. He soon established his own reputation in the legal community and after only four years with the firm had tried dozens of cases. His list of successes included several murder cases and he boasted a perfect acquittal record in all his homicide trials that had gone to verdict.

Zamloch's most notable success had been his representation of Joseph Finkel, "the Green Glove Rapist," in 1943. Finkel was a serial rapist, who terrorized the exclusive Pacific Heights District of the City for months during World War II. He was finally captured and tried. The case was hopeless, one of the most difficult that the young lawyer had ever handled. After a trial that lasted fifty-nine days, Zamloch was able to obtain an acquittal on nearly half the charges brought against his client. By the end of 1945. Zamloch was rewarded with a partnership in the firm. After less than six years in practice, he was a partner in a fine firm and a respected member of the San Francisco trial bar.

8
—

With the case set for trial, the new defense attorneys had a great deal of work to do and very little time within which to do it. There was no question that the court would grant the newly appointed attorneys a continuance, but no one expected a delay of more than two months. During that time, Sullivan, Zamloch, and Vinkler would have to learn the case from the ground up and Spagnoli would face the chore of reacquainting himself with the matter.

In an era predating the copy machine, reproduction of Burns's files and notes was time consuming. Everything had to be typed and it was a laborious process. Meanwhile, the newly appointed attorneys were busy clearing their trial calendars for the next several weeks in anticipation of a November or December trial. Both Zamloch and Sullivan immediately prepared written motions for a continuance, with affidavits apprising the court of when they would be available for trial. Spagnoli, knowing the court would grant additional time, relied on his co-counsel to do the work and chose not to file a motion. His trial calendar was a meager one, and he was not concerned as to the trial date.

The motions to continue were heard by Judge Goodman on the morning of September 18. Before the judge appeared on the bench, Zamloch and Sullivan huddled with their clients, whom they had previously interviewed on Alcatraz, and explained what would be going on that day. Spagnoli used the time to patrol the spectator section and hallways, seeking out members of the press. The motion had only been scheduled the day before, and as a result, the press was not well represented. Nevertheless, Spagnoli managed to locate three newspaper reporters covering the case and made himself available for interviews.

The hearing was brief. The U.S. Attorney presented no opposition to the requests for continuance. At the outset, Goodman addressed himself personally to the defendants Shockley and Carnes and obtained their approval of their new attorneys. The judge then announced that the motions would be granted and the trial would be continued. He scheduled September 23 as the date when a new trial date would be set and directed all counsel to be present at that time. After the hearing, Hennessy, the defense attorneys, and Warden Johnston gathered in the back of the room to discuss possible trial dates. The first date available to all counsel was the third week in November, so November 20 was agreed upon as the date to be suggested to the court for trial. Ever the professional, Hennessy made it clear to all opposing attorneys that they would have complete access to not only their clients but any convict witnesses they wished to interview on Alcatraz. He assured them that the Alcatraz authorities would be cooperative in scheduling meetings, and that if any difficulties developed, he would be personally available to assist with scheduling problems. Warden Johnston confirmed Hennessy's assurances.

After Hennessy and Johnston left, Spagnoli suggested that all the defense attorneys meet with Ned Burns sometime within the next few days. This, he advised, would give everyone an opportunity to discuss the case, obtain Burns's input and get everyone going in the same direction. A mutual defense was not what Zamloch had in mind. His preliminary review of the case indicated that he was better off distancing Carnes from the other defendants. He believed that his defense would differ sufficiently from the other two, that close cooperation might not be wise, or even possible. He also felt that there would probably be instances where Carnes's testimony would be adverse to the others. On the other hand, he had no desire to alienate his co-defendants, and readily agreed to a meeting and brainstorming session. Since Sullivan was undertaking his first capital case, he was eager to participate in the meeting and gain whatever knowledge or advantage he could. They all agreed, therefore, that such a meeting would be held as soon as possible. A week later, Goodman ordered the trial to begin on November 20, and on September 30, in Ned Burns's office, the Alcatraz defense corps had its first and only team meeting.

Spagnoli assumed the role of chairman of the meeting and immediately began pontificating as to how the case should be handled. He spoke in grandiose terms, describing the high visibility inmates he intended to call as witnesses, and referring to the convicts by their first names as if he was part of their prison society. Zamloch, though thirty years younger than Spagnoli and far less experienced, was unimpressed with the older man's approach.

"I don't mean to be impertinent, Ernie," he broke in politely, "and obviously you've had a lot more experience in the courtroom than I, but I think it might be well if we listened for a time to Ned to get his views on the case, and his ideas on tactics. After all, he came within a few days of taking this case to trial so obviously he had given it more thought than all of us combined."

"I agree," interjected Sullivan, also unimpressed with Spagnoli's monologue. "Ned, why don't you give us your thoughts on the case and any advice you have. We've all interviewed our clients and have been through the file; but I, for one, would like to hear your thoughts on the various issues and defenses available to us. I'd like to know what you think of the case and how closely you think we can work together."

"Yeah, yeah, I think that's a great idea," responded Spagnoli, concealing his annoyance at losing his center stage position.

Burns, a quiet yet highly effective trial lawyer, had never really had the opportunity to immerse himself in Thompson's defense, since for much of the time, he had been represented by Spagnoli. Soon after Burns focused his preparation on Thompson, the conflict developed and he withdrew. So when asked to present his thoughts on the inmate's defense, he began with a disclaimer.

"Frankly Ernie, given your background in the case, you know as much about Thompson's defense as I do. My experience with him hasn't been too good. In my opinion he's a lot of mouth and I don't know how well he'll work with the other defendants. At the same time he's ring-wise and well thought of by the prisoners, so lining up witnesses shouldn't be too difficult. What they have to say, however, may present some problems. I think he'll be the hardest sell of the three. He's arrogant and will take a lot of preparation."

He noted that Thompson's primary defense would be alibi, his claim being that he had abandoned the escape and returned to his cell by the time Cretzer shot the hostages. Burns added that he wanted to re-interview some of the witnesses, but a number of those he had talked to would place Thompson in his cell when the shooting took place.

To Sullivan, Burns shook his head and smiled sadly. "Shockley is a total lunatic and his defense, in my opinion, will depend on you convincing the jury that he's crazy. Everybody out there I've talked to believes that Sam is insane. Even before the riot everybody referred to him as 'Crazy Sam.' He's been cooped up in isolation for the last three years, which hasn't done anything to improve his sanity. I've been told that his intelligence test results place him in the moron classification, so he's retarded as well as crazy. You may even get some help from the guards as to Shockley's sanity. I haven't talked to any of them in detail, but their informal comments suggest to me that even most of the staff considers Shockley crazy. You've interviewed him, what do you think?"

"I've only spent a couple of hours with him so far," responded Sullivan, "but I'm convinced he's either crazy or faking. So far I haven't been able to get anything out of him as to his version of the facts. He tells me he doesn't remember anything and I don't know whether he's telling the truth or not. My preliminary thinking is that I should get the court to appoint a psychiatrist to examine him on the question of his competency to cooperate in the preparation of his own defense. Right now he's either not capable of cooperating or refusing to cooperate. Maybe he's trying and just has no recall. I don't know, but right now things are pretty much the shits."

Burns agreed. "He never made much sense to me when we talked about the break and most of what he said was 'I don't know.' I'm not sure Hennessy has a murder one case against Shockley." Burns advanced. "I'm certain Shockley wasn't part of the original plan and I think he just ran out like a crazy man when Cretzer racked open the cells in D block. I like your idea of getting a psychiatric exam, because I never got much cooperation from him either.

"The other thing," Burns added, "is that he's a real squirrelly guy and I don't know how well he'll be received by a jury. He's not the arrogant asshole that Thompson's going to be—sorry about that Ernie—but he's going to come across weird. Those eyes of his are the eyes of a madman and I don't know whether he's going to frighten the jury, piss them off, or draw their sympathy. All his weirdness fits an insanity defense well, but there are so many unknowns. You've got your work cut out for you Bill."

Sullivan nodded understandingly at Burns's analysis. These were basically the same conclusions that he had reached on his own. Somehow he was going to have to package this piece of human flotsam into someone who would be favorably received by a jury. Given his inexperience, and what he had to work with, Sullivan wasn't sure how he would accomplish this.

There was an air of confident sophistication about Archer Zamloch that made him seem taller than his diminutive 5'4". Years earlier he had been impressed by a comment of legendary San Francisco trial lawyer Ingemar Hoberg, whom he greatly respected. In speaking to a group of lawyers, Hoberg had stated that to be a really effective trial lawyer a man had to be taller than six feet or shorter than 5'6". Zamloch took pride in his stature and was once described by a disgruntled opponent as "...the only guy I ever knew who could strut while he was sitting down." He believed he had properly analyzed his client's case but was also keenly interested in what Burns had to say.

"Carnes's best defense is probably his age," suggested Burns. "He's only nineteen and if you get some parents on the jury they're not gonna want to execute a kid. The other big thing going for him is that at one point he checked on the hostages and reported them all to be dead when they were all alive. That came out in Lageson's testimony at the coroner's inquest and should be extremely helpful. There's no question, though, that Carnes was in on the deal almost from the beginning, although he denies being part of the planning. He was there at the start of the break, he used at least two weapons, he was in on the capture of several guards, and he was there for some of the shootings. He's also got a shitty background including a murder conviction when he was only sixteen, incarceration at Alcatraz at age eighteen, and a life sentence plus ninety-nine years. He's a sullen kid and I don't know how well he'll do in front of a jury. On the other hand, he seems bright and I think you can work with him. But, I'll tell you, Archer, in the several meetings I've had with him we certainly have not become good buddies. What's your make on him?"

"Well I agree with most of what you say," Zamloch answered quietly, "and I think the major chore will be to warm him up and make him a little more human than he's appeared in the interviews I've had with him. I think he's got potential as a witness, but I'm a little concerned abut the fact that he was obviously in on this thing from the beginning and is up to his eyeballs in the conspiracy count.

"Another thing," Zamloch continued, "he claimed during one of our meetings that he tried to help Lageson just before Cretzer shot him. Did he ever say anything to you about that?"

"Yes he did and, to be honest with you, Archer, I didn't understand for sure what he was talking about. He told me that he arrived outside the hostage cells just as Cretzer was about to shoot Lageson. As Cretzer reloaded, Carnes claims he motioned Lageson to duck and when Cretzer fired Lageson lurched forward. He thinks he did Lageson a favor, but at the same time he doesn't seem to be pushing it as part of his defense. Number one, I'm not sure it amounts to anything, and number two, I doubt that Lageson will go along with that testimony. Lageson's gotta be one pissed off guy by this time and I'll be shocked if he acknowledges that Carnes did anything to help him, assuming that what the kid did can be considered help. But yeah, he's made that same claim to me. If you can get him to admit that he tried to help Lageson and the other hostages, and stress his age and his deprived background you may well have something going for you. You're going to have to hammer the hostility out of him, and pound a little 'good guy' up his ass, but if you do it right, Archer, you may be able to save the kid's life."

"I feel the same way about Shockley, Bill. I think that case can be won on insanity. Ernie, I don't know about Thompson. I think he's an asshole and I think the jury's going to think he's an asshole. But, if anybody can save him, you're the guy."

The meeting went on for the entire morning, and as it proceeded, Burns became more of an observer than a participant, with the other four taking more dominant roles in the discussions. Spagnoli eventually focused on his favorite theory of defense, an attack on Alcatraz and the Alcatraz personnel. "I think our best bet is to get some of these 'big shot' convicts in here like "Machine Gun" Kelly, Bob Stroud, Tom Robinson, Floyd Hamilton and the like to talk about the Alcatraz brutality. There have been a couple of Alcatraz homicide cases tried in the federal court in the last few years where the juries have been so pissed off at conditions out there that they virtually let the defendants off. That's the way we ought to go. Cretzer acted alone, our guys had nothing to do with the shootings and whatever our guys did wrong was forced on them by the brutality of the Alcatraz prison system."

"I think that oversimplifies the situation," replied Zamloch, "but if you want to pursue that theory you ought to talk with Jim MacInnis, who as you know, along with Sol Abrams, defended Henri Young. You also ought to talk to Harold Faulkner and Joe Sweeney, who got "Whitey" Franklin and Jimmy Lucas off with life for killing a guard during a break a few years earlier. That's not going to be a big part of my defense, but I'm for anything that hurts the prosecution."

"The Young case is something you might want to pursue, Bill," Burns suggested. "Jim and Sol did a helluva job with an insanity defense in that trial and it had a lot of parallels with Shockley. Young had been in isolation and solitary for three years and claimed abusive treatment. When he got out, the first thing he did was stick a knife into Lucas McCain, one of his partners in an earlier escape attempt. The defense was temporary insanity and Young claimed no knowledge of the details of the crime. It looked like a clear case of murder one, but the jury accepted the insanity and brutality arguments and found him guilty of involuntary manslaughter."

Throughout most of the meeting Sullivan had remained quiet. Because of his inexperience he was content to listen and learn from his more experienced co-counsel, and contribute only when he felt he had something valuable to add or when he had a question relative to Shockley's defense. "I seems to me," Sullivan finally broke in, "that one of the most important things in handling this case is to stay out of each other's way and be sure that we don't do anything to hurt one another. My guy's not gonna hurt either Carnes or Thompson and I would hope that neither of them take any shots at him." Sullivan knew from the coroner's inquest there would be testimony that Shockley urged Cretzer to shoot the hostages and he hoped the other defendants would not corroborate this very harmful fact.

"I agree that we should cooperate to the greatest extent we can," responded Zamloch, "but this early in the case I don't know for sure what everybody's gonna say. As I understand it, there's going to be evidence that Shockley struck Weinhold when he was being put in one of the cells and that he called for Cretzer to shoot the hostages. I haven't discussed this with Carnes, so at this point I don't know what he'll say about that." It was obvious that Zamloch was willing to cooperate, but just as obvious that he was leaving his options open.

The attorneys all agreed that Burns would stay on the case, working in the background. He would be available to assist in the preparation of voir dire questions, motions during trial, jury instructions, legal research and any matters pertaining to the defense effort in general, including an appeal in the event of a death penalty verdict. Ethically he could not work for any one defendant to the exclusion of the others, but all counsel felt there would be no problem with his helping on issues and aspects of the defense common to all three defendants. Burns also agreed to be an information clearinghouse, and act as a sounding board for any attorneys who wished to test out arguments.

9
—

By the first week in October, trial preparation was well underway, and both the prosecution and defense attorneys had cleared their calendars through the end of the year. In the U.S. Attorney's office, Hennessy had Dan Deasy working full time reviewing the FBI report and interviewing witnesses. Deasy, the son of a former San Francisco Superior Court judge, was a relative newcomer to the office. He had, however, tried a number of homicide cases and Hennessy had confidence in his ability. Hennessy planned to handle most of the case, although Deasy would examine some of the witnesses. The two men worked well together and Deasy was comfortable working as the number two lawyer on the case. With the full resources of the FBI, Alcatraz, and the U.S. Attorney's office, the government's preparation was smooth and thorough.

Hennessy had spent time with both Lageson and Burch during the coroner's inquest. He was satisfied that both men would be effective witnesses. They had dramatic stories to tell and Hennessy believed that their testimony along with that of the other hostages would present an overwhelming case of first degree murder. He felt that Associate Warden Miller, who had also testified at the inquest, would have a more difficult time as a witness. Hennessy had tried a number of Alcatraz cases and Miller was always vigorously attacked during cross-examination. In his role as chief of prison discipline, he incurred the wrath of every inmate who suffered any punitive measures, and was constantly accused of brutality toward the convicts. Considering the number of times he had heard these allegations, Hennessy was beginning to wonder if the charges might be true.

The interviews with all of the hostages had gone well, but Hennessy was concerned about three of the witnesses. Lieutenant Simpson and Captain Weinhold had been very badly wounded and were still hospitalized as the trial date approached. Initially, Hennessy was concerned as to whether the two men would be strong enough to testify, but they appeared to have recovered sufficiently to appear in court.

Cecil Corwin, on the other hand, presented a different problem, one that Hennessy feared was certain to be taken advantage of by the defense. The FBI had interviewed numerous inmates who were confined in D block when Coy overpowered Burch, and their versions of the facts were all contrary to that of Corwin. "You know Dan," Hennessy had worried, "I'm concerned about Corwin's testimony. He's going to be our weak link. He is such a nice guy, but he performed so badly during the break that I'm afraid it's going to hurt the case. The defense guys will come after him like gangbusters, and if Goodman lets them go, they'll have Corwin for lunch on cross-examination." Deasy shared Hennessy's concern and listened intently as the U.S. Attorney analyzed the aging guard as a witness.

"The ruckus in the gun gallery lasted for two or three minutes, and every con in D block knew some kind of a fight was going on up there. The phone was right there, but Corwin never touched it. He didn't call the armory or any other duty station. He claimed Fleish prevented him from doing so, but the evidence is totally to the contrary. If Corwin had done his job and turned in the alarm, the escape attempt would probably have ended right there with little or no injury or loss of life."

"What do you think happened?" Deasy inquired. "Did he panic?"

"That's my take on it," Hennessy responded. "The cons in the cells closest to him heard Corwin ask Fleish what he should do, then he did nothing. Obviously Corwin's conduct is no defense to the charges, but I expect the defense lawyers to stress his inept conduct and attempt to blame Miller's death on the guards."

Corwin was a highly intelligent man who was both articulate and cooperative. A jury would probably respond well to him, but Hennessy was concerned that he would be vulnerable on the facts. "It's going to be his word against Fleish, who emphatically denies that he interfered with Corwin in any way. Fleish made the same denial to the FBI right after the break, and the D block inmates corroborate his version. It should all be irrelevant, but if the defense gets into it, they'll be able to lead the jury off into the boondocks and away from the real issues of aiding and abetting and conspiracy."

The biggest unknown for Hennessy was what Shockley would say and whether the Government could establish that he was anything more than a highly vocal bystander. Hennessy was satisfied that he could make a case against Shockley for both conspiracy and aiding and abetting, but it would not be nearly as strong as the cases he had against Thompson and Carnes. Shockley had refused to discuss the case with the FBI investigators so Hennessy had no idea of his version of the facts. He also didn't know if Sullivan planned to rely on insanity as a defense. From reviewing Shockley's prison file, Hennessy recognized that insanity was a likely defense. He had expected Burns to request the court for a psychiatric examination of the defendant and was sure that Sullivan would make such a motion.

Hennessy never became emotionally involved in the cases he prosecuted. However, he had experienced personal embarrassment at the result in the Franklin/Lucas case and the incredible verdict in the Henri Young matter. Verdicts like those, he felt, made penal work on Alcatraz more dangerous than it already was. He was determined to prevent another unfavorable result. These prior cases were on his mind as he prepared for trial and planned how he could keep the hostile Alcatraz testimony out of evidence. In Hennessy's mind, such evidence was irrelevant to the escape attempt and the murder of Miller. Hennessy believed that the Alcatraz insurrectionists were simply hardened criminals serving long terms for serious crimes. Two officers had died as a result of the conduct of these men and Hennessy was dedicated to evening the score. These three men would pay with their lives for their crimes.

Although initially interested in the brutality defense, Zamloch soon realized that it would not fit with Carnes's defense. Carnes had only been on Alcatraz for a year and during most of that time had been in idle status. He had never been in isolation or solitary and had never even seen the inside of D block. The conditions on Alcatraz had played no role in Carnes's decision to join the escape attempt. He was serving a ninety-nine year sentence for kidnapping and escape after which he faced a life sentence for murder in Oklahoma. It was the length of his sentences and a desperate feeling of hopelessness that he would never attain freedom that had motivated the young Indian. As much as Zamloch would have liked to have been able to blame Carnes's surroundings, he knew he could never make such a defense work.

Zamloch's analysis of the case led him to the conclusion that Carnes would probably be found guilty of homicide. His job as defense attorney, therefore, was to save the youngster's life. To accomplish this he would need more than the fact that his client was only nineteen years old. He needed to establish conduct by Carnes or some factual evidence upon which the jury could rely to arrive at a sentence less than death.

Even with his life on the line, Carnes presented a tough, sullen countenance that was difficult for Zamloch to break through. Carnes's experience with defense lawyers in the past had not been rewarding. In both his prior cases his attorneys had listened to his story, then recommended guilty pleas. These pleas resulted in his terms of ninety-nine years and life. Carnes had never selected his own attorney. All his prior lawyers had been court-appointed. He recognized that Zamloch was his only hope in the present case, but still viewed defense attorneys as "part of the system." After several hours with Zamloch, however, Carnes developed a greater feeling of comfort with him than with any of the attorneys who had represented him in the past.

During one of their early meetings, Zamloch was questioning Carnes regarding his contacts with prison authorities following the riot, with a view to uncovering any statements or admissions the young man may have made. When asked about the associate warden, Carnes flew into a rage as he recounted the terrible beating he had received from Miller after the riot. "I hate that son of a bitch," Carnes fumed, "I saved that asshole's life and his thanks was to beat the shit out of me. I wish Hubbard had blown his head off."

"What do you mean, you saved his life?" Zamloch inquired in total disbelief.

"Well, when we was comin' out of the dining hall after Coy had shot at the tower guards, we seen Miller running towards us down Broadway. Hubbard stopped real quick and took a shot at him from point black range. He couldn't miss that fat target. I seen it happening and I didn't believe killing even Miller made sense, so I kinda bumped into Marv and screwed up his aim. He only got off one shot and it went wild. Miller turned around and ran for the main gate before Marv could get off another shot."

Zamloch stared into Carnes's deep set black eyes, hoping to convince himself that the young man was telling the truth. If true, that evidence could go a long way in countering the prosecution's argument that Carnes acted with malice and intent to kill. If he could argue that Carnes had saved the life of the associate warden, Zamloch felt he had a chance of saving him from the gas chamber. "Did anybody other than Coy see you bump into Hubbard?" asked Zamloch, fearing a negative answer.

"I don't know," responded Carnes, "there was five or six guys still in the kitchen but they was all hiding and I don't think any of them could see us from where they was."

Zamloch immediately determined to request the names of the kitchen detail and follow up on Carnes's story. The attorney was not even sure that the event had happened, let alone that it was an intentional act by Carnes to save Miller, but he was determined to thoroughly investigate his client's claims. He interrogated Carnes further as to any other humanitarian acts he may have performed during those critical hours.

"Is there anything else you did that day, Clarence, by way of helping any of the guards or doing anything to save any of them like you did for Miller?" As soon as he asked the question, Zamloch could detect a tension develop in Carnes. The young convict didn't answer the question. Sensing a problem, Zamloch pressed on and repeated his request.

"Well, like I told you before, I kinda signaled to Lageson that he oughta duck just before Cretzer shot him. But listen, I don't want any of this shit comin' out in the trial," directed Carnes.

"What do you mean you don't want it coming out during the trial? That's the kind of evidence that can save your life, Clarence," the lawyer responded with a tinge of annoyance in his voice.

"Well the guys'll say that I sold out and that I'm a screw lover. They'll call me a fink and stuff like that," the young defendant explained. "I'd get blamed for all them screws not gettin' killed."

Zamloch had tried several homicide cases and, over the years had dealt with hundreds of criminal defendants, but he had never faced a situation quite like this before. *The Alcatraz society is indeed a strange one, he thought, where a man will face the death penalty before he'll let it be known that he performed some act of kindness that saved the life of a prison guard.*

Zamloch studied his young client and chose his next words carefully. He needed the boy's cooperation, and to gain it he felt he had to break through the youngster's tough façade. He stood up and walked to the other side of the room. Drawing himself up to his entire 5'4" height he turned slowly and faced Carnes. He stood silently for a moment and then spoke.

"Look, Clarence, you're charged with a capital crime here and the death penalty is a realistic possibility. Let me be totally frank with you. This is not the time for you to be worrying about some piss-ant prison social status and whether those guys out there on the Rock are going to like you or not. If we lose this case you're not even going back to Alcatraz, because the next cell you'll see will be on Death Row in San Quentin. Believe me, Clarence, you are in deep shit. You have a choice to make and you have to make it right now. You have the alternative of possibly being known as a screw lover and fink and being alive or being a hard nose tough guy and being dead. If you did something to help any of those guards it could very well save your life if you let me use it as part of our defense. If we don't use it, your defense will suffer. You gotta decide what it's gonna be, because I can go either way. I can only defend you if you cooperate with me."

The two men stared silently at one another for what seemed to the young attorney to be an eternity. Finally a hint of a smile crossed the young convict's ruddy face and he said, "Okay, Mr. Zamloch, we'll do it your way." Zalmloch breathed deeply and slipped his hands into his pants pockets to dry his sweaty palms. Both men were smiling now and as Zamloch resumed his seat they both relaxed visibly. "Call me Archer," he smiled.

Carnes's grin broadened. "Mr. Zamloch is just fine with me," he responded in a quiet voice barely above a whisper.

10

The more he studied the Henri Young case, the more impressed Sullivan became with the striking parallels between Young and Shockley. Both were docile, non-aggressive individuals. Both had been confined for lengthy periods of time in isolation with periodic stays in solitary. Both had long records of minor misbehavior for which they suffered harsh punishments. Finally, both inmates claimed almost complete lack of recall of the events for which they were on trial. Sullivan felt his case was even stronger because Shockley was of such limited intelligence that he could not feign insanity or derangement. Sullivan wasn't necessarily impressed with Shockley's honesty, but was impressed with the fact that he wasn't bright enough to lie successfully.

After a number of interviews with his client, Sullivan concluded that Shockley was not sane enough to assist in his own defense. Their sessions together were totally unproductive and Sullivan's frustration was turning to despair. Shockley seemed to want to help, but there was very little he could contribute that would help prepare the defense. He repeatedlly described the riot that took place in D block three days earlier and how he had managed to destroy virtually everything in his cell, as if this was in some way crucial to his defense.

Sullivan was convinced that Shockley did not grasp the magnitude of the situation. He was unable to discuss with him the various defense theories and tactics. Shockley couldn't suggest the names of very many potential witnesses, since he had no recollection of the events on the day of the riot. Sullivan made a motion requesting a mental examination to establish that Shockley could not adequately participate in his own defense. He was confident that this would be the finding of any qualified psychiatrist, and that Shockley's trial would be delayed until he was found competent to cooperate with his attorney. Sullivan continued his trial preparation, however, on the outside chance that the psychiatric findings would be different than he expected.

In the absence of Judge Goodman, the matter was assigned to Judge Roche, who heard the motion on October 28, 1946 on only three day's notice. There was no opposition from Hennessy and the motion was routinely granted. So confident was he that Shockley would be found incapable of assisting in his defense, that Sullivan had let more time pass than he should have before filing the motion. With the motion granted and the order on file, Sullivan wasted no time in scheduling the examination. Roche had ordered that the examination be conducted by Dr. John Alden, a forty-three-year-old, well-respected psychiatrist.

The examination was conducted in the Alcatraz hospital on November 5. Alden was courteously received by Warden Johnston, who offered his full cooperation. He furnished the doctor with Shockley's entire prison file, including various intelligence test results and background information developed by the Bureau of Prisons and Department of Justice. After a thorough review of the records and a lengthy discussion with the warden, Alden conducted an in-depth interview of Shockley. He found the patient to be totally cooperative and willing to answer all questions, with the exception of those related to the break. Each time the conversation drifted to the events of May 2, Shockley politely declined to respond, stating that he did not feel that it was right for him to talk about the break because of the impending trial. Following his examination, Alden prepared a report for the court with copies to be delivered to Sullivan and Hennessy. Unfortunately, because of scheduling problems and the time it took the doctor to prepare the report, Sullivan did not receive his copy until just a few days before the trial was set to begin.

It was Monday morning, the 11th of November, nine days before the trial. Arriving late at his office, Sullivan positioned himself behind his desk and began thumbing through the mountain of notes he was organizing for the trial. He had conducted his trial preparation with the belief that the case would be continued once Alden's report was filed. As a result, his preparation had not been the intense type that he would have performed had he been confronted with a date certain for trial.

He was just finishing his second cup of coffee, when his secretary dropped a bundle of mail on his desk. Near the top of the pile he saw the return address of the Federal District Court. *John Alden's report*, he thought, as he ripped into the envelope with excited expectation. Having read many medical-legal reports in both civil and criminal cases, he automatically turned to the last two pages for the reporting physician's opinions and conclusions. He felt a stab of nervous apprehension in the pit of his stomach as he read with shock and dismay the final paragraph of Alden's report:

> In my opinion, at the time of my examination on November 5, 1946, Sam Richard Shockley was able to understand the nature and consequences of his actions, was capable of understanding the nature of the charges against him, was able to confer with his attorney and was capable of preparing his defense.

"Jesus Christ," Sullivan whispered aloud as he slumped back in his chair. "We're going to trial next Wednesday, and I'm defending a goddam crazy man that the doctor thinks is sane." More than at any time during his short tenure as counsel for Sam Shockley, Sullivan realized the magnitude of the task facing him. He read the final paragraph again in disbelief and stared at the final page of the report. For the next hour he read and re-read the entire report, studying and analyzing every line and phrase.

He was particularly concerned about two aspects of the report. First he was upset because the doctor had concluded that Shockley was legally sane and could participate in the preparation of his defense. Regardless of Alden's opinion, Sullivan knew Shockley couldn't adequately participate in his own defense. But there was nothing he could do about that now. Second, since Sullivan had not raised the question of Shockley's sanity at the time of the riot, the doctor had not considered this aspect of the case. There was nothing in the report regarding Shockley's sanity on May 2 when the killing took place. Not only did he have to prepare his case with a client who was incapable of cooperating with him; he had no expert evidence of his client's sanity or insanity at the most critical time of all, the time of the killing. The mental exam upon which he had placed such great hopes had turned out to be a total disaster.

11

John Driscoll, deputy clerk of the U.S. Federal District Court, sat at his desk, alone in the ornate courtroom of Judge Louis Goodman. Outside raged the worst winter storm of the season. Rain, driven by forty mile per hour winds lashed the Bay Area, bringing with it periodic heavy hail showers. In the mountains, snow blocked all the Sierra passes, disrupting both travel and communication. Driscoll perused the final morning edition of the *Examiner*, reading with interest about the storm that was punishing Northern California. Already ten deaths and heavy property damage had been attributed to the weather disturbance. Thirty Muni trolleys had been disabled, and numerous automobile accidents contributed to congested streets and traffic chaos. Noting that two more storms were approaching the California coast, Driscoll felt fortunate to be employed indoors rather than outside battling the elements like his brother on the San Francisco Police Force. He was also happy that there was no morning calendar today, as he prepared for the start of the Alcatraz murder trial the next day. There were a few brief hearings set on the afternoon calendar, but everything for them had been prepared, giving Driscoll the luxury of reading the paper this morning.

He turned to the sports page and began reading an article about The Big Game, set for Memorial Stadium in Berkeley next Saturday. As he concluded the article, he heard the door to Judge Goodman's chambers close, indicating that the judge had arrived. Although there was no prohibition against reading the newspaper during working hours, the heavy-set, red-faced Irishman quickly folded the paper and slipped it into the bottom drawer of his desk. He gathered up the Alcatraz files, walked slowly into the combined office/cloak room, which he shared with the court reporter, and poured a cup of coffee for the judge. He knocked on the door and, without waiting to be acknowledged, walked into Goodman's chambers with the files and the steaming hot coffee.

"Good morning, John," greeted Goodman. "The weather out there is absolutely frightful. We sure took a beating down our way last night. Two trees in my neighbor's yard were blown down by the storm."

"It's pretty bad all right," Driscoll agreed, "and the paper says we can expect two more storms over the next few days." The big man with his tie slightly askew proudly presented his boss with the coffee and set the files on an open spot on the Judge's cluttered desk. "I brought in the Alcatraz files, Your Honor. The attorneys have filed proposed *voir dire* questions and have indicated that they will have a few pre-trial motions. As you know there's nothing on the calendar for this morning so you'll have plenty of time to go over the files. There's only a handful of brief hearings this afternoon; you've got a real light schedule today."

"That's fine, John," the judge announced as he sipped his coffee, "but I'm basically ready to go with this case."

Goodman, appointed to the bench in 1942 by President Franklin Roosevelt, had an illustrious academic background. A champion debater in high school and college, he received his bachelor's degree from the University of California in three years, then passed the bar examination after only one year of law school. His undergraduate classmates included Earl Warren, later chief justice of the U.S. Supreme Court; J.D. Zellerbach, a leading figure in the commercial paper industry; and Robert Gordon Sproul, who later served as president of the University of California. Following admission to practice, he joined the law offices of Louis H. Brownstone and maintained a law practice for more than twenty-five years. As a practitioner, Goodman represented primarily corporate and affluent clients, but once on the bench he displayed an uncommon concern for the indigent defendant. Describing his feeling to a friend, he once stated, "It is the little fellows, the great mass of small offender, who give me the sleepless nights. No one knows or cares about them; the burden of terrible power is much greater than in the instance of a man who moves with the world and can hire lawyers."

As Driscoll excused himself, Goodman set his coffee on his desk and picked up the Shockley file. He thumbed idly through it, then looked quickly at the other two files. He had thought about this case a great deal during the last few days and he had also reflected on the earlier trial involving Henri Young. Goodman had not been on the bench when the Young case was tried, but had followed the trial in the newspapers. Like many San Franciscans, he had been interested in the testimony since so little was known about Alcatraz. Also like many others, he had been surprised at the verdict and the subsequent conduct of the jury. As an attorney, however, he considered the result an anomaly, contrary to the facts and law of the case. Even though he respected Judge Roche, he had questioned many of the judge's evidence rulings in the case, and wondered whether the defense adopted by MacInnis and Abrams was proper. The defense attorneys had been permitted by Roche to put Alcatraz on trial; thereby shifting the jury's focus away from the crime of the defendant and onto the alleged conditions that prevailed in the prison.

In preparation for the present case, with the Young trial in mind, Goodman had taken the time to read several chapters of *McBain on Evidence* as well as a few other evidence texts. He had presided over several homicide trials in the four years he had been on the bench, but made a special effort in this case to refresh his understanding of the evidentiary rules that might arise. He had also recently declined the opportunity to discuss the case with Judge Roche during lunch. Roche had mentioned the case, knowing it was coming up for trial, and Goodman had quickly changed the subject. When he thought about it later, he was puzzled by his conduct, but for some reason had felt uncomfortable discussing the matter with his fellow jurist.

Finishing his coffee and sliding the Alcatraz files aside, he unfurled his copy of the morning *Chronicle* and glanced over the front page. The lead story described John L. Lewis announcing that he was terminating the contract between the government and the United Mine Workers. Lewis's action, as president of the union, was in violation of an existing court order and the Department of Justice indicated they would file contempt charges against him and the union. It was the beginning of a showdown between Lewis and President Truman, who had previously stated he would neither back down from the government's position nor compromise with the union. Truman contended that Lewis was in violation of a federal District Court restraining order prohibiting the miners from striking. Lewis had called the miners out anyway.

Although a political liberal and always sympathetic to the labor movement, Goodman reacted negatively to the situation. Regardless of politics, he was a law and order judge and was uncomfortable with the story. He put the front section aside, and turned to lighter reading on the sports page. The lead story there was about the Big Game. As a California alumni, his sympathies were with the Golden Bears as they prepared for what surely would be a mud and bloodbath at the hands of the Stanford Indians. Living on the Peninsula, Goodman resided in Stanford territory, but his heart was with the Bears. It had not been a good year for California football, and their coach, Frank Wickhorst, was under considerable pressure from the student leaders. A loss in the Big Game would also be a loss of employment for Wickhorst and his staff. Severe weather was predicted for Saturday, and Goodman had already decided not to attend the game.

Following his review of the newspaper, he turned back to the Alcatraz files and began making notes for his opening comments to the jury and the *voir dire* procedure, which would commence at 10:00 A.M. the following morning.

Voir dire, a French term meaning "to speak the truth," was the essence of jury selection. It was the process of individual interrogation of each prospective juror designed to determine his or her qualifications to serve and to reveal any bias or prejudice. In federal court, the judges conducted the *voir dire* examination on their own. They would, however, allow the attorneys to submit questions in advance and on rare occasions permit them to ask clarifying questions of prospective jurors. Generally, however, the attorney's role in the questioning process was severely restricted, to prevent the lawyers from trying to influence the jurors. Goodman noted that Zamloch was seeking permission to participate in the *voir dire* procedure, and although he rarely granted such a request, because of the seriousness of the case, veiwed the motion favorably. It was late morning by the time Goodman completed his review of the files and the pre-trial motions. It had taken much longer than he had anticipated. This was in part because he had taken the time to read all the motions and pleadings that had previously been made and ruled upon. This was not his usual approach, and he wondered why he had been so inordinately thorough.

As he set the files aside, his mind wandered and he found himself thinking about how the case would play out. The only one of the lawyers that Goodman didn't know well was William Sullivan. He had only seen the young Army veteran in court a few times. Sullivan was somewhat inexperienced and quick tempered, but had boundless energy and enthusiasm. Goodman was confident he would do a good job. Zamloch had appeared in his court many times, as had Spagnoli. He considered Zamloch to be an extremely competent trial lawyer, who would conduct himself in a highly professional manner. Spagnoli, he thought, would probably spend a lot of time on his feet making spurious objections. Goodman knew Vinkler better socially than professionally, as both men were active in Jewish affairs in the City. Hennessy, the wily old prosecutor, a consummate professional and acid-tongued fighter, could be depended upon to put on a strong case for the government.

This should be an interesting case, Goodman thought to himself, *and with that crew of lawyers there may well be some fireworks*. As he leaned back in his large leather chair he thought again of the Henri Young trial. *There will be no re-run of that case in my court*, he thought. *No way in hell.*

12

—

Wednesday-Thursday, November 20, 21

The final vestiges of the killer storm were passing through the Bay Area, as the principals in the Alcatraz murder case began arriving at the Post Office Building. Sullivan wolfed down a doughnut and a cup of coffee at the small cafe across the street, wishing he had gotten a little more sleep the night before. The howling storm had been partially responsible for his fitful sleep, but nerves had also taken their toll. He was starting the biggest trial of his career, one that would receive daily attention from the press. The challenge and visibility were exciting, but also made him nervous. He had lain awake much of the night, worrying. He would be trying his first capital case along with veteran criminal lawyers who had been in this position many times before. He had thought of little else but the trial for the last ten days and, although he hoped he had done everything necessary, could not be sure that he was adequately prepared. It was inevitable in trial work that no matter how hard you worked and how thorough your degree of readiness, something unexpected would come up, requiring improvisation. The finest trial lawyers, Sullivan believed, were those who handled the unexpected situations the best. Any good lawyer could handle familiar problems, but the great ones could handle the unanticipated with cool brilliance.

Sullivan met Zamloch as he entered the building and the two walked to the courtroom together. Zamloch appeared relaxed and confident and Sullivan wondered if his fellow counsel really felt as calm as he looked. Although it was thirty minutes before the case would be called, the other attorneys were all present when the two entered the courtroom. The spectator section was almost empty, as the prospective jurors were still in the jury assembly room on the floor below. A handful of the "courthouse regulars" sat in the rear row, chatting about the upcoming trial. There were a dozen or more senior citizens that frequented the City's courtrooms. All retired men, they would divide their time between the federal trial courts housed in the Post Office Building and the San Francisco County Superior Court located a few blocks away in City Hall. None of them were interested in the appellate courts, but were fascinated with observing the trial courts at work. Whether these old fellows were frustrated attorneys or litigants, they had a burning affection for the litigation process. They were equally at home watching civil or criminal cases, and a trial as noteworthy as the Alcatraz murder case was of particular interest. They all recognized Hennessy and Spagnoli, but not all of them were familiar with the other attorneys. Hennessy and Spagnoli recognized the professional observers as well, and exchanged greetings with them.

The defense lawyers began arranging their files at the counsel table, automatically positioning themselves at the table in accordance with custom. Although no written rule dictated the order to be followed by the defense attorneys in the event of multiple defendants, over time, the custom developed that the defendants would proceed in the same sequence as they were named in the charging allegations. The court always retained the right to alter this order if cause was shown and the attorneys could agree to a different order if they wished. Generally, however, the progression would be established by the order the defendants were named in the indictment, which meant that Sullivan would go first during each phase of the defense case, followed by Spagnoli or Vinkler, and finally Zamloch.

Another procedure dictated by custom rather than rule, was the positioning of the attorneys at the counsel table. Over time it became the practice that the party with the burden of proof occupied the portion of the counsel table nearest the jury. Therefore the prosecutor in a criminal case and the plaintiff's attorney in a civil trial sat closet to the jury.

While the attorneys quietly and somewhat nervously arranged their materials and positioned themselves at the counsel table, additional observers began to filter into the courtroom. Soon the spectator section was more than half full. Included in the audience were federal employees eager for a glance at the Alcatraz inmates and a contingent of journalists assigned to cover the trial for the local press and national wire services. Two floors below, under heavy security, the defendants arrived for what was expected to be nearly a month's "vacation" from their island home.

For the duration of the trial, they would be housed under special security in the San Francisco County jail. Today, as always, the trio arrived in handcuffs and heavy shackles, chained together at the wrists and ankles. They were led into the holding cell where they waited, manacled and under armed guard, for court to begin. Under the watchful eyes of three Alcatraz officers, three specially assigned deputy U.S. marshals, and the bailiff, the defendants were marched to their appointed places. They sat in chairs away from the counsel table, against the wall to the right of the judge, with two marshals seated next to them. The rest of the custodial force sat in the front row of the spectator section.

Promptly at 10:00 A.M. the door to the judge's chambers swung open and Judge Goodman, his black robe flowing behind him, moved swiftly across the courtroom and mounted the four steps to the bench. Those familiar with courtroom protocol rose immediately without waiting for the cry of the bailiff. "Hear Yea! Hear Yea! All rise! The District Court of the United States of America for the Northern District of California, Southern division, is now in session, the Honorable Judge Louis E. Goodman, presiding." As the judge took his seat on the bench, the bailiff concluded his proclamation with, "All be seated and be in order."

Goodman's court was strikingly ornamented. It was paneled in white marble with elaborately carved columns supporting ornate statuary. The arched ceiling was covered with baroque carvings. Multi-colored skylights along with three large windows permitted natural light to flood the room.

The spectators resumed their seats, amid the rustle of raincoats, umbrellas, and newspapers. Driscoll, in a soft, firm voice, markedly different from the sonorous tones of the bailiff, quietly called the case at hand, "The United States of America versus Sam Richard Shockley, Miran Edgar Thompson and Clarence Victor Carnes." As he finished speaking, all the attorneys rose and one by one stated their appearance and the party they represented.

From the bench, the judge looked down on the counsel tables in front of him and the jury box to his left. The clerk and court reporter sat in front of the judicial dais, between the judge and the attorneys. The witness stand, slightly elevated, was located to the judge's left, between the bench and the jury. Outside the rail were rows of seats sufficient to hold two hundred and fifty spectators. Today the panel of prospective jurors occupied sixty of those seats. The trio of defendants looked like they had been stamped out of a mold, in their black three piece suits, white shirts, black ties, black shoes, and white socks. Without speaking, they glanced nervously at the standing room only crowd in the spectator section.

After a few preliminary remarks to the jury, during which he introduced the attorneys and their clients, and described the general nature of the case, Goodman inquired of the attorneys as to whether any of them had any preliminary motions.

The first motion to be heard, was one to continue the trial. Spagnoli made this on the grounds that a petition for habeas corpus was pending on behalf of Thompson and the issues raised in that proceeding should be resolved before the present case proceeded to trial. Spagnoli had filed the habeas corpus petition to challenge Thompson's sentence for kidnapping and transporting a stolen motor vehicle across state lines. Initially Thompson had received a sentence of ninety-nine years, which was subsequently changed by the trial judge to life imprisonment. Spagnoli contended that this modification constituted an illegal sentencing and, as such, Thompson was being illegally held on Alcatraz when the riot of May 2 occurred. The petition had been argued before Goodman only a few days earlier, and he had taken the matter under submission until after the trial. He summarily denied Spagnoli's motion.

Spagnoli immediately launched into a second motion, challenging the composition of the federal grand jury that had handed down the indictment. He contended that the grand jury was drawn improperly from the federal jury list, which was undemocratic because it did not contain the names of "the laboring classes." Goodman allowed Spagnoli to argue his emotional plea for dismissal of the charges against Thompson, but summarily denied the motion even before Hennessy could rise to present his opposing argument.

At the conclusion of Spagnoli's fruitless arguments, Zamloch requested that the attorneys be permitted to actively participate in the *voir dire* questioning of the jury. Goodman announced that, although it was contrary to his customary procedure, he would permit the attorneys to ask questions after he had completed his inquiry of each juror. However, the attorneys were barred from revisiting any matters that the court had already covered. This was satisfactory to Zamloch, whose major concern was that as the questioning proceeded the court would tend to cut short the examination in an effort to speed things along. Goodman had a tendency to hurry *voir dire* and was often not as thorough in his interrogation of prospective jurors as Zamloch liked. He wanted to be able to cover areas he knew the judge would skip over as the process became repetitive and time-consuming. His victory, however, was only temporary. Halfway through the selection process, Goodman reversed himself, concluding that the attorneys were repetitive and wasting time in their questioning of the prospective jurors.

The final defense motions came from Sullivan. He requested that the defense be granted additional peremptory challenges beyond the twenty allowed by law. A peremptory challenge permitted a party to excuse a juror without explanation. In this case, Goodman ordered that peremptory challenges be exercised jointly by the defendants. Goodman reserved his ruling on the motion until later, indicating that he would reconsider the question in the future if the number of challenges became a problem. Sullivan also moved to exclude all witnesses from the courtroom while testimony was being taken. This motion was granted with the exception of Warden Johnston and two investigating FBI agents, Thomas Dowd and William Dillon, who were permitted to remain in court throughout the entire trial as representatives of the government.

The last preliminary motion was made by Hennessy, requesting that the defendants be remanded to the custody of the U.S. Marshal during the trial so it would not be necessary for them to be returned to Alcatraz at the end of each court day. With the granting of this motion the court was prepared to commence selection of the jury and the trial was officially underway. Activated by a nod of the judge's head, Driscoll selected twelve names at random and the eight men and four women took their seats in the box.

The judge had only thirty minutes to question prospective jurors before the noon recess. At the request of the defense, he cautioned the jury before dismissing them that "...guilt or innocence of these defendants is not to be determined by the circumstances under which this trial is held, nor shall your verdict be influenced by these circumstances." Whether such an admonition would be effective was speculative, but there was grave concern on the part of the defense attorneys that their clients would not get a fair trial. These fears were exacerbated by the negative press coverage such as the hangman's noose photograph. Anti-Alcatraz sentiment always ran high among a segment of the Bay Area public, and had heightened after the May riot.

The noon recess produced a logistical problem for U.S. Marshal George Vice. Now that the defendants had been remanded to his custody, it was his responsibility to provide them with the noon meal. They were fed breakfast and dinner in the county jail, but lunch would be served in the holding cell. Vice's budget provided a scant $.21 per day for a prisoner's meal and he found it impossible to locate a caterer to work for such paltry pay. It was necessary, therefore, for him to contact Alcatraz, where box lunches were hurriedly prepared and messengered across the Bay. Forced to gulp down his sandwiches just before the start of the afternoon session, Carnes suffered through the afternoon first with hiccups, then with indigestion.

Much of the afternoon session was devoted to Goodman's continued questioning of the jury. At the outset, Spagnoli requested that Thompson be permitted to sit at the counsel table so he could actively participate in the jury selection process. Goodman granted this request, to the obvious pleasure of the Texas killer. He smirked and strutted arrogantly to the counsel table, taking his place with the lawyers. He shot a priggish glance at his two confederates, and looked around the courtroom with self-important pride. Shockley sat with a fixed stare watching the proceedings, most of which he did not understand. Carnes appeared bored and squeezed his lower lip with his fingertips as he stared at the ornate ceiling. At the counsel table, Thompson was animated. He studied the list of prospective jurors, and made whispered comments to Spagnoli. As the judge questioned the members of the panel, Thompson made notes that he passed along to his attorneys. Occasionally, he would turn and wink at his two co-defendants.

The judge had completed his examination of the jury by mid-afternoon and permitted the attorneys to ask follow-up questions. He repeatedly admonished them for covering matters that he felt he had adequately reviewed, and finally cut off their questioning completely, directing counsel to begin exercising peremptory challenges. The defense challenges were dictated by Thompson. He had listened carefully to the questioning and had taken extensive notes. The name of each juror to be excused by the defense was announced by one of the lawyers, but in every instance Thompson made the determination.

At the end of the first day, forty-seven prospective jurors had been examined. Thirteen had been excused peremptorily by Thompson, who smugly enjoyed his role as the center of attention at the counsel table. Hennessy used his challenges to excuse eight venire-men and women. A total of fourteen jurors were excused by the court for cause, all but two of whom expressed opposition to the death penalty.

By the middle of the second day, Goodman had quickened the pace of jury selection to the point of absurdity. When one of the prospective jurors, a middle-aged businessman, expressed some question as to whether he could be fair, Goodman interrupted the juror with the suggestive inquiry, "If you're selected, you will be fair won't you?" The man timorously responded in the affirmative, but his answer failed to reassure the defense. Sullivan sought to question the juror further but was abruptly cut off by Goodman, who announced that "We're taking too long with this process. We've got to move things along." The defense, therefore, was compelled to exercise a peremptory challenge to excuse the man. In like manner, when the widow of a California Highway Patrolman killed in the line of duty guardedly indicated that she could be fair and serve without bias, the judge brusquely curtailed the attempted questioning by Sullivan and Spagnoli, stating impatiently, "We must proceed faster." Again Thompson directed that the prospective juror be excused.

As the procedure continued, the supply of venire-men and women began to diminish, and it was necessary to bring in additional jurors from other departments. Finally, after sixty-seven jurors had been examined, a jury of six men and six women was selected. The six women were all housewives. The male jurors included two corporate executives, an architect, an engineer, a retired businessman and a clerk for the War Department, who had lost both legs in World War I and was confined to a wheelchair.

The court suggested that two alternate jurors be selected, and for the first time, a question arose as to the adequacy of the number of peremptory challenges for the defense. One of the proposed alternates, Mrs. Violet Hauptli, was the sister-in-law of a San Francisco police officer. Although she had answered all the judge's questions to everyone's satisfaction, Thompson sought an additional peremptory challenge in order to excuse her from the panel. The other two defendants, however, indicated that they were satisfied with Mrs. Hauptli, and the court denied Thompson's request. The now surly convict scowled angrily at his fellow defendants. With no recourse, Thompson was forced to accept the jury as constituted, including Mrs. Hauptli.

The San Francisco Sheriff's Department did not adhere to the Alcatraz rule forbidding inmates to read newspapers. As a result, the defendants had the opportunity to see copies of the local papers every day while confined in the county jail. Angered by the nickname "Tex" given him by the press, Thompson penned the following note that Spagnoli delivered to the newsmen covering the trial:

"The prosecution has put the name Tex on me. I have never been under the name Tex Thompson. My name is M. E. Buddy Thompson."

Thompson's protestations went unheeded by the press, who continued to refer to him alternately as "Buddy" and "Tex."

Despite the superficial nature of Goodman's *voir dire*, the defense felt that they had obtained as good a jury as the situation permitted. With the exception of Mrs. Hauptli, even Thompson was satisfied with the panel. All the jurors on the panel had repeatedly denied any bias, promising faithfully that they would "…well and truly try the case." Outside the hearing of the attorneys, Thompson boasted to Shockley and Carnes about the excellent jury that he had selected. They paid little attention to him.

13

___

Friday, November 22

The end of the week brought a return of violent winter weather. Across the Bay in Richmond, fourteen power poles were toppled by high winds and heavy rain, causing power outages that closed most of the city's schools. In the Sierras, snow two and a half feet deep on highways 40 and 50 blocked both routes through the mountains, isolating many communities.

In Judge Goodman's court, the jury sat in quiet anticipation. Nodding to Hennessy, the judge announced, "All the jurors and the two alternates are in the box and you may proceed with your opening statement."

Gathering his notes, Hennessy strode slowly to the lectern, and in a formal, legalistic style, began to lay out his case. He started with a recitation of the indictment and a brief statement of the crime, then declared emphatically: "We intend to prove, Ladies and Gentlemen, that the defendants herein charged are guilty of murder in the first degree."

After a detailed description of the interior of the cell house, Hennessy focused on Thompson's repeated requests over a three day period for a lay-in from his tailor shop work assignment so he could be in his cell the afternoon of the escape attempt. "We will show that Thompson repeatedly sought a lay-in from his foreman, Haynes Herbert, and when his requests were denied, he convinced Dr. Stuart Clark, one of the prison doctors, that he was ill in order to receive a medical lay-in that afternoon."

Hennessy then delineated the events of that afternoon, carefully tying each of the defendants into the conspiracy, by describing their involvement in the capture of the various hostages and the weapons they carried. "When Sundstrom reached the west end of the cell house, Thompson came out from behind B block with the rifle and covered him. Cretzer came from

79

behind C block with the .45 and Carnes was there with a billy club to put him in cell 402. As he was entering the cell, Shockley stepped up behind him and clouted him over the back of the head. And as Weinhold was being put into the hostage cell, Shockley ran up behind him, struck him repeatedly over the back of the head, and cursed him. Captain Weinhold attempted to speak to Cretzer and dissuade him from attempting further violence, but Shockley intervened, standing beside Cretzer urging, 'Kill every goddamned bastard in there.' Then Thompson joined in, 'Yeah, kill every goddamned son of a bitch. We don't want any witnesses.' When Cretzer hesitated, Shockley attempted to grab the pistol saying, 'If you haven't got the guts to kill them, I will.' With Shockley on one side of him and Thompson on the other side, both urging him to kill every guard, Cretzer pointed the pistol at Captain Weinhold and shot him in the chest. Then he shot Miller, the man who is dead and for whose murder we are prosecuting these defendants. He fired again and shot Corwin in the face, shattering his jaw and causing him to bleed profusely. He then moved to cell 402 where, again at the urging of Shockley and Thompson, Cretzer shot Simpson and Baker.

"Returning to cell 403, Shockley observed Lageson alive in the back of the cell and demanded that Cretzer shoot him. When Cretzer saw who it was, he balked and protested, 'No that's my friend Mr. Lageson, he's a good guy.' But Shockley persisted, 'Friend hell! He'll go over to court and swear your life away just like the others. Kill the motherfucker!' Prodded by Thompson and Shockley, Cretzer aimed his pistol and apologized, 'I'm sorry Mr. Lageson,' then pulled the trigger."

After describing the remaining events of the afternoon, during which the wounded hostages lay bleeding and feigning death, Hennessy detailed the recapture of the cell house. He related how the assault team entered the west gun gallery, ultimately recapturing the gallery and bringing D block under control. "About 7:00 P.M., a group of guards led by Associate Warden Miller entered the west gun gallery through the outside door in an effort to rescue Burch and recapture the cell house. They were met by a fusillade of bullets. As he moved from one part of the gallery to another, officer Harold Stites was hit by a bullet from either D block or the open cell house door and fell over dead."

At this point the defense attorneys leapt to their feet objecting to Hennessy's erroneous assertion that inmate fire had killed Stites, explaining to the court that the evidence established that Stites was shot by fellow officers firing into D block from the hillside. It was error, they claimed, for Hennessy to blame Stites's death on any inmate, when the evidence was clearly to the contrary. "If Stites had died from inmate gunfire, the defendants would have been charged with his murder as well as that of Miller," Zamloch argued. The defense attorneys also requested that Goodman admonish Hennessy and explain to the jury that the defendants were not charged with causing Stites's death.

Hennessy responded to the objections by urging that Stites's death was part of the *res gestae* or the overall facts of the event. Since the defendants were charged with a criminal conspiracy, everything that occurred in the course of that conspiracy was admissible, and as members of the conspiracy they were all responsible for everything that happened.

Accepting Hennessy's explanation, although not yet conversant with the facts, Goodman overruled the objections and permitted Hennessy to proceed. He also refused to explain to the jury that the defendants were not accused of shooting Stites and that his death was not to be considered as part of the case against the defendants.

Following his description of the facts, Hennessy set forth the government's legal theories. "We believe we will be able to establish that each of these defendants, while they did not fire the actual shots, aided, abetted, and encouraged the shooting of William A. Miller, and in law are responsible as principals. We will show that each of these defendants actively participated in a criminal conspiracy to escape from this penitentiary, and under the law are responsible not only for their own acts, but for the acts of all their co-conspirators. We will ask you, Ladies and Gentlemen, to consider carefully all the evidence in this case, and to bring in a verdict of guilty as charged." To the surprise of all the defense attorneys, Hennessy did not ask for the death penalty. On the other hand, he did not suggest a life sentence, leaving each defense lawyer to speculate as to the prosecutor's intentions.

The defendants sat grim and silent during the prosecutor's opening. Thompson, no longer animated, listened intently, hanging on Hennessy's every word. A leaden-faced Shockley stared blankly around the courtroom with wide eyes. Carnes fidgeted with a pencil and seemed bored. Although able to maintain a strong façade, internally the youngster was experiencing growing apprehension. For the first time in his young life he was facing the realistic possibility that he might die.

≈

As Sullivan moved to the rostrum to give his opening statement, he appeared ill at ease and unsure of himself. He began by re-introducing all the attorneys and parties to the jury, despite the fact that the trial had been in progress for two days. He requested that each lawyer and defendant rise and face the jury, and surprisingly, the judge permitted this unnecessary and amateurish conduct without comment. It appeared to the other attorneys that Sullivan was using the introductions to overcome his nervousness.

Sullivan commenced his opening with a discussion of the law of conspiracy, which he attempted to explain by using a fictional case as an example. "Ladies and Gentlemen, the killer of Mr. Miller is Joseph Paul Cretzer, so why then, are these defendants on trial? It is the theory of the law from the days of King John that anybody who combines with another to do something which is unlawful is himself criminally responsible for everything that naturally follows in an unbroken chain of causation. For example, If A meets B in a hotel down here on Jones Street, and one says, 'Look, there's a tavern down the street here, that has a lot of money in the...'"

"I submit, Your Honor," Hennessy objected, "this is not an opening statement, it is an argument."

When Sullivan protested that he was doing nothing more than Hennessy had done during his opening, Goodman ruled that while the prosecutor's remarks on the subject of conspiracy had not been improper, Sullivan's were, and he should confine himself to a statement of the facts rather than become involved in a premature argument of the matter.

Frustrated, Sullivan abandoned any further effort to explain the law of conspiracy and, with a damning and unnecessary concession, accepted Hennessy's earlier statements. "So assuming that in this case there was a general plan to escape, everything that was done in the furtherance of that conspiracy would be the responsibility of all the conspirators and they would all be guilty for any acts committed. But if the facts show that the original escape plan had failed and the others abandoned it, then whatever happened thereafter is something for which none of the defendants can be held responsible."

By admitting the conspiracy and that Shockley was a part of it, Sullivan was required to defend on the theory that Shockley and the others had abandoned the plan. "What Cretzer did was utterly foreign to the plan of escape," Sullivan protested, "and therefore, his conduct released the defendants from responsibility." He went on to attack Cretzer as a madman with a violent past, whose conduct was so far beyond the plan to escape that it could not possibly be attributed to the defendants.

He denied that Shockley had made any of the statements attributed to him by Hennessy and stated that "...the only evidence of Shockley's statements will come from the guards in the cells, and because there was so much confusion you can't believe any of them as to what happened." Since Sullivan knew that Shockley had no recollection of the events and could not convincingly deny making the incriminating statements, the wisdom of this assertion was questionable. A more plausible approach would have been to explain Shockley's statements as the uncontrolled exclamations of an insane man.

Sullivan then launched into a discussion of the brutal conditions on Alcatraz, contending that when Shockley was released from his cell, he acted like an animal. He explained that as a result of spending years in solitary confinement and isolation, Shockley was deranged. "We will show that when the cells in D block were opened that afternoon by Cretzer and Sam raced out to freedom, he had no realistic idea of what he was doing, nor could he distinguish between right and wrong."

While he referred to Shockley's failure to understand the nature of his conduct, Sullivan did not explain his insanity theory in any detail. Seemingly unable to make up his mind as to his ultimate defense theory, Sullivan shifted from his discussion of insanity and returned to the abandonment notion. "But all of that isn't material in so far as these defendants are concerned, for the reason that this plan of escape had been totally abandoned by them when key #107 could not be found and the escape siren had sounded."

The further Sullivan went in his opening, the more rambling and confused his presentation became. Believing there was strength in numbers, the young lawyer sought to align Shockley's defense with the other two defendants, arguing that all three defendants were victims not participants. Finally he drifted into a disjointed emotional outburst. "You're going to have to bear with us as to how we can prove our facts. Cretzer, Coy, and Hubbard are dead. Miller is dead. Many men were wounded over there. The guards were in a little cell, feigning death, playing dead, excited. The inmates were excited. These men are on trial for their lives. They have committed crimes against society. I will say this: I have never yet met a creature who did not have a desire to live. I have seen men wounded; I have seen men die, but they all had a desire to live. These men want to live. The cause of the underdog is not an easy one. These men have been in court prior to this. They are serving life sentences. They are serving time at Alcatraz, which is segregated and set apart for the nation's most hardened criminals. I know you are going to sit and weigh the evidence dispassionately, even though there may be clashes between counsel. There is no enmity between myself and Mr. Hennessy, between myself and Warden Johnston, between myself and the FBI. You are the sole judges of the credibility of every witness who takes the stand…"

Unable to endure Sullivan's emotional and disordered ramblings any longer, Hennessy finally objected. "Your Honor, again I submit this is not an opening statement, but argument."

"Yes," Goodman immediately responded. "Counsel cut out this arguing. If you have anything more to say by way of an opening statement, go ahead."

Embarrassed and flustered, Sullivan muttered an apology, and brought his opening statement to an inglorious conclusion. "I respectfully submit to you, Ladies and gentlemen, that if you bear with us in our efforts to get the facts in this case, you will find these defendants not guilty of the crime as charged."

As Sullivan returned to his seat at the counsel table, Spagnoli rose and reiterated his earlier objection that the indictment was invalid and as such, he objected to the introduction of any testimony. Goodman, paying even less attention to him than before, overruled the objection without comment, and called the noon recess.

Since Vinkler had spent the most time with the witnesses and had developed the Alcatraz brutality theory, he made the opening statement on behalf of Thompson. Spagnoli's habit was to do his trial preparation during the prosecution's case, so at this stage of the proceedings Vinkler had far more knowledge of the facts and legal theories.

Vinkler's opening, while more orderly and organized than Sullivan's was poorly conceptualized. Whether due to overzealousness or misinformation, Vinkler committed the trial lawyer's mortal sin of misleading the jury as to what he would prove, thereby jeopardizing his credibility. He told the jury that on the day of the escape Thompson was ill, and had requested a lay-in for that reason. "On this particular day Thompson had been certified as sick by one of the prison physicians and that is the reason he was in his cell, not because he had agreed with anyone else to make a break from Alcatraz." Unfortunately for Vinkler, Thompson had previously told the FBI that he had known of the break in advance and had sought the lay-in in order to participate.

Vinkler also mischaracterized Thompson's participation in the escape. He stated that when his cell was gratuitously opened, Thompson stepped out to see what was going on. As he did, Coy immediately directed him to move the large scaffold. While Thompson and another convict, whose name he did not know, were in the act of moving the scaffold, the escape alarm sounded and Thompson returned at once to his cell. Vinkler minimized his client's involvement in the escape almost to the point of non-participation, and assured the jury that, "We will prove to you that any shooting that took place at Alcatraz took place after the siren blew and long after Thompson was back in his cell."

It was never clear why Thompson and his attorneys chose to revise history in this way. There was no question that Thompson had participated in the escape attempt. To deny advance knowledge of the breakout after he had already confessed could only raise questions in the minds of the jurors as to his credibility.

Following his brief and misleading description of Thompson's participation in the escape attempt, Vinkler focused on what he planned to be an important defense theory, the brutal living conditions imposed on Alcatraz inmates. In this phase of his opening, Vinkler was emotional and effective.

He described conditions on the island as "...worse than any German concentration camp. Alcatraz is a graduate school for hardened criminals, run by brutal guards who hate and mistreat the inmates. The guards of Alcatraz, our evidence will show, have an innate sense of hostility toward the prisoners. Any break that took place on Alcatraz was the result of the mistreatment and indignities inflicted upon these men. The escape attempt was the culmination of years of brutality. Coy, Cretzer, and Hubbard planned the whole break. Cretzer is dead and far better off than when he was in prison. This is an issue of the convicts versus the guards. The convicts hate the guards just as much as the guards hate the convicts. There will be some lying here, but it will be up to you, Ladies and Gentlemen, to find out who is telling the truth."

As he went on and his level of emotion escalated, Vinkler admonished the jury that the defendants were presumed innocent until the government had proven them guilty. He urged the panel to maintain open minds, regardless of how the deliberations went in the jury room. Without any objection from the prosecution, Goodman suddenly interrupted the emotional Vinkler, chastising him for going beyond the realm of opening statement and engaging in argument. "Counsel, I do not want to shut off attorneys, but this is the time to tell the jury what, if anything, you are going to prove. If you have arguments to make, there will be a time to make them. Now if you have anything further that you wish to present to the jury having to do with what you intend to prove, you are free to do that."

The interruption had a chilling effect on the lawyer's opening. Surprised and shaken, Vinkler stammered to the jury, "I want to stress again this fact, that at the time of the shooting, Thompson was in his cell. I want you to remember that. We will prove that when the siren went off, that is when the shooting took place. The shooting took place after the siren went off, not before. That is all." With this impotent conclusion to his opening, Vinkler dropped dejectedly into his chair and stared at his notes. Thompson smiled broadly at his two fellow prisoners, unaware of the problems Vinkler had created.

When the judge called on Zamloch for his opening statement, the attorney announced that he would reserve his opening until he put on his case. This was a departure from his normal practice, but under the circumstances Zamloch felt it was a wise thing to do.

Since it was accepted among trial attorneys that between fifty and seventy percent of jurors made up their minds based on the opening statement, Zamloch always made his opening immediately following that of the prosecution to be sure the jury heard the defense's story early in the trial. Because the jury here had already heard the general defense theory from two lawyers, he exercised his option to give his opening just before putting on his witnesses. In doing so, he would be able to address the jury after he had heard the prosecution's case and could delay revealing the details of his own case to the prosecution. Zamloch was also comfortable reserving his opening because there was a significant amount of the prosecution's case with which he would agree.

While there is no unanimity among trial lawyers regarding the psychology of the order of witnesses, most feel that the party with the burden of proof should begin with a strong witness. Hennessy eschewed this philosophy and chose instead to present his case in strict chronological order. His first witness was Herbert Cole, an obscure Deputy U.S. Attorney called for the purpose of establishing that he had served the indictments on the various defendants. The government compounded its lack-luster beginning by next offering an executive order signed by President Millard Fillmore in November of 1850 to establish that Alcatraz was federal property. Although half-heartedly objected to by Spagnoli, the order was admitted.

The first significant witness called by the prosecution was Dr. Jeanne Miller, the young deputy coroner who performed the autopsy on William Miller. Not long out of the University of California Medical School, Dr. Miller was completing her pathology residency at the University of California Hospital. As part of her residency she had served as an autopsy surgeon in the coroner's office for a year and a half. Despite her youth, she was a skilled physician as well as a competent and relaxed witness.

Dr. Miller testified that the bullet entered the decedent's right arm, passing horizontally through both lungs and the forward part of the vertebral column, and lodging just above the left shoulder blade. She described the cause of death as shock and hemorrhaging into the pleural cavity. The single bullet that she had removed from the body was identified and admitted into evidence.

There was no evidence of external bruising or injury, despite Warden Johnston's assertion to the press that Miller had been subjected to a severe beating. The autopsy also suggested that the wound may not have been a fatal one had the victim received timely medical care. Dr. Miller testified that the "...gunshot wound to the right arm and thorax and laceration of the lung resulted in bilateral hemothorax." This was a collection of blood in the lung cavity that developed over time. With the passage of time and the bleeding, Miller went into shock, which was one of the causal factors in his death. His pleural cavity filled with blood, resulting in lung collapse and oxygen deprivation.

Dr. Miller's direct testimony was brief, and Zamloch immediately sought to cross-examine her on the autopsy she performed on the body of Harold Stites. Since the death of Stites had been injected into the case by the prosecution, Zamloch moved quickly to demonstrate that the autopsy established that Stites had been shot in the back.

Hennessy objected at the first hint of anything related to Stites's death, and Judge Goodman sustained his objection, shutting Zamloch down abruptly. Stites's death continued to hang over the heads of the defendants, and they were being prevented from defending themselves against Hennessy's unsubstantiated accusation.

~

In mid-afternoon, Hennessy called Warden Johnston to the stand. His intention was to use Johnston for the personification of Alcatraz. Johnston sat at the counsel table as the personal representative of the institution, and Hennessy wanted to identify Johnston with Alcatraz so that any mention of the prison would trigger a picture of the white-haired, grandfatherly warden in the jurors' minds. If the defense attempted to attack the "horrors and brutality of Alcatraz," it would be the kindly Warden Johnston they would be accusing.

In creating this favorable image, Hennessy felt it was important that Johnston make a good impression during direct examination and be protected from damaging cross-examination by the defense. He determined, therefore, to limit the warden's testimony to a few routine, non-controversial areas. Since the rules of evidence restricted cross-examination to those matters covered on direct, he hoped to prevent cross-examination on the sensitive issues the defense was so eager to explore. It was a calculated risk, with success totally dependent on Goodman's evidentiary rulings.

Hennessy's plan worked to perfection. On direct examination he had the warden identify himself and describe the prison in general terms. He then established that William Miller was a federal employee at the time of his death, and that his duties included supervising activities in the cell house when he was there alone or assisting officer Lageson. Johnston also testified that late in the evening of May 2 he had observed Miller on a stretcher after he had been wounded, and that early the next morning the officer died as a result of his wound.

All three defense attorneys took turns trying to break through the protective barrier Hennessy had created for Johnston, with no success. Zamloch repeatedly attempted to reproduce testimony the warden had given during the coroner's inquest, where he discussed the riot and Alcatraz procedures in detail. Again and again, Zamloch queried the warden as to the harsh conditions in D block and the rigors of daily existence on Alcatraz. He sought to question Johnston about inmates who had gone insane, and "the many shattered souls who had given up and attempted suicide." All his efforts were fruitless. Goodman sustained each of Hennessy's objections on the ground that the material was irrelevant and outside the scope of the prosecutor's direct examination.

Zamloch's efforts to establish the warden's bias or prejudice also met with failure. After repeated objections by Hennessy, all of which were sustained by the court, the judge admonished the struggling Zamloch, "Do not ask any more of those questions. I do not want to admonish you again. I appointed you as an attorney in this case because I thought you had diligence and were a conscientious lawyer."

"I think that is what I am doing now," responded Zamloch in exasperation.

There followed a heated exchange between the attorney and the judge, during which Zamloch implied that Goodman was obstructing him from an adequate cross-examination. "If the court instructs me that I cannot examine as to this witness's bias I can only enter an objection as to the obstruction."

Flushed and outraged by the accusation that he was obstructing the defense, Goodman stared down at the feisty Zamloch with a look that would wither most lawyers. Zamloch, chin elevated, drew himself to his full height and awaited Goodman's wrath.

"I so instruct you. You may enter an objection to it."

Zamloch's cross-examination was over and he had done nothing to tarnish the glow of the kindly Alcatraz warden. As he resumed his seat at the counsel table, the frustrated attorney muttered to himself, "You son of a bitch, you don't give a shit for anything but moving this case along and getting these guys over to San Quentin."

Hennessy had accomplished what he had set out to do. He had given Alcatraz a face and a personality and Warden Johnston had escaped without having to answer any difficult questions about the prison. In the first real skirmish of the trial, the advantage had clearly gone to the government.

The prosecution next focused on Thompson. Hennessy sought to support the prosecution's claim that Thompson had falsely obtained a medical lay-in on Thursday afternoon to participate in the escape. Three witnesses, Haynes Herbert, Glen Pehrson, and Dr. Stuart J. Clark, gave brief testimony regarding their contact with Thompson and how they saw his effort to obtain a lay-in.

Herbert, a journeyman tailor, was in charge of the tailor shop. He testified that on Monday, Tuesday, and Wednesday of the week involved, Thompson had approached him at least once each day with the request that he be given a lay-in on Thursday afternoon. On Thursday morning, however, Thompson said nothing about a lay-in. Under Spagnoli's cross-examination Herbert conceded that lay-in requests were not at all unusual. Thompson operated one of the two tacking machines in the shop. Frequently the tacking machine operators would be caught up with their work, and would be granted lay-ins. Herbert could not specifically recall any prior occasions when he had allowed Thompson to lay in, but was sure he had done so in the past.

Glen Pehrson, the officer on duty in the hospital the afternoon Thompson received his medical lay-in, was not a convincing witness. He testified that he had seen Thompson in the hospital that day and overheard him relate his symptoms to the doctor. Of the many prisoners who visited the hospital that day, he claimed a clear recollection of Thompson because "…he appeared nervous and agitated. It was his whole demeanor that just made him stand out." When asked by Spagnoli why he had such specific recall of Thompson, Pehrson's contentious response was "…it was my job to observe and I've been doing it for five years."

The final witness of the afternoon was young, arrogant Dr. Clark, the physician on duty that day. Like Pehrson, Clark gave a recollection of Thompson being nervous and agitated as he related his symptoms. When challenged by Vinkler on cross-examination as to why he was so specific in his recollection of Thompson, his manner became hostile. "I recall especially that he was quite flushed and somewhat apprehensive and nervous and he asked for a half a day off. And I just remember, that's all," the doctor snapped at Vinkler. Also like Pehrson, he could not recall any of the numerous other inmate patients that day, and when asked again how he could recall Thompson so well, he responded with flippant finality, "I just do!"

Clark had very little independent recall, and his testimony came almost exclusively from his woefully inadequate records. He had no recollection of Thompson's specific complaints or medical history. The more detailed the cross-examination became, the more hostile and argumentative his answers were. Believing that Clark would be a routine witness, Hennessy had spent minimal time preparing him. He assumed the doctor would recall his treatment of the patient and would have kept adequate records. However, Clark's supercilious manner and poor record keeping supported the defense's claim of the harsh treatment at Alcatraz, including inadequate inmate medical care. By the end of the day, Clark had been made to appear an uncaring institutional physician, who provided marginal medical treatment.

The moment the last juror left the courtroom, the marshals surrounded the defendants and swathed them in chains and manacles. As the convicts were led away, Sullivan, one week into his first capital case, relaxed in his chair and addressed his friend and co-counsel. "Well, Archer, what do you think?"

"I don't know, Bill," Zamloch responded. "As far as the jury is concerned, I like the women, but that guy MacLean bothers me. I didn't like him during *voir dire* and I still don't. Obviously it's too early to tell much about the evidence, but I don't think we can count on Goodman for much help."

"I agree," Sullivan concurred. "Letting Hennessy get Stites's death into the case was really bad. In my opinion it was clear error, but Goodman had his mind made up and there was no keeping it out. We've really gotta' stay on top of Hennessy. He is one sly son of a bitch."

Zamloch nodded affirmatively, but his mind was elsewhere. He was thinking of how he could best capitalize on the six women jurors, all of whom were mothers. As he had from the beginning, Zamloch was concerned about how well Carnes would be received by the jury. He was not the hardened killer Hennessy would portray him to be. Beneath the surface hostility and toughness, Zamloch saw a frightened boy who had lied to Hubbard and the others during the riot when he told them the hostages were all dead. Carnes had no stomach for murder and had clearly demonstrated it. How best to get that across to the jury? A major aspect of his case would be the sympathy he could generate for his young client, and he felt the women jurors would be key to this. Although the jury would be instructed not to allow feelings of sympathy affect their deliberations, Zamloch would do everything he could to plant the seeds of sympathy in their minds. It was his best hope of keeping Carnes out of the gas chamber.

14

The weekend brought not only a respite from the trial, but also The Big Game, one of the Bay Area's major social and sporting events of the year. While not necessarily considered a big game by those outside the Bay Area, the annual football battle between the University of California Golden Bears and the Stanford University Indians was a cherished tradition for the local population.

Zamloch, who received both his undergraduate and law degrees at Stanford and had participated in intercollegiate athletics, was an ardent Stanford fan, and attended the game with his wife. Sullivan, who matriculated at Stanford but obtained his law degree at the University of California Hastings School of Law, had a more ambivalent approach to the game. Judge Goodman, a 1913 graduate of the University of California, and also a Hastings alumni was a fair-weather Bear fan. Given the prediction of a substantial Stanford victory, the muddy field and threatening weather, Goodman spent his Saturday afternoon on the links at the Lake Merced Golf Club. The game was played on the soggy turf of Cal's Memorial Stadium in Berkeley under leadened skies.

It was a sad performance by California. On the field the football team performed ineptly, outmanned by the opposition. On the sidelines, Frank Wickhorst seemed confused and befuddled as he stumbled through what was to be his final game as the U.C. football coach. In the stands, thousands of disgruntled and drunken students laid waste to the rickety wooden seats in the rooting section, destroying and torching them. The police and fire departments were summoned to quell the disturbance. As predicted, the Golden Bears lost to Stanford. The score was 25 to 6.

Tuesday morning, as the attorneys waited for the trial day to begin, the game was a major topic of conversation. "As much as I enjoyed the game and the Stanford win," lamented Zamloch, "it was truly a sad display by the students in the stands. Toward the end of the game they totally lost control of things."

"It looked like a lot of drunken vets upset with their team," injected Sullivan. "Believe me, I've seen my share of drunken military conduct and this was as bad as anything I'd seen in the past."

"Yeah," responded Zamloch, "they were calling for Wickhorst's scalp and were even bitching that President Sproul was spending too much time and money on professors and not enough on athletics."

The Big Game festivities seemed to extend into the new week. Thursday was Thanksgiving and a court holiday. Since Mondays were normally reserved for court matters other than the trial, it would be only a three-day court week. This would allow the attorneys additional preparation and afford more free time in the county jail for the defendants. Enjoying more freedom in the county jail than they ever experienced at Alcatraz, the three convicts welcomed the extra day off.

The first witness of the day was Special Agent William B. Dillon, a ten-year veteran of the FBI and one of the two agents in charge of the post-riot investigation. Dillon was called by the prosecution to explain the physical layout of the cell house and describe the areas where the significant events took place.

Using a diagram prepared by another agent, Dillon described the arrangement of the cellblocks and the corridors. He also described the configuration of the west gun gallery, explaining to the jury the location of various ladders and doors. The defense attorneys all objected to the diagram, claiming it contained inaccuracies, was too small to be seen by the jury, had not been prepared by the witness, and contained notations made by someone other than the witness. Fearing that the diagram would create more confusion than enlightenment, Sullivan moved the court for a jury view of the location. "I move that the jury be allowed to view the Alcatraz Penitentiary itself for the purpose of further familiarizing themselves with the facts shown in that document. I believe the jury has that right, particularly in a capital case, to see the place where the alleged crime took place."

"Well, Mr. Sullivan," the judge responded, "I will rule on that after we have heard all the evidence. I will not make any order at this time.

After familiarizing the jury with the general physical layout of the cell house, Dillon identified numerous photographs showing interior views of the cellblocks, hostage cells, D block, gun gallery and other significant venues.

Throughout Dillon's testimony, Spagnoli made numerous spurious objections challenging the admission of the photographs. Failing in his effort to block the pictures, he repeatedly interrupted Dillon, demanding to know whether any photographs of the "dungeons" had been taken. He and Hennessy engaged in an open colloquy over the existence of the alleged dungeons and whether they had been photographed. Hennessy steadfastly denied that anything comparable to a dungeon existed on the island, but Spagnoli persisted. "I'd like to find out, if Your Honor please, if the District Attorney has any photographs of the exterior and interior of these dungeons over there."

"Unfortunately we have no dungeons over there," responded Hennessy in sarcastic exasperation. "I do not know what you mean by these so called dungeons."

During the colloquy, Goodman ignored the bickering attorneys. Finally Hennessy returned to his direct examination, offering additional photographs into evidence. It was nearly noon and the court declared the midday recess without ever ruling or commenting on the dungeon issue.

Toward the end of the morning session, Joe Bailey, one of the elevator operators in the building was confronted by a nondescript middle aged man wearing a long tweed overcoat. The man stepped into Bailey's elevator and asked politely, "Could you tell me where the Alcatraz trial is being held?"

"On the third floor. It'll be around to your left and down to the end of the hallway," responded Bailey, studying his passenger. It was unusual for a spectator to arrive this late, as most observers arrived early each day to assure themselves a seat. Additionally, the man's appearance was somewhat mysterious. He wore a hat pulled down over his eyes and a full-length overcoat buttoned to the neck with the collar turned up.

As the elevator jerked upward, Bailey faced his lone passenger, and noticed a distinct bulge in his overcoat, just under the left arm. Having seen that same bulge in the clothing of countless U.S. marshals who frequented the building, Bailey knew immediately that the man was carrying a gun. This was just the thing that the marshals and many of the employees in the building feared, an escape attempt or other violent act by a confederate of one of the Alcatraz defendants. Neither man spoke as the elevator lumbered slowly up two stories and came to an abrupt stop. Careful not to stare at the bulge and alert the gunman, Bailey looked away from the man when the elevator stopped and he slid the inner door open. As the passenger stepped out of the elevator he removed his hat. Still without making eye contact, Bailey pointed in the direction of Goodman's court. "Around to the left sir, and right down that hall," instructed Bailey, striving to prevent his anxiety from showing in his voice.

Bailey's heart was racing. After a few seconds, he stepped out of the elevator into the hall, relieved to see the man in the long coat walking down the hallway, oblivious to Bailey's observations. He stood in the hall, his gaze fixed on the retreating figure, not sure of a course of action. His trance was abruptly interrupted by the call bell in his elevator, indicating passengers waiting on the main floor.

Ignoring the summons, he headed down the hall toward Goodman's court as the man in the overcoat disappeared into the courtroom. Bailey experienced a feeling of relief as he observed Fred Henderson, a burly deputy marshal, coming toward him down the hall. Henderson was one of two marshals assigned to monitor the activity in the hallways and maintain a vigil outside the courtroom. The marshal smiled broadly as he approached and quipped, "Hey Joe, what are doing out here in the middle of the hall? Who's driving that elevator of yours?"

"Come'ere Fred," Bailey whispered, despite the fact that there was no one within earshot of the two men. Surprised at Bailey's obvious concern, the smile melted from the big man's face. "What's the matter, Joe?" Henderson asked with serious interest, "you look like you just saw a ghost."

"Did you just see that fellow in the long overcoat go into Goodman's court? Well, he's packing a gun. I saw the bulge under his coat. I've never seen him here before. He's not one of the regular courtroom guys and he asked me where the Alcatraz trial was being held. You better check it out. There may be trouble."

Henderson turned immediately and ran the short distance to Goodman's court, then disappeared into the courtroom. As the call bell rang again and again Bailey stood frozen in the middle of the hallway, his eyes fixed on the courtroom door.

The marshal slipped quietly into the courtroom. The large room was full and the new spectator was forced to become part of the standing room crowd. Henderson quickly spotted him leaning against the back wall, a few feet from the door. He moved swiftly and unobtrusively to the spectator's side. Grasping the man's arm firmly with his right hand, he displayed his marshal's badge with his left, and whispered, "I'm a U.S. marshal. Please come with me." Surprise and apprehension spread over the suspect's face as he stared into Henderson's steel gray eyes and unsmiling face. Without saying a word and offering no resistance, he allowed himself to be led from the courtroom. The entire episode was accomplished in a matter of seconds and with such precision that none of the other spectators were even aware that there had been a confrontation. It was not until they were several steps down the corridor that the man turned to Henderson and, in a quaking voice, asked, "What's going on? What's this all about?" Seeing the pair exit the courtroom and turn in his direction, Bailey darted for the safety of his elevator and, with the call bell still ringing, headed for the ground floor.

Henderson, meanwhile, hustled his prisoner down a side corridor into an empty jury deliberation room. Once in the privacy of the jury room, Henderson again displayed his badge and asked the man to remove his coat.

"Sir, my name is Fred Henderson, I'm a Deputy U.S. marshal. We have received a report that you may be armed and I would appreciate it if you would remove your coat. The confusion in the man's face began to dissipate and his brow furrowed in anger. "What are you talking about, armed? I'm not armed. Who the hell said I was armed?" As he spoke the man began to unbutton his coat. He stood facing Henderson, glaring into the marshal's eyes. When the coat fell open, Henderson caught a glimpse of what was causing the ominous bulge. Tucked into the man's breast pocket was a rolled-up copy of the previous day's *Chronicle*.

A feeling of embarrassment and annoyance swept over Henderson when he realized what he had done. Without giving any hint of his true feelings however, he stated in a firm voice, "Well sir, if you're not armed you won't mind then if I pat you down." The man by this time had deposited the large coat on the table in the center of the room.

"Naw, go ahead," the man consented, "you won't find anything more dangerous in my pockets than yesterday's newspaper."

"I'm sorry, sir," Henderson apologized, as he lightly patted the man's chest and the areas under his arms. "We can't be too careful, you know, with those killers in there on trial. One of the building employees saw the bulge under your coat and reported it to me. As you can understand, I would certainly have to check it out. Sorry for the inconvenience. You are free to go."

At the commencement of the afternoon session, Vinkler advised the court that he had a matter of some importance to discuss. "If Your Honor please," he began, "Defendant Thompson has asked me to draw Your Honor's attention to the fact that certain papers, which he deems necessary to his defense in the matter, have been taken from him and have not been returned."

Hennessy was immediately on his feet, denying any knowledge of the allegations.

Vinkler repeated the accusation, claiming the papers had been taken from his client and were now in the custody of the security people or the prosecutor's office.

"What is it you wish me to do, counsel?" asked a disinterested Goodman.

"Your Honor, I'd like you to issue an instruction..." Vinkler began, only to be interrupted by the judge.

"He's entitled to have these notes and be free from interference by anyone. The court will make an order to that effect."

Later in the day the papers were returned to Vinkler by one of the marshals. Sanctions were not imposed, nor did the judge take any steps to investigate the matter. No explanation of the incident was ever offered by the prosecution, the marshal's office, or the Alcatraz authorities, nor did the court ask for one. The matter received no further attention from the court. It was as though nothing had ever happened.

During cross-examination of Special Agent Dillon, it became clear that the FBI diagram was, in many respects, inadequate. Judge Goodman therefore ordered that a second diagram be prepared, based on a schematic done earlier by Ned Burns. That diagram, prepared by Klein's Attorney's Legal Service, was ultimately admitted into evidence. Spagnoli also attempted to establish that Dillon had deliberately limited his photographs of D block so that the jury would not see how small the cells were. He also claimed that the authorities were withholding pictures to conceal the extensive damage to the D block cells during the retaliatory bombardment by prison authorities.

At the conclusion of Dillon's testimony, Spagnoli proposed that the court consider early daily adjournment. "If Your Honor please, without encroaching on the power of the court, I was going to make a suggestion in the interest of everyone connected with the trial that the court adjourn somewhere around four o'clock for the reason that traffic is so congested. I know a good many of the jurors live out of town, and the witnesses find it inconvenient to get to their homes. It took me over an hour and a quarter just to get from the court down to the jail last Friday. I think it might be better if we adjourned a little earlier."

"I join in that, Your Honor," Zamloch added.

Spagnoli's suggestion brought an immediate response from juror number five, Don MacLean. "Your Honor," urged the irritated juror, "I object to leaving at four o'clock. I would like to see this trial ended as soon as possible and I think we ought to stay here as long as we can." The juror, a corporate executive, had been a questionable selection in the minds of the defense attorneys, but was one of the jurors Thompson wanted to keep. The already apprehensive defense team quickly branded the upstart panel member a prosecution juror. "I knew we shouldn't have kept that asshole, Spagnoli whispered to Vinkler. Looking down the counsel table, Spagnoli's glance met Sullivan who rolled his eyes as if he had heard and agreed with Spagnoli's remark. Turning to Zamloch, Sullivan inquired quietly, "What in the hell is his big hurry?"

Reminding everyone that he had previously announced he would adjourn between four and four-thirty each day, depending upon the circumstances, Goodman attempted to both allay the juror's concern and explain the court's need to conduct other business and accommodate other litigants. But the juror's comment was disconcerting to the defense attorneys.

As his last witness of the day, Hennessy called Officer Carl Sundstrom for the limited purpose of establishing that the defendants were properly convicted federal prisoners incarcerated at Alcatraz at the time of the riot. This was one of the formal elements of the crime and the proffered evidence consisted of certified copies of the convictions and sentencing of the three. The information in these documents was obviously unfavorable to the defendants and consequently the defense should have quietly stipulated to their admission.

Instead, Spagnoli took a confrontational position, making repeated, groundless objections that drew unnecessary attention to Thompson's former crimes and long sentences. An irritated Goodman summarily overruled his objections. When Hennessy sought to introduce similar evidence as to Carnes and Shockley, the judge rejected the offers of Zamloch and Sullivan to stipulate to the prior convictions. Hennessy was then free to read the documents in their entirety to the jury. As a result, the jury heard details about the defendants' crimes that would not have been highlighted if, at the outset, Spagnoli had simply stipulated that the defendants had been properly convicted and sentenced.

Encouraged by his success, Hennessy proceeded to introduce the same evidence as to Hubbard, Cretzer and Coy. Over Zamloch's strenuous objection, Hennessy was again successful and was able to acquaint the jury with the sinister details of the crimes and sentences of the three dead rioters. The correctness of this ruling was questionable and the evidence was harmful to the defense.

Following adjournment, Spagnoli presided over an impromptu press conference. He presented a note allegedly written by Thompson responding to media reports that of the fifty convicts subpoenaed by the defense, half were unwilling to assist in the case. The note read as follows: "...I will bring every inmate and officer from the island, from the lowest to the highest, to ascertain if there has been any brow beating, tampering and scaring of my witnesses. They will be here for sure to testify unless such punishment here to the aforementioned arises."

While the language sounded more like that of Spagnoli than Thompson, the attorney claimed it was from his client and discounted the importance of the supposed problem. "We're not at all concerned about witnesses," boasted Spagnoli. "They're all lined up and they'll be here. Buddy Thompson just wanted me to be sure that the air was cleared, because of rumors that have appeared in the papers about a problem with defense witnesses. There is no problem and the defense of the case is going very well."

Spagnoli then announced that ex-Alcatraz inmate William Simmons, recently discharged from the federal penitentiary at Atlanta, had contacted him. Simmons, now a resident of Albany, New York, had written to Spagnoli offering to testify, "...to prison brutality and why men on the Rock blow their tops." Simmons had spent fourteen years on Alcatraz and expressed his willingness to "gladly do my best to help Sam and the other two fellows." Simmons knew both Shockley and Carnes and had been friends with Coy and Cretzer.

"Will you be calling Mr. Simmons as a witness?" inquired one of the reporters.

"Well we'll be looking into this," responded Spagnoli. "I'll be meeting with my fellow counsel and our decision will be forthcoming."

15

___

Sundstrom returned to the stand in the morning for cross-examination. Sullivan and Zamloch attempted to introduce portions of their clients' prison files in an attempt to develop some favorable information. Sullivan sought to highlight Shockley's test scores and psychiatric evaluations in support of the insanity defense. Zamloch tried to introduce evidence regarding Carnes's conduct and disciplinary record at Alcatraz in an effort to establish his good record. Hennessy successfully objected that such questions were beyond the scope of his direct examination, and prevented the defense from mitigating the effects of the previously admitted documents.

Spagnoli sought to examine Sundstrom regarding the modification of Thompson's sentence, but was stopped abruptly by Hennessy's objection. It was the third time he had raised the issue and it brought a stinging rebuke from Goodman.

"Counsel, you can see from the prior rulings that the court considers, as it should, that this habeas corpus proceeding is entirely irrelevant to this proceeding. Now I rule that it is also entirely incompetent. The clerk will enter an order denying the petition on the ground that it is entirely without merit. It is not necessary to ask any further questions along this line; it just takes up time. I wish to state for the record, that I have not ruled on this matter previously because I wanted to give you every opportunity to present whatever additional arguments you might wish to advance. I also strongly believed that to rule on the petition during the trial would serve to confuse the jury. I believe that a ruling on the matter should have been delayed until after this trial, but you have relentlessly pursued the matter and forced a ruling, which I have now made."

Playing the role of the wounded warrior, Spagnoli gave a feeble wave of his hand and capitulated. "We have to bow to the court's ruling."

Unimpressed with Spagnoli's histrionics, Goodman replied icily, "Yes counsel, I think you do. Mr. Hennessy, call your next witness."

The petition had been meritless from the outset. Sensing defeat, Spagnoli had pushed for a ruling in open court hoping to play on the jury's sympathy. The wisdom of this tactic was questioned by his co-counsel, who made eye contact with one another, rolled their eyes, and shook their heads. Their reactions were subtle and even the astute Hennessy failed to read the silent communication. *What an idiot*, thought Zamloch. *Ernie is so full of shit.*

Hennessy rose and dramatically announced his next witness, "Call Mr. Bert Burch to the witness stand." The entire courtroom stirred with anticipation of Burch's dramatic testimony describing the beginning of the bloody riot. As the thin, lanky officer, dressed in a pinstriped suit, strode to the witness stand the jury watched his every move intently.

In a slow Oklahoma drawl, Burch carefully responded to Hennessy's questions. He had been employed at Alcatraz since September 1939, and on the date in question was assigned to the 8:00 A.M. to 4:00 P.M. day watch in the west gun gallery. He had relieved Officer Frank Prindle that morning receiving the latter's weapons: a Springfield 30:06 rifle with fifty rounds of ammunition and a .45 caliber Colt automatic pistol with twenty-one rounds. In the gallery, Burch also had custody of numerous billy clubs, gas masks, and all the significant cell house keys. Key #107 to the yard door and #88, which opened the door between the cell house and D block, were kept along with two dozen other keys on a board mounted on the cell house side of the gallery. Burch testified that about 2:00 P.M. on the day in question, he was patrolling on the D block side of the gallery when he approached the door leading to the cell house side. "As I got to the door, possibly put my hand on it, the door swung open suddenly. It opened in on me toward D block. Coy hit the door and landed it in on me," Burch stated calmly.

"You could identify the man who came through the door as Coy, could you?" asked Hennessy.

"Yes, definitely."

"How was he dressed?"

"He was in his underwear."

Asked to continue his description of the events, Burch went on.

"Well, Coy hit it suddenly from the other side. The door hit me, threw me off balance and I went back against the bars. I wound up against the bars, and he was on top of me. He swung at me with a club or a weapon of some kind. I had my rifle in my right hand. As I remember, I threw my rifle up more or less instinctively as he hit at me. He struck me across the head at the same time as he grabbed the rifle. I had hold of it and he had hold of it. He struck again, more or less on the back of my head. I finally went down on my back with Coy on top of me in the gun gallery. As I landed, my gun, a .45 automatic was under me. I was trying to reach around and get ahold of the gun and he was clawing at my hand, trying to keep me from getting ahold of it. After struggling around, I got the gun out of the holster and then lost it, because I remember at one time feeling the gun down under my legs. By that time he had a good hold on my wrist. When he saw that I didn't have the gun he already had my wrist and he twisted my arm back behind me, you know, like in a hammer-lock, and turned me over on my face."

The veteran officer spoke quietly, and the jury listened raptly, some of the jurors leaning forward intently. Thompson furiously took notes on his yellow tablet. The other two defendants stared into space and avoided making eye contact with the witness.

"Coy was on top of me now, on my back. He was hitting me in the back of the head with something. During the course of the struggle I called out to Mr. Corwin on the floor below."

"Who is Mr. Corwin?" interrupted Hennessy.

"Mr. Corwin was the officer on duty in D block, on the floor in D block. I had called to him 'telephone' or something like that. I remember when Coy turned me over there he was saying, 'I'll fix your telephone,' or words like that. And then I remember he twisted my shirt collar up with his hand, and that is about the last I remember. I was struggling to get my breath; he was twisting my shirt and hitting me."

"You became unconscious?"

"Yes sir, I did," Burch answered slowly.

Burch testified that he recalled regaining consciousness some time later on the floor of the gallery on the cell house side. His hands were tied behind him and his head was tied against an electric conduit line mounted on the wall. As his head cleared, he realized that his hands were only loosely tied, but his head and neck were bound tightly to the pipe with the heavy cord used to raise and lower keys between the cell house floor and the gallery. He was able to loosen his hands, but even the slightest movement of his head or upper body caused the rope around his neck to tighten, making it difficult for him to breathe. Because of his position, he could only work at the knots around his neck with one hand at a time. "Finally I was able to untie the rope from the pipe and ease my position to where I could get my breath. Then I just lay back on the floor. I don't know for how long, but it seemed like a long time." His uniform and shoes were gone as were all the keys, clubs, gas masks, and guns.

"I crawled back into D block on my stomach and raised up to look over the edge of the steel plate at the bottom of the gallery. As I raised up, Cretzer was right in front of me, standing at the end of the first tier. He was no more than ten or twelve feet from me and at the same level. When he saw me he snapped off a quick shot with the .45 and hollered something like, 'Stay away from the phone or I'll blow your head off.' I dropped back down on the floor of the gallery behind the steel shield and laid there for I don't know how long.

"Finally I crawled a little further along the gallery and raised up again. As I did I saw a convict named Pepper standing on the top tier, and he yelled out, 'Look out for the gun guard.' Then I saw Cretzer again, this time up on the upper tier above me. He fired again and I dropped flat on the gallery floor again. I heard him say, 'I told you I'd blow your head off.' I laid there very quiet for a long time."

Burch then explained how he returned to the cell house side of the gallery and crawled all the way across the cell house to the north end. Once again he lifted his head up over the steel shield and once again drew gunfire. He believed this shot came from the general direction of D block, but could not be sure. He abandoned any further attempts to observe what was going on and returned to the D block door where he lay on the floor of the gallery on the cell house side. In this position he was directly above the door to the prison yard and could overhear the voices of various inmates. At one point he heard Cretzer complain, "Frisco's as far away as ever." He also heard the jingling of keys and the cursing and complaining of the inmates when they were unable to open the outside door. For the next several hours, Burch lay shivering in his underwear, out of sight of those on the cell house floor, and too afraid to again look over the steel shield.

At dusk, Burch heard heavy gunfire in the vicinity of the gallery entrance as the assault team was entering. Soon thereafter he was discovered by Phil Bergen, who provided Burch with a .45 automatic pistol and ammunition, and arranged for clothes to be brought to him. Bergen and

Burch immediately relocated to the D block side of the gallery, where they periodically fired into the D block cells to provide cover for the officers attempting to enter the gallery from outside.

"While you were firing into the D block cells," Hennessy inquired, "did you see any other guards?"

"Well, in a little while I saw Stites. He was down the gallery from me at the time I saw him, probably ten or twelve feet away. It was sort of dark because we'd shot out one of the overhead lights. There was some light though, and I could see Stites silhouetted against a window on the south wall. As I was busy myself, I didn't pay too much attention to him. As a matter of fact at first I didn't even know for sure who it was, and shortly thereafter I heard Stites drop. I heard his gun hit the floor. It seems to me that I heard him moan. He was dead."

Zamloch leapt to his feet, objecting that any testimony regarding Stites was immaterial and highly prejudicial to the defendants.

Goodman responded, "From what I understand, the U.S. Attorney is having the witness describe the events that led up to or had something to do with the matters that are alleged in the indictment."

Sensing serious trouble, Sullivan joined in. "I also object to the testimony on, among other grounds, Your Honor, that my client is charged only with the murder of William A. Miller and is not charged with killing Stites." Sullivan went on, requesting that if the judge did admit the evidence, that he instruct the jury that any testimony regarding what happened to officer Stites was not to be considered by them in determining the guilt or innocence of the defendants.

Looking over at Hennessy, Goodman asked, "Have you anything to say?" When Hennessy responded, "I object to that," Goodman summarily denied Sullivan's request.

Vinkler was on his feet with basically the same demand. "Your Honor, I agree with Mr. Sullivan, that unless the ladies and gentlemen of the jury are properly instructed, this testimony will be highly prejudicial." Goodman was unimpressed with the defense concerns. "I have already told them what the charge is. I don't have to keep on telling them that the defendants are not charged with the killing of other people."

Zamloch again attempted to intervene. "Perhaps it is not much, but—"

"Well, I don't care to hear any further argument," Goodman interrupted, "I have ruled on this. You have your objections in the record. Proceed with the questioning."

All three of the defense attorneys sunk into their chairs in a state of disbelief. The jury could clearly conclude from Burch's testimony that Stites was shot by one of the convict rebels. Goodman allowed this evidence, despite the fact that the FBI investigation had clearly established that Stites was shot in the back as he stood in front of a window facing the hostile gunfire.

"What's going on here?" Sullivan whispered to Zamloch. "The judge is really sticking it up our ass!"

"I know," lamented Zamloch, "I can't believe it's happening."

Flushed with success, Hennessy asked a few innocuous questions, and terminated his examination. "Take the witness," he announced to the reeling defense counsel.

The defense attorneys had expected Burch to be a routine witness, who would simply describe Coy's attack. They did not plan an aggressive cross-examination, because they were not challenging his account of Coy's actions. Now, however, Burch's testimony took on unexpected importance. The defendants had been tacitly charged with killing Stites. Hennessy had referred to Stites's death during his opening statement, but none of the defense attorneys expected any evidence on the subject. All the attorneys knew that Stites had died from a bullet in the back, which could only have come from outside the building. But now Hennessy made it appear that Stites was killed by an inmate, and the defense had to defend against two murders though they were charged with only one.

Zamloch was particularly concerned and he turned to Sullivan as Hennessy settled comfortably into his chair at the counsel table. "Do you want me to take him first, Bill?" he inquired. "I want to go after him on this Stites thing." Sullivan had no problem letting Zamloch lead off and, with a nod of his head, watched his co-counsel stride to the podium.

Zamloch's cross-examination of Burch began slowly and tentatively. With time, however, his questions became more focused and he was ultimately able to cast doubt on the claim that Stites had been killed by inmates. Burch admitted that he had seen no flashes of gunfire from the D block cells. He also recalled that the windows in D block were broken by gunfire from outside and that no one in D block, guard or convict, fired at the windows. Zamloch also brought out that at the time of Stites's death it was unlikely that any convicts were firing into D block from the main cell house. Burch agreed with Zamloch's suggestion that if any inmate was firing into D block through the door, he would have been in full view of the east gun gallery, which by then was manned by four armed officers.

If an inmate was shooting from behind the end of C block, out of the view of the east gun gallery, he would not have been able to see Stites. Zamloch's cross-examination of Burch established to the defense's satisfaction that Stites could not have been shot from D block or the main cell house. Nevertheless, the issue of Stites's death was never definitively resolved, leaving a lingering question in the minds of the jurors.

Under the rules of evidence at the time, the defense attorneys were not permitted to review the FBI investigation report. FBI investigators found numerous bullet indentations on the inside portion of the steel shield in the gallery, which could only have been made from outside. This was clear evidence that gunfire was coming into the gallery from the hill below, but the information never got to the jury. The defense attorneys never saw the FBI report, and therefore were never able to develop the true facts of Stites's death.

Zamloch led Burch through a detailed description of his frantic pleas to Corwin to sound the alarm. As Hennessy predicted, the defense planned to attack Corwin with the argument that if he had reacted properly at the outset and turned in the alarm, the riot could have been stopped before any blood was shed. Knowing he had done an effective cross-examination, Zamloch wanted a dramatic finish. Noting the time, and aware that the noon recess was at hand, he wrapped up his questioning with a description of Burch, under attack by Coy, calling to his fellow officer for help, and begging Corwin to use the phone to turn in the alarm. Because of Corwin's failure to act, help never came.

During the noon recess the new diagram from Klein's Legal Service arrived. After lunch, it was Sullivan's turn to cross-examine Burch and he used the diagram to establish Burch's location at various times. At one point in his questioning, Sullivan had Burch demonstrate his position in the gallery at the time he was fired at by Cretzer. "I want you to demonstrate to the jury exactly what your position was when he fired at you. Stand over here in front of them and demonstrate," directed Sullivan. He positioned Burch in front of the jury box, which was approximately the height of the steel shield. He instructed Burch to demonstrate how he peered over the shield and came face to face with the gun wielding Cretzer. It was unclear what Sullivan hoped to accomplish with the demonstration, but it was a tactical error. Crouched on his knees in front of the jury box, the aging guard presented a helpless sight. At one point he lost his balance and almost fell. As the jury looked down at Burch and imagined the terror he must have felt as he faced Cretzer's blazing .45, he presented a dramatic and highly sympathetic picture. He was anything but the picture of Alcatraz brutality, that the defense team sought to portray.

The final witness of the day was Chief Steward Robert Bristow. As he somberly took the witness oath, Bristow glared at the defendants. His serious countenance masked his normally convivial, outgoing personality. A husky man, he loved a good time and enjoyed singing. Bristow was a devoted fan of the young singer Mel Torme, and sought to emulate his style. On more than one occasion he was known to have attempted a Mel Torme impression on the last boat to Alcatraz after a night of revelry and bar hopping in San Francisco. Today, however, he was humorless as he sat on the witness stand.

Bristow told a dramatic story of entering the cell house and after proceeding to the west end, being captured by Carnes. He described how Carnes grabbed him from behind and placed a sharp weapon against his throat, before moving him into a cell with the other hostages. He identified the homemade shiv used by Carnes, and it was admitted into evidence.

He described how he was placed in a cell with Miller, Moyle, and Egan. Within minutes Burdett, Corwin, and Lageson were brought to the cell at gunpoint. He described Cretzer holding the .45 automatic, demanding that Lageson reveal to him which key opened the outside door to the exercise yard and Lageson refusing to tell him. In a quiet, unemotional voice, the witness described the events leading up to Cretzer's shooting spree. Over the objection of all defense counsel, the witness was allowed to testify to the conversation that took place between Cretzer and Weinhold immediately after the siren sounded. "Don't you boys go out into that yard. You're going to get hurt," warned Weinhold.

"There's gonna be a lotta guys hurt before this is over, there'll be a lotta guys killed," Cretzer responded unemotionally.

Bristow testified that as Cretzer and Weinhold talked, Shockley stood by, urging Cretzer to "...kill all the sons a bitches." Urged on by Shockley, Cretzer leveled the gun at Weinhold, announcing, "And you're gonna be the first son of a bitch to die." Then he pulled the trigger, shooting the captain in the chest from a range of about three feet. As Weinhold slumped to the floor, Cretzer fired blindly into the cell, hitting Miller in the right arm and Corwin in the face. Everyone in the cell fell to the floor, wounded or pretending to be dead."

Bristow described Cretzer's reluctance to shoot Lageson. "Well, Shockley looked into the cell and yelled to Cretzer, 'There's a son of a bitch in there that ain't been shot. Shoot him.' But Cretzer hesitated and said, 'That's Mr. Lageson, he's my friend.' 'Friend hell,' Shockley said, 'he'll go over to the court and squawk just as loud as anyone else; shoot the son of a bitch.' Well he starts shooting Mr. Lageson and the clip was empty. So he took the clip out, dropped it on the floor, put in another clip and told Mr. Lageson, 'I'm sorry,' and he shot him."

During his cross-examination, Sullivan attempted to establish that since Bristow had never held a conversation with Shockley and never had occasion to visit D block, he could not be sure of his identification of the inmate.

"Oh, yes I can," was Bristow's firm response.

"Mr. Bristow, there's 280 prisoners on Alcatraz. Can you identify them all?" Sullivan pressed the witness.

"Well not unless they make themselves totally conspicuous, like Shockley did," came Bristow's stinging response.

Wounded by the answer, Sullivan pleaded to the court, "I move to strike that answer out."

"No," ruled Goodman. "You were arguing with him. You asked an argumentative question and he answered you."

"Well, it was an argumentative answer, Your Honor, and you know that it was," snapped Sullivan, raising his voice and beginning to lose his composure.

Sullivan's impertinence brought an immediate and irritated response from the bench. "Now see here, Mr. Sullivan, what you have just said was not only uncalled for, but when you reflect upon it you will realize that you should not have done it. You shouted at me, when you spoke to me as the judge of the court. You know that is wrong," Goodman lectured the now contrite defense lawyer. "I'm not asking you to withdraw, but just calm down and don't get yourself excited. Remember this is a court of justice."

Slowed by the judge's fierce temper and the dressing down in front of the jury, Sullivan's cross-examination became subdued as he attempted to show that Shockley was disturbed during the events surrounding the death of Miller. "How was Shockley acting when you first saw him? What did he do?" inquired Sullivan.

"Well," Bristow responded thoughtfully, "he acted definitely sane as far as I could tell. He just acted like he wanted to get rid of a bunch of guards."

Wounded again by the sly Bristow, Sullivan appealed once more to the court. "May I ask that that statement be stricken as the conclusion of this witness or am I still walking into one of his traps."

"You are walking into your own trap," Goodman responded. "You asked how he was acting and Mr. Bristow tried to answer your question. Mr. Sullivan," Goodman continued condescendingly, "I am being very patient with you. If you happen to be, let us say, not quite apt at the moment, you cannot ascribe the results that flow from that to the judge or the witness or your opponent. As a result of some question that you ask that is not done skillfully, if you get an answer that you do not expect or do not like, don't blame me for that. Don't blame the witness for that. Do not blame your opponent. It is your fault! I have tried to be patient with you, now I'm going to make my rulings firm."

"Very well," the humbled Sullivan went on, "I respectfully ask the court to delete from the record the last answer as not being responsive."

"Motion denied," Goodman shot back, glaring down at the flustered young defense lawyer.

Shaken badly, Sullivan asked a few last questions and brought his cross-examination to a limping conclusion.

Zamloch fared no better during his cross-examination. "Mr. Bristow," Zamloch asked in an accusatory manner, "you realize, do you not, that if you had put up a struggle and had given the alarm at the outset, none of these people who are now dead would have been killed?"

"Well if I had done what you suggest, I probably would be dead," Bristow answered. Seeing Zamloch recoil from the answer, two of the male jurors smiled and glanced at the judge. Goodman was expressionless.

16

Friday, November 29

Thursday was Thanksgiving and court was not in session. While the inmates at Alcatraz dined on traditional Thanksgiving turkey and the trimmings, the three defendants in the San Francisco County jail ate a marginally appetizing dinner of roast pork. As always, however, they were treated to the privilege of the daily newspaper. Even Shockley with his limited intellect, found the paper a joy. Most of his reading was limited to the comics, but he also struggled through a few articles on the sports page and perused the ads for the new movies.

By Friday, November 29, the series of storms had passed, but heavy fog closed both the San Francisco and Oakland airports. Near zero visibility caused scores of automobile accidents on Bay Area highways, with more than a hundred vehicles involved. Commercial air traffic was initially diverted to the Sacramento airport, but by mid-morning, Sacramento was also fogged in. On Alcatraz, the heavy fog shut down the prison industries and the inmates who worked outside the cell house were confined to their cells, except for trips to the dining hall for meals. Only those prisoners who worked inside the cell house were released from their cells.

Despite the fog and resulting traffic congestion, all the jurors were in their places when court resumed. Hennessy took a deep breath and rose to call his first witness of the day. "Your Honor, we call Officer Cecil Corwin to the stand."

Now serving in a clerical position as he recovered from his massive wound, the fifty-two-year-old Corwin appeared considerable older. He seemed tentative and ill at ease as he identified himself and was sworn in. Although he had been the subject of quiet, yet harsh, criticism by many

Alcatraz officers for his failure to sound the alarm, formal disapproval was never leveled at Corwin. Furthermore, his conduct was never questioned in any of the official reports. From his review of the FBI report and his pre-trial interviews with witnesses, Hennessy knew that Corwin's testimony could present problems. He had determined, therefore, to keep the officer's testimony as brief as possible and the questions simple.

Corwin testified that his first awareness of something unusual on May 2 was at 2:00 P.M. when he heard the shutter on the cell house door window open and close. Believing that an officer wished to enter D block from the cell house, he called to Burch to lower key #88. When he opened the door, he saw Carnes standing in front of the officers' toilet and Cretzer in front of the dining hall with another inmate whom he did not recognize. Not seeing Bill Miller, he became concerned and immediately closed the door.

Next he heard a commotion above in the gun gallery, and Louie Fleish, who was cleaning up after the noon meal announced, "There's somebody in the gun gallery disarming the guard up there." Corwin testified that he realized there was trouble and started for the telephone mounted on the west wall of D block. Before he got there, however, Fleish blocked his way, extending his arms out to the side and directing, "The best thing you can do is sit down here. You can't do anything about it, just sit down. Go over there and sit down and you won't get hurt."

Corwin stated that almost immediately he heard someone insert a key into the door from the cell house side, so he moved back toward the door to hold it closed. He was holding key #88 and momentarily considered inserting it into the lock to prevent whoever was on the other side from unlocking the door. This aspect of his testimony was clearly erroneous since Corwin had the only key to that door.

He stated that he then heard Coy's voice from above demanding, "'Open that goddam door and be goddam quick about it.' I never saw Coy, but I recognized his voice and I knew he had Burch's guns." Following Coy's order, he opened the door and was confronted by Cretzer with a .45 automatic, Hubbard with a rifle, and Carnes with a club. The three inmates rushed into D block, and made him their prisoner.

According to Corwin, while the others remained on the flats, Cretzer climbed up to the second tier of the D block cells. "He walked the full length of the line of cells to the south end, and then he called to Carnes to bring me up to the second tier to open the cells. Well, Cretzer started asking me to unlock the box that controls the cells. They call it the dead lock. There's a lever in there that you put in the on-key position and you can open the cell doors. Then he changed his mind and said, 'Pass it up, we're running behind schedule.' Then he ordered me back downstairs." Corwin stated he was taken out of D block and placed with the others in cell 404. Just before leaving D block, he observed Lageson in D block being questioned by Cretzer. "Cretzer wanted Lageson to operate the necessary controls to open the D block cells, but he refused."

Shortly after Weinhold was brought to the cell, Corwin recalled hearing the siren. "At that time Captain Weinhold started talking to Cretzer, trying to get him to give up the escape attempt and surrender. He said, 'You don't have a chance, Joe. You'd be foolish to go outside now. You'll be killed.' Cretzer answered him, 'If we can't go, if we are going to be killed, we are going to kill you too.' The captain then said, 'Well we can only die once.' Cretzer said, 'Go ahead and die, you son-of-a-bitch,' and shot the captain. Then he shot me and I went down. I don't know how many times he shot. He shot me underneath the left eye and the bullet came out of my right cheek."

Asked about Shockley's involvement, Corwin testified, "Yes, he participated in the conversation. He told Cretzer 'Kill every one of the yellow-bellied bastards. We won't have any testimony against us.'" Corwin stated that despite the seriousness of his wound he never lost consciousness.

Knowing that Corwin was vulnerable on the issue of his conduct during the early stage of the break, Sullivan attempted on cross-examination to show that nothing but his own fear prohibited him from sounding the alarm. He brought out that Corwin outweighed Fleish by thirty pounds, and that at no time did Fleish attempt to use force of any kind to prevent Corwin from using the phone. Sullivan questioned Corwin as to his custodial and physical training. Time and again his questions were blocked by objections from Hennessy, which were sustained by the court. In frustration, the young lawyer reacted emotionally. "You know judge, I'm handicapped. I can't try this case the way I would like to, because of all these objections."

"I know you can't," responded the judge, "and I'm not going to let you." It was as if Goodman and the young barrister were now at war. The judge was sustaining nearly all of the prosecution's objections, whether or not they were well taken. Sullivan's frustration was mounting.

"I have a perfect right to probe this man…" protested Sullivan.

"I have warned you before," Goodman interrupted rudely, now becoming emotionally involved himself. "I will not permit this trial to degenerate into loud arguments to the jury. The case must still be conducted with propriety. Now if you feel you haven't the necessary experience or knowledge, or qualification to conduct this examination, I will ask some-one else to help you and assist you during the rest of the trial of the case."

Goodman's scolding was insulting. To question the knowledge and com-petence of a trial attorney in front of the jury was a humiliating indignity likely to strip the attorney of his credibility and make him appear inept. The seething Sullivan chose not to respond to the judge's attack, and did not acknowledge the offensive comments.

"May I proceed?" he inquired coldly. Without waiting for a response, he continued his cross-examination.

As the morning session drew to a close, it was obvious that Corwin was badly shaken. Despite Hennessy's objections, Sullivan was repeatedly able to call attention to Corwin's inept handling of the emergency. "Isn't it a fact, Mr. Corwin," he demanded, "that if you had not been intimidated, and had phoned for help, Mr. Miller would never have been killed?" This brought a bitter objection from Hennessy and a further admonition from the judge. "I'm going to sustain the objection," ruled Goodman, "and I'm going to caution the jury on every such occasion, that questions of this kind are clearly improper. The conduct of the attorney in asking them is clearly improper and you are to disregard them entirely." Although he knew he had succeeded in unnerving the witness, Sullivan was not sure he had been able to convert Corwin's questionable conduct into a viable explanation for Miller's death.

As Corwin emerged from the courtroom at the noon recess, Ernie Lag-eson, who had spent the morning in the corridor outside waiting his turn to testify, met him. A brief glance at his friend told Lageson that things had not gone well, and he felt immediate compassion for the older man. "How's it going, Cec?" he asked sympathetically.

"Not too well, Ernie," Corwin responded, despondently. "Those bastard lawyers are making it sound like I was the cause of Miller's death. It was really an unpleasant experience. I hope it goes better for you." Lageson could see tears in Corwin's eyes, and the veteran guard looked exhausted.

"Come on Cec," urged Lageson, "don't let them get to you. That's what they want to do; shake you up and screw up your testimony. We didn't kill Miller, the cons did. And you can't ever forget that."

"Yeah, I know what they're trying to do, Ernie, and unfortunately, they're succeeding. But you know, maybe I should have grabbed that phone and called the armory. Louis Fleish didn't really stop me; I just froze. Maybe they're right. Maybe it could have been different."

Lageson suggested that they put the trial out of their minds, go to lunch, and talk about something more pleasant. "You're right, Ernie," Corwin agreed, his voice gaining strength. "Let's get outta' here and go get something to eat. I'm glad you're here, Ernie. I sure prefer spending time with you rather than with Hennessy or the Warden," he said with a smile. Just as he had taken strength from Lageson's conduct during the riot, Corwin now received comfort and courage from the younger man's presence. Moved by his appreciation, Corwin instinctively put his arm on Lageson's shoulder as the men walked down the hall. "Yeah, Ernie, I'm really glad you were here."

Lageson was not a career law enforcement officer, but was an educator. Born and raised in the midwest, he had worked for years as a teacher, administrator, and superintendent in various rural school districts of North Dakota. In 1941, he accepted a position with the Bureau of Prisons as a custodial officer with the hope that he would be able to contribute to the education and rehabilitation of prisoners. He was sent to Alcatraz, where his duties turned out to be custodial, there being little or no rehabilitation of the Alcatraz inmates. He served in the Navy during World War II and upon discharge from the service returned to Alcatraz intending to stay only a short time and then return to the field of education. The riot changed his plans and he stayed on at the prison to be available as a witness at the trial.

It was 2:30 in the afternoon when Hennessy called Officer Ernest Lageson as his next witness. Lageson's residual military bearing showed as he stood at attention in front of the witness stand to be sworn in by the clerk.

In response to Hennessy's questioning, Lageson testified that on the day in question he was the officer in charge of the cell house, and was returning from lunch about 2:10 P.M. He stopped briefly at A block to chat with inmate orderly Thomas Wareagle, then proceeded down Broadway to release another of his orderlies, Ramon Remine, to spend the afternoon in the recreation yard. As he approached the C block cut-off, he saw a number of inmates milling about at the west end of Broadway. Thinking there could be a problem, Lageson ran to the west end of the cell house to investigate. He stated that as he neared the end of the cellblock, he was met by Coy, wearing trousers but no shirt. Coy grabbed his arm, and when Lageson attempted to pull away he was suddenly confronted by Hubbard holding a rifle, Cretzer with the .45 automatic pistol and Carnes carrying a billy club.

Lageson added that Cretzer appeared to be in charge and directed him around the end of C block and through the open door into D block. After only a few moments in D block, he was directed by Cretzer to enter cell

404. Later Coy ordered the hostages moved to cell 403, because the door on 404 could not be locked. "As we got to the officers' toilet, Cretzer handed me a bundle of keys and told me to go up and release Hamilton. I handed the keys back to him and told him to go get Hamilton himself. Coy then said, 'Mr. Lageson, don't be a fool.' I told Coy, 'No you can lock me up, but I'm not going to get Hamilton.' Cretzer then said, 'Oh, have it your way, Mr. Lageson,' and he went to get Hamilton himself." Lageson also testified to seeing Carnes armed with one of the billy clubs and Shockley running back and forth in front of the hostage cell waving a monkey wrench. The wrench was admitted as U.S. Exhibit #24.

Lageson also witnessed Shockley's assault on Sundstrom. "Then Mr. Sundstrom was brought in. Coy was holding him by the necktie and brought him in. As he was putting him in the cell, Shockley ran up and hit Sundstrom at least twice on the side of the face."

The witness stated that as tension among the convicts mounted they congregated in front of the hostage cells. Lageson heard Cretzer expressing frustration over the key crisis, "They've got us fucked on this key; we're as far from Frisco as ever."

He described how Weinhold attempted to talk Cretzer into surrendering, warning him that the alarm would soon sound and they would never get out of the cell house. "When the alarm sounded, Mr. Weinhold told Cretzer, 'There is the alarm now. You haven't got a chance.' Shockley said 'We'll kill every one of you sons of bitches.' Thompson was there and he joined in too. 'We don't want any living witnesses, kill them all.' Mr. Weinhold said, 'Well, you can only die once.' At that moment, Cretzer pulled the trigger and Weinhold dropped to the floor. He then shot into the rear of the cell and Mr. Corwin, Mr. Bristow, Mr. Burdett. and I dove or fell. Then he turned the gun on Mr. Miller, who was sitting on the bunk and shot him. He sagged back on the bunk."

The witness explained that after firing several rounds into cell 402, the group returned to the front of his cell, number 403. Shockley looked into the cell and shouted, "There's one son of a bitch who hasn't been hit yet, shoot him."

"Oh, that's Mr. Lagseon," Cretzer responded, "he's a pretty decent screw. He's always treated me right."

But Thompson intervened, "We don't want any living witnesses, kill 'em all."

Shockley also persisted. "No matter if he's your friend or not, he'll go to town and squawk just as loud as any other son of a bitch. Kill him."

"With that," Lageson continued, "Cretzer aimed the gun and apologized, 'I'm really sorry Mr. Lageson,' and pulled the trigger. The gun was empty and the mechanism only clicked. So he took out the old clip and put in a fresh one. He cocked the gun, drew another bead on me and fired again. I ducked or dove or something. The bullet grazed the side of my head and struck my ear. I was stunned by the force of the bullet and I just lay there as if I were quite dead." The courtroom was silent as the officer described his brush with death. At the counsel table the three defendants sat motionless, none of them able to meet Lageson's unwavering gaze.

Sullivan's cross-examination of Lageson was ineffective. Initially, he sought to criticize the officer for his failure to turn in an alarm when he first spotted what looked like trouble.

"Was there a reason you didn't call in an alarm?" Sullivan asked.

"I thought it was only a small commotion at the other end," Lageson responded, "and I went to investigate before I turned in any kind of an alarm. I knew there was a guard in the gun gallery and also Mr. Miller was down there."

"It has occurred to you, hasn't it Mr. Lageson," Sullivan continued, "that if you had blown your whistle and sounded the alarm before walking down to investigate that perhaps this shooting would never have happened?"

In response to Hennessy's objection, Goodman angrily remarked, "If that is urged as a defense to the charge in the indictment, I will hold that it is wholly incompetent, irrelevant, and immaterial." As Sullivan sought to respond, the judge, raising his voice, commanded, "There is no use arguing about it any more, I have ruled on that." Once again, the defense was rebuffed in an attempt to shift blame from the defendants to the officers.

Zamloch was more successful, and was able to develop an inconsistency in Lageson's testimony. At the coroner's inquest, Lageson had estimated that the shooting of Weinhold took place at 2:40 P.M., approximately thirty minutes after he returned from lunch. In answer to Hennessy's question on direct examination, however, he estimated that the shooting occurred some ten to fifteen minutes earlier. When the discrepancy was called to his attention, Lageson denied that his prior testimony was false, and explained, "It's pretty hard to give accurate times."

"Of course it is," Zamloch agreed. "In other words there was a great deal of excitement. You were all under a great deal of stress. You naturally could not make notes at that time and you had to rely on your reconstruction the next day, the best you could remember, isn't that about it?"

"Yes, true," Lageson conceded, ending the cross-examination on a high point for Zamloch. In addition to admitting the error, Lageson made the more significant admission that he was under stress, allowing the defense to argue that he may have made other mistakes in his recall of the facts.

Honing in on Zamloch's innocent comment about Lageson not making any notes, Hennessy succeeded in introducing one of his most damning pieces of prosecution evidence. His tactic was highly dramatic and effective. On re-direct, Hennessy called Lageson's attention to Zamloch's earlier questions. "Mr. Zamloch, in his examination of you, asked if you had made any notes while this thing was occurring."

"I made no notes," was Lageson's response.

"Well did you make any notes at all," Hennessy persisted.

"I wrote the names of the six men on the wall of the cell," Lageson answered.

Hennessy then produced a photograph of the list of names and asked if it was an accurate depiction of what he had written on the wall that night. "Yes, sir, that is my handwriting. I wrote those names on the wall of the cell sometime after the shooting that night. The names of Cretzer, Coy, and Hubbard were circled and a large check appeared beside Cretzer's name. The names of Carnes, Thompson, and Shockley also appeared on the list, with no identifying characteristics."

Instantly all the defense attorneys were on their feet voicing objections and stating various theories as to why the photograph should not be admitted. Goodman listened patiently to the objections and the supporting arguments but was unmoved. Without waiting for Hennessy's response, the judge overruled all the objections and admitted the photograph into evidence. The prosecutor hastily retrieved the photograph from the witness and thrust it in front of the clerk to be marked as the next exhibit in order. "I offer this in evidence and ask that the jury be permitted to see it," Hennessy rattled on, pushing to get the photo into the hands of the jury before the defense found a way to prevent it.

"The photograph will be United States Exhibit #25," the clerk announced, handing it back to Hennessy. As the prosecutor moved to place the photograph in the hands of the jury, the defense attorneys vigorously renewed their objections. Spagnoli asked that the photograph not be considered as to Thompson, since the question regarding Lageson making notes was not asked by him. Zamloch sought to delay a jury view until after he'd had an opportunity to cross-examine the witness on the photograph.

Sullivan demanded clarification as to what the markings by the names meant. The scene was confused, almost frenzied, as the defense team sought to regroup and blunt the effect of the damaging evidence.

"Show it to the jury," the judge finally ordered, bringing the bickering to an end and allowing the now fascinated jury to study the list of names.

It was late in the day and the defense was in turmoil. The photograph was an unexpected blow. The attorneys had hoped to argue that the hostages were confused as to the times and involvement of the defendants. The list of names, however, was demonstrative proof of the three defendants' involvement. It was also substantiation of Lageson's testimony, as the names had been written contemporaneously with the events. Lageson had written the names during the night in an effort to memorialize his personal observations. One by one, the attorneys agreed with Goodman's suggestion that adjournment for the weekend was in order. Cross-examination of the witness on the issue of the photograph would resume the following Tuesday morning.

Lageson was surprised by the furor that the photograph had created, but took it in stride. Hennessy had not discussed the list in detail with him and, in fact, Lageson had nearly forgotten that he had written the names on the wall. Hennessy had deliberately delayed in admitting the photo, hoping for the dramatic impact that it would have on the jury and adverse counsel. The tactic paid off, and he was able to end the week on a theatrical note, with the defense scrambling in disarray.

While it had not been a good week for the defense, it had been a particularly bad week for Shockley. At the beginning of Friday's session, Warden Johnston handed Sullivan a sealed envelope and advised him that it contained a letter from inmate #561, Joseph Moyle. Sullivan considered Moyle to be a very important witness for Shockley, and he was justifiably concerned. "What's this?" he asked in surprise.

"This is a personal uncensored letter that Joe Moyle wanted delivered to you and rather than trust it to the mail, I'm delivering it in person. Please be aware, Mr. Sullivan, that nobody on Alcatraz has seen the contents of this letter and I have no idea what is contained in this envelope."

Sullivan tore open the envelope. "Dear Mr. Sullivan," it began, "I know you are intending to call me as a defense witness in the case for Sam Shockley. After thinking the matter over, I have decided that it is not in my best interest to testify or take any part in the trial. For that reason I am telling you I do not wish to testify and I ask that you do not subpoena me.

If you call me I will refuse to testify." Moyle went on to explain that it was his opinion that he would be transferred from Alcatraz in nine years or less and he did not want to jeopardize his future. Also he pointed out in the letter, "I got to live over here."

"Shit!" Sullivan whispered to himself, "Somebody's gotten to this guy and frightened him into not testifying." Sullivan had been impressed with Moyle during their interview and believed he could have been a great help to Shockley's defense.

As one of the warden's passmen, Moyle enjoyed a high degree of credibility and trust within the institution. His work assignment was that of cook and housekeeper for the warden, a job reserved for only the most trusted and well-behaved prisoners in the prison. Sullivan believed this would make him a highly credible witness for Shockley. At the time of the shooting he and Egan were in Cretzer's cell, only twenty-five feet from the hostages.

Moyle made a good general appearance and told his version of the facts in a straightforward, believable fashion. Although he heard all the conversation that took place, including Captain Weinhold's attempt to talk Cretzer out of shooting the guards, he emphatically denied that he ever heard Shockley urge Cretzer to shoot anyone. "Shockley didn't say anything," Moyle had assured Sullivan. "He was just standing there and I don't think he knew what was going on." Now that evidence was gone, which meant Sullivan would be forced to place greater emphasis than ever on the brutality and insanity defenses.

17

The trial was scheduled to resume on Tuesday, December 3. It was a gray rainy day, with a cold steady wind out of the south. Much of the Bay Area was in a state of turmoil, brought on by a general strike called by the Alameda County American Federation of Labor union leadership. For several weeks, the A.F. of L. Retail Clerks Union had been striking against two East Bay department store chains, Kahn's and Hasting's. With the passage of time and the employment of non-union workers, relations between the parties had grown ugly.

Open hostilities developed on Monday morning, December 2, when the Oakland police escorted a number of trucks carrying merchandise through picket lines, outraging the picketers and union leadership. By late afternoon, downtown Oakland had become a battle zone, with more than 500 pickets and 250 police officers confronting one another in a series of violent clashes.

The Retail Clerks union called for a general strike throughout the East Bay, and on Tuesday, December 3, more than 130,000 workers in all walks of retail, commercial, and manufacturing commerce went out on strike. The four daily newspapers in the East Bay did not publish. Restaurants and markets closed. Retail trade ground to a standstill. Shipyards as well as manufacturing, industrial, and commercial firms closed. Transportation workers stayed off the job. The San Francisco-Oakland Bay Bridge experienced the worst traffic jam in its history, with vehicles backed up for miles. As 10,000 union members and sympathizers demonstrated in downtown Oakland, the entire East Bay was hopelessly stranded, including Alcatraz juror Raymond Willis.

Willis, an East Bay architect residing on High Street in East Oakland, did not own a car and traveled to and from court on the Key System, the public transportation complex serving transbay travelers. With the system shut down, Willis had no way to get to court and so advised Goodman's clerk by telephone.

Also missing on Tuesday morning was juror #4, George Bain of Ross, located across the Golden Gate Bridge in Marin County. Bain, a retired businessman, was suffering from a heavy cold and had called earlier, advising that he was too ill to come to court. Faced with two absent jurors, Goodman had no choice but to declare a recess and order the parties to return the following day.

Although the strike raged on, order was established and traffic began to flow again over the next twenty-four hours. Goodman ordered the marshal's office to provide transportation for Willis, and the other East Bay jurors, civil engineer Frank Varney of El Cerrito, and housewife Della McVittie of Richmond. With a deputy U.S. marshal serving as chauffeur for the East Bay jurors, the court's normal routine was reestablished and the trial resumed on Wednesday morning.

Before testimony began on Wednesday, Sullivan again moved to exclude the Lageson photograph. Although he had no written authorities, he cited several applicable cases and two legal grounds in support of his motion. Goodman listened with only moderate interest and hastily denied the motion on both grounds.

Sullivan had given considerable thought to his motion, and the judge's cavalier treatment of the matter irritated the young attorney tremendously. As the case had progressed, Sullivan was becoming more and more frustrated, watching Hennessy run roughshod over him. It seemed that whatever Hennessy said or did was accepted by the court, while Sullivan's arguments met with rejection and frequently an embarrassing lecture form the judge. *That son of a bitch Goodman wants these guys gassed*, Sullivan thought to himself. *He's going to let Hennessy do whatever he goddamn pleases*.

When Lageson resumed the stand, Zamloch was the first to cross-examine him, attempting to establish that it had been Carnes who had spoken on his behalf just before Cretzer fired. "Didn't you hear someone outside the cell say, 'He's a good screw, let him live, he never hurt anybody?'" asked Zamloch.

"Yes, I heard Cretzer say, '...he is a good screw...'" Lageson responded.

"Isn't it a fact that those words that I have just quoted to you were spoken by Clarence Carnes?" continued Zamloch.

"No, not that I can recollect," the witness responded firmly. "I'm certain that Cretzer said, '...he's a good screw.'"

Getting nowhere with that line of questioning, Zamloch asked the witness if it wasn't true that just before he was shot, while Cretzer was reloading the gun, that Carnes had motioned to him with his hands, indicating that he should duck when Cretzer fired. Again Lageson responded negatively, stating that he recalled no such action or signal by Carnes.

Finally Zamloch was able to make some progress when he developed an inconsistency in Lageson's testimony. Under Zamloch's cross-examination the officer had described hearing one of the insurgents come to the front of the cell, then leave and report to the other inmates, "I guess they're all dead, because they are all still lying the way we left them." Lageson also stated to Zamloch that he *believed* the voice to be that of Clarence Carnes. At the coroner's inquest, held only a few days after the riot, the witness had stated he *was sure* the voice was Carnes's. Zamloch emphasized this inconsistency to make the point that Carnes sought to save the lives of the guards rather than aid and abet in the taking of any life.

Still smarting from Goodman's abrupt denial of his motion, and shaking with pent-up rage, Sullivan rose to cross-examine Lageson. Holding the photograph in his hand, he lashed out at the witness. "At any time after you were rescued, did you walk up to Thompson or Shockley or Carnes and say 'These are the men who tried to kill me'?" he probed bitterly.

"No, Sir, I did not," Lageson calmly responded.

"As a matter of fact, the first time you did such a thing was in court here the other day, isn't that correct?" Sullivan aggressively demanded.

"You mean when he identified them?" the judge interjected, without waiting for any objection from the prosecution.

"Identified them and accused them of trying to kill him," responded the rancorous attorney.

"I won't allow that question," ruled Goodman, glowering at Sullivan. "The record speaks for itself. The witness was asked to identify the men and he identified them by pointing them out. There is no private individual who accuses anybody in the federal court, it is done by the process of the law."

"The Grand Jury," Hennessy added.

"You have the answer to your question, Mr. Sullivan," Goodman continued, ignoring Hennessy. "Now proceed if you have any other questions."

Sullivan returned to his seat at the counsel table.

Finally, in an effort to inject some confusion into the list of names that Lageson had written on the cell wall, Vinkler brought out that there were three inmates on Alcatraz named Thompson. Unfortunately for Vinkler, Lageson knew them all and was able to describe and identify all three of them. The identity question was put to rest for good.

Vinkler was the first attorney to seek an explanation of the various marks Lageson had made along with the names. The witness testified that the check behind Cretzer's name indicated he was the shooter and the circles around Coy and Hubbard identified them as the individuals who had overpowered Miller. Lageson was never asked to explain the circle around Cretzer's name.

Lageson had been a strong witness for the government. He positively identified all three defendants as participants in the riot. He placed weapons in the hands of both Carnes and Shockley, and described Shockley's attack on Sundstrom. He described Shockley and Thompson as urging Cretzer to kill the hostages, thereby aiding, abetting, and furthering the death of Miller. Additionally, Lageson knew all the defendants personally and, given his demeanor on the stand, it was a near impossibility for the defense to successfully argue that he had misidentified any of the participants. Finally, his identification of the defendants was confirmed by his handwritten list scribbled on the wall of the death cell, and presented to the jury by way of photograph.

As Lageson walked away from the witness stand and past the counsel table, Hennessy rose to acknowledge his departure. As the two men made eye contact, Hennessy winked and nodded at the departing witness, a hint of a smile on his lips. Lageson made no response, displaying no emotion as he left the courtroom.

The prosecutor's next witness was Joseph V. Burdett, the custodial officer in charge of the kitchen and dining hall. Burdett was a big man, with a bull neck and a deeply lined face. Standing 6'3" and weighing well over 200 pounds, he was powerfully built and strong, but possessed of a gentle personality and soft voice. Burdett was in his mid-forties and had been with the prison service for sixteen years. He was cordial with his fellow officers, but mainly kept to himself. He and his wife were not an active part of the Alcatraz social scene, preferring to spend their time together and with their only child, Joe Jr.

Burdett's testimony was generally consistent with that of the other hostages, particularly as to the conduct of Thompson and Shockley. He testified that when he made a routine check of the cell house at about 2:15 that afternoon he was captured by the armed prisoners. Entering cell 404, he observed Moyle and Egan standing at the front of the cell and Miller and Bristow near the back wall. Miller's hands were tied behind his back.

"Tell us what happened next," Hennessy inquired.

"Well, Mr. Miller asked me to untie his hands. So I turned to Carnes, who was standing in front of the cell holding a club, and asked if it would be all right to untie his hands. He said yes. When I slipped the cord off his thumbs, Mr. Miller handed me key 107, which was the key to the outside door."

"What did you do with the key?"

"Well, I put the key under one of the seats that was mounted on the wall. I laid it against the wall under the seat. Shortly after that we were moved out of cell 404 and into 403."

When Burdett identified Carnes as the man who unwittingly allowed the break to fail, the young defendant drummed his fingers on the counsel table. Then he turned to his attorney and broke into a stream of rapid whispers. As he did, Thompson shot Carnes a withering look of scorn. Thompson's disdainful stare silently let the youngster know how strongly the older man disapproved of his giving the guards an opportunity to hide the key.

According to Burdett, the inmates returned several times to cells 402 and 403 looking for key #107. None of the inmates, however, thought to search for the key in cell 404.

Immediately following Burdett's testimony, Zamloch requested permission to recall Lageson. Hennessy offered no objection and the bailiff went out into the hall to locate the young officer. During the noon recess, Lageson had contacted Hennessy concerning certain parts of Zamloch's cross-examination questions. Hennessy passed Lageson's comments along to Zamloch, suggesting that he might wish to recall the officer.

With Lageson back on the stand, Zamloch asked him if he recalled being asked earlier whether Carnes signaled to him to duck just prior to being shot. Lageson, who had earlier stated that he did not recall such a gesture, acknowledged that upon reflection he did recall that Carnes may have made such a motion with the club in his hand, responding, "It could be construed that way, yes." This revised testimony was extremely important to Carnes's defense. Zamloch now had solid evidence upon which to argue that Carnes actually tried to help the guards.

To his consternation, Carnes was being described, not as an aider or abettor of the murderer, but as an aider of the guards. He knew this was his counsel's theory of defense and he had agreed to it, but he was, nevertheless, embarrassed and ill at ease. He accidentally made eye contact with Thompson, and the latter smiled scornfully, rolling his eyes to signal his utter disgust. "What a fucking pussy," he snarled under his breath, the comment audible only to Spagnoli.

"You should be so lucky as to have a guard come in and say something good about you," Spagnoli muttered instinctively.

"Yeah, I guess so," whispered Thompson. He slumped in his chair and glanced at the clock on the far wall. It was almost three o'clock and the afternoon session would be wrapping up within the hour.

Lieutenant Joseph Simpson was the government's last witness of the day. A friendly, outgoing individual, Simpson was well liked by the custodial force, but feared and distrusted by many of the prisoners. He was considered by the inmates as a leading member of the "goon squad," a group of senior officers called upon from time to time to quell cell house disturbances. While not abusive to the convicts, he was a firm, no nonsense disciplinarian. As the bailiff pushed open the door at the rear of the courtroom, Simpson slowly shuffled down the aisle to the witness stand. He appeared pale and drawn, much older than his fifty-two years. Slightly overweight with a jolly countenance before the riot, he was now gaunt. His normally round, florid face looked wan and sunken. The bullet wounds he had suffered during the riot had almost taken his life and he was still a long way from complete recovery. He continued as an outpatient at the Marine Hospital. Until very recently his ability to appear in court had been in question.

Hennessy had a finely-tuned flare for the dramatic. As soon as Simpson took the stand and identified himself, Hennessy announced that Simpson had been badly wounded during the riot and was still suffering disability from his wounds. Addressing the witness he suggested, "During the course of your testimony it may arise that you will suffer pain or inconvenience. If so, please call it to the attention of the court if you should desire a recess." The attorney then turned to the judge and went on, "I may state, Your Honor, that it is possible he might request a recess during the course of the examination."

"Very well," responded the judge, in a supportive manner, playing into Hennessy's agenda. The crafty prosecutor, capitalizing on the witness's physical condition, got Simpson's testimony off to a dramatic and sympathetic start.

Simpson described how he and mail censor Robert Baker entered the cell house between 2:15 and 2:20 P.M. on that Thursday and walked down Broadway. He looked to his left as he reached the west end of the cell house and the first thing he saw was Thompson standing near the cell house officer's desk, holding a rifle. He went on to describe the other inmates he observed, including Cretzer with the pistol, as well as Shockley, Carnes, and Fleish. There were others too, he indicated, but he could not now recall who they were or what they were doing.

As the testimony continued, Spagnoli and Vinkler engaged in an animated, whispered conversation with their client. In addition to all the other problems he was facing in the case, Thompson was now, for the first time, being accused by a witness of having the rifle in his possession. Simpson explained that Thompson ordered him to stand behind C block. He then herded Simpson and Baker around the west end of C block into cell 402, jabbing them in the back with the rifle and ordering them to "Step it up."

Simpson testified that the prisoners became agitated when they were unable to fine the key to the outside door. As they were trying various keys in the lock, the siren sounded, and Simpson heard one of the inmates announce, "It's all up to us now." Simpson did not recognize the voice, but he heard Cretzer address Hubbard in apparent response, "We might as well go the hard way, Marv." This was Simpson's first awareness of Hubbard's involvement.

Simpson then heard the sound of gunfire. "There was some shooting going on down at the west end of the cell block, but I couldn't tell where it was from. The next thing I remember, Cretzer was standing in front of the cell pointing the .45 at us. Then Shockley says, 'That's Lieutenant Simpson, he ain't no good, kill the son of a bitch,' and Cretzer fired." The bullet struck Simpson in the chest, knocking him backward against the wall, although he did not lose consciousness.

He then heard Shockley cry out again, "That's Baker, the goddamn mail censor. He ain't no good neither, kill him too," and again the .45 thundered. Baker was jolted off the bunk by the force of the bullet, and landed on the floor. Simpson soon lost consciousness.

At some point Simpson awoke and was aware of pain in his leg. "Later on it felt like my leg was asleep," he explained, "and I went to move it. There was a prisoner standing out in front and I heard him say, 'That son-on-a-bitch ain't dead yet,' and they shot me again."

"Where were you shot this time?" asked Hennessy.

"In the side, over here," responded Simpson, indicating his left side just under the arm.

The cross-examination of Simpson was ineffective. Sullivan concentrated on Shockley's mental condition, but Simpson declined to give any opinions regarding the inmate's sanity. When Sullivan asked him if he had observed anything unusual when Shockley came out of solitary he responded, "What I observed of Shockley was that he resented any kind of authority."

Spagnoli, stung by the testimony that placed the rifle in his client's hands, sought to cast doubt on Simpson's identification of Thompson. "No, there is no doubt in my mind about it." Simpson assured the attorney, "I saw Thompson every day that I was on duty and there's no question in my mind that he was the man holding the rifle." Spagnoli was equally unsuccessful in his efforts to establish that Thompson had left the front of the hostage cells and returned to his cell before the shooting began.

As the day drew to a close, Simpson was physically exhausted but exhilarated, knowing that his testimony had gone well. Zamloch indicated that he would have only a few minutes of questioning, but needed to review the transcript before he could proceed. This was a ploy by Zamloch to delay his examination of the witness until the next day, to allow himself additional preparation time. Since it was late in the afternoon, Goodman declared an end to the court day. He inquired if the witness would be able to return the following morning. "I'll be here tomorrow," responded Simpson in a strong voice.

As he left the stand, Simpson was careful to watch his step on the stairs. While looking down, he caught a glimpse of the new tie clasp he was wearing. He smiled to himself, recalling how lucky his old one had been for him on May 2. He was alive today because of that small piece of jewelry. It was a facsimile of a silver dollar given to him by his wife Marian. Simpson had referred to it as his "lucky tie clip" after he experienced good fortune while wearing it during a trip to the casinos at Lake Tahoe. On May 2, however, the clip's luck was life saving. The first slug pumped into him by Cretzer struck the tie clip and was deflected to the right. The bullet curved around his rib cage and lodged in the thick musculature of the right upper back. Had the bullet not struck his tie clip, it would have torn through his heart. Now bent, distorted, and no longer functional, the jagged piece of metal was kept by Simpson in a small jewelry box; a souvenir of that agonizing night, and a symbol of the luckiest moment of his life. "It's almost over," he thought to himself, "a few more minutes tomorrow morning and I can put it all behind me and concentrate on getting back to work." He stepped into the gathering darkness of the winter evening and waited, along with the other Alcatraz officers, to be driven to the dock in the Marshal's van. He considered himself a lucky man. *Things sure could easily have gone the other way*, he thought, *the way they went for Bill Miller.*

18
——

Zamloch's cross-examination of Simpson was brief, and except for pointing out a minor inconsistency regarding when he first saw Hubbard, was ineffectual.

Following Zamloch, Vinkler undertook to examine the witness, even though the initial questioning on behalf of Thompson had been conducted by Spagnoli. He got nowhere with his questions regarding the existence of alleged dungeon cells. Hennessy successfully objected to most of his questions. On the few occasions when the attorney was able to frame a proper question, Simpson managed to sidestep the issue. "Oh, yes, I have heard prisoner talk of the old Spanish dungeons," he conceded, "however, I've been there since 1934 and I have no idea where they are, or if they exist at all."

Vinkler also failed to advance the Alcatraz brutality defense. Simpson admitted that he sat on disciplinary boards from time to time, but denied participating in brutal treatment of prisoners. He also specifically denied beating Thompson. "I've never touched Thompson in my life," Simpson responded contemptuously, treating the question as an affront to his dignity. After only a few minutes, his testimony was complete and the lieutenant departed the courtroom, his face reflecting his relief.

Hennessy's next witness was Robert Baker, the prison mail censor. Baker was a tall, lean man who had worked on Alcatraz since the prison opened in 1934. As mail censor, he knew more about the prisoners than any other officer on the island. He was also one of the officers most well known by the inmates. He was liked and respected by the other officers, but his reputation among the prisoners was not good. It was his job to periodically excise portions or entire pieces of correspondence. It was also occasionally necessary for him to meet with prisoners and discuss violations of correspondence regulations. These interventions were poorly received by the inmates and frequently construed by them as unfair. The inmates also believed, albeit mistakenly, that Baker took pleasure in delivering bad news, which contributed to his negative reputation.

Baker's testimony concurred with that of Simpson. He too, placed the rifle in Thompson's hands, and described the "...semi-circle of cons." confronting them at the west end of the cell house. He described Shockley's attack on Sundstrom, and confirmed Simpson's description of Shockley just before Cretzer's shooting spree. "Shockley was carrying a Stilson wrench and was screaming, '...shoot the sons of bitches.' Cretzer didn't say anything, he just opened fire. He kept shooting. I don't know how many shots. And then he went away."

On cross-examination, Sullivan sought unsuccessfully to advance Shockley's insanity defense. He attempted to argue that because of the intimate knowledge Baker gained through reviewing Shockley's mail, he was qualified to express an opinion as to the inmate's sanity. Goodman sustained all of Hennessy's objections, again frustrating the young attorney's efforts.

Hoping to finish on a positive note, Sullivan inquired sarcastically, "Oh, by the way, did Shockley hit you over the head with that Stilson wrench you said he was carrying?"

"No, but he threatened to," was Baker's mocking response.

Concerned by Baker's assertion that Thompson held the rifle, Vinkler attacked the reliability of his observation. "Why do you particularly remember Thompson among the two hundred or more prisoners that you have over at Alcatraz?"

"I remember him because he had a rifle pointed at me," Baker carefully recited, convincing Vinkler to terminate his questioning.

Taking advantage of the opening provided by Vinkler, Hennessy had only one question on redirect. Holding the weapon aloft for the jurors to see, he asked, "I show you defendant's Exhibit G, and ask you if this rifle bears any resemblance to the one you saw in the hands of the defendant Thompson."

"Yes, sir, the one he held looked just like that one."

When Baker's testimony was finished, Hennessy recalled Carl Sundstrom to the stand. His earlier appearances had been to authenticate prison records and inmate files, but Hennessy now wanted him to recall his experience as a hostage.

"Sunny" Sundstrom was easygoing, and well liked by both guards and inmates. He had been on Alcatraz since 1938, initially as a custodial officer and now full time as the prison record clerk. Sundstrom was in his mid-thirties and handsome, with sandy hair and bright blue eyes. He kept himself in good physical condition and was an avid tennis player.

Sundstrom recounted that on the day in question, armory officer Cliff Fish received a call reporting possible trouble in the cell house. In response, Simpson and Baker entered the cell house. Sundstrom remained at his desk in the administrative offices. After six or seven minutes and no report from the other two officers, Sundstrom armed himself with a gas billy and entered the cell house. He testified that he passed through the main gate at approximately 2:24 P.M. and was captured at the west end of the cell house by Thompson, who was holding a rifle. Coy grabbed him by the necktie and led him around C block to cell 402, while Thompson followed behind with the rifle and Cretzer walked beside him with the .45. "They took me past the officer's toilet and cell 403 to cell 402. Just before we got to cell 402, Shockley came up to me and yelled, 'You son of a bitch,' and hit me twice on the chin, right here on the chin. Then they opened the door of the cell and I went inside. I just stood there looking at the bars with Mr. Baker and Lieutenant Simpson."

Sundstrom then described how Cretzer demanded his uniform trousers. While removing them, the gas billy and his wallet fell out of his pockets onto the floor. Cretzer ignored the gas billy, but confiscated the $92 contained in the wallet.

"What did he say, if anything?" Hennessy queried.

"As he handed the empty wallet back to me he smiled and said, 'You can call this highway robbery.' "

The witness went on to describe the events that followed. While his version was generally consistent with the other hostages, he recalled Cretzer firing first into cell 402 then moving to 403. Hennessy realized that Sundstrom's recollection of the sequence of shots was erroneous, but made no attempt to correct him. Sundstrom's testimony was cumulative, and the principal reason for putting him on the stand was to permit the jury to hear from each of the hostages. Hennessy noticed that it was just about time for the noon recess, so he quickly concluded his examination of the witness before the midday break.

∽

At the commencement of the afternoon session, Sullivan elicited from Sundstrom that at no time did he ever see a weapon in Shockley's hands. In an effort to mitigate the impact of Shockley's assault on Sundstrom, Sullivan again managed to incur Goodman's wrath. Responding to the attorney's questioning, Sundstrom reiterated that Shockley had cursed at him and struck him twice in the jaw. He admitted that he was neither stunned nor badly injured by the blows. At that point, Sullivan called to his client, "Step up here, Sam." With Shockley standing near the witness, Sullivan suggested, "As a matter of fact, Shockley is kind of a weakling, isn't he?" He then inquired as to Sundstrom's weight and the officer testified that he weighed 162 pounds. Sullivan then directed Shockley to remove his coat and vest and roll up his sleeves in order to demonstrate his weak physique. Shockley's face was blank and pale as he stood within a foot of the jury box. As ordered, he removed his suit coat and began unbuttoning his vest.

Goodman was caught off guard. "What is the purpose of this?" he inquired of Sullivan.

"The purpose of this is to show that this man was not strong enough to hurt this witness," responded Sullivan, waving his hands in the air.

"How is taking off his coat going to demonstrate that?" demanded the judge. "Tell him to put his coat back on."

Sullivan refused to be dissuaded. "This individual has dramatically come in here and put his finger on…"

Raising his voice, Goodman ordered Sullivan, "I don't want any more argument. Tell him to put his coat and vest back on. I am not going to have any demonstration of this kind in my courtroom. Have him put his coat and vest back on."

Sullivan refused to back down and he continued his cross-examination. "Would you say Shockley was a strong man, Mr. Sundstrom? Do you want to feel his muscles?"

"Not necessarily," Sundstrom stammered in confused reply.

"No! No! No! Stop that sort of thing at once!" Goodman called out, feeling he was losing control of his courtroom.

"If Your Honor please, I have authorities to submit on this point. I can prove I have a right to do this," Sullivan shot back.

"The witness is not going to feel somebody else's muscles. This is silly. It is undignified and I will not permit it!" exclaimed Goodman, now nearly shouting. Hennessy jumped to his feet objecting. The courtroom observers sat stunned, yet clearly amused, by the chaos.

"Sit down, Sam," Sullivan called out in mock retreat. As Shockley went back to his seat at the counsel table, Sullivan calmly returned to the podium and resumed his cross-examination. The incredible demonstration had accomplished nothing beyond further alienating Goodman.

"I wonder who's crazy here, Shockley or his attorney?" Hennessy whispered to Deasy.

Sullivan next sought to establish that Shockley was merely a bystander, running around in an irrational manner, and behaving as a madman. "When I saw him, he was just standing there," Sundstrom stated. "I would say he acted mean and vicious." Despite Sullivan's pressing, Sundstrom refused to yield, insisting that Shockley demonstrated no signs of deranged or irrational behavior. He also denied that Shockley was a follower, describing him as just as much a leader as Cretzer.

Sundstrom's testimony on this point was, at the least, disingenuous. In a detailed statement given to FBI investigators two days after the riot, Sundstrom described Shockley as "running around and acting like a crazy man." The rules of evidence did not, however, permit Sullivan to review this statement, and the inconsistency was never revealed to the defense or the jury.

Finally as part of his continuing effort to place the Alcatraz authorities in an unfavorable light, Sullivan interrogated Sundstrom regarding the officers with whom he spoke after his rescue. Sundstrom testified that the associate warden was one of these individuals. Sullivan then inquired, "Did Mr. Miller participate in the subsequent executions of Coy, Cretzer, and Hubbard?"

"I don't know what you mean by participation. He was over there." There was no objection to the question, and Sullivan was satisfied. The question was what was important, not the answer.

There was a stir in the press section when Hennessy announced his next witness. Associate Warden Edward J. Miller was well known to the members of the press, as he, along with the warden, was always on the Government's witness list when the U.S. Attorney prosecuted an Alcatraz case.

The heavyset, square-jawed Miller was a strong yet fair disciplinarian. However, the stories of his brutality, all of which he denied, were legion. Despite this, most of the inmates liked the bellicose administrator. There were, however, several inmates who claimed they had felt the sting of his violent hand and others with tales of his sinister "goon squad."

This squad was composed of a lieutenant and two or three senior officers as needed to establish order in cases of abnormal inmate violence. Force was often required in maintaining prison discipline, but there were occasions when excessive force was applied at Alcatraz. In his role as the chief operating officer of the prison, Miller absorbed the blame for every custodial excess. In fact, however, he was not an advocate of excessive force.

Miller was a perfect complement to Warden Johnston, who was not active in the daily operation of the prison, and maintained an aloof and somewhat condescending attitude toward inmates and officers alike. Miller was earthy and related well to people. Beneath his rough exterior he was a fair, evenhanded administrator, well-suited to manage both the desperado population of Alcatraz and the custodial force that controlled it.

Miller testified that he first became aware of trouble on May 2 when he heard the escape siren while performing a routine inspection at the northern end of the island. He ran up the steep hill to the main entrance and, without taking time to be briefed on the status of the situation, drew a gas billy from the armory and entered the cell house.

He stated that at the west end of Broadway, he observed a man coming out of the dining hall door dressed in a prison officer's uniform coat and hat. "When I saw this man, I thought at first it was the captain. As I turned down the corridor the man started walking faster and when I was about halfway to the end of the cell house he stepped out of the dining hall into the cell house and drew a rifle from behind his back. He pointed it at me and hollered for me to stop."

Under further questioning by Hennessy, Miller stated that he recognized the gunman as Bernie Coy. "He threw down the rifle on me and fired. I turned and ran, and he fired another shot that hit the cellblock over my head. I attempted to throw the gas billy at him and it hit the railing above me and bounced back at me." Miller went on to explain that he was certain the shooter was Coy and was equally certain that he was alone. As the rifleman continued to fire, Miller was able to reach the main gate and exit the cell house.

Hennessy then took the associate warden through the facts of the hostage rescue. Miller testified that he led a force of approximately a dozen officers who entered the cell house through the main gate and rescued the nine hostages. Initially, the rescue team headed down Seedy Street, between C and D blocks, and determined that the hostages were in cells 402 and 403. When fired upon by the insurgents from the top of C block, the group retreated and went around the other side of the cell house, down Michigan Boulevard, the corridor between A and B blocks, to reach the hostages. Lageson, Bristow, Burdett, and Sundstrom were able to walk and the other five were carried out on stretchers. As the rescue party departed, Lieutenant Faulk closed and locked the door to D block, isolating that area from the rest of the cell house.

The final minutes of Miller's direct examination concerned the morning of Saturday, May 4. By that time, the prison authorities were satisfied that the three holdouts had taken refuge in the east end of the C block utility corridor. Calls for their surrender had gone unanswered and there was no indication that anyone was alive in the cramped space. At approximately 10:00 A.M., Officers Mowery and Spencer entered the corridor. As the two officers made their way slowly through the dark passage, they found the bodies of Coy, Cretzer, and Hubbard.

By the time Hennessy finished Miller's direct examination it was late in the day. There was only time for Spagnoli and Sullivan to question before court adjourned. Spagnoli's cross-examination was brief. He was able to establish that the east gun gallery was manned just after the siren sounded, no later than 3:00 P.M. "The guards in the east gun gallery," inquired Spagnoli, "could see anyone, any of the prisoners or anyone else who might be in the vicinity of the library or in the vicinity of those cells 402, 403, or 404, is that correct?"

"That is correct," responded Miller. Spagnoli hoped to later use this testimony as support for Thompson's contention that he was not present in front of the hostage cells when the shooting took place.

Sullivan attempted to highlight the brutal recapture of the cell house and demonstrate that excessive force was employed against the lightly armed holdouts. Under his questioning, Miller acknowledged that he had forty officers with incredible firepower at his disposal, including shotguns, pistols, rifles, submachine guns, tear gas, bombs, and grenades. In addition, officers from penal institutions around the country had been flown in to assist. Miller conceded that against this overwhelming force, the inmates had only two guns and seventy-one rounds of ammunition. He also admitted that the authorities did considerable damage to D block during the re-capture. Sullivan was able to bring out the fact that Coy, Cretzer, and Hubbard all received multiple gunshot wounds to the head and that Miller had ordered his men to shoot to kill.

Unnoticed by all but the most knowledgeable courtroom observers, a sullen, bedraggled Kay Benedetti spent the day unobtrusively slouched in a seat at the rear of the spectator section. The thirty-eight-year-old former wife of Joe Cretzer was spotted as she slipped from the courtroom by an *Examiner* reporter, and was photographed as she left the building.

The former madam and gun moll had moved to San Francisco to be near Cretzer and her brother Arnold Kyle when they were transferred to Alcatraz in 1940. Many insiders believed she was a part of Cretzer's abortive breakout attempt in 1941, and was standing by to pick up the escapers in a boat. Although she severed her relationship with Cretzer in 1945 and was later married to truck driver Elmer Benedetti, she apparently encountered difficulty in breaking with her former life-style. In May of 1946 she and long-time friend Helene Wallace entered not guilty pleas to several counts of shoplifting and requested a jury trial on the charges. During the break she had volunteered to assist the authorities by trying to talk Cretzer into surrendering. Her offer, however, came just before the bodies were removed, too late to accomplish anything. Following the riot, she claimed Cretzer's body and attended to the details of his funeral and burial.

19

As he began his cross-examination of Miller, Zamloch had a single goal. He had to attack Miller and tarnish him in any way possible. Miller vigorously disputed Carnes's contention that he had attempted to save the associate warden's life. So, while urging that his client saved Miller's life, Zamloch also had to prove the associate warden a liar.

Zamloch began by again forcing the reluctant Miller to admit that the rioters could not have possessed more that two guns and a limited amount of ammunition. This he hoped would demonstrate that the custodial bombardment was an act of revenge. Next, he accused Miller of subjecting Carnes to a severe beating after order was restored. When Miller denied this accusation, Zamloch suddenly inquired if he owned a pearl handled pocket knife. The astonished associate warden admitted he did, whereupon Zamloch demanded that it be produced and marked for identification as an exhibit. "Isn't it a fact, Mr. Miller," demanded Zamloch, "that on the third tier of A block, which is generally uninhabited, you administered to Clarence Carnes a merciless beating and kicking?"

"That is not true," the flustered Miller responded.

"Isn't it also a fact that you took this knife of yours, opened it, placed the blade across Carnes's throat, and told him, 'I will put a scar on your throat you will have for the rest of your life'?"

"That is not true," was Miller's adamant denial. "I treated him just the same as any other inmate."

"Then Lord help the inmates!" Zamloch muttered, loud enough to be heard by the jury. Moved by his macabre humor, two of the male jurors smiled slightly, their eyes riveted on the bantam attorney.

"Mr. Miller," he inquired, "you know that among the inmates over there you carry the appellation of 'Jughead,' don't you?" Zamloch had asked the question in order to demean and embarrass the witness, but the effect was just the opposite. Upon hearing the question, Miller threw his head back in uproarious laughter. His reaction was infectious and immediately the three defendants joined in the hilarity, bringing smiles or laughter to the faces of all the jurors.

Seeking to get his cross-examination back on track, Zamloch raised his voice slightly and inquired, "Mr. Miller, you know, as a matter of fact, that you are the most hated and feared man at Alcatraz, by guards and convicts alike, don't you?" The smile disappeared from Miller's face. Hennessy's objection was sustained by Goodman, who sought to soften the effect of the question. "I suppose no prisoner in jail likes the jailer, but it won't help us any to go into that. I will sustain the objection."

Despite diligent effort, Zamloch was unable to budge Miller from his firmly entrenched position that it was Coy, not Hubbard who shot at him after he entered the cell house, that there were at least two shots, and that Coy was standing alone. In an effort to cast doubt on this testimony, Zamloch suggested, "You saw a man that you took to be Coy in a guard's uniform."

"I didn't take it to be Coy," Miller snapped. "I knew it was Coy." It was Coy who fired the shot at me," Miller reiterated. "I only seen Coy. I didn't see Hubbard."

As he brought his cross-examination to a conclusion, Zamloch realized that Carnes's claim of disrupting Hubbard's attempt to kill Miller would rest entirely on the credibility of Carnes and his convict witnesses. Any hope of assistance on the issue from Miller or any other members of the custodial force had been thoroughly dashed.

Vinkler took over when Zamloch was finished and established that a Coast Guard cutter stationed off the island had fired its deck guns into D block. Following restoration of order within the cell house, a number of large unexploded shells were found lying on the floor of D block. This Vinkler sought to prove, was further evidence of the vengeful overkill sponsored by the prison authorities when they knew that none of the rioters were in D block.

Before Miller left the stand, Spagnoli sought once again to revisit the issue of the legality of Thompson's sentence. "Mr. Miller, can you tell us what difference there is between a life sentence and one of ninety-nine years?"

"I have already ruled on that," Goodman angrily announced. "I have ruled it is incompetent, immaterial, and irrelevant."

Persisting, Spagnoli shifted to another improper line of questioning, inquiring, "Will you tell us, Mr. Miller, why some important defense witnesses for Mr. Thompson have been transferred from your institution since the May 2 riot, and have been transferred to other institutions around the country where we cannot locate them? For instance 'Lefty' Egan, 'Joe Blow' Bell, and I don't know how many others. I would like to find out."

Goodman responded immediately to Hennessy's objection, and chastised Spagnoli for making an unfounded accusation. He assured Spagnoli that he could issue a subpoena for any inmate witness and that individual would be brought to testify for the defense.

Spagnoli recognized at once that his ploy was backfiring. He suggested that he would have to consider the matter, sheepishly retreating from his earlier accusation.

Hennessy glanced at the clock, and saw that it was almost time for the noon recess. Catching the defense attorneys off guard, he hastily slipped some damaging statistics into evidence before the defense could react. "How many guards were wounded during this affray on May 2?" Hennessy asked Miller.

"I think it was fourteen," recalled the associate warden. "I believe that to be the whole total."

"And two were killed?" Hennessy queried.

"Two killed, yes," echoed Miller.

Annoyed with himself at permitting Hennessy to remind the jury that two guards had died, Zamloch momentarily considered a motion to strike, but decided not to highlight the harmful evidence and remained silent. Scanning his notes, Zamloch concluded that contrary to their hopes, Miller had been a disaster for the defense. He had provided no support for Carnes's claim of jostling Hubbard. In fact, he adamantly denied that either Hubbard or Carnes were anywhere in sight when Coy fired. If the jury believed Miller, one entire aspect of Carnes's defense would evaporate.

Additionally, none of the defense attorneys had succeeded in portraying Miller as the brutal leader of the custodial force, who drove Coy and Cretzer to try to escape from the tyranny of Alcatraz. *Shrewd old 'Jughead' held his own*, thought Zamloch, *even through he sure as hell lied when he denied ever striking an inmate. Maybe the jury will see through it.*

Miller's testimony was complete, and Hennessy had a few minutes to fill before the noon recess. Anticipating that Miller would be on the stand for the entire morning session, Hennessy had arranged to have Weinhold testify at the commencement of the afternoon session. The captain was still a patient at the Marine Hospital, and the medical staff had urged that his time on the stand be brief. Hennessy intended to limit Weinhold's testimony to the afternoon session.

To fill the time until the recess, he called Lieutenant Phillip Bergen. When the afternoon session began, he would interrupt Bergen's testimony for Weinhold. Bergen's involvement in the May 2 outbreak was to lead the assault team into the west gun gallery. When the riot began, Bergen was enjoying a day off with his wife on the mainland. He arrived on the island at approximately 5:00 P.M. after learning of the uprising through a news broadcast on his car radio. Hennessy called Bergen for the sole purpose of highlighting the death of Harold Stites.

From the earlier testimony and photographs presented by Agent Doud, the jury had been given the physical description of the west gun gallery. In D block the gallery had three levels, the lowest being the main floor. Entry from the outside was into this lowest level. On the main floor the bars of the gallery were covered with heavy-gauge wire mesh.

On the stand the lieutenant indicated that shortly before 7:00 P.M. he entered the gallery through the southern exterior door. "Who entered with you?" Hennessy inquired.

"Mr. Stites and Mr. Cochrane."

"Just tell us what happened when you entered the D block portion of the gallery?" Hennessy continued.

Anticipating more testimony about Stites, Zamloch addressed the court. "We object to this question as incompetent, irrelevant, and immaterial. I assume the court will rule as it has in the past, but I want my objection to appear in the record."

"It's part of the *re gestae*," Hennessy announced, confident of a favorable ruling.

Sullivan joined in the objection and Zamloch continued. "The testimony is now coming in as to the shooting that happened at 6:00 P.M. That is hardly still part of the *res gestae*."

Goodman, however, was ready to accept all of Hennessy's arguments on the subject. Ruling in the prosecutor's favor, the judge cited as his authority the fact that he had let the evidence in earlier. The defense attorneys were not surprised at the ruling, and knew they stood no chance of blocking the evidence. As the morning session concluded, the mood at the defense end of the counsel table became increasingly somber. Once the jury and defendants were out of the courtroom, Sullivan and Zamloch remained seated at the counsel table, discussing the Stites problem.

"This is really unfair," Sullivan complained. "That damn Goodman is buying everything Hennessy has for sale. There's no way that all this Stites evidence should be coming in. It's irrelevant and it's prejudicial."

"You're absolutely right, Bill," Zamloch agreed. "The problem is he let it in back there during Burch's testimony and there's no way he's going to back down now. Hennessy's going to push it as far as he can and he's gonna have the judge with him the whole way."

"Yeah, that's another thing that pisses me off," grumbled Sullivan. "He's giving Hennessy every break in the book and he's really leaning on us. I don't know how far we're going to get with this brutality theory of ours; he's really been shutting us down there."

The two went on for several minutes, complaining and consoling one another over what had become a pattern in the case. Goodman was giving Hennessy wide latitude in admissibility of evidence, while placing a tight rein on the defense attorneys and unduly limiting their cross-examination.

"Maybe things will get better when we start putting on our case," Zamloch suggested hopefully.

"Yeah, I hope so," Sullivan agreed, "because up till now we've been taking a shit kicking. But it is the prosecution's turn at bat and you've gotta expect things to go well for them. I really hope my psychiatric testimony goes well, because I'll tell you, Archer, I think that's gonna be Shockley's only hope."

"Well Bill," Zamloch went on, "if Carnes was on the jury you'd have a solid vote for insanity. That kid is far more concerned about Shockley than he is about himself. He's mentioned several times how Sam doesn't know what's going on and how he's not in touch with reality. He was even crazier, according to Clarence, during the riot, running around, yelling and getting in everyone's way. Clarence feels strongly that to find Sam guilty would be a real miscarriage of justice, and as I said, he's really bothered by it."

∽

When the afternoon session began, Hennessy requested permission to call Captain Weinhold out of order. There being no objection from the defense, Hennessy nodded to the bailiff and announced, "Call Captain Henry Weinhold."

The door swung open revealing the frail figure of Captain Weinhold. As everyone in the courtroom watched, he walked haltingly down the aisle toward the witness stand. Now, six months after the riot, he had only recently received clearance to leave the hospital for brief periods. The heroic officer would never recover sufficiently to return to his rigorous duties at Alcatraz. Despite his doctor's cautioning, Weinhold was determined to make the trip to court. "There's no way in hell that I'm going to be kept off that witness stand," he decreed. The young public health physician supervising his case had no stomach for a conflict with his patient, even in his severely weakened condition, and reluctantly signed the order permitting Weinhold to be transported to court.

Weinhold suffered a massive chest wound during the riot, and his recovery had been both slow and agonizing. The bullet had done near fatal damage. He hovered for days between life and death. After several weeks of recuperation, he developed a serious kidney infection. He was now solidly on the road to recovery, but faced many more months of rehabilitation and recuperation.

The courtroom was cathedral quiet as the captain shuffled slowly down the aisle. Although pale and emaciated, Weinhold maintained his military bearing. He stood at attention in front of the court clerk's desk as the oath was administered, and with labored steps climbed the three steps to the witness stand. Having heard much about him from previous witnesses, the jury sat in eager anticipation of Weinhold's testimony.

Hennessy led Weinhold through his recollection of the events. After he was alerted that there was trouble in the cell house, he entered through the main gate and proceeded down Broadway. Weinhold testified that he saw nothing unusual until he reached the west end of the cell house. There, Hubbard stepped out from behind C block, holding a rifle. Hubbard was followed closely by Shockley and Carnes. Weinhold was taken first to Coy's cell at the west end of B block where Hubbard took his uniform coat and trousers. He remained in the cell with Carnes guarding him for several minutes. Then, in the distance, he heard an unidentifiable voice call out, "Bring that son of a bitch Weinhold over here." Carnes escorted him across the west end of the cell house to the officer's toilet cell. When they arrived, Shockley ran up behind the captain and struck him in the back of the head. He was first placed in the end cell, then moved to 403 with the other hostages. The door was locked behind him, and most of the convicts departed, leaving only Cretzer and Shockley standing in front of the cells.

Weinhold described his conversation with Cretzer. "Well I said to him, 'You know you can't make a go of this. Even if you get outside, every one of you will get killed.' Cretzer said, 'If we can get outside we can make it, and we'll kill a couple of you guys while we're going out.' Then I told him, 'you're not going to get away with it. You know nobody does. You can't get away with anything on Alcatraz. The best thing for you is to give me that gun and call this thing off. You'll be done for and everybody will be done for.'

"All the time I was talking," Weinhold went on, "Shockley was standing in back of Cretzer keeping up a constant chatter. 'Kill the bastards! Go on; kill the dirty goddam bastards! Kill them all. Kill all of them, they're no goddam good. Kill them all.' He kept it up and kept it up, taunting Cretzer. Finally Cretzer said, 'Well we're going to kill you all.' Then I said to him, 'Well that doesn't mean anything; you can only die once. But the best thing for you to do, Joe, is to give me the gun. About that time the siren blew and when the siren went off, Shockley yelled, 'There it is! Go ahead, shoot him!' Then Cretzer pulled the trigger and I felt a shock here in my chest. Everything went a little hazy. My knees melted away from under me, and I lost interest in the proceedings for a while."

Weinhold went on to describe his wound and his limited recollection after being shot. "The bullet entered here in my chest on the left side, just slightly left of center. It passed through my body and came out under my right armpit, then passed through my right arm and shattered the right humerus and lodged on the outside of my arm at the elbow. I remember waking up, finding myself on the floor with my head on Corwin's knees, and being aware that I'd been injured. While I was lying there in that position, I saw three inmates tiptoe past the cell going east and then later turn around and run past the cell going west. I saw Thompson who had the rifle and Shockley with nothing in his hands and Cretzer still carrying the .45."

The jury sat enraptured as the captain spoke in a strong, quiet, voice. Although frail and weak, his face lined and shoulders hunched, he was still a dominant and impressive witness.

"Do you remember being rescued and taken out of the cell house?" asked Hennessy.

"Yes," responded Weinhold, "I had regained consciousness and everything was perfectly clear to me. I recollect being terribly cold and asking for someone to put a blanket over me."

The defense attorneys were afraid to cross-examine Weinhold. None of them felt anything helpful could be developed on cross-examination. Furthermore, Weinhold was such a charismatic witness that they wanted him off the stand and out of the courtroom as soon as possible. Sullivan and

Vinkler each asked a few innocuous questions, and Zamloch announced, "No questions, Your Honor."

Although brief, Weinhold's testimony was highly effective for the prosecution. He was particularly harmful to Shockley, whom he positively identified as encouraging Cretzer to kill the hostages. This, coupled with the testimony of Shockley's physical attack on Weinhold, put the inmate in a very negative position. Vinkler was surprised by Weinhold's testimony that Thompson was armed with the rifle, but could do nothing to nullify the captain's version of the facts. Carnes fared the best of the three, but nevertheless was described by Weinhold as an active and armed participant.

With Weinhold's dramatic testimony still ringing in the juror's ears, Bergen returned to the stand. He described how he, Stites, and Cochrane burst through the outside door into the main floor enclosure of the west gun gallery. Immediately upon entering they were met with gunfire, which seemed to come from two directions. One line of fire came from the cell house door directly in front of them, while additional fire came from the upper tiers of D block.

Bergen testified that once inside Stites turned to the left and assumed a covering position while he and Cochrane turned to the right to ascend the ladder to the first tier. Bergen and Stites returned the inmate fire, and Cochrane started up the ladder. As he mounted the ladder, he was shot in the arm and Bergen directed him to retreat and seek medical treatment. Bergen then scrambled up the ladder. Within a couple of minutes, Stites climbed the ladder, followed by officers Mahan, Clark, Oldham, and Bloomquist. Bergen positioned the officers along the south and west walls, firing into the D block cells and at the cell house door. He testified that they received hostile gunfire and he could see muzzle flashes coming from the eastern end of the upper tier of D block.

Bergen immediately set out to locate Burch. Under cover of the protective steel shield, he crawled through the door into the darkened cell house portion of the gallery, and found Burch, who was wearing only a shirt and underwear. He determined that Burch was uninjured, and the two men crawled back to the D block side of the gallery, careful to stay below the steel shield. Burch provided Bergen with what information he had regarding the inmate takeover and Bergen armed him with a .45 and ammunition.

While talking with Burch, Bergen's attention was called to Stites. "I saw Mr. Stites standing behind the wall that reaches about waist high."

"You mean that steel sheet that is on the bottom of the gallery?"

"Yes. He was standing almost erect and I heard him say, 'Well, boys, they got me.' Then he sort of slumped down and fell on his head about half way down the ladder. Oldham was standing at the corner of the gallery and in a couple of minutes, he was shot too."

Bergen testified that he then returned to the cell house side of the gallery. "Well, after Stites and Oldham were shot, we figured the shots were coming from D block, which made it impossible to go up the ladder to the top tier of the gallery. So I took the long route and went all the way across the cell house and up the ladder and back to the south end of the gallery."

Upon his return to D block he reported by phone to the armory that the gallery was secure and Burch was unhurt. He and his men remained in the gallery until 11:00 P.M. on Friday, approximately twenty-nine hours. He saw various inmates moving about from cell to cell and tier to tier in D block, but none of them were armed. At no time did he see any inmates out of their cells in the main cell house.

The clear inference created by Bergen's testimony was that Stites was shot by a prisoner either from the cell house or from D block. On cross-examination Sullivan concentrated on this aspect of his testimony, but Goodman intervened without any objection from Hennessy, blocking Sullivan's entire line of questioning. Despite continuous interruption from the judge, Sullivan was able to bring out that at the time he was shot, Stites was moving from the southern extension of the gallery toward Bergen. As he did, he stood erect, rather than crouching behind the shield as Bergen had directed. He was, therefore, visible to those outside. Sullivan also brought out that the light in D block was bright, supporting the argument that standing in front of the window, Stites would present a silhouette to the officers on the hill outside who were firing into D block.

Spagnoli's cross-examination of Bergen was brief, and focused on the bombardment. He sought to establish that although there were no rioters or weapons in D block, countless rounds including rifle fire, grenades, tear gas, and deck gun shells from the Coast Guard cutters were fired into the area. Spagnoli claimed that the bombardment was not an effort to quell an escape attempt, but a vengeful attempt to slaughter the occupants of D block. Bergen, however, insisted that during the night he saw gunfire coming from the cells in D block, thereby justifying the bombardment.

At the end of the day, Hennessy advised the court and counsel that he would conclude his case in chief on Monday. Grandstanding for the press after the defendants and jury left the courtroom, he announced, "We had a meeting this afternoon with the judge and I advised him that I had a few short witnesses and would be resting my case in chief at the close of the day Monday. I've got another twenty or twenty-five witnesses under subpoena, but I think we've put on a strong enough case on behalf of the government and additional testimony will simply be cumulative."

20

Goodman directed the jury and counsel to resume on Monday, December 9th rather than starting on Tuesday. "We've been in trial on this matter for three weeks and I want to move along," he instructed the attorneys. The government's first witness on Monday morning was Roy B. Sievertson, the Alcatraz plumbing foreman. Sievertson was a roughhewn individual, well over six feet tall, with large hands and tremendous upper body strength. He was a highly skilled plumber, who was seriously dedicated to his work. He also enjoyed an excellent relationship with the inmates he supervised. His florid complexion gave him the appearance of an outdoorsman, but he chose to spend the bulk of his spare time indoors, in the many bars and cafes along the waterfront, often in the company of his friend and drinking companion, Alcatraz chief electrician, Joe Steere. There he was well known to the longshoremen and merchant seamen who lived and worked in the area.

Hennessy considered Sievertson to be a minor witness, and permitted Deasy to conduct the direct examination. Sievertson was a member of the rescue party who along with Associate Warden Miller led the posse of officers that freed the hostages. In addition to rounding out the story of the rescue, Hennessy had another objective in selecting Sievertson as a witness.

In response to Deasy's questions, Sievertson described the rescue and how the officers encountered inmate gunfire from the top of C block. Spagnoli objected, urging that these events occurred hours after the crime with which the defendants were charged and were therefore too remote in time to be relevant. Without explanation, Goodman overruled the objection. Sullivan then sought an advisory ruling to later permit him to introduce matters that occurred several hours after the shooting as part of his case. Goodman refused to consider this inquiry with the terse response, "I do not answer questions, Mr. Sullivan. If you have an objection you wish to raise, I will rule on it."

Deasy proceeded with his examination of the witness. "What did you do after taking the guards out of cells 402 and 403?"

"We came back after we got them all out; we went back again, around into those cells. And the last time we were in there Mr. Roberts got shot. I think it was in front of—"

Immediately Sullivan rose again moving to strike the testimony and requesting that the jury be admonished that the statement of the witness had no bearing on the guilt or innocence of the defendants and was not part of the issues of the case.

"The sole purpose of these questions, Your Honor, is to call to the attention of the jury the shooting of Mr. Roberts and create the inference that the defendants are responsible for his being shot. We are only being charged with the shooting of Mr. Miller. There are so many issues being dragged into this case, that I would like to have the jury instructed at the present time."

Unwilling to admit that there was anything erroneous about any of his rulings, Goodman summarily rejected Sullivan's argument. "No, I don't think it's fair to say there are so many issues being tried at this time. You can argue the case and I will give proper instructions to the jury at the proper time. Overruled."

The prosecution had once again wounded the defense. As with the Stites evidence, the government had managed to get before the jury the shooting of another officer, and the defense had another phantom allegation with which to deal.

Goodman had even more unfavorable rulings in store for the defense. On cross-examination, Spagnoli elicited testimony from Sievertson that Sundstrom, Baker, and Simpson had all told him that it was Coy with the rifle who captured them. Ignoring the fact that Sievertson was a government witness and Deasy was conducting the examination, Hennessy objected and moved to strike the answer on the grounds that it was nonresponsive.

"It is responsive, and it contradicts the testimony of the prior witnesses," explained Spagnoli in an effort to hold onto the favorable testimony.

"I agree it is not responsive, and it is not contradictory to any prior testimony," ruled Goodman. "The statement may go out and the jury is instructed to disregard it."

As quickly as the evidence appeared, it evaporated. Whether Sievertson was in error or whether the three hostages had made prior inconsistent statement would remain a mystery. The issue had been taken away from the jury and Spagnoli would never be permitted to challenge the former testimony with the inconsistency.

"How can he rule that there is no inconsistency?" an outraged Sullivan whispered to Zamloch. "I can't believe this guy's rulings! They all three testified that Thompson had the rifle and yet this witness says they all told him it was Coy. I don't believe it!"

On direct examination, Sievertson had identified the tools used in the escape as having been stored in the utility corridor of C block. On cross-examination he was interrogated by Sullivan regarding the security of the corridor and what steps he had taken to prevent entry into the area. "Didn't it occur to you that these various items here might be dangerous in the hands of an inmate who might decide to attempt to make an escape?"

"Could be, yes."

"But you never before May 2 took steps to prevent that occurrence?"

"Yes, that is correct."

Zamloch also questioned the witness on the security issue. "Mr. Sievertson, would it be an accurate thing to say that the only person who had access or occasion to use these various tools was yourself and a convict assistant?"

"Yes."

"What was the name of your assistant at that time?"

"Ed Mrozik."

Mrozik worked indoors, usually under Sievertson's supervision, although there were times when he was alone and unobserved. No charges were ever brought against Mrozik, but his presence outside his cell during the riot was noted by several of the hostages. During the FBI investigation, his possible involvement had been widely suggested. There was never sufficient proof of Mrozik's involvement for the U.S. attorney to seek an indictment, but there was ample reason to believe that he assisted Coy in moving the bar spreader parts from the kitchen to the utility corridor.

This was not Mrozik's first brush with notoriety. Only a few years earlier, fate had propelled him and another inmate plumber to celebrity status within Alcatraz convict society. One summer, he and inmate plumber Sam McAllister were assigned to the outside plumbing detail, under Sievertson's direction. The two inmates accompanied Sievertson to Building 64 to resolve a minor plumbing problem in one of the apartments. The guard who occupied the apartment worked days and his wife was home alone.

Most of the work to be done was in the crawl space beneath the apartment, but one of the inmates needed to crawl up under the sink to work on the drain line. A trap door under the sink provided access from the crawl space to the apartment. As Sievertson explained to the woman what would be taking place, the two convicts stood beside him. He explained that McAllister, a handsome, dark-haired man in his late twenties would enter the apartment through the trap door to work on the drain line. One look at the virile, well built prisoner and the thought that he may soon be lying on her kitchen floor generated a rush of sexual fantasy in the young housewife's mind. She made sensual eye contact with the young convict and he returned her look with a smile of willing anticipation.

Closing the door she hurried into the bedroom and quickly slipped out of her bra, panties and slip, then put back on her plaid skirt and soft woolen sweater. Anxiously she snatched the pillows off the bed and placed them on the kitchen floor near the sink. She closed the curtains on the window above the sink, and lowered the narrow shade on the glass paneled kitchen door.

With everything ready, a wild excitement swept over her unlike anything she could remember. Her hands trembled and she felt both weak and exhilarated. She could feel her body preparing for what she both wanted and feared. The consequences of such an act with a prisoner, if it became known, were too fearful to consider. As her desire for the young convict grew, so did her apprehension. She walked into the living room, turned on the radio, then cranked up the volume. The music was loud enough to muffle sounds inside the apartment, but not so loud as to draw the attention of anyone outside. She returned to the kitchen and stood silently at the sink listening for the sound of movement beneath the floor.

Soon she could hear voices and the sound of hammering on the pipes. Suddenly her fear was gone and all that remained was her desire for the handsome man she had seen so many times working as part of the plumbing crew. She was about to live out a fantasy.

McAllister lifted the trap door and climbed out into the kitchen. As he emerged from the crawl space, she positioned herself on the pillows, and raised her skirt to her waist. It was Christmas in July for McAllister and he made the most of the situation.

Meanwhile, back in the crawl space, Mrozik waited for McAllister's report on the progress of the job. He soon realized what was going on and covered for McAllister with Sievertson.

Word of the spectacular event spread throughout the prison like wildfire. McAllister became a celebrity without peer and Mrozik was famous for facilitating the astonishing event. Eventually, the story was passed to the officers and administration through the prison network of informers. No disciplinary action was ever taken and over time the story became part of the color and history of the island.

The next witness for the prosecution was Donald Mowery, one of the officers involved in the hostage rescue, and the leader of the team that located and recovered the bodies from the utility corridor. His testimony regarding the hostage rescue added very little to the government's case and was cumulative of the testimony by Miller and Sievertson.

Mowery also described the carnage he observed when he and the others discovered the bodies of Coy, Cretzer, and Hubbard. Mowery was a skilled marksman, who volunteered to enter the utility corridor to either capture, kill or bring out the bodies of the insurgents. By early Friday, the administration was satisfied that the holdout inmates were in the C block utility corridor. It was not known, however, whether they were still alive. Repeated calls for their surrender went unanswered and the last shooting from the corridor was a single rifle shot at 9:00 P.M. Friday. Mowery testified that on Saturday morning, Associate Warden Miller asked for volunteers to enter the corridor. "Several of us volunteered, and I was the first to enter, followed by Mr. Spencer."

When he entered the corridor, Mowery encountered total devastation. The hundreds of hand grenades and other explosives had left the area a twisted mass of steel and debris. With his flashlight aimed ahead of him and officers Spencer and Steere covering him from behind, Mowery moved cautiously down the passage. "I saw something that looked like part of a man's head at the end of the corridor. After I got down about half way through I could see that it was Coy."

"Can you describe him any further?"

"He had on a prison officer's coat and inmate trousers. He didn't have a hat on. He had a .30 caliber rifle across his knee in a position to shoot. He was dead."

"After you found Coy what did you do?"

"I just proceeded on down there until I could see the top of Hubbard's

Federal District Court Judge
Louis Goodman, trial judge
for the Alcatraz murder case.

Attorney Aaron Vinkler,
one of the attorneys for the
defendant, Miran Thompson.

Attorney Ernest Spagnoli, lead counsel for the defendant,
Miran Thompson. Spagnoli is shown on the MV Warden
Johnston, the Alcatraz launch, following one of his many
visits to the island in preparation for the trial.

Attorney James "Ned" Burns, who initially represented all the defendants. Burns was substituted out of the case as attorney of record prior to trial, when it was determined that each defendant required separate counsel.

Attorney Archer Zamloch, counsel for Clarence Carnes.

Warden Johnston, Associate Warden E. J. Miller and U.S. Attorney Frank Hennessy.

Attorney William Sullivan, counsel for defendant Sam Shockley.

Assistant U.S. Attorney, Dan Deasy, who assisted U.S. Attorney Frank Hennessy in the prosecution of the case.

Dr. John Alden, the court appointed psychiatrist who examined Sam Shockley and testified as to the defendant's sanity. Dr. Alden was the only medical witness to testify regarding the issue of Shockley's sanity.

The names of the inmates involved in the escape attempt were written on the wall of the hostage cell by custodial officer, Ernest B. Lageson. The FBI photograph of the names was introduced into evidence by the prosecution during the trial.

Officer William Miller, one of the hostages shot by inmate Joseph Cretzer. Officer Miller died as a result of his wounds, and the surviving inmates, Thompson, Carnes, and Shockley were tried for his murder.

Officer Harold Stites who was killed during the escape attempt. Although denied by the government for many years, officer Stites was killed by gunfire from other officers.

Officer Ernest B. Lageson.

Officer Bert Burch, Associate Warden E. J. Miller, and officer Ernest B. Lageson.

B.A. Burch   J.U. Burdett   C.G. Fish

Officer Bert Burch was the officer on duty in the west gun gallery who was overpowered by inmate Bernard Coy. Coy knocked Burch unconscious, tied him up, and commandeered his rifle and pistol. With these weapons Coy and his confederates took control of the cell house. Officer Joseph Burdett was the officer on duty in the kitchen and was taken hostage by Coy and the others when he made a routine visit to the cell house. Officer Cliff Fish was the officer on watch in the armory during the escape attempt.

I. B. Faulk   J.H. Simpson   E.F. Stucker

Lieutenant Ike Faulk was the officer in charge of the dock
at the time of the escape attempt and in the temporary absence
of the warden and associate warden, ordered that the escape
alarm be sounded. Lieutenant Joseph H. Simpson entered the cell house in
response to concern expressed by Cliff Fish and was taken hostage. Lieutenant Simpson was shot by inmate Joseph Cretzer and seriously wounded.
Officer Ed Stucker was in charge of the basement facilities and was the
first officer to warn officer Fish that there was trouble in the cell house.

C. W. Sundstrom   **H.W. Weinhold**

Officer Carl Sundstrom was the records clerk at the time of the escape.
He entered the cell house to assist other officers and was taken hostage.
Captain Henry Weinhold entered the cell house to investigate the apparent
problem described to him by armory officer Fish and was taken hostage.
Weinhold was later shot by Cretzer and seriously wounded.

Defendants Miran Thompson, Sam Shockley, and Clarence Carnes, followed by Alcatraz custodial Officer Zubke and led by Officer Levinson, disembarking the MV Warden Johnston en route to arraignment on murder charges following the death of Officer William Miller. Note rope hanging over their heads resembling a hangman's noose, which was highlighted in the local papers that carried the photo and story of the arraignment.The headline over the photo read "ALCATRAZ KILLERS...AND THE SYMBOL" unequivocally suggesting the guilt of the defendants.

Defendants Thompson, Carnes, and Shockley along with Alcatraz custodial
Officer Zubke leaving the courtroom
following their arraignment carrying the indictments that were read and
handed to them in court.

File photo of
Clarence Carnes taken
approximately 1945.

File photo of Clarence Carnes
taken in 1987, the year before he
died. Carnes died in 1988 at the
age of 61.

Bernard Coy

Sam Shockley

Miran Thompson

Joseph Cretzer

Marvin Hubbard

Photo of the capture of Marvin Hubbard by the FBI and local authorities in 1942. Hubbard claimed he was beaten into signing a false confession by the FBI. He was scheduled to have a Federal Court hearing in San Francisco on his appeal two days after he was killed attempting to escape from Alcatraz.

Attorney James Martin McInnis, (left) defendant Henri Young, (center) and attorney Sol Abrams, (right) conferring during Young's trial in 1941. Young was charged with murder arising out of the death of fellow inmate, Rufus McCain. Young's defense was based on the theory that he had been rendered temporarily insane by the conditions under which he had been confined at Alcatraz. The defense was successful and the jury found him guilty of involuntary manslaughter. The attorney for Shockley attempted to use the same defense theory in his case.

Kay Benedetti, also known as Edna Kyle, Edna Cretzer, Kay Wallace, and various other aliases. She was married to Joseph Cretzer in the early 1930s and was actively involved in his criminal exploits. When he was transferred to Alcatraz from McNeil Island in August of 1940, she moved to San Francisco to be near him. Prior to the 1946 escape attempt, however she divorced Cretzer and married a local truck driver by the name of Elmer Benedetti. After the abortive escape attempt in which her former husband was killed, she claimed his body and had him interred in a south San Francisco cemetary. She also made a clandestine appearance at the trial.

Louis Fleish, D Block orderly, who observed the early events of the escape attempt and testified on behalf of the defedants at the trial. He had been the leader of the notorious Purple Gang in Detroit. His brothers, Sam and Harry also served time on Alcatraz.

View of the west gun gallery
showing the general area
where Bernard Coy broke into
the gallery, overpowered
Officer Burch and obtained the
guns that made possible the
escape attempt of 1946.

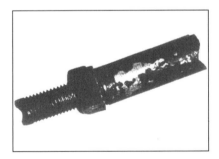

Bar spreader fabricated in
the prison machine shop
used by Coy to spread the
bars and gain access to the
west gun gallery.

Night view showing the crowds of
people that lined the streets, hills,
piers, and bridges of San Francisco to observe the gunfire that
went on throughout the first
night of the 1946 uprising.

View of the C block utility corridor
where inmates Bernard Coy,
Joseph Cretzer, and Marvin Hubbard
died from custodial officer gunfire.

Warden Johnston in front of the hostage cell
where officers Lageson, Corwin, Miller,
and Captain Weinhold were shot.

View of the MV Warden Johnston bringing the bodies of
Coy, Cretzer, and Hubbard to San Francisco for delivery to the morgue.

The family of deceased officer Harold
Stites at the time of the Coroner's
Inquest. From left to right.
Mrs. Bessie Stites, son James, 17
and son Robert, 15.

Warden Johnston in front of the
rear door of the cell house leading
to the recreation yard. The escape
attempt failed when the prisoners
were unable to find Key #107,
which would unlock this door.

head. He was seated with his back to Coy. He had nothing in his hands. The French knife was laying alongside of him."

After Hennessy placed the knife in evidence he continued with his interrogation. "What did you do then?"

"It was evident that he was dead. Part of his head was gone. After that I went down a little farther and I could see Cretzer facing in the same direction as Coy. He had a .45 automatic pistol in his hand."

"Would you say that the shotgun blasts you fired into the corridor the night before killed all three of these men?" inquired Sullivan on cross-examination.

Without hesitation the sharpshooter responded, "I wouldn't say definitely, but I think they did. There was no more shooting that night except what I did. I'm quite sure of that."

Instead of ending his case with a strong witness, leaving a powerful impression on the jury, Hennessy concluded his case with a series of "housekeeping witnesses," who gave testimony on minor points. It was an anti-climatic finish to match the lackluster beginning.

"The Government rests," Hennessy announced, satisfied that he had put on a strong enough case for a triple conviction.

After all, he thought to himself, *this is an Alcatraz murder case with two dead guards. There is no way this case can be lost.*

As soon as the prosecution rested, Zamloch advised the court that he wished to make a motion outside the presence of the jury. The jury was dismissed, and Zamloch immediately moved for a reduction of the charge against his client from first to second-degree murder. The motion was a longshot and the diminutive barrister knew it, but with Carnes facing the death penalty, he could leave no stone unturned in defense of the case.

He based his argument on the contention that the government had failed to prove premeditation by Carnes, and therefore had failed to carry their burden of proof as to first degree murder, "Premeditation," he argued, "is the act of meditating in advance. It involves deliberation on the contemplated act of plotting to take a human life. The loss of life in this case resulted from the impulsive, spontaneous act of a crazed killer acting alone and without input from the others involved in the escape. Not only was there no contemplation of killing by Carnes, but the evidence was to the contrary. The government witnesses have established that after Cretzer's shooting rampage, Carnes succeeded in saving the lives of several of the officers by reporting to the others that the guards were all dead, and assisting officer Lageson by motioning to him to duck before Cretzer fired at him a second time." Contending that the prosecution had presented no direct evidence of premeditation by Carnes, and stressing the youngster's humanitarian conduct, Zamloch argued for dismissal of the first-degree murder count in favor of a second-degree charge.

The argument went even better than Zamloch had hoped. Whether because of surprise or lack of preparation, Hennessy did not present a vigorous opposition to the motion. Even though the facts as to Shockley differed significantly from those as to Carnes, Sullivan found himself caught up in the excitement of the moment. Impressed by Zamloch's presentation and surprised by the weakness of the government's response, he joined in what now seemed to be a possible winning motion.

Looking toward Spagnoli, Goodman inquired of the older man, "Have you a motion to make, too?"

"No, we have not," Spagnoli answered, a tone of mild disinterest in his voice.

Goodman quickly banished the defense's enthusiasm. "I think it is a matter for the jury to determine in this case. I can't assume the prerogative of determining the weight of this evidence. I will deny both motions. Mr. Bailiff, return the jury to the box. Do you wish to make an opening statement, Mr. Zamloch?"

"I believe so," Zamloch responded, rising to address the jury. From the outset he disassociated his client from Shockley and Thompson. "I concern myself in this opening statement only with the defendant, Clarence Carnes," Zamloch began, "and, as far as possible, will avoid even mentioning the other defendants. By way of preamble, let me remind you that each of these defendants is entitled to your separate consideration. You may not lump them all together and consider them as a whole. Clarence Carnes demands his right, that you consider him separately." Zamloch's strategy was in stark contrast to the tactics adopted by Sullivan, who in his opening statement sought to ally Shockley with the others, arguing that the defendants, along with the guards, were victims of Cretzer's violence.

Assuring the jury that his client would take the stand, Zamloch told them that they were entitled to know "the tragic story that has brought this nineteen-year old full-blooded Choctaw Indian, not only to the last outpost of the United States prison system with only a future of life in prison to look forward to, but has also brought him to stand before you charged with the crime of murder."

Knowing that Hennessy would impeach Carnes with evidence of his prior felony convictions, Zamloch chose to blunt the effect of it by introducing the information himself. Employing his superb skill as an advocate, he presented a sanitized version of Carnes's criminal background, characterizing the murder Carnes committed as an accidental killing by a frightened sixteen-year-old-boy. "When Carnes ducked, his gun went off, and the man died," Zamloch explained, describing how Carnes fired when his victim threw a bottle at him. Zamloch followed this description with an understated history of Carnes's criminal exploits, including a description of his prison break as "slipping away" from the harsh conditions at Granite State Reformatory. He pointed out that no harm came to the people who were kidnapped during that escape. Although he did an excellent job of minimizing Carnes's past crimes, Zamloch could not alter the fact that his client had been convicted of murder, kidnapping, escape, assault, and theft.

Zamloch convincingly portrayed Carnes's role in the Alcatraz uprising as a follower, who saw an opportunity to escape and took it. When the attempt failed he abandoned the plan and did his best to save the lives of the hostages. "The defense will establish, Ladies and Gentlemen, that not only would Mr. Miller be just as dead had Mr. Carnes never left his cell, but without Clarence's intervention, many more guards would have died. Nothing Clarence did contributed to the death of Mr. Miller, and throughout the entire uprising he consistently maneuvered to save the life of every important prosecution witness that testified here against him."

He reminded the jury that it was Carnes who allowed Miller's hands to be untied, an act of compassion that ultimately foiled the escape attempt. As he outlined the evidence he would present, Zamloch emphasized Carnes's role as one dedicated to saving lives, not a person aiding or abetting in Miller's death.

Zamloch explained that Carnes abandoned the escape attempt when the alarm sounded with the intention of returning to his cell. "Sidetracked when Coy directed him to come along into the kitchen, Clarence attempted to dissuade Coy and Hubbard from shooting the tower guards. Returning to the cell house, with Hubbard now in possession of the rifle, the trio came face to face with Associate Warden Miller. Realizing that Hubbard intended to kill Miller, Carnes intentionally jostled his arm, causing his shot to go wild, and thereby saving the associate warden's life. He faced the anger of Hubbard and Coy in order to save Miller's life. He got his reward that Saturday night when Miller took him out of his cell and unmercifully beat and kicked him and held his knife at his throat, hysterically demanding that he falsely confess to being present at the time of the shooting of officer Miller."

Zamloch described how after Carnes returned to the cell house he went back to the hostage cells where Cretzer had already shot the hostages and was preparing to kill Lageson. "Again Carnes intervened, exhorting Cretzer, 'Let him live, Joe. He's a good screw. He never hurt nobody.' Realizing that Cretzer intended to shoot Lageson, Carnes surreptitiously signaled to the officer to duck.

"Finally, when a question arose as to whether all of the officers were dead, Carnes volunteered to check the cells. Doing so he could see that all the hostages were alive and feigning death, but he reported back to the others, 'I guess they're all dead. They're all still laying the way you left them.' In so doing, Carnes prevented a total massacre and saved the lives of eight men."

Zamloch emphatically announced that Carnes's defense would not be based on any theory of Alcatraz brutality. "Now you have heard much during the early portions of this case concerning brutality and negligence. You have heard much of the Alcatraz inhumanity toward man, which I am convinced is all true and should be investigated. Clarence will not rely upon the treatment that he has received at Alcatraz nor the conditions to which he has been subjected. He is content to rely upon the facts and the evidence as it comes to you in this case. There was no murder in the mind or heart of Clarence Carnes. He is guilty of nothing more than attempting to escape, which every man in that institution would do if even the slightest opportunity presented itself."

As Zamloch concluded his opening statement, Buddy Thompson stared with cold eyes, first at the attorney, then at Carnes. The two inmates made brief eye contact, and Thompson's sneer became a mocking smile. He held Carnes in disdain for the mercy he had shown to the officers, but envied and coveted the strong defense argument it provided the teenage convict.

When the jury was gone and the defendants were being shackled for their return to the county jail, Sullivan turned to Zamloch. "Nice job on your opening, Archer," he said with a weak smile.

"Yeah, good job," added Vinkler. Spagnoli said nothing, and busied himself with stuffing his notes and files into his battered old brief case. It was a tense moment, but no one articulated what was on all their minds. Zamloch had broken ranks.

It seemed that Zamloch might even be planning to turn on the other two defendants by suggesting that they urged Cretzer to fire the fatal shot. The government had no evidence that Carnes had urged Cretzer to fire any of the shots. Was Carnes going to testify that one or both of the other defendants did goad Cretzer to commit Miller's murder? This was the reason Ned Burns had sought relief of the court many months earlier. He had seen the possibility that the time would come when the defendants would go their separate ways. That time had arrived, and, while all the attorneys were aware of the situation, none of them spoke of it.

Sullivan had too much on his mind to worry about Zamloch's opening statement. Tomorrow was a critical day, perhaps the most important day of the trial for Shockley. Dr. John Alden, the court appointed psychiatrist, was scheduled to testify. Sullivan believed that Alden's testimony would make or break Shockley's insanity defense. There would also be testimony from an array of convict witnesses, all trying to help "Crazy Sam." The pivotal testimony, however, would come from Alden. *It will be a long night of preparation*, Sullivan thought as he headed out into the deepening darkness of the chill December night.

Sullivan headed up 7th Street, and arrived at Market Street to find an eastbound N car waiting for the stoplight. He hopped aboard just as the light changed. It was a ten block ride down Market to Fremont, then a three block walk to his office. Before hunkering down to begin his trial preparation, Sullivan took the elevator to the Bar Association lounge for a couple of drinks and some light-hearted conversation. He spotted the O'Gara brothers and his old friend Elmer Delaney, all on their second drink of the evening. They immediately called Sullivan to their table, eager for news of the Alcatraz trial.

"Well, things are going as well as can be expected," Sullivan responded. "Hennessy rested today and I start putting on my case tomorrow. It'll be a big day with John Alden on the stand and my psychiatric defense pretty much on the line."

"Well if it's like any of the cases I've worked on with you Bill," Delaney began, "I'd say you're totally prepared and ready to go. My advice is to have a couple of stiff shooters, relax, and go home for a good night's sleep."

Sullivan took part of his friend's advice, and downed three cocktails. He then returned to his office for three hours of concentrated work before surrendering to fatigue. He slept fitfully, but at dawn awoke from a brief period of deep sleep and felt rested. Although he was tense and apprehensive, he was also ready.

21

Tuesday, December 10

That morning there was an air of anticipation in the courtroom. The spectators were aware that the defense case was beginning, as was the long awaited stream of Alcatraz criminals. It was another standing room only crowd, as the curious lined up for a glimpse of the convict witnesses. The members of the press had scoured their files for background information on the anticipated witnesses. Finally, they would be able to file the stories they had all been waiting to write. The jury too, was keenly interested in what was to come. They also looked forward to the upcoming array of America's badmen and wondered what they would have to say.

At the outset, Sullivan renewed his motion for a jury view of the cell house. "I make this motion in good faith and for the purpose of enabling the jury to more carefully follow the testimony of certain witnesses that we expect to bring here on behalf of the defense, as well as to corroborate the statements concerning that chart by various witnesses who have already testified."

Appreciating the value of a jury view and recognizing that diagrams and photographs could not totally acquaint the jury with the scene, Hennessy addressed the court. "Your Honor, we have no objection to that." Hennessy realized that several areas of the west end of the cell house and much of D block, which had been the subject of testimony, were neither shown on the diagrams nor depicted in the photographs.

Consistent with his earlier opinion, however, Goodman refused. "I see no reason to take this jury over to Alcatraz Island. The possibility of extraneous matters being injected into the case is too great. I haven't had any difficulty following the events as described by the witnesses, and I think the jury understood the testimony as to the events that have been described. I will deny the motion without prejudice at this time."

Goodman's denial "without prejudice" left open the possibility that the motion could be renewed at a later time. It was clear, however, that in the absence of some dramatic development, he would never permit a jury view. In keeping with his judicial style, Goodman made no inquiry of the jury as to whether or not they felt a site view would be helpful. It was apparent that he did not wish to delay the trial, which he felt had already gone on too long, by scheduling a field trip.

The ruling was damaging to Shockley's case. Sullivan felt that the only way he could adequately portray the conditions in isolation and solitary was to show them to the jury. Mere photographs of D block could not convey the true nature of the life Shockley had lived for the past three years. Sullivan also felt that the drama of a visit to the island, the cell house, and D block would engender feelings of sympathy for the defendants, a consideration obviously not overlooked by the judge.

Sullivan's first witness was Warden Johnston, through whom he intended to establish Shockley's harsh living conditions. Sullivan had been blocked from developing this information during his cross-examination of the warden. He needed to show that Shockley had spent several confinements in solitary and had lived for more than three mind-numbing years in isolation. This was key foundation evidence for the insanity defense.

Through Johnston, Sullivan established that Shockley was transferred to Alcatraz in 1938 and, during the next five years spent five separate periods in solitary, ranging from seven to eighteen days. On July 1, 1943, he emerged from solitary and was placed in an isolation cell, where he remained from that time on. Johnston admitted that during his three year confinement, Shockley only left his cell for a weekly one hour visit to the recreation yard, and a weekly ten minute shower. Beyond that, Shockley never left his six by nine foot cell between July 1943 and the riot of May 2, 1946.

Sullivan invited the warden to explain how it was determined which prisoners would be sent to Alcatraz. The warden thoughtfully responded that he would try to provide the jury with as brief, yet thorough, an explanation as he could. Johnston explained to the attentive jury that careful and exhaustive analysis was given each prisoner to best meet his custodial and rehabilitation needs. Committees comprised of psychiatrists and psychologists, as well as educational and medical experts considered each case and placed each inmate in one of twenty-five institutions.

Describing Alcatraz, he emphasized, "…we have a good educational program, an excellent library, and good industrial shops under competent foremen. And if we find aptitude for a particular kind of work, we try to put the inmate into that. Now I am not claiming that we do a perfect job, but we do make that serious effort."

Sullivan's examination of the warden backfired. Johnston had testified many times and the young defense lawyer was no match for the shrewd veteran. Try as he did, Sullivan simply could not break through Johnston's gentle façade. Nor could he depict Alcatraz as anything more sinister than a maximum security penitentiary designed to hold highly dangerous lawbreakers.

Things did not improve during Hennessy's cross-examination. Questioning Johnston on the subject of D block, Hennessy brought out that those who found their way into isolation did so by proving themselves either obstructive, destructive, assaultive, or dangerous. Johnston also revealed that three of Shockley's trips to solitary confinement were because he refused to work. Focusing on Shockley's three year period of isolation just prior to the riot, Hennessy established that this was entirely because of his refusal to work. "In other words, the only reason he was kept in a D block isolation cell, was because he refused to work?" queried the U.S. Attorney.

Frustrated, and realizing that Hennessy had taken control of the witness, Sullivan sprang to his feet objecting to the question. "Just a minute, I have to call these witnesses—you can appreciate my position, Your Honor. I have to call witnesses who are prosecution witnesses to prove part of my case. Mr. Hennessy thinks he therefore is qualified to hit me with a shillelagh and have a lot of fun with this thing. I am not bound by answers of that nature."

Irritated, Goodman delivered another stern reprimand. "Mr. Sullivan, I do not know why you continue to make these speeches to me and the jury. I have warned you time and time again. I will overrule your objection. You yourself asked the witness what the reasons were that Mr. Shockley was put in solitary and now you want to shut off cross-examination by the prosecution. Overruled."

Hennessy restated his question.

"If he was willing, at any time, to go back and do the job assigned to him, could he have been taken out of D block?"

"Yes," responded Johnston. "If he had indicated a willingness to accept an assignment, he would have been taken out."

It was a poor start to Sullivan's case, and the feisty young Irishman knew it. He had been denied his jury view. Johnston's testimony had been a disaster, providing no foundation for the psychiatric testimony to follow. Additionally, Johnston had pictured Shockley as a recalcitrant, who voluntarily removed himself from the general population. The jury was left to draw the conclusion that Shockley could easily have gotten out of isolation by simply agreeing to work.

"Call Dr. John Alden," Sullivan announced, and the bailiff scurried to the courtroom door. Throwing open the door, he repeated the call into the sparsely populated hallway. "The court calls Dr. John Alden!"

Dr. Alden, a graduate of Harvard Medical School, maintained his primary practice at the University of California Medical Center, and enjoyed an excellent professional reputation. On frequent occasions he was appointed by the courts to perform independent examinations of parties in criminal and civil litigation where sanity was at issue. A small man, 5'6" and 140 pounds, he was fashionably dressed in a gray, three piece suit, and carried a small briefcase. He smiled at Hennessy and Spagnoli, both of whom he knew from prior cases. As Alden passed the counsel table, Sullivan greeted him politely, but was concerned as to how the doctor's testimony would unfold.

When he requested the psychiatric examination, Sullivan had mistakenly limited the request to an analysis of Shockley's present mental capacity and ability to assist in his own defense. That, therefore, was the scope of Alden's examination. He took no history regarding Shockley's mental status at the time of the riot, nor did he inquire in-depth into the facts of the riot. Having determined that Shockley was mentally sound enough to assist with his defense, Alden terminated the examination.

Sullivan, however, needed to establish that Shockley was insane at the time of the riot. It was necessary, therefore, for him to provide the doctor with sufficient information to permit him to form an opinion as to Shockley's sanity at the time. This would be accomplished through hypothetical questions containing a combination of assumed and proved facts. The questions had to be carefully worded so as to provide the doctor with all the relevant facts to enable him to form an expert opinion. The usual procedure in preparing such testimony was for the attorney and doctor to work together to review the facts and develop the questions. However, Alden had refused to discuss the case with Sullivan without Hennessy present. Because he was court-appointed, Alden felt he should not meet with either of the attorneys separately.

"I don't know what I'm going to do," Sullivan had confided to Gerry O'Gara the night before. "I don't have the slightest idea what he's going to say about Shockley's sanity at the time of the riot. Without some input from him I can't be sure what information he considers important and I really can't be sure exactly what to put in the questions. If I don't have everything just right in those hypotheticals, he may go against me and I'm screwed. I'm really up against it, Gerry. Or rather, poor old Sam's up against it."

If Sullivan could establish the right facts, and if based on these facts Alden considered Shockley insane, Sullivan would have his expert opinion and the possibility of a successful defense. Otherwise, he was looking at a first-degree murder conviction. Sullivan was about to embark on the most important witness examination of his young legal career. Shockley, the man whose life hung in the balance, sat at the counsel table, his vacuous stare and open mouthed expression proof to Sullivan of his mental deficiency. Sullivan was certain that Shockley lacked any appreciation of the fact that his life depended on what would happen during the next few hours.

The direct examination began with a series of formal questions to qualify Alden as an expert witness. Satisfied at the outset with the witness's qualifications, Hennessy rose and with a wave of his large hand, declared, "The government will stipulate to the doctor's qualifications." Before Sullivan could respond, the prosecutor announced to both the court and jury that the witness was "a very well-qualified alienist."

"Yes," added Sullivan, "a specialist in the field of psychiatry," fearing that not all of the jurors would understand the archaic term.

Sullivan then inquired if Alden had received any compensation from the defendant. Again, Hennessy interrupted, stating that the government would compensate Alden. "You need not worry about that, Mr. Sullivan, the witness will be paid."

"I'm not worrying about that," responded Sullivan, "I just want to bring to the jury's attention the fact that the doctor is not being paid by me or anyone connected with the defense of this case." This was Sullivan's unsubtle way of advising the jury that Alden was appearing as a witness called by the court and was not a "hired gun" for the defense.

With the preliminaries over, Sullivan moved on to the substance of the doctor's testimony. He first established that prior to his interview with Shockley, Alden reviewed his medical and prison records. In addition to his social and family history, Alden reviewed Shockley's intelligence and mental examinations. In a 1938 test, Shockley demonstrated an I.Q. of 68, comparable to a mental age of ten years, ten months. By 1942, his I.Q. had deteriorated to 54, a mental age of eight years, ten months. "This," Alden testified, "classified Shockley as feeble-minded, or the mental status of a high-grade moron."

The records also disclosed other information Alden considered significant. Prior examiners considered Shockley's reasoning skills and judgement defective and found him to be emotionally unstable. He had been hospitalized for observation because he was fearful, disoriented, and assaultive. The records indicated that his conduct had been erratic and unpredictable, with episodes of hallucination during which he heard voices and experienced bizarre sensations. He displayed classic symptoms of paranoia. Shockley's doctors felt that he might break down under conditions of confusion or tension and become dangerous to those around him. Alden noted evidence of irrationality in the fact that shortly after the May outbreak, Shockley directed the warden to, "Please drop all my correspondents from my correspondence list and return all mail—and don't give any of my relations permission to visit me."

During Alden's testimony, Sullivan frequently glanced over at the jury. All of them were listening intently. He felt that the testimony was going well. Optimistically, he moved on to the next phase of the doctor's testimony, a description of the interview and examination of the defendant.

Comfortable with Alden's style, Sullivan allowed him to describe the interview in a narrative response. The decision was a wise one. The doctor began by describing Shockley's bizarre statements. "Well, I thought he would talk about the break or something like that, but he began talking about minerals that were placed in his food. He said these kept him in pain day and night and that his large intestines were filled with rays from lights, which he believed were directed at him from the light bulb in his cell. He said he could feel the rays of these lights in his head, feel them throughout his spinal column. When I asked him who he thought was responsible for these rays, he responded that it was being done by the 'Public of Health.' When I pressed him for a further explanation of the rays, he said they were automatically arranged, so that when lights were turned on they would start a fire that would go into his body."

As the doctor spoke the jury hung on every word. Even Judge Goodman seemed fascinated with Alden's testimony. "Then he made mention about radio voices and what he was describing to me as voices that he heard that sounded to him like they came over a radio. He described how after

the riot three officers approached him with drawn guns and one of the officers had the hammer of his gun drawn back. At the time, the voices called
out 'let it go off.' Shockley said that he heard the voices and he thought the
officer could hear them too. He described how the voices irritated him
because they were evil voices. Evil voices that he felt made trouble
between the inmates."

With no prompting from Sullivan, Alden continued his narrative. "He
then expressed an idea which I thought was quite significant, because it
isn't something we hear very often, but we do see it in some patients with
this kind of difficulty. He insisted that, not only did he hear the voices, but
he was putting out voices himself, as if he was a radio, explaining, 'I am a
walking radio at times.' The idea, as I understood it, was that other people
could hear the things that he was thinking about. 'I get the news,' he
insisted, 'and that's the education system we have here. It isn't the inside
news, it's mostly irritable news. It's put into your mind by radios.'"

Since the testimony was going well, Sullivan let Alden continue to tell
the story his own way. "When I asked him to tell me what happened at
the time of the break, he said, 'I don't care to go into that just now,
because I got that indictment against me and some of the words I use
might be used against me. But I don't think I will be tried for it, because
I don't think the court has jurisdiction over here. I think only Spain or
Mexico has jurisdiction.'"

Alden testified that he immediately considered the possibility that Shockley might be faking his symptoms. "I wanted to see whether he would give
me deliberately false answers to simple arithmetical questions, so I asked
him a number of questions designed to determine the reliability of the
information he had given me. It was evident to me that he was not trying
to falsify, but was being totally honest in his responses. As a result, I did
not further pursue that line of questioning."

Alden stated it was his conclusion that Shockley was mentally ill, diag-
nosing his condition as dementia praecox, more commonly known as paranoid schizophrenia. He stated that he believed Shockley to be in the active
phase of the disease, demonstrating psychotic symptoms including delu-
sions, hallucinations, incoherence, illogical thinking, and grossly disorganized behavior. Alden described Shockley's mental illness as one of the
most serious and violent known to medicine. He also stated that he believed emotional breakdown and instability were quite likely in Shockley's
case. He felt there was more than adequate evidence to establish that his

disorders were real and not faked. "In the first place, there was the record that showed that he had experienced hallucinations and other symptoms long before he was charged with the present crime. Secondly, the symptoms were totally consistent with those we find in other patients with this type of mental illness. And finally, I thought his intelligence was insufficient for him to malinger that well. I mean, he would have to learn a lot about how to fake the disease and with such a low-grade of intelligence, it doesn't seem likely to me that he would be a very good malingerer."

As helpful as the doctor's testimony was, Sullivan realized he also had to bring out the negative rather than allow Hennessy to do so. For that reason, he asked Alden about Shockley's mental condition at the time of his examination in early November, a few weeks previously. "In my opinion, at that time, Sam Shockley was able to understand the nature and consequences of his actions, was capable of understanding the nature of the charges against him, was able to confer with his attorney and was capable of preparing his own defense."

Sullivan then proceeded to the most critical part of his examination, the hypothetical questions concerning Shockley's mental condition at the time of the riot. He felt confident based on how Alden's testimony had gone so far, but was still fearful of making a fatal mistake.

"Did you form any opinion as to his mental condition at the time of the May 2 break?" Sullivan asked.

"No, I did not have any information concerning his actions at that time or immediately preceding or following that time, and I had no evidence upon which to base such an opinion."

"Well, Doctor, I'd like to ask you a few hypothetical questions," Sullivan continued, "Assuming that Sam Shockley—"

"Mr. Sullivan," Goodman interrupted, "I imagine this will take a little while and I think this might be a good time for the morning recess." With that he admonished and excused the jury. Sullivan buried himself in his file, taking a final few minutes to review the questions that he hoped would produce the testimony necessary to establish an insanity defense. He appeared outwardly calm, but churned internally with fear that the final phase of Alden's testimony would be ineffective. The first half had gone well, he conceded to himself, but the critical portion lay ahead.

As the jury filed back into the courtroom, Sullivan glanced at his client. The inmate stared dumbly at the jurors as they resumed their seats and Sullivan felt a stab of pity. Instead of a convicted armed robber and kidnapper, Sullivan saw a confused child of eight years, ten months, trapped in the body of an adult. He wondered how much Shockley understood of what was taking place.

Sullivan's reflections were interrupted by Judge Goodman's brusque announcement. "The jurors are all present; you may proceed."

Absorbed with his thoughts about his client's mental deficiency, Sullivan shifted his line of inquiry. "Doctor, before asking these hypothetical questions, I want to call your attention to the tests showing Shockley's mental age as ten years, ten months in 1938 and eight years, ten months in 1942 and ask if there is any significance to that?"

"That would indicate mental deterioration between those dates. He is mentally deficient and in addition probably has other mental illness; feeblemindedness in and of itself should keep the same mental age all the way through. But with schizophrenia, although it is not primarily a disease of intelligence, there usually is some deterioration of intelligence. And the Stanford-Binet Tests do show a definite deterioration of his intelligence." The evidence was clear. Shockley was mentally deranged and getting worse.

"I want you to assume, Doctor," Sullivan resumed, "that Sam Shockley was confined for three years in the segregation block of Alcatraz and on several occasions prior to that period of confinement spent lengthy periods in solitary confinement for up to eighteen days at a time; that during his eight years of imprisonment at Alcatraz he was the victim of hallucinations and frequently heard voices that he described as radio voices; and that suddenly on the second of May of this year he finds the door to his cell open and is confronted with the exciting opportunity to obtain freedom. In your opinion as a psychiatric expert would there be any reason to suspect that Shockley, under those circumstances, would not know what he was doing?"

"Yes," responded Alden emphatically, "I'm very sure that there would be a psychiatric reason to suspect that he did not know what he was doing."

Excited by the ease with which he had elicited so valuable an answer, Sullivan pressed on. "Assume that Sam Shockley had been confined in the isolation section of Alcatraz, forbidden to fraternize with other inmates, forbidden to go out of doors other than once a week for an hour; that he was otherwise kept in his cell twenty-four hours a day, seven days a week, and that in addition to this confinement he heard voices, suffered from hallucinations, and displayed symptoms of dementia praecox; and that he is suddenly faced with the opportunity to escape this confinement under terrifically exciting conditions and circumstances. Would it be possible, in your opinion, that his judgement could be so distorted that he would be unable to comprehend the nature and consequence of his actions?"

"Yes," Alden replied, "I believe it would be not only possible but probable."

"Would you say, Doctor, that it would be probable under those circumstances, that he would be less able to understand the nature and consequences of his actions than at the time of your examination on November 5?"

Again the doctor answered in the affirmative, "Well, I believe that would be quite probable."

"Well, would it be possible, Doctor, that under those circumstances described, that Sam Shockley at that time and place and under the circumstances, could be so mentally deranged as to be unable to distinguish right from wrong?"

Again, without hesitation, the psychiatrist responded in the affirmative. "Yes."

"You may cross-examine," Sullivan announced in a calm voice that masked his wild excitement. Alden had testified to the magic words, "right from wrong," that legally established insanity. The prosecution had the burden of proving that Shockley was sane. Alden was the only psychiatrist in the case, and based on the expert testimony he had just given, Sullivan knew that Hennessy would have an extremely hard time establishing Crazy Sam's sanity. *I pulled it off!* Sullivan thought to himself. It had been a day beyond his wildest hopes.

Hennessy's cross-examination of Alden was fruitless. The doctor admitted that his one hour examination of the patient was less desirable than a more detailed interview. "Yes, my opinions are less certain than if I had seen him a lot of times." Alden also agreed that the intelligence test scores alone were not determinative of sanity or insanity, and admitted that many of the statements in his report were not his own observations, but those of medical practitioners who had seen Shockley in the past.

Hennessy was hesitant to vigorously cross-examine the doctor as to Shockley's mental condition at the time of the riot for fear of making the situation worse, and instead focused his questions on Shockley's mental state on November 5. Alden reiterated that on that date he found Shockley able to understand the nature and consequences of his actions and capable of understanding the nature of the charges against him so as to cooperate with his attorney. This testimony did little to detract from Alden's earlier damaging testimony. Realizing that his cross-examination was accomplishing nothing, Hennessy concluded his questioning, hoping to get Alden off the stand as soon as possible.

To eliminate any misunderstanding, Sullivan revisited the issue on re-direct examination. "You definitely take the position, Doctor, that your conclusion that Shockley was legally sane on November 5 when you examined him had no reference to the situation that existed as to his sanity on May 2, the day of the break."

"That is right," Alden responded.

"Well, is it your opinion then, Doctor," Sullivan went on, "that under all the circumstances surrounding his incarceration and experience, that he was legally insane at the time of the break?"

"Yes," Alden agreed, "but I did not express an opinion on that point in my report."

"In other words, under all the circumstances it is your opinion that he was unable to distinguish between right and wrong at that time."

"Yes, I believe that to be so," the doctor further agreed.

Alden's testimony ended at five minutes to twelve and Sullivan, successfully concealing his jubilation, suggested to the court that it might be a good time to declare the noon recess. There followed a brief discussion between Sullivan and Goodman concerning the witness list for the afternoon session.

As Sullivan and the judge conferred, Hennessy turned to Deasy and dejectedly whispered into his ear, "Thank God that's over! Considering what he said in his report, I didn't dream Alden would come on that way and give Sullivan that kind of testimony."

"Yeah, Frank," Deasy agreed. "This was not a happy morning."

"That understates it, my friend," the prosecutor snapped. "Alden has established that insanity was probable as of the time of the escape, and that's all Sullivan needs. I can't believe it."

By now the jury and spectators were gone, but the chatter of the defense lawyers at the far end of the counsel table continued. Sullivan's excitement was infectious, and, although Alden's testimony meant nothing to Thompson and Carnes, their attorneys were equally excited over the events of the morning.

"That was a helluva job, Bill," Zamloch acclaimed, extending his hand in congratulation. "You really set it up. Your questions on redirect totally matched the insanity instructions. All you've gotta do in argument is read 'em both to the jury. It was really a fine job."

Spagnoli and Vinkler added similar laudatory comments, and a joyous Sullivan relished every minute of it. "Yeah, we've had some tough innings, prior to today," Sullivan reflected, "but we knocked it out of the park this morning. You know, Alden wouldn't meet with me before the trial, so I had to wing it. I had no idea as to his opinions of Sam's sanity at the time of the riot. His report hurt us, but his testimony was golden!"

At the commencement of the afternoon session, Spagnoli interrupted Sullivan with a problem regarding his inmate witnesses. He reported to the court that of the twenty-four witnesses he had subpoenaed, it was his understanding that two and possibly four had been transferred to other institutions. Playing to both the jury and the press, Spagnoli stated, "Mr. Thompson requested me to address the court as follows: He would like to be assured of the fact that these prisoners will be assured safe passage back to the penitentiaries from whence they might come, instead of being re-confined at Alcatraz. He is fearful that they might be re-confined on Alcatraz if they are brought back here to testify. I do not know what Your Honor would do in that respect, but we would like to ascertain whether Your Honor would have them returned to Atlanta or Leavenworth or wherever they might be now before we send for them."

Impatient with Spagnoli's repeated grandstanding, and having no control over the Department of Justice, Goodman snapped, "Of course, the court has no authority over the prisoners after conviction and sentence. They are committed to the custody of the attorney general, and he has the exclusive determination as to the place of confinement." The judge was all the more irritated because the court clerk had previously provided the same information to Spagnoli, who nevertheless made his speech in open court.

Questioning Spagnoli's good faith in subpoenaing the witnesses, Goodman shot back, "I think that before the court orders these witnesses brought here to testify, there ought to be some showing made as to the necessity of having them brought here. While the court is perfectly willing to issue the writ, I think there ought to be some statement as to what these witnesses will testify. It may be that the U.S. attorney will stipulate to the testimony."

Spagnoli hastily backed away from his demand that the witnesses be made available. "May it please, Your Honor, I would have to talk with them first in order to determine what their testimony would be. Thompson's position is this: that he would rather do without these witnesses than have them brought back here and have them re-confined to Alcatraz."

No longer concealing his annoyance, Goodman leaned forward and replied sharply, "Counsel, I have no control over that matter at all."

With a tone of resignation in his voice, Spagnoli responded, "In that event, Mr. Thompson would ask those witnesses not to come and also, Your Honor, strike from the petition for the writ of habeas corpus and the order Your Honor made this morning, the names of those witnesses. I think "Joe Blow" Bell is one and "Lefty" Egan is another and possibly two others."

Controlling his irritation, Goodman declared that the court would order the presence of any witnesses he desired. Spagnoli resumed his seat at the counsel table, unaware of the three jurors who rolled their eyes in an obvious display of impatience.

Sullivan's first inmate witness was twenty-seven-year-old San Francisco native, James Quillen, who was serving time for armed robbery, kidnapping, auto theft, and escape. Quillen and his long-time criminal partner, Jack Pepper, were confined to D block after a failed attempt to tunnel to freedom from their place of employment in the kitchen. During the riot, Quillen, Pepper, Howard Butler, Edwin Sharp, and Shockley had barricaded themselves in Shockley's cell, where they had waited out the bombardment and recapture of the cell house. Sullivan hoped that Quillen, the acknowledged leader of the group, could provide alibi evidence as well as testimony concerning Shockley's insanity.

Quillen testified that he first became aware of trouble when he heard a disturbance in the west gun gallery. Believing that the guards were beating a prisoner, the D block inmates began shouting. Shortly, however, they learned from Louis Fleish that an inmate was in the gun gallery disarming Burch, and that an escape attempt was underway.

Quillen stated that in a few minutes he saw Cretzer on the main floor of D block waving a .45 automatic. Soon thereafter, the doors of the two upper tiers of cells racked open. Quillen, along with most of the other D block inmates, went down to the main floor, or flats as it was referred to by the inmates, and took a look into the main cell house. Quillen had returned to the second tier of D block and was standing with a group of inmates when he heard the sound of gunfire. He described the shots as being fired at the Road Tower from the dining hall and stated that the inmates standing near him became concerned. "Later on we heard a lot of shooting coming from inside the main cell house. We wanted to get as far away from the gun gallery as we could." All five prisoners, including Shockley, gathered up mattresses and blankets from nearby cells and piled them in front of the door of Shockley's cell as protection from the anticipated gun battle.

Having established that Shockley was in D block when the shooting began and that he remained there throughout the riot, Sullivan turned to Quillen's opinion regarding Shockley's sanity. A lay witness who was intimately acquainted with a defendant could express an opinion as to the defendant's sanity. By his own admission, Quillen was not an intimate acquaintance of Shockley, and Goodman did not permit him to express an opinion as to Shockley's sanity. He was permitted, however, to testify to Shockley's weird behavior, both on the night of the riot and on previous occasions.

In response to questions by Vinkler, Quillen provided support for the contention that the D block bombardment was excessive and retaliatory. "Afterward a Navy lieutenant came into D block and collected the unexploded shells. They were about a foot long and three inches wide. There were seven of them that I saw."

"And you also told us they fired hand grenades into D block?"

"Yes sir."

"And did you hear anything the guards said that night?"

"Yeah. First they said, 'D block, do you want to surrender?' Everybody was too scared, so nobody said anything. Then he yelled again, 'D block, I don't care if you don't throw out your rifle. We're going to kill all of you. I got the whole United States military behind me and we're going to kill all of you convict bastards.'"

Ed Sharp was a tall, slender man, well regarded by the other inmates. He was not a troublemaker, and was confined to D block at the time of the riot at his own request. He had been experiencing problems with some other inmates, and felt that for his safety and theirs he should be in D block.

Sullivan called Sharp to support Shockley's contention that he returned to his cell immediately after the siren sounded. Sharp's direct examination went well. He confirmed Quillen's testimony that as soon as the siren sounded, the D block prisoners returned to their cells. He recalled that Shockley arrived immediately after the siren sounded and that the inmate was in an agitated state. "… he arrived very soon after the siren sounded. He acted like he was highly nervous and was trembling and carrying on. I don't know how to describe it. I just know he didn't act right."

Sharp also provided valuable testimony on the issue of Shockley's sanity. He celled next to Shockley in D block, and testified to the defendant's hallucinations and aberrational conduct. "He thought he heard somebody calling to him out of the sink and toilet." Sharp's homespun style seemed to be well received by the jury. As his direct examination ended, Sullivan felt good about Sharp's testimony, since it fit so well with that of Quillen and Alden.

On cross-examination, however, Sullivan's confidence in Sharp suffered a severe blow. Hennessy asked a number of questions about a statement Sharp had given the FBI just after the riot. In it he was quoted as saying that Shockley returned to his cell approximately thirty minutes after the other four. While Sharp denied having made that statement, he admitted other portions of the interview recorded by the investigators. His denial lacked conviction. Hennessy pressed on. "And after he'd been in the cell about thirty minutes, isn't it true that Shockley told you that some of the officers had been shot?" By this time, Sharp's easygoing manner had given way to indecision and confusion. "I absolutely did not! No!" he answered. "I didn't make no such statement as that." Satisfied he had badly damaged Sharp's credibility, Hennessy further impeached him by bringing out his criminal background, and ended his examination.

Sullivan interrupted his progression of convict witnesses to call Dr. Gus Theodore Kerhules, the autopsy surgeon who did the autopsies of the deceased convicts. The wisdom of calling him was questionable. Kerhules was a lifeless, boring witness and at 3:15 in the afternoon it was difficult to keep the jury interested in his testimony. Sullivan took him laboriously through the three autopsies, with the doctor reciting medical terms that many of the jurors did not understand. All three men died from multiple gunshot wounds to the head, face, and shoulders. Sullivan sought to prove that the guards were instructed to shoot to kill, not to capture the rioters. What he succeeded in proving was that after hiding in the utility corridor with only their heads and shoulders exposed, the convicts suffered fatal wounds to the exposed portions of their bodies and perished. Satisfied that Kerhules's testimony had accomplished nothing, Hennessy chose not to cross-examine.

Sullivan's final witness of the day was Quillen's friend and long time criminal partner, Jack Pepper. Bald, with deep-set eyes, Pepper had handsome, rugged features. He was not a big man, but was healthy and athletic looking. His three-piece gray suit fit him well, and with his smartly tied black tie, he looked more like a successful businessman than a hardened criminal. At one time, Pepper had been a promising professional boxer. His fondness for alcohol and fast women, coupled with his refusal to train seriously, led him from boxing to crime.

Pepper testified that shortly after the siren sounded, Shockley and the rest of them barricaded themselves in Shockley's cell and waited for gunfire. He stated that after the shooting began, Shockley's actions became irrational. "He acted sort of like a crazy man, like he wasn't right. We were all hungry after laying up there and one of the boys said he had a potato sandwich in his cell. There was a lot of shooting going on and Shockley wanted to run out and get the potato sandwich. Anyone in his right mind wouldn't do a thing like that."

Sullivan suddenly began asking conclusionary questions calling for Pepper's opinion of Shockley's sanity. He had not laid a proper foundation for such an opinion, and when Goodman sustained Hennessy's objections, Sullivan protested. "Don't argue!" the judge sternly admonished. "I've had enough of argument. I have suggested to you what you can ask him. Now if you don't want to accept my suggestion, turn to something else."

Sullivan persisted with his argument, implying that the court's ruling was wrong, but Goodman cut him off, and delivered another blistering rebuke in the jury's presence. "Why don't you ask him simple questions that the man can answer and then you will get an answer. Ask him what he said to Shockley, what Shockley said to him and about things he observed. After you've practiced a little longer, you will learn. Consult with one of the other lawyers and maybe you won't waste so much time."

Hennessy's brief cross-examination established that Pepper had seen Shockley dispose of money, suggesting the defendant's involvement in the operational details of the escape. "Did you see Shockley tear up any money while he was in that cell with you?"

"Yes."

"What did he do?"

"He just pulled some money out and tore it up."

"What did he do with the money?"

"Threw it down the toilet."

It had been an exhausting day for Sullivan and he was happy to see it end. The testimony of the high risk Alcatraz convicts had been an unsettling experience for the court employees, who were aware of the extraordinary security measures. More than a dozen Alcatraz officers and deputy marshals had ringed the courtroom.

As usual, Spagnoli made himself available to the press at the end of the court day. Stating that he would probably start his case before the end of the week, he announced that his witness list included at least three of the most notorious Alcatraz inmates: George R. "Machine Gun" Kelly, Thomas H. Robinson Jr., and Floyd Hamilton. After sparring playfully with the press for fifteen minutes, Spagnoli suggested to Sullivan that they go for a drink. Zamloch was already gone, and Vinkler, not much of a drinker, headed for home. "You had a pretty good day, Bill," Spagnoli remarked. "That guy Alden did a helluva job for you."

"Yeah, thanks, Ernie, it did go well. I was happy with Alden's testimony. I can't say I'm pleased with the inmate testimony so far, though. That goddamn judge is really going with Hennessy on keeping out the insanity testimony. I hope I do better with the cons I've got coming in tomorrow, particularly Henri Young. Goodman's just not cutting me any slack at all and when I push back he gets pissed off and chews me out. At least he let me go with Alden and that really did work out well."

It was well after 5:00 P.M. as the two weary attorneys entered the elevator. As they rode to the ground floor without speaking, Deputy Marshal Fred Henderson inquired of the smiling elevator operator, Joe Bailey, "See any armed spectators today, Joe?" As Bailey and Henderson chuckled together, the lawyers left the elevator, oblivious to the joke.

"Where to, Bill?" inquired Spagnoli.

"Let's hop a streetcar down to Hoffman's for a couple drinks and have dinner there"

It became a more festive night than either Sullivan or Spagnoli had contemplated. It was not until each of them bought two rounds of drinks that the subject of dinner arose. At Sullivan's suggestion they ate dinner at the bar. Spagnoli, a bourbon drinker of some repute, continued celebrating Sullivan's triumph well into dinner, and was still at the bar when Sullivan left for the evening.

22

Wednesday, December 11

Sullivan's first witness in the morning was Howard Butler, one of the D block convicts in Shockley's cell during the bombardment. Butler was a black man serving twenty-two years for armed robbery. He was a tall, slender, effeminate homosexual who was ostracized by the hetero-sexual inmates, and lustfully sought after by the homosexual ones. Homo-sexual prisoners were celled together in an area sequestered from the general population. Black and white prisoners were similarly separated. Black inmates were all assigned cells in a designated area of B block. The prison administration was faced with a choice in Butler's case. Initially he was placed in the homosexual section of the prison. In time, his multiple sexual liaisons created so many conflicts with other inmates that he was assigned to D block for his own protection. There he celled on the top tier next to Henri Young.

Butler's testimony concerning the early stages of the riot was similar to that of other inmate witnesses. He recalled that the calm of a typical D block afternoon was shattered by the sounds of the frenzied altercation in the gun gallery. Soon after the commotion began, Butler observed armed convicts on the main floor of D block and then the doors of the two upper tiers of cells opened. He described seeing Cretzer come to the front of Young's cell, and point the .45 at him with a "murderous look in his eye." After pointing the gun at Young, Cretzer smiled, snapped the safety on, and walked slowly away.

Butler testified that all of the inmates in the upper tiers came out of their cells and milled about. Some of them peered out into the cell house, but only Shockley actually left isolation and entered the main cell house. After a while Butler went down to the west end of the middle tier and joined a small group of inmates. He was standing there when the siren sounded.

"Well when the siren blew, about five minutes after it blew, some firing started. Naturally, when that happened everybody knew that something unusual was happening so we took steps to barricade ourselves in our cell to protect ourselves as best we could."

"Did you see Shockley at any time?" Sullivan asked.

"No, he wasn't there," Butler responded.

"How soon after the siren blew did you see Shockley?"

"Well, I couldn't say for sure, with all the excitement and everything, well, I would say about fifteen or twenty minutes after the siren," the convict replied.

A smile appeared at the corners of Hennessy's lips. He relaxed back in his chair and watched Sullivan awkwardly shuffling his notes, obviously surprised by Butler's answer. The youthful attorney was unable to hide his distress from the keenly observant Hennessy.

Butler was confused, and his testimony was inconsistent with what he had told Sullivan earlier. Fearing he would confuse the inmate further, Sullivan chose to move on. He shifted his inquiry to Shockley's conduct and conversation during the night. Unfortunately for Sullivan, Butler denied hearing any of Shockley's comments throughout the evening. He confirmed the testimony of the prior inmate witnesses that Shockley had to be restrained from leaving the cell to go for food during the night, but then volunteered that he did not view Shockley's conduct during the night as unusual.

Satisfied with the testimony, Hennessy limited his cross-examination to Butler's claim that he heard gunfire from the cells in D block Thursday night and early Friday morning. Although it was factually impossible, Butler had told the FBI investigators that he heard prisoners firing during the night from cells in D block. Knowing full well that this could not have happened, Hennessy carefully developed the misinformation. Butler's mistaken testimony corroborated Bergen's erroneous evidence and provided justification for the night-long barrage of gunfire into D block from the hill below. As Sullivan asked a few final questions on redirect, the prosecutors fell into a hushed, but jubilant conversation. "I can't believe he called this guy," Hennessy whispered laughingly. "If I'd known he was going to be that good, I'd have called him myself."

"Yeah, he went even further than his statement," Deasy responded, excited by the unexpected testimony. "Either Bill wasn't paying attention when he interviewed him or Butler changed his story."

Louis Fleish was one of the big names on Alcatraz. The leader of Detroit's notorious Purple Gang for many years, he was implicated in countless homicides, robberies, rackets, and drug deals throughout the 1930s, but managed to escape conviction. In November of 1939 he was stopped while carrying unregistered machine guns in the trunk of his car, and was subsequently convicted under the National Firearms Act. He received the thirty-year maximum sentence for the offenses. Because of his background and extensive criminal connections, he was sent to Alcatraz, where he joined his brothers, Sam and Harry.

Fleish was a compulsive gambler, whose habit continuously led him to violate prison regulations. Eventually, he was transferred to isolation. He soon became the D block orderly, which afforded him several hours outside his cell each day, as well as the opportunity for conversation with the officer in charge of the block.

Sullivan considered Fleish an important witness whose articulate, intelligent style would impress the jury. He planned to use Fleish's testimony to attack Corwin's credibility. He hoped that Fleish would lay a foundation for the argument that the escape attempt was facilitated by the ineptness of custodial authorities, whose bungling allowed the rioters to take control of the cell house. Sullivan would then argue that in an effort to conceal this ineptness, the authorities now sought to place responsibility on the mentally deranged Shockley, who at the time of the uprising was merely acting out one of his many hallucinations.

Fleish performed admirably. Despite his vicious criminal history, he had a warm and gentle manner that appealed to the jury. His testimony differed significantly from Corwin's, but based on the FBI report, Hennessy knew that Fleish's version of the facts was correct.

Fleish testified that as he and Corwin waited for the afternoon laundry delivery, they heard a loud knock on the cell house door. Assuming the laundry had arrived, Corwin called up to Burch to lower key # 88 so he could open the cell house door.

"What happened after Burch lowered the key to Mr. Corwin?" Sullivan inquired.

"When Mr. Corwin opened the door, we saw several inmates running around in the main cell house and realized that something funny was going on. I told Mr. Corwin to close and lock the door, which he did. The minute he locked the door, well, that is when Coy burst through the door in the gun gallery and overpowered Mr. Burch.

"Where was Mr. Corwin? Was he near you when this scuffle took place?" Sullivan probed.

"Well, when the scuffle started, Mr. Corwin and I went under the upper level of the cage, where they have the water basin and the lavatory facilities. We were standing there and Mr. Corwin turned pale as a ghost when he heard the racket taking place up in the cage. He was very nervous and all I could tell him was to take it easy and let's wait to see what happens, because I was as surprised about things as he was. While we were standing there, several of the inmates in D block who could hear the scuffling up in the gun cage started yelling and hollering, 'What's happening down there?' At that point, I left Mr. Corwin where he was and walked over to the flats in front of the tiers and told the inmates in the upper tiers what was going on."

Fleish repeatedly denied that he had done anything to prevent Corwin from using the telephone. He denied ever being between Corwin and the telephone, stating that at all times Corwin was only a few feet from the phone. During the latter part of the scuffle in the gallery, Fleish was out in the middle of the D block area, describing the action to the eager D block audience. During this entire time, according to Fleish, Corwin stood frozen, making no effort to sound an alarm.

Fleish then described seeing Coy walk over to the cell house portion of the gallery carrying Burch's guns. "He must have handed the guns down to Cretzer and Hubbard, because in a minute or so, the two of them had the guns and were facing us through the glass slit in the cell house door. They were pointing the guns at us through the glass slit. Corwin and I were standing by the door and he had the key to the door in his hand. He kind of looked at me as though for me to tell him what to do. When I saw those guns facing us, I told Mr. Corwin he better open up the door."

By the time he finished testifying, Fleish had painted a convincing picture of a terrified and ineffectual Corwin. Sullivan felt sure that the jury would believe him. His testimony on the insanity issue, however, did not go as well. Sullivan was unable to lay an adequate foundation to permit Fleish to express an opinion as to Shockley's sanity. Fleish characterized Cretzer as the ringleader of the escape, whose orders were followed without question by both Hubbard and Coy. Sullivan hoped this would weigh in on the issue of aiding and abetting, demonstrating that no one was taking orders or even suggestions from Shockley.

Henri Young was Sullivan's next witness, and one in whom he placed a great deal of hope. It had been five years since Young's own murder trial ended with the jury returning an astonishing involuntary manslaughter verdict. Following his trial, Young was returned to D block, where he had been confined ever since. Intrigued by the psychiatric testimony during his trial, Young devoted himself to the study of psychiatry and mental disease. As a result of intense self-education, he corrected his own mental disorder and became, at least in his own mind, an expert in the field. His reputation as a student of mental disorders extended to the Library of Congress, where he was listed as one of a limited number of persons entitled to receive copies of all unpublished psychiatric manuscripts deposited with the library. Young had confidently predicted to Sullivan during their pre-trial meetings that the court would qualify him as an expert witness in psychiatry. As such, he was prepared to testify that Shockley was insane.

Young's educational pursuits went beyond psychiatry, and included the study of religion. In 1944 he became a Catholic. As part of his conversion he confessed to a murder he had committed many years earlier in the state of Washington, of which the police were unaware. He then voluntarily returned to that state and stood trial for the killing. Despite his confession from the witness stand, the jury deliberated for six and a half hours before finding him guilty. For his crime he received a life sentence to be served following the completion of his federal term.

Over Hennessy's objection, Sullivan was able to get much of Young's background into evidence and was also able to get before the jury the long-standing hostility between Young and Cretzer. For years the men were friends. They were both intellectually superior to most of the other prisoners, and frequently competed at chess. Because of Cretzer's strong anti-religion feelings, the cordial relationship was shattered when Young converted to Catholicism. Young testified how Cretzer appeared at his cell during the riot. "I was sitting on the bed when he pointed the gun at me. He just smiled. I sat there looking at him. I thought he was going to shoot, so I jumped up and started to walk toward the door rather than get killed sitting down. Then he turned around and walked away."

Sullivan questioned Young about his study of psychiatry and his efforts to assist Shockley. After establishing Young's educational background, as well as the extent of his reading and analysis of mental disorders, Sullivan asked about conversations with Shockley. "Have you had occasion to have conversations with Shockley regarding the subject of his sanity?"

"Yes, I've had occasion to talk with him many times, because we used to go to the yard together. I was interested in helping the man and having him tell me about some of the difficulties I knew he was having. I was interested, also, in the subject of his sanity, and I was making many efforts to help. What I had explained to Sam was that the sadistic environment of the institution was the direct cause of most of the insanity that I had observed in the prison. Sam replied that he was worried because of the state of his mind and asked me if, from my study, and the fact that I'd been able to cure my own three year period of insanity without the benefit of a doctor, I could help him overcome his mental difficulties."

"What did Shockley tell you about his mental condition?"

"He was very, very worried about it," Young responded.

Hennessy suddenly realized that Sullivan was proceeding on two legal theories, both of which would permit Young to express his opinion as to Shockley's sanity. Although Goodman had not found any of the earlier convict witnesses to be intimate acquaintances of Shockley, Sullivan was convinced that Young was, and should be allowed to testify as to his sanity. Hennessy was rapidly coming to the same conclusion.

Sullivan's second theory was more tenuous. He was attempting to use Young's education and research to establish him as an expert in the field of mental illness, who was qualified to express an expert opinion as to Shockley's sanity. This testimony would place Young in the same category as Dr. Alden.

Young was an intelligent and articulate witness. Hennessy realized that if he was unable to block Young's testimony the prosecution would suffer another setback on the issue of Shockley's insanity. Alden's testimony had been damaging, and if Young was allowed to capture the jury's interest, Hennessy's case would be in serious jeopardy.

The objections and legal wrangling became heated, and Goodman ruled that the issue should be argued outside the jury's presence. He excused the jury for the noon recess, and directed that Young also be removed from the courtroom.

As soon as Young and the jurors were out of the courtroom, Sullivan explained that he intended to introduce conversations between Young and Shockley as evidence of Young's status as an intimate acquaintance. He also argued that Young was a qualified expert in the field of mental illness, who, because of his special knowledge and study, could give expert testimony regarding the defendant's sanity.

Goodman then expressed his major concern, which was time. "The witness, for reasons I am not concerned with, appears to want to be quite talkative about the matter. I do not want to have this get into a long-winded answer and discussion of the whole field of psychology and insanity. So if you can confine yourself to specific matters that are not opinions on the part of the witness or on the part of the defendant, then that would be proper."

Hennessy pressed his argument. "He is not an expert and he should not be testifying as such. We object to Young getting up there and posing as an expert and going into a long dissertation on a subject of which he knows very little, and getting it before the jury."

"Well, Your Honor," Sullivan fought back, fearing that as usual the judge would accept the prosecution's argument, "I can appreciate Mr. Hennessy's attitude toward the witness, because Henri Young was previously on trial in this court himself and escaped the death sentence. So perhaps there is some special reason for Mr. Hennessy's attitude toward this witness."

"There's no attitude about it!" Hennessy snarled in response, the old wound ripped open.

"There certainly is," Sullivan shot back, raising his voice in anger.

"No, my objections are purely legal objections."

Tired of the bickering, Goodman brought the morning session to a close by announcing, "I will allow conversation evidence to the extent that it has to do with statements Shockley may have made and actions of Shockley that the witness may have observed that are of an abnormal or unusual character."

At the commencement of the afternoon session, Sullivan's initial question could not withstand Hennessy's objection. "Mr. Young, I want you to tell us the conversation you had with the defendant Sam Shockley regarding his mental condition."

"I object to that as incompetent, irrelevant, and immaterial," interrupted Hennessy.

Despite his statement made at the close of the morning session, that he would permit the witness to testify to statements made by the defendant,

Goodman sustained the objection, ruling that the question called for general conversation rather than for anything unusual.

There followed a series of questions during which Sullivan was permitted to bring out the same information testified to earlier by other witnesses. But as soon as Sullivan sought to obtain Young's opinion regarding Shockley's sanity, Goodman interrupted the questioning.

"The trial judge has wide discretion in determining the qualifications that render a witness competent to testify concerning the sanity of an individual. As in the case of the other witnesses from whom you sought to elicit an opinion, I hold that this witness does not possess the qualifications which in my opinion warrant the giving of an opinion."

In a desperate attempt to understand Goodman's ruling, Sullivan probed, "Perhaps Your Honor could give me some clue as to how well a man has to know another man to be considered an intimate acquaintance. For the record, Your Honor, could I know if that ruling applies to every inmate that I bring over here?"

"I don't know," Goodman responded, "it depends. There might be somebody that the court might find is an intimate acquaintance, I can't rule academically on that. I have ruled, counsel."

Sullivan made one last, flailing attempt to establish Young as an expert, by requesting leave to present the court with a legal definition of an expert. This request was denied and the entire matter was concluded when Goodman announced, "In the discretion of the court, he is not qualified to testify."

Sullivan sat down at the table and turned to Zamloch in disbelief. "That son of a bitch wants Shockley to die," he whispered. "There's no question but that he should have let Young's opinion in on one or both grounds. The cases are full of authority and on much weaker facts than I've got. The bastard is simply hiding behind 'judicial discretion' because he knows it's impossible to overturn such a ruling on appeal. You notice how he didn't give any explanation as to why Young wasn't qualified. There was an army of inmates who came over and testified on Young's behalf during his trial and they were all permitted to give their opinion as to his sanity at the time of the killing. Goodman is as wrong as he can be and there's not a goddamn thing I can do about it."

Sullivan's next witness was Meloy Kuykendall, a big, burly redhead, serving life for robbery, murder, and kidnapping. An Oklahoma native, Kuykendall was well liked and respected by the inmates. For several years he had worked as an orderly in the prison hospital and was able to describe Shockley's conduct while a patient in the psychiatric ward. "Well, Sam was checked into the ward for a while and the doctor gave him some medicine one morning. He smelled the medicine, then threw it against the wall. He said there was something wrong with it. He claimed we were trying to give him dope or poison him so they put him in the cage."

"They put him in the cage?" Sullivan repeated. "What is the purpose of the cage?"

"Well that's where they put the insane men."

"How long did they keep him in the cage?" Sullivan asked.

"Around thirty days. The only time they used those cages was when somebody was really crazy."

On cross-examination, Hennessy sought to establish that the cages were employed for security reasons. "No, he was never in there for security reasons, no sir! He was in there for the way he acted. Everybody out there thought he was crazy."

Kuykendall's testimony was corroborated by Hugh Gant, a medical patient in the hospital while Shockley was receiving psychiatric care. "Yes, Sam would call me over and whisper to me that the doctor was trying to kill him. He claimed that Dr. Ritchey was trying to kill him with the medicine he was giving him. He would tell me all kinds of wild tales about rattlesnake dens he used to sleep in and how the snakes wouldn't bite him, because he was one of them. Another time I was there, they had him in the 'bug cage,' you know where they keep the crazy guys."

The presence of Rufus "Whitey" Franklin as Sullivan's next witness highlighted one of the historical ironies of Alcatraz. During the 1938 escape attempt led by Franklin, Harold Stites was the custodial hero when he single-handedly thwarted the breakout by killing Thomas Limerick and wounding Franklin. In the 1946 attempt in which Franklin was scheduled to participate but couldn't, Stites was again on the front line, but this time he was killed. Cretzer had wanted Franklin as part of the escape, but when they were unable to release him from his cell in D block they went without him.

Franklin had a quiet, high-pitched voice, and spoke with an Alabama drawl. He was handsome and boyish, appearing much younger than his thirty years. Outwardly he was a docile prisoner, but was capable of vicious conduct and was serving two life terms for a pair of first-degree murder convictions as well as thirty years for bank robbery. Franklin had been in D block for eight years, since his escape attempt of 1938, and knew Shockley well. They celled next to one another and conversed on a daily basis.

His testimony regarding Shockley's bizarre conduct corroborated that of the convicts who had testified earlier, and he contributed further examples of the deranged man's ramblings. "Mr. Franklin," Sullivan finally inquired, "based on your knowledge of Sam Shockley, the fact that you have talked to him on many occasions, the fact that you have observed his intimate actions, have you formed an opinion as to his sanity?"

"Yes."

"What is your opinion?

"I think he's crazy."

The evidence had sailed in so smoothly that Sullivan couldn't believe it. Hennessy and Goodman had both allowed the evidence to come in without comment. One of Sullivan's most articulate witnesses had just emphatically announced that Shockley was crazy. Hennessy briefly considered a motion to strike, but thought better of it, not wanting to highlight the opinion and have it repeated to the jury.

In an effort to generate sympathy, Sullivan called Shockley's older brother, Patrick. Pat Shockley was of limited financial means, but had readily agreed to travel to San Francisco from his farm in Oklahoma to help save his brother's life. Drawing from his meager savings and borrowing additional funds from friends and relatives, Shockley scraped together the money for bus tickets to the West Coast for himself, his former wife May Ballard, their teenage daughter Anna Lee, and Ballard's sister Maggie Jeans. They arrived the day before the trial began, and rented rooms in a rundown hotel for the duration of the trial. The four were in court every day, occupying the same seats in the front row of the spectator section.

Although Sam was not close to his siblings, he and Patrick got along well as children. Pat was the only family member with whom Sam corresponded. There had been occasional letters between the brothers, but they had not seen each other since Sam entered prison in 1938. Pat had hoped to visit his brother before testifying, but the authorities denied him visitation rights.

On the stand, Pat Shockley was nervous and uneasy. His suit purchased for the occasion at a used clothing store, was dated and ill fitting. He looked older than his thirty-nine years, a result of the hard life of an

Oklahoma dirt farmer. He immediately captured the jury's attention, and they studied him carefully.

May Ballard was a frumpy, sad-eyed woman who sat stone-faced, glancing only occasionally at her former brother-in-law. She wore a shapeless print dress under a heavy coat, which had seen many winters and was threadbare at the cuffs. Anna Lee, seventeen years old with bleached blond hair, squirmed nervously in her seat, pouting at the inconvenience of having to sit all day at the trial of an uncle she hardly knew. She would have preferred to spend her time touring the Market Street department stores. Given the magnitude of the charges pending against her uncle, however, Sullivan insisted that the entire family be in court every day. Unfortunately, Pat's testimony was not particularly well received by the jury. The jurors appeared much more interested in the defendant's niece. As she tossed her chemically-enhanced locks while crossing and re-crossing her legs, she engendered speculation as to her life-style. She certainly did not share her parents' back county image.

Pat Shockley's testimony was brief. He described his family as consisting of six siblings, three boys and three girls, as well as a half-brother. He testified that Sam quit school at age twelve, having progressed to only the third grade, and immediately ran away from home. He returned after several months and resumed his life on the farm. Pat related that when Sam was seventeen or eighteen he was sent to reform school. He suffered a severe beating inflicted by another inmate while serving his sentence at the Granite State Reformatory, the same institution where Clarence Carnes did time in 1944. When he was released from Granite, Sam had numerous scars on his head and neck, and demonstrated a complete personality change. "Well, I wouldn't say he was completely insane after that, but he definitely was no longer normal like he had been before. His behavior was okay, but it seemed like he couldn't hold a conversation too long."

Shockley went on to describe a second beating suffered by his brother at the hands of a local police officer. After this experience, Sam's condition was further altered, and it appeared to Pat that his brother's mental condition was much worse. Pat added that his paternal aunt had been insane and was institutionalized prior to her death. Sullivan was unable to draw a strong comparison between Shockley's symptomatology and that of his aunt, so the family history of insanity did not prove to be strong evidence. Hennessy asked no questions on cross-examination.

~

A stir passed through the spectator section as Sullivan announced to the court, "I call as my final witness the defendant, Sam Shockley." The jurors stared intently at the thin, pale convict as he rose and walked hesitatingly toward the witness stand. He looked first at the judge, then the jury, then stared back at Sullivan as if seeking directions as to what to do next.

"Raise your right hand, please," droned the clerk prior to administering the oath. "State your name to the court and jury," he then ordered in the same monotone.

"Sam Richard Shockley," responded the witness nervously.

In an effort to put Shockley at ease, Sullivan began in a friendly and informal tone, "Sam, you are the defendant in this case aren't you?"

"Yes sir."

"I'm going to show you three letters that have been marked for identification and ask you if you can identify them. Did you write these letters?"

"Yes, I did."

"Who did you write these letters to?"

"You."

Although he had seen all three letters previously, Hennessy asked to review them again before they were presented to Shockley. After a brief review of the documents, he interposed an objection.

"I have no objection to two of the letters, but that longer letter is nothing but a self-serving declaration by the defendant," Hennessy protested.

The first two letters were innocuous pieces of correspondence dealing with routine trial matters, but the third was a lengthy, rambling monograph, detailing Shockley's views on the trial, the conditions of his incarceration, and an alleged plot by prison authorities to control and poison him. Sullivan planned to present the deranged and fanciful comments as support for his insanity defense. He had earlier sought unsuccessfully to admit the letters into evidence through Baker. He had then tried, without success to elicit Baker's opinion as to Shockley's sanity. Now, with only Shockley himself to authenticate the letters, Sullivan was making one last effort to get the writings into evidence.

"Let me look at them before I rule on them," demanded Goodman.

"They all concern the mental status of this man, whom you have appointed me to defend," explained Sullivan, a note of desperation in his voice.

Noting the dates on the correspondence, Goodman handed them back to Sullivan, sneering, "These letters were all written after the filing of the indictment in this case." Hennessy had not even stated the basis for any objection, but it was clear that Goodman did not want the letters in evidence. While the letters were probably admissible, Goodman obviously felt Shockley had written the third one as support for his insanity defense.

"I will sustain the objection to the introduction of these letters, without prejudice, on the ground that they are incompetent, irrelevant and immaterial." Goodman relied on the catchall objection permitting him to keep the letters out of evidence without having to explain why. Such a ruling was so vague and broad, that it was unlikely ever to be disturbed on appeal.

More evidence, thought Sullivan, *that Goodman is intent on seeing Sam Shockley die in the gas chamber.*

Frustrated, Sullivan moved to a new subject area, asking a simple question to which he felt no successful objection could possibly be made.

"Do you hear voices, Sam, at any time?"

When Goodman sustained Hennessy's objection, Sullivan lost his composure. "Oh! Christ! Let's call a recess right now, Your Honor! I can't continue this case."

The emotional outburst alone was inflammatory. But Sullivan's reference to the Deity was too much for Goodman to handle. Leaning forward and glaring down at the offending attorney, the judge fumed, "Mr. Sullivan, I heard that! I heard what you said! And I have cautioned you before. Now I shall hold you for Supplementary Proceedings at the conclusion of this trial! I can't help it if I have appointed you as attorney or not. You cannot use language such as you have just used in front of me in this courtroom. It is unbecoming a lawyer. You are entirely not in condition, at the present time, to carry on the important responsibility of an attorney and an officer of this court."

Realizing he had exceed the bounds of accepted conduct, and fearing he might be spending the night with his client in the county jail, Sullivan immediately repented. "I apologize, if I said anything—"

"You should apologize! And it required more than that!" Goodman interrupted reproachfully. "You have a grave responsibility, sir. You served in the armed forces of the United States; you have taken an oath. And you have a responsibility as an officer of this court. You're not some sixteen-year-old law student! Behave yourself in this courtroom! You are not doing your client or yourself any good."

As Sullivan struggled to explain to the court that, because of his client's limited mental capacity, he needed greater latitude in his questioning, Goodman realized that the original question had been a proper one, and his ruling had been wrong. But he was still upset by Sullivan's offensive language. Without admitting his error, Goodman announced in a calm voice, "I shall allow the question you asked to be answered, and if you will just contain yourself and not do the things you do—I have been tempted several times during the trial of this case to declare a mistrial and appoint another counsel to represent this defendant. Now if you feel you cannot perform your duties as an officer of this court, even at great expense to the United States, I might be tempted to declare a mistrial on the ground of your conduct as the attorney for the defendant on the stand. Now please try and do your duty to your client and at the same time conduct yourself as an officer of the court. You make the burden of this court very much heavier. It is the duty of an attorney to try his case expeditiously and fairly and without all of these exhibitions. Now the last question was whether or not he ever heard any voices, and he may answer that question."

The courtroom was deathly quiet and all eyes were fixed on Goodman. Everyone, including the jury, felt embarrassed for the proud young defense lawyer. It was another devastating verbal whipping, administered in the presence of the jury. And this time the tongue-lashing was magnified by Goodman's decision to hold the frustrated young attorney in contempt, reserving his punishment until after the trial. And it had all resulted from Goodman's erroneous ruling as to a proper question asked by Sullivan.

Hennessy's face was expressionless as he observed the exchange. But even the hardened prosecutor felt pity for the young defense lawyer. *Jesus Christ, the judge is tearing him up*, Hennessy thought to himself, *at this rate the jury won't pay attention to anything he says in closing argument*.

As Shockley turned his pale face and gazed earnestly at the jury, he responded in his slow, soft drawl as to whether he had ever heard voices.

"Yes, Sir."

When asked to describe the voices, his brow wrinkled as he struggled to phrase an answer. "Well, it is just like a radio would enter your mind. Evil words would enter your mind; stay on in your mind for, oh, I don't know, a long time."

"What evil words do you hear, Sam? Don't be afraid, tell the jury," Sullivan led him carefully.

"Well homosexual words, like Queers, Punks, Fruits, names like that. When I was in the cage, I was in bed, and I remember things would enter my mind of past crimes. And I couldn't see, but I remember being choked. I was being accused of kidnapping that Matson boy and murdering that little Weyerhauser boy."

"Who accused you of that, Sam?"

"Well, I don't know. It entered my mind. I would say it was the radio system."

Sullivan then had him describe his concerns about the food at Alcatraz. "Well, it would cause me misery and pain. Too many minerals in my food. The words entered by mind and told me not to eat the food because it may kill me."

"Do you know who put the minerals in your food, Sam?"

"Well, yes. I suppose it was the Public of Health."

"Do you have any enemies over there, Sam?"

"Well, yes I do. I think I do. I would say I have prisoner enemies and officer enemies." When asked to name his enemies, however, he was unable to do so without prompting.

"Do you consider Mr. E.J. Miller one of your enemies?" Sullivan asked.

"Yes sir, I do," Shockley quickly responded.

"How about Mr. Corwin? Do you think he is one of your enemies?"

"Well, I believe he is."

Shockley expressed reservations as to whether or not mail censor Baker was his enemy. Sullivan then returned to the radio voices and inquired as to whether they had ever suggested to Shockley that he was born in a different century.

Hennessy, fearing that Shockley's rambling and incoherent testimony might convince the jury that he was insane, rose again to object. "I object to this. I think this has gone on long enough." To Hennessy's surprise, Goodman allowed Sullivan to continue. However, when Shockley testified that some of the prison bath towels and blankets bore the U.S. Army logo and by using them he believed he was committing a felony, Goodman terminated the entire line of interrogation.

Shockley had virtually no recollection of the events of May 2. He recalled the door to his cell being racked open, but little of what followed. "I recall being up in the west end of the cell house, and I heered the door being opened and from then on I didn't know anything until I got to the door. When I got to the door, somebody said something to me about some shoes. I don't know who it was at the door. I recall having some kind of a tool, but I don't know what type or kind it was. But I remember picking up something, I don't remember what it was."

"Do you remember what happened from there on, Sam?" Sullivan asked.

"No sir, I don't."

"Do you remember, at any time, hearing a siren go off?"

"No."

"Do you remember anyone telling you to go back to your cell?" Sullivan went on.

"Seems like I heered a voice. I wouldn't say whose it was, but somebody told me to go back to my cell."

He denied any recollection of striking Weinhold or Sundstrom and professed no knowledge of the events of the riot.

With regard to the events that followed the riot, Shockley displayed a fairly keen recollection. Sullivan asked if he recalled the guards coming into D block on Saturday.

"Well, Saturday, yes. Late Saturday afternoon sometime, I think it was in the evening. Well there was two of them that I knew and one that I didn't know his name. They had guns pointed at me and E.J. Miller came up to my cell and I heered him say, 'Shoot that son of a bitch if he moves.' I stepped out of my cell onto the tier and there was water and broken glass everywhere. Then he told me to pull off all my clothes and throw them over the gallery. Well, we all stripped down naked, then Mr. Miller, he takes his hand and hit me, shoved me up against the wall and said, 'You glass-eyed son of a bitch, go on up there.' So I walked barefooted over the glass and sharp pieces of glass and steel, pieces of bullets and things like that was all over the gallery floor."

"Did Mr. Miller or anybody else take you out of your cell and into a visiting room shortly after that?"

"In the night I was awakened by two or three officers. They taken me to the visiting room at the east end of the cell house and there was two FBIs there—two FBI men. And they asked me a lot of questions about the break. And I told them that I didn't care to say anything and that I didn't want to talk to them. They told me that Carnes had snitched on me about the break and that I was in on the break. Then they told me that I was going to die in the gas chamber over at San Quentin, that is what they told me."

"What else did they tell you?' Sullivan queried.

"Well," Shockley drawled, "he told me they were gonna take me out and work me over, and then I'd be happy to talk to them."

Sullivan asked Shockley for a description of his years in solitary and isolation. The defendant described how for the first seven or eight months he had had no exercise at all. "I didn't have no exercise at all. I stayed in my cell. All the exercise I had was just to go down and get a haircut and take a bath. And I didn't do that very often."

"Sam, did they used to question you about crimes that you were supposed to have committed in other states and because of that were you unable to sleep at night?"

"Yes, sir."

"Could you explain that for the jury?"

"Well, I was tortured over there about past crimes. I have been accused of committing past crimes and I got extreme punishment to confess to the crimes that I was accused of. I got a mental picture of a man that I was supposed to have murdered years back and it was put on my mind. Then the radio system would say it to me over and over. Dr. Roucek, he was the doctor over there. He used to say he was going to put me in the gas chamber. I have been tortured. They kept questioning me. I was put in the hole for eighteen days. I was accused of murdering a couple of officers in the state of Virginia, but I ain't never been in Virginia. And the radio system, if you want to call it that, put that in my head. And I have a mental picture that I'm going to be punished after this trial is over, because we had those blankets that said U.S. Army on them."

By the time Shockley's rambling direct examination ended, it was well past 4:30 P.M. Goodman agreed that Hennessy's cross-examination would take place the following morning, and declared a recess. As the jury filed out of the courtroom, a number of them stared at the obviously confused Shockley. Seemingly unaware of the jury's presence, he stared blankly into space. Sullivan studied each juror's face as they passed by, seeking a sign to indicate their reaction to Shockley's testimony. Although he made eye contact with several of them, their expressionless faces provided no clue to their thoughts.

23
—

Hennessy's cross-examination of Shockley was brief but effective. He questioned the defendant regarding his life before prison and Shockley responded in considerable detail. He was able to recall dates and locations of prior employment as well as past events of his life. "Where were you employed when you lived in the state of Idaho?" Hennessy asked.

"I worked at the harvest, at the hay harvest and the bean harvest and the potato harvest. And I worked for the City of Jerome in Idaho in 1936 and 1937, that's when I worked there."

"When did you leave Idaho?"

"In 1938, I think in the month of January or February of 1938."

"And you returned to what place?"

"Returned to the state of Oklahoma," Shockley responded without hesitation.

"Then subsequently in that year, you got into trouble and you were convicted of bank robbery and kidnapping, is that correct?"

"Yes."

But when asked to recall the events of May 2nd, Shockley displayed a total lack of recall. More than fifty times, he responded, "I don't know" or "I don't remember" to Hennessy's questions. Twice he could not answer questions that he had answered for Sullivan the day before.

As Sullivan listened to the cross-examination, he was pleasantly surprised at how Shockley's repeated "I don't know" answers seemed to fit his personality and mental capacity. Perhaps it was wishful thinking, but by the time Hennessy's cross-examination was finished, Sullivan felt that "Crazy Sam" hadn't performed too badly.

Hennessy's last question was an attempt to demonstrate that Shockley was faking his confusion. "Mr. Shockley, your recollection is quite clear as to a great number of incidents that happened many years ago in the state of Oklahoma and also in the state of Idaho; how is it that you don't remember what happened in the United States Penitentiary at Alcatraz Island on the afternoon of May 2, 1946?"

"Well, I really don't know, sir," Shockley responded, mystified. His response created the definite impression that he was as confused by his memory lapse as was Hennessy.

Shockley's inability to recall the details of the riot was also consistent with the opinions expressed by Dr. Alden. His expression of confusion at not being able to recall these events fit perfectly, like a missing piece in the insanity defense puzzle. Sullivan could not believe how well everything had come together.

"Step down, Sam," Sullivan directed paternalistically, "and go sit over there at the table." As the convict moved haltingly back to his seat, Sullivan reflected briefly. He had done all he could, and he felt that the defense had gone well.

"If Your Honor please," Sullivan addressed the court, "I have concluded the defendant Shockley's defense." Making one final request for the jury view, Sullivan ventured, "I respectfully ask the court at this time to allow the jury to go over and inspect D block for the purpose of seeing Shockley's cell 26 and seeing the cell he was occupying prior to April 27. Also it is important they see the location of the table at which Officer Corwin was seated, the location of the telephone, and the actual proximity of the telephone to the door. I think those are vital things for the defense in this case. I have previously given my reasons to this court and I believe the jury should be permitted to make that inspection."

Unimpressed, Goodman ruled without hesitation, "I will deny the motion, without prejudice."

Spagnoli, nattily attired in a three-piece suit, rose to present his case. Unable to pass up the opportunity to make a speech, he addressed the court. "As Mr. Vinkler announced in his opening statement, Your Honor, we intend to produce, at this time, six witnesses who will testify to the alibi of Thompson that he was in his cell at the time of the shooting and at the time of the homicide of William Miller, deceased in this case." Although Spagnoli's comments were improper and nothing but a restatement of his co-counsel's opening statement, Hennessy wisely chose not to object. With theatrical formality, Spagnoli called his first witness; "We ask leave at this time, Your Honor, to produce Mr. Gerald Peabody as our first witness."

"Ernie can be such an asshole," Hennessy whispered to Deasy, "but if he doesn't get any worse than this we'll be okay."

Gerald Peabody was one of the more interesting convicts in the Alcatraz population. He was a member of a wealthy Baltimore family that had substantial holdings in mining and seaport operations. Peabody was both bright and well educated, but decided not to involve himself in the family businesses. Instead, he pursued a career as a bank robber and con man. He was initially successful in both endeavors, but eventually became another of the FBI's conquests, and in 1940 received a twenty-two year sentence for bank robbery. He was transferred to Alcatraz in 1945, and at forty-six years of age became one of the senior members of the island society. His congenial manner, maturity, and education placed him a cut above most of the other prisoners. He was a model prisoner at Alcatraz, and did extensive reading. He also became one of the better legal writers on the island, frequently researching and preparing legal briefs for other inmates.

After a few preliminary questions to identify and introduce Peabody to the jury, Spagnoli inquired, "Tell us why they removed you from Atlanta to Alcatraz?"

In response to Hennessy's objection, Spagnoli launched into yet another speech. "It is just preliminary. We intend to prove that this witness was sent from Atlanta by the Federal Bureau of Investigation, simply because he testified on behalf of some lawyers, who, along with Mr. Peabody, were falsely accused of having so-called stolen money from this bank robbery for which Mr. Peabody was convicted. He would not stand for any frame-up of these lawyers. Because of that he spent eight months in solitary confinement in Atlanta, then was mysteriously sent over to Alcatraz and has been confined there as punishment."

When Hennessy again objected, Spagnoli declared, "This is an offer of proof." Goodman, however, was unimpressed with Spagnoli's antics, and sharply admonished him to refrain from making future offers of proof until the court had ruled on the objection. "The jury will disregard and ignore these remarks of counsel. The issue in this case is the guilt or innocence of the defendants of the charges set forth in the indictment and that is a plenty big enough job to do without trying other cases."

In an effort to prepare Goodman for what he hoped would be a future favorable ruling, Spagnoli again addressed the court. "I might call Your Honor's attention, without asking Your Honor to change his present ruling, but as a feature of our case, as Mr. Vinkler mentioned in opening statement, we intend to show the conditions that exist at Alcatraz and at other institutions in the United States and why they are sent there and how many of them have become insane."

"You can save your time and breath on that," Goodman declared, "because I now rule that that is wholly immaterial and incompetent and will be excluded from this case. It is not one of the issues in this case."

Spagnoli gave no indication that he heard the judge's ruling, but both he and Vinkler were keenly disappointed with the court's comments. The Alcatraz brutality defense was slowly evaporating. Neither of them considered the cause lost however, and intended to press the issue in the hope of turning the judge around. At the very least, they hoped to be able to slip some evidence past him.

Posturing, Spagnoli continued with improper questions. "Were you guilty of this bank robbery with which you were charged?"

"No sir, I was not," the witness responded ignoring Hennessy's objection.

Annoyed, Goodman again admonished Spagnoli. "I will sustain the objection. I thought this was a witness for defendant Thompson. Try his case. Never mind the witness's case."

Peabody occupied cell #387, immediately below Thompson, and on May 2 was on idle status. He testified that he saw Coy walk by his cell wearing nothing but a pair of trousers. Coy went to the east end of C block and operated the cell controls. Peabody heard Thompson's cell door rack open. At the same time, he observed Hubbard running down Seedy Street carrying a rifle, urging everyone to be quiet. Within a few minutes he saw Thompson and Carnes moving the large scaffold from its storage place near the library toward the west end of the cell house. Just as they moved the scaffold opposite Peabody's cell, the siren sounded. Peabody testified that he heard one of them say, "This calls for a change of plans," and both Thompson and Carnes abandoned the scaffold and ran toward the west end of the cell house.

Peabody was soon aware of footsteps directly above his cell and then heard Thompson's cell door clang shut. He stated that immediately after Thompson's cell door closed, he heard a single shot ring out from a distant point at the west end of the building. Five to seven minutes later, he heard two short bursts of gunfire. Sometime after these shots, he heard heavy shooting which sounded as though it was coming from both inside and outside the cell house.

Although Peabody was a credible witness, his testimony was little more than an inference of an alibi. He created the strong impression that before the gunfire at the west end of the cell house, Thompson had returned to his cell. He could not, however, say with conviction that this is what happened, since he had not actually seen Thompson enter his cell.

Unimpressed with Peabody's testimony, Hennessy did not cross-examine.

Percy Geary, a New York gangster, was Spagnoli's next witness. Born and raised in Manhattan, Geary was a member of an Irish gang that operated mainly in the borough of Queens. In 1946, Geary and fellow gang members John Oley, Charlie Harrington, and Tommy Duggan, were all doing time at Alcatraz. Geary despised his given name and went by "Jack." Use of the hated name Percy by a fellow inmate usually provoked a fight.

Geary celled on the middle tier directly above the hostage cells. From this location he could observe the door to D block and could have seen and heard everything that took place leading up to the shooting of the hostages. At the time of the riot, he was employed as a cell house orderly and was enjoying free time in his cell. He had chosen not to go to the recreation yard, and testified that he was reading a book that afternoon. His surly attitude and limited recollection did not anoint his testimony with the ring of truth.

Geary testified that he was first alerted when he overheard Cretzer and Thompson arguing below his cell. He claimed to have heard Thompson complain, "If anyone is going to get hurt, then I don't want any part of it whatsoever." To this statement Cretzer angrily responded, "Then get the hell outta here!" Immediately thereafter, Geary was aware of Thompson ascending the staircase at the end of the gallery and passing in front of his cell.

"Did you have any conversation with him?" Spagnoli inquired.

"Well, he says to me, 'It's pretty hot down there. I'm gonna' go to my cell before there's any shooting.' He asked me for advice, you know, what to do in a position like that. So I told him the sensible thing to do was to get out of the spot of any fire." According to Geary, Thompson then walked away. He soon heard the clanging of a cell door closing. He admitted he could not see that far down the tier, but believed it was Thompson's cell door that he heard close.

Geary was an ineffective witness and some of his testimony seemed to come as a surprise to Spagnoli. He denied seeing the scaffold being moved or seeing any inmates other that Thompson and Cretzer. He even denied hearing the escape siren until prompted by Spagnoli's leading questions. Zamloch glanced down the counsel table to Sullivan and both attorneys shook their heads. *That was really a shitty job of witness preparation,* thought Zamloch, *Geary's contribution was limited at best, but Ernie should have had him better prepared.*

On cross-examination, Hennessy brought out that during the FBI investigation Geary stated that his first awareness of trouble was the sound of a single gunshot. The FBI report also quoted him as stating that when he looked out of his cell he saw nobody and could not identify any voices. Geary denied these statements, but even Spagnoli doubted his veracity.

On direct, Spagnoli had foolishly attempted to minimize Geary's criminal background by referring to his crime as a "technical kidnapping." On cross-examination, Hennessy forced the reluctant witness to admit that he was serving seventy-seven years for five felonies: grand larceny, burglary, kidnapping, escape, and extortion. By the time Hennessy's cross-examination was finished, Spagnoli faced the hopeless task of rebuilding Geary's shattered credibility.

"Is everything you have told the jury today from the witness stand the truth?" Spagnoli asked the battered witness.

"Yes," was Geary's ineffective answer.

Spagnoli ended the examination and resumed his seat at the counsel table. As he did, he announced to the court, "Gerry Myles will be our next witness, Your Honor," and turned the questioning over to Vinkler.

Myles proved to be a strong defense witness and Vinkler conducted an excellent examination. Born January 15, 1915 in a home for unwed mothers, Myles was raised by adoptive, then foster parents. His criminal record dated from 1929, when at the age of fourteen he was sentenced to eighteen months in the Kansas Boys' School. Thereafter, he spent most of his life either incarcerated or living as a vagrant. On Alcatraz he became a model prisoner and looked forward to discharge in 1952, with parole possible before that time.

Myles occupied cell #420 on the middle tier of C block. This was two cells west of the C block cut-off and only a few cells from Thompson. He testified that he was first alerted when he observed Coy opening the locked library door. Later he observed Coy in the west gun gallery, passing a rifle down to Hubbard. He provided a series of narrative answers to Vinkler's well-crafted questions and told a story that was generally consistent with that of many of the hostages.

Myles's testimony provided alibi evidence as well as corroboration for Geary's shaky evidence. Myles testified that when the siren sounded, Carnes and Thompson abandoned the scaffold they were pushing and ran toward the west end of the cell house. Shortly thereafter, he observed Thompson walking east along the middle tier of C block. He stopped in front of Geary's cell and Myles overheard Thompson's side of their conversation. "Those guys are going crazy down there, they're going to kill somebody." According to Myles, Thompson asked Geary if he was doing the right thing in abandoning the escape effort. Thompson then passed in front of Myles's cell, and proceeded down the tier to his cell. His recollection as to the timing and spacing of the gunshots differed slightly from that of the hostage witnesses, but he unequivocally stated that Thompson was back in his cell before any shots were fired. Myles stated that he heard a single shot, from somewhere at the west end of the building. Thereafter he heard Cretzer, whom he knew well, talking in an excited voice at the west end of the C block flats. This conversation was followed by two bursts of pistol fire and Cretzer's cry, "I got all them sons of bitches." He then heard someone declare, "There's one more left," after which he heard a single pistol shot.

The remainder of Myles's direct examination described the rescue, the bombardment, and the re-capture of the cell house. He joined in the attack on the associate warden, whom he quoted as stating to one of his officers who threatened to kill Thompson, "Hey, there's no need to kill him now, I can kill him when we get him in court."

On cross-examination, Hennessy questioned Myles about his FBI interview. Myles had taken a hostile position with the investigators, insisting that he hadn't seen anything significant and even if he had, he would never reveal information to them. Hennessy attempted to use this statement to impeach Myles's testimony. The strategy was only marginally successful. Technically there was an inconsistency, but it was clear to the jury that Myles simply refused to cooperate with the FBI, and later cooperated with the defense.

∽

Spagnoli's next witness was Floyd Hamilton. As the sole surviving member of the Bonnie Parker and Clyde Barrows gang and formerly #1 on the FBI's list of America's most wanted criminals, Hamilton was a part of America's criminal folklore. Even the most seasoned of the regular courtroom observers eagerly awaited his testimony.

Hamilton had been privy to the escape plans from the beginning, a fact he never admitted, but had waited until the last minute to decide if he would participate. Like Thompson, he obtained a lay-in slip from the hospital and was in his cell when the riot began. As soon as the escape got underway, Cretzer directed Lageson to release Hamilton and when the officer refused, released him himself. Once out of his cell, the Texas bank robber took a careful look around. Not impressed with what he saw, and lacking confidence that his aging body could survive the physical rigors of another Alcatraz escape attempt, he chose to return to his cell. He walked with a slight limp as he made his way to the witness stand, and looked confidently around the courtroom, at the judge, jury, and spectators.

Basking in the glow of Hamilton's notoriety, Spagnoli began by bringing out the witness's criminal background and the fact that he was serving a thirty-year sentence. "Did they send you to some other prison before they sent you to Alcatraz?" the lawyer inquired, gesturing to the prosecution end of the counsel table.

"Yes sir, I was first sent to Leavenworth."

"What did they send you over to Alcatraz for?"

"I don't know. Just to fill the joint up, I suppose," Hamilton replied arrogantly. Although Spagnoli found the response amusing, a number of the jurors did not. Serious about their sworn responsibility, they resented Hamilton's flippant comment and were unimpressed by his reputation. Spagnoli was so overcome with his own self-importance that he failed to notice the frowns crossing the faces of several disapproving jurors.

Hamilton testified that he had occupied cell 418, two cells west of Thompson on the middle tier. After obtaining his lay-in he took the medicine prescribed by the doctor and lay down on his bunk. He stated he was startled when he heard Cretzer calling out, "Is Hamilton in his cell? Go get Hamilton out." Confused, he looked out of his cell, but observed nothing. About five minutes later he again heard Cretzer call out, "Go get Hamilton out of his cell." He claimed he had no view to the west so did not know what was going on there. In fact, Hamilton had been well aware of what was going on, but there was nothing to suggest this to the jury.

"In about ten or fifteen minutes," Hamilton continued, "I heard the locking mechanism make a noise indicating someone was unlocking the doors at the east end of the cell block. I heard a cell door nearby open, and immediately after that, Thompson walked by my cell, very slowly, looking over the railing toward the west end of the block as if he was trying to see what was going on down there. He was gone, I would say, about ten or twelve minutes and then the escape siren sounded. About three or four minutes after that, Thompson again appeared in front of my cell and I asked him what was going on down there. He told me that Coy, Cretzer, and Hubbard had guns and they were fixin' to make a break. Then he asked me, 'What would you do? Would you join them if you was me?' And I told him if he wanted to stay out of trouble, he'd better get back to his cell. Then I saw him go to the east end of the gallery and lock himself in his cell."

"Did you actually see Thompson enter his cell?" Spagnoli asked.

"Yes I did," Hamilton responded emphatically.

"Was that before or after any shooting took place?"

"That was before any shooting took place, yes, that was before any shots were fired at all."

"And you actually saw him enter his cell before any shots were fired at all?"

"Yes."

Concluding the alibi testimony, Spagnoli took Hamilton through the events after the riot, focusing on the mistreatment of Thompson by prison authorities. Thompson was specifically denied sandwiches and coffee when they were distributed on Saturday afternoon. Additionally, Hamilton heard the FBI roust him from his cell at midnight Saturday for what he heard described as an "interrogation." He recalled at least one other occasion when Thompson was removed from his cell.

Hamilton also overheard comments by Associate Warden Miller when he and Lageson visited Thompson's cell Saturday morning.

"Tell us what happened between those two gentlemen and Mr. Thompson," Spagnoli inquired.

"Well, they walked up in front of Thompson's cell and Miller said, 'I'll teach you to kill my officers.' He reached through the bars, I couldn't tell you where they caught him, but they punched him twice. Lageson started to pull out a blackjack and Miller pushed him back and said, 'We won't have any of that.' Miller reached through the bars and I saw his hand punch twice."

"Did you pick anything up from in front of Thompson's cell later on when you went out?" the lawyer asked.

"Yes I did. There was a handful of hair laying there. I picked it up and gave it to Thompson."

Spagnoli then held up a small clump of hair, which Hamilton stated appeared to be the hair he had recovered, although he couldn't be sure. Without objection, the unsightly exhibit was marked for identification.

Anticipating a blistering cross-examination by Hennessy, Spagnoli concluded, "You talked with Mr. Vinkler, an attorney for Mr. Thompson on the 9th of November of this year over there at Alcatraz, is that correct?"

"Yes."

"And I was present during that conversation, isn't that correct?"

"Yes sir, you were."

"And we asked you to tell the truth here, didn't we?"

"Yes sir, that is correct."

"Have you told the truth?"

"I have."

Spagnoli's concerns regarding cross-examination were without foundation. After only a few general queries, Hennessy terminated his questioning of the witness. A confident and smiling Floyd Hamilton left the courtroom to be swallowed up once again in the monotony of life on Alcatraz.

William L. "Dub" Baker, one of the two librarians on duty May 2nd, provided additional corroborative evidence for Thompson's alibi. Although Baker was a good witness, Spagnoli's questioning detracted from his effectiveness. From the outset, Spagnoli chose to perform for the gallery and provoke Hennessy rather than develop Baker's testimony.

When Baker admitted to a kidnapping conviction, Spagnoli again referred to the crime as a "technical kidnapping," which drew an immediate response from Hennessy. In his bickering style, Spagnoli chided the prosecutor, suggesting that his questioning might well prove that Baker was innocent, a feat he claimed to have accomplished during Peabody's testimony.

"Your clients are always innocent, I presume," Hennessy responded sarcastically. Spagnoli's antics worked only to his disadvantage, disrupting the flow of his case with useless arguments, distracting the jury's attention from the testimony.

Spagnoli brought out that Officer William Miller had locked Baker and fellow librarian Edward Cook in the library for their afternoon shift at approximately 1:30. Baker recalled conversing through the wire mesh wall of the library with Thompson, Hamilton, and Peabody, all of whom celled across from the library. Thompson complained of a headache and advised that he had just received some aspirin from the hospital. He asked Baker to keep a lookout for him while he made a cup of coffee. Complying, Baker pressed his face against the wire mesh and looked to the west end of the corridor. As he did, he observed Coy walking quickly toward the library, shuffling keys in his hands. He realized something highly unusual was happening.

Coy unlocked the library door. He spoke briefly with Cook, and the two men headed for the west end of the cell house. Distancing himself from the action, Baker moved to the opposite side of the library. Cook soon returned and reported that Coy and Cretzer had captured Miller, and that he wanted no part of it.

The most significant portion of Baker's testimony concerned his recollection after he heard the siren. The siren sounded about 2:30 P.M. Baker testified that within five minutes he heard shots. He first heard a single shot, which he estimated came from the kitchen. Almost immediately thereafter, he heard two bursts of gunfire from the vicinity of cells 402 and 403. Realizing that the situation was serious, he went to the sink and wet his handkerchief to protect his face and eyes from tear gas. As he did, he looked across the corridor and saw Thompson sitting in his cell. "You looked up and saw Thompson in his cell?" asked Spagnoli.

"Yes sir, I did."

"And this was right after you heard those shots?"

"Yes it was."

Baker had also seen Thompson outside his cell before the siren and gunfire, when he happened to glance out at the rolling scaffold. For some reason Spagnoli did not follow up on this, ignoring the issue of Thompson's abandonment of the scaffold at the time of the siren.

Again Spagnoli ended the questioning seeking to strengthen the witness's credibility. "Everything you have told us here is the truth, isn't that correct?"

"That is correct," was Baker's reply.

"You have not been asked to tell anything that was not correct, have you?"

"Never have, no."

"And I spoke with you a few Saturdays ago over at the prison and you told me the same story that you just told here, isn't that correct?"

"We object to this build-up, Your Honor," Hennessy finally blurted out, bringing Spagnoli's examination to a close.

Hennessy's cross-examination consisted primarily of clarification until he got to the subject of prior convictions. "What felonies were you convicted of besides kidnapping?" he asked.

"Murder and manslaughter," was Baker's answer.

"And who did you murder?" Hennessy probed.

"My father."

"That is all," Hennessy stated, resuming his seat at the counsel table and leaving the entire courtroom in a quandary as to the details.

"But you've never been convicted of perjury, have you?" Spagnoli struggled lamely. "And you are telling the truth here, are you not?"

"Yes I am," responded the shaken witness.

The last few questions for Baker were from Zamloch. He focused the inmate on the gunfire timeline, which was critical to Carnes's defense. Zamloch brought out that Baker first heard muffled gunfire from the kitchen area, followed by two bursts of pistol fire from the area of the hostage cells. This was followed by a single shot from the dining hall and another single shot from the hostage cells. This would permit Zamloch to argue that Carnes was in the kitchen with Hubbard and Coy up to the time that the single shot was fired from the dining hall, which was the shot fired at the associate warden. That being the case, Carnes could not have been present at the hostage cells until the final shot was fired at Lageson, and would have been in the kitchen when Cretzer shot officer Miller and other hostages.

At the conclusion of Baker's testimony, Goodman called the afternoon recess. Spagnoli was scheduled to conduct the examination of the next witness, Thomas Henry Robinson Jr., but as the jury filed out he turned to Vinkler and suggested, "Aaron, why don't you take this guy? He's basically going to testify as to the brutality aspect and conditions in D block, which is more your area than mine." Although he had been present during Robinson's interview, Vinkler had not participated in his preparation and felt ill equipped to examine the witness. He also resented Spagnoli's abdication of responsibility. Given Goodman's rulings, it would be difficult to get the brutality facts into evidence, and Spagnoli was simply passing the buck. Always the team player, however, Vinkler accepted the assignment.

Robinson was a highly intelligent man, who could have helped the defense. However, the combination of Spagnoli's poor preparation and the fact that Vinkler interrogated him on short notice nullified his effective-ness. He was called to testify as to the harsh Alcatraz conditions, but con-tributed little information. He gave a few examples of prejudice and hos-tility by the guards, but basically his testimony was ineffective.

Spagnoli called his next witness, inmate Ray Stevenson, then with a dramatic air of self-importance, requested permission to leave the court-room. "May I be excused, Your Honor, for a minute? One of my witnesses, "Machine Gun" Kelly, wishes to confer with me before he takes the stand." In response to Goodman's scowl, Spagnoli quickly assured him that Vin-kler would examine Stevenson and there would be no delay in the pro-ceedings. Goodman readily granted his request. Hennessy and Deasy exchanged glances. It was obvious to the two prosecutors that Spagnoli's case was going downhill. Spagnoli scurried from the courtroom and Vin-kler, surprised and confused, rose to examine the witness, this time with no advance notice or preparation.

After identifying Stevenson's cell and having him mark it on the dia-gram, Vinkler focused his questioning on the day of the riot. To everyone's surprise, Stevenson testified that he was working in the laundry when the escape siren sounded about 2:30 P.M. The laundry was immediately locked down, and he was moved to the yard about 6:30 that evening.

When Vinkler asked Stevenson if he had observed gunfire coming from any of the boats in the bay, Goodman interrupted demanding, "What are you going to prove by this witness? That he saw shooting from the boats?"

"Yes, Your Honor," Vinkler replied. "I wish to show that they were shoot-ing two-inch shells."

"What you intend to show from this witness is that he saw gunfire from a boat?" Goodman asked incredulously.

"That is correct."

"Is there anything else you want to show from this witness?" the judge demanded, clearly irritated.

"I will develop it as I go along," Vinkler stammered in reply, attempting to keep his response as vague as possible.

"Just answer the question," the judge ordered. "Is there anything else you want to show from this witness except that he saw gunfire from a boat? Because as to that matter, I rule it incompetent and irrelevant. What else have you got?"

Realizing he was in trouble, Vinkler shifted his approach. "Yes, Your Honor, there are some other matters I wish to go into with this witness."

But when Vinkler asked Stevenson about Alcatraz prisoners who had been transferred from Alcatraz to the psychiatric facility in Springfield, Missouri, the judge again caustically intervened. "Do not bring anybody else over here to testify as to these matters and cause the government unnecessary expense. You should know by now, that I am ruling this testimony incompetent, irrelevant, and immaterial. If you have something material to bring out I do not want to shut you off. I just do not want to take the time of the court and jury for you to go into extraneous matters."

Vinkler's flustered distress was evident to even the most unsophisticated observer. In a final effort to salvage Stevenson's testimony, Vinkler announced that he intended to focus on Stevenson's conversations with various guards.

"Just ask the question," the annoyed Goodman responded coldly.

"Mr. Stevenson, since May 2, have you ever discussed this matter with any of the guards on duty on Alcatraz?"

"No," was his devastating response.

"Have you ever been questioned by the FBI, regarding what happened on May 2?" Vinkler asked hopefully.

"No," Stevenson again replied.

Thoroughly embarrassed, Vinkler terminated the examination.

By this time Spagnoli had returned to the courtroom, unaware of the debacle that had just occurred, and announced that his next witness would be Edward Cook, the other inmate librarian.

Infuriated by Stevenson's testimony, Goodman lashed out at the unsuspecting Spagnoli. "Is this witness being called to cover the same subject matter as the last witness?"

Oblivious, Spagnoli responded, "I did not hear his testimony."

Outraged by Spagnoli's lack of preparation and disorganized presentation, Goodman ordered that he would no longer require the government to produce the witnesses subpoenaed by Spagnoli until he demonstrated that they each had something relevant to say. "At this time the court will vacate the writ that has heretofore been issued, and I will require some evidence as to the materiality of the witnesses before I order any further men to be brought over here." This was a highly unusual order, and a requirement rarely imposed on a criminal defendant.

To add to the chaos, Spagnoli sheepishly advised the court, "Before Your Honor finally vacates it, I wish Your Honor to vacate the order insofar as George "Machine Gun" Kelly is concerned. I assumed Mr. Vinkler had seen him. We have been over to the island both together and separately. Kelly tells me he was in the yard and knows nothing. He was inadvertently brought over here. He got a nice little trip out of it. That is about all. We do not want to bring him in here and have him say he knows nothing. I have never discussed the matter with him, except a few minutes ago. So we will ask that he be sent back to the island. That will leave only nineteen witnesses."

Barely restraining his fury, Goodman adjourned for the day and restated his order that no further Alcatraz inmates would be brought to testify until Spagnoli had made an adequate showing that they had something relevant to contribute.

Spagnoli then addressed the court with a preposterous evidentiary request, almost as if to intentionally irritate the judge. "Just a minute, Your Honor, as long as the warden is here, would Your Honor instruct the warden to bring over all of the records from the hospital that have been developed since he has been warden, so that we may develop evidence to prove, as part of our defense, how many prisoners have gone insane over there and have been sent to the insane asylum at Springfield? We ask that he bring all of the hospital records and that he be prepared to testify."

"I will deny that request," the outraged judge ruled, even before Hennessy could respond. Spagnoli persisted, urging that he wanted to make a record, but Goodman cut him off rudely, ordering, "I have denied your request, now you have your record. It will not serve any purpose to put a witness on. The record is complete. If I am wrong about it, some other court can correct me."

As the court day ended, Thompson's defense lay in chaotic shambles. Although some of the earlier witnesses had provided helpful evidence, the closing witnesses had contributed nothing. Beyond that, they had highlighted Spagnoli's confusion and lack of preparation. Spagnoli had completely alienated the judge, and had compounded his transgression by attempting to blame Vinkler.

Enjoying the sideshow, the prosecutors smiled knowingly at one another. "Ernie really stuck his foot in his mouth," whispered Deasy.

"You're far too generous, Dan," Hennessy responded, "I'd say he stuck his head up his ass. And tomorrow is Friday the 13th. How much unluckier can he get?"

24

The morning brought more heavy fog, which had blanketed Northern California for days. At least one traffic fatality and numerous injuries were blamed on the severe weather conditions. It was a gloomy morning at the courthouse as the attorneys and jurors made their way to Judge Goodman's court.

Calling Edgar Cook to the stand, Spagnoli adopted a contrived air of familiarity with the Alcatraz prison society. "Now, you were working in the library on May 2 of this year when some of the boys over there attempted to escape?"

"Yes."

Cook had been approached by Coy in the summer of 1945 and invited to join the escape. He had only been on Alcatraz for about a month and his initial reaction was affirmative. "Sure, count me in. I wanna get the hell outta here." He and Coy discussed the plan in detail over the next several months, but Coy never revealed the names of the other participants. In time, Cook began to have reservations about participating, unwilling to rely entirely on Coy's selection of personnel. He finally decided not to join the breakout, but never shared this information with Coy.

Cook's testimony was of limited benefit to Thompson's defense.

The only relevant testimony he provided was his statement that after the shooting started he overheard Baker talking with Thompson. He testified that Thompson's voice came from his cell, although he admitted that he could not actually see him.

Zamloch examined Cook, concentrating on the timing of the gunfire. Cook's recollection as to the sequence of the various gunshots was consistent with Carnes's version.

~

The next three witnesses, inmate George Hollingsworth, officer John Mullan, and officer Virgil Cochenour, were all called to establish the fact that within five to fifteen minutes of the siren sounding, the east gun gallery was manned. Mullan and Cochenour occupied the lower tier, and officers Zubke and Long the upper tier. Spagnoli's intent was to demonstrate that by the time the gallery was manned, Thompson was back in his cell. The testimony, however, was not dispositive of much of anything.

As Vinkler examined Cochenour, the last of the three witnesses, Goodman, eager to move the case along, interrupted. "Counsel, do you have to question him regarding all these matters again, that have been testified to time and time again? If you have some special matter that you want to bring out, let's get to it."

Vinkler refused to allow the judge to interfere with his presentation, and silenced Goodman with a stinging reply. "During the prosecution's case they presented continuous testimony as to alleged inmate gunfire, until I heard gunfire in my sleep. At that time the court expressed no need to move the case along nor any concern that the jury might be subjected to cumulative testimony." Thoroughly but politely chastised, Goodman had no more to say on the subject, and Vinkler concluded his examination uninterrupted.

Spagnoli's choice of Robert Stroud as his next witness was a further example of the attorney's obsession with high visibility witnesses, regardless of their value to the case. It was unclear whether he sought self-gratification by associating with famous criminals or whether he felt that they would impress the jury. What was clear, however, was that he went out of his way to call the notorious and the noteworthy, even if their contribution to the defense case was meager. So it was with Robert Stroud.

Stroud was the author of two leading volumes on bird diseases, and was a recognized authority on the subject. His fame both as a murderer and an intellectual was well known. In 1909 he was convicted of killing a rival over the affections of a prostitute in the Yukon Territory. He was initially incarcerated at McNeil Island and later transferred to Leavenworth. Seven years later, in a fit of rage, he killed a Leavenworth guard in the prison dining room. He was convicted of murder and received the death penalty. After Stroud's mother appealed to Mrs. Woodrow Wilson, President Wilson commuted his sentence to life imprisonment in isolation. In 1942 he was transferred to Alcatraz.

Vain, arrogant, and enormously egotistical, Stroud was generally disliked by the other inmates. Eventually, his interpersonal dealings were limited almost entirely to the custodial force, which didn't care for his company either. In addition to his bird research, he produced numerous writs and legal briefs for himself and others, diagnosed his own physical ailments, and prescribed his own medications. Stroud trusted no one, individual or institution.

Spagnoli's first question of Stroud was essentially an invitation for him to make a speech to the jury. "Mr. Stroud, will you give us a little background about yourself, who you are?"

Immediately aware of Spagnoli's intention to showcase Stroud in an effort to impress the jury, Goodman stopped the witness before he could respond and directed, "No, just ask direct questions."

When Spagnoli tried again to bring out Stroud's background, the judge terminated the line of questioning, "Now counsel, I am not belittling the witness's activities. I know he has written a lot of books, and studies on birds. We are confronted in this case with a specific issue. Ask him about the events that have to do with the charge contained in the indictment, nothing else. We have got to proceed."

Forced to limit his interrogation to relevant matters, Spagnoli was at a loss, since Stroud had no significant knowledge. The only subject area that Spagnoli was ultimately able to cover related to the extensive shelling of D block. Stroud testified that a few minutes after the alarm sounded, all the convicts involved in the riot left D block. By the time Associate Warden Miller was shot at from the west end of Broadway, Stroud insisted that all of the rioters were out of D block. He also testified unequivocally that, except for a shot fired by Hubbard at the very outset, no gunfire came out of D block throughout the entire affair.

Stroud insisted that the fusillade into D block was concentrated in the eastern corner of the block, where his cell was located. He testified that he saw personnel on gunboats in the Bay watching him through binoculars and firing at his cell. "My cell was singled out for individual bombardment. There were more than 400 slugs hitting that cell, over 79 bullet holes through the wall of the cell." A considerable amount of gunfire was concentrated into that area of D block, and the D block inmates all believed that the bombardment was an attempt by prison officials to retaliate against the inmates for the deaths and injuries suffered by the officers. However, no proof of such a conspiracy was ever uncovered.

Following Stroud's appearance on the stand, Spagnoli made a demand to inspect Thompson's FBI statement. In a departure from his usual activist roll, Goodman became a spectator as an argument raged between Hennessy and Spagnoli over whether the defense would be permitted to see the statement. Initially Hennessy stated simply, "I haven't any statement." While the statement may not then have been physically present in Hennessy's file, it was certainly in the possession of the prosecution team. As the argument continued without intervention from the judge, Hennessy began referring to the statement as "the confession." This drew an outraged protest from Spagnoli. "There is no confession! Your Honor, we assign that comment as gross misconduct on the part of the district attorney and prejudicial to defendant Thompson. He has never made a confession. He has nothing to confess to."

Finally acknowledging that the statement existed, Hennessy declared, "If the FBI has it, we decline to turn it over to you at this time." Insisting that he be permitted to review Thompson's statement, Spagnoli implored Goodman to intercede, "We have a right to see whatever the prosecution has, that might aid or assist the defendant in this case."

Goodman responded with disinterest. "I don't agree with you counsel, proceed with your next witness." In hopeless resignation, Spagnoli sagged into his chair, and indicated that Vinkler would present the next witness, inmate Lawrence DeCloux.

The testimony of DeCloux proved to be one of the greatest mysteries of the trial. Perhaps he was intended as a living example of the insanity that the defense claimed pervaded the island. He appeared with a sealed bundle of papers, which he had previously turned over to the warden, stating that they were relevant to the issues of the case. Warden Johnston presented the papers to Vinkler, who advised the court, "I don't know what the papers are. Will Your Honor permit the witness to open them? They are sealed."

"No," Goodman responded, impatient with the continuous disruptions. "The witness is summoned here to testify and answer such questions as may be put to him." With that, the documents were passed off to Spagnoli, who reviewed them and placed them in his brief case. They were never seen or referred to again.

DeCloux's testimony added nothing to the case, a situation that was becoming more and more frequent as Spagnoli's case unfolded. The witness stated that on May 2 he had been confined in D block and, like the others, had stepped out of his cell when the doors racked open. He recalled seeing Cretzer point the .45 at Young and pull the trigger. The gun did not fire and, after pointing it at DeCloux, Cretzer walked away and left D block.

Soon after taking the stand, DeCloux became noticeably anxious and began to gaze wildly around the courtroom. Vinkler, observing the witness's agitation, became uncomfortable, and quickly terminated the questioning. On cross-examination, Hennessy asked him for his recollections regarding the gunfire into D block on the day of the riot, and DeCloux became unmanageable. Obviously believing that the authorities had fired needlessly into isolation, DeCloux released an irrational tirade. "Well there was a lot of it that came in the top tier, where they tried to murder me. You hear that? They were throwing bombs in there. You couldn't hear anything. I was there. I went through that inferno. There was no shooting coming out of D block, only coming in."

The more DeCloux talked, the more disturbed he became. Finally, he was totally out of control, making many in the courtroom nervous. The bailiff, marshals and armed Alcatraz guards tensed in anticipation, carefully monitoring the wild-eyed, unshackled convict on the stand.

The courtroom tension was exacerbated when Zamloch rose and addressed the court. "May it please the court, I beg leave to cross-examine this witness as to his ability to testify prior to making a motion to strike."

Puzzled, Goodman inquired, "Well do you consider it has any bearing on your defendant in this case?"

"Well I think this man is insane and it may have a bearing. This witness testified that he observed Carnes in D block, and it's not clear to me whether he meant Carnes or Cretzer." Zamloch wanted it clearly understood that he was not bound by the testimony of Thompson's witnesses.

"Now I have remained silent during this parade of witnesses here," Zamloch resumed, "but I have a document here, which this man has prepared and I think it pretty clearly demonstrates that he is mentally unbalanced." Turning to the witness, Zamloch continued, "Did you mean to say Joe Carnes or Joe Cretzer?"

"Joe Cretzer," DeCloux responded. "Did I say Carnes? That was an unintentional error on my part."

Satisfied that the matter had been clarified, Zamloch terminated his examination. DeCloux however, was not finished. "If Your Honor please, I have a statement, that I am required by law to make. I wish to make it now."

"No! No!" Goodman exclaimed. Then he called out to the bailiff. "Take the witness back! Remove this man from the courtroom!"

But DeCloux would not be silenced. As the bailiff and two marshals approached the stand, he continued to rant. "Are you going to leave those people who attempted to murder us over there and let them go and get away with it? I can't bring it out? This looks to me like a German people's court! You can cite me if you want!"

With that, DeCloux was lifted forcibly from the stand by the marshals and carried out a side door amidst gasps from the spectators' gallery. Two of the male jurors smiled nervously and one of the women fumbled with her purse.

Goodman acidly addressed the shocked and contrite Vinkler. "I don't know why you produce a witness of this kind. I asked you yesterday to give me assurances that the testimony of your witnesses would be material. To have a display like that here in the courtroom, I have to instruct the jury to disregard the incident which occurred."

"Your Honor," Vinkler began apologetically, "when I talked to the man originally, he appeared to be sane to me. I am not responsible for his conduct here, and I want the court to realize that. I don't like to be criticized unjustly. If I am wrong I will take my criticism, whatever it is. If Your Honor feels that way, I won't call these witnesses."

"It is not a question of how I feel," Goodman responded, somewhat calmer. "I know you were appointed in this case at the request of the defendant Thompson. I am not trying to hinder the testimony. But you were asked to use the normal amount of discretion in selecting your witnesses and to aid in the expeditious trial of this case."

"I asked him and he said he knew Coy. That is why I presented him, Your Honor." Vinkler's excuse did not satisfy the judge.

Vinkler next called inmate Audrey Aeby to establish that Thompson's lay-in on the day of the riot was taken so that he and Aeby could play dominoes. Aeby was a quiet, surly man. He was employed in the kitchen, and therefore had his afternoons free. While this evidence could have been helpful to Thompson's defense, the shoddy handling of the issue rendered his testimony completely worthless.

After identifying Aeby to the jury, and establishing that he and Thompson frequently played dominoes together, Vinkler inquired, "About two weeks prior to May 2, did you and Thompson have a date to play dominoes on May 2, 1946?"

"I don't know," Aeby answered.

"Did you make any date with Thompson as to whether you were to play with him—"

"No," the witness interrupted before Vinkler could finish his question.

Vinkler had relied on Thompson's representation that there was a domino game, and had not reviewed the testimony with Aeby. Now he had to try to educate Aeby and lead his testimony without seeming to do so.

"Well, Mr. Thompson tells me that he had a date with you to—"

"We object to what Thompson may have said," was the anticipated objection from Hennessy.

"Well, I want to refresh his recollection," Vinkler explained, hoping that Aeby would take the hint, and agree that there was to be a domino game on May 2.

"Well," the judge interceded, "he said he has no remembrance." Turning to the witness, Goodman inquired, "Did you have a date to play dominoes with Thompson, the defendant?"

"I don't know."

Attempting to mask his embarrassment, Vinkler retreated. "This is all I have of this witness." When Hennessy had no questions, Aeby was excused.

A restlessness passed through the jury box, prompted by embarrassment for Thompson's lawyers. Hennessy and Deasy again exchanged puzzled glances, surprised at the utter chaos of Spagnoli's case. Deasy, unable to restrain himself, leaned over and whispered his thoughts to Hennessy.

"They must be letting Thompson call the shots as to the witnesses they're putting on. I can't believe they're calling all these cons without knowing what they're going to say. They can't seem to make up their minds on how they want to go with the lay-in. First they try to show that he was really sick and now they're going on 'the domino theory.' It doesn't make any sense. It looks to me like they've lost the jury."

Hennessy only smiled.

Hilliard Sanders was another witness that Thompson's lawyers had apparently never interviewed. He celled on the north side of C block on the second tier overlooking Broadway. He had neither seen nor heard anything significant except the siren and Hubbard holding a rifle. He never saw Thompson. After a few minutes of fruitless questioning, Vinkler sadly inquired, "You do not know very much about what happened that day, do you?"

"No, not very much," Sanders responded. Vinkler terminated the examination.

The next four witnesses contributed nothing but further evidence of the lack of preparedness of Thompson's lawyers. Hughes Hilliard heard the siren, but had neither seen nor heard anything else. Paul Davis was awakened by a flurry of activity and voices. He looked out of the corner of his cell to the west and saw Coy emerge from the gun gallery. Later, he observed Hubbard carrying a rifle. Once again the witness had nothing to contribute, and Vinkler terminated his interrogation after only a few minutes.

Vinkler called Roy Sievertson in an attempt to impeach Baker. It was Vinkler's intention to establish that Sievertson had earlier testified that Baker told him Coy had the rifle rather than Thompson. However, in answer to Vinkler's question, Sievertson stated that he did not remember such a conversation with Baker. Vinkler had not been in court the day Sievertson testified, and had neglected to obtain a copy of the transcript. As a result, there was no way he could substantiate Sievertson's earlier testimony. Flustered and confused, Vinkler abandoned the entire line of questioning. "Your Honor, I will have to excuse this man until I can get a copy of the transcript. I have misplaced it. I haven't got it." Sievertson was excused. For whatever reason, he was never recalled and the issue faded away.

Harry Cochrane was called as another impeachment witness. Cochrane and Baker had shared a room at Marine Hospital while they convalesced from their wounds. Vinkler hoped to establish that Baker told Cochrane that someone other than Thompson was wielding the rifle.

Fumbling with his questions, Vinkler confused Cochrane. At one point he testified, "Baker never had spoken to me that Thompson had the rifle, no, no sir." But then, a few moments later, Cochrane stated, "He didn't say anything about the rifle being thrown on him. He said he did see Thompson with the rifle." Totally confused, Cochrane then testified, "He just told me that Thompson shot the gun at somebody else and the bullet passed through this other person and hit him in the leg."

"He said Thompson shot him?" Vinkler asked in shocked disbelief.

"No, Cretzer shot him with the .45 and the bullet passed through another man and hit him in the leg," Cochrane corrected himself.

Totally confused himself, Vinkler abandoned his attempt to impeach Baker. "That is all I have of this witness, Your Honor."

"Have you any more witnesses?" Goodman inquired.

"I have changed my mind about these other witnesses," responded Vinkler, in obvious retreat. "I do not think I will call these other witnesses now. I am not going to call them. We will call Warden Johnston after the recess. I will not call these other inmate witnesses."

At this point Spagnoli resumed control of the defense, rising to add, "I'm going to call Warden Johnston, but it will take a little time, if Your Honor please. Then we will have Thompson, the defendant as our final witness."

"Do you wish me to call the noon recess at this time?" Goodman asked.

"I think that would be advisable," Spagnoli replied, seeking time to regroup and prepare.

The plan was to divide the examination of Warden Johnston with Spagnoli taking the lead. His would be an aggressive examination, designed to put the warden in an unfavorable light. Vinkler would follow, developing evidence of the brutal conditions at Alcatraz and the high level of insanity among the prisoners.

After establishing that Johnston was a licensed attorney and a member of the California bar, Spagnoli asked rhetorically, "When you were admitted as an attorney at law, you took your oath of office such as all lawyers must take and you are familiar with that oath are you not?"

"Certainly," the warden responded.

"And you know the constitutional right of parties accused of crimes, that they cannot be compelled to testify against themselves." This question was never answered because Hennessy's objection was sustained, but Spagnoli felt he had made his point.

"Well, then, did you violate your oath as an attorney at law, when you permitted within the walls of your institution at Alcatraz, officers of your institution and the Federal Bureau of Investigation to browbeat, threaten and otherwise—"

"I object to that," Hennessy interrupted.

Not waiting for the prosecutor to finish his objection, Goodman lashed out at Spagnoli. "Don't ask that kind of question, or make that kind of statement. It is not becoming to a lawyer. It is not becoming to speak of the public officials of the government in the manner that you were speaking of them, and it is not becoming to slur them in that way. If you have any legitimate questions to ask, you may proceed. Don't ask any questions of that nature anymore."

Spagnoli shifted his line of inquiry.

"On May 2 of this year, Mr. Johnston, you had four inmates in the institution; I'm not sure of their correct names, but known as 'Lefty' Egan, 'Joe Blow' Bell, Raymond Pyle, and James Walsh."

"That is correct."

"Well how soon after May 2," Spagnoli sneered, "was 'Lefty' Egan removed from your penitentiary to some other penitentiary in the United States?"

Hennessy jumped to his feet with an objection, and again Goodman admonished Spagnoli. "What are you trying to do now, go back to the same thing I cautioned you about before? Don't make anymore of those slurring statements. The court has offered to bring any witness that you wanted whose testimony would be material. You did not avail yourself of that offer. Now discontinue this line of questioning."

As Spagnoli began to respond, Goodman harshly cut him off. "I will hear no more. Proceed."

Turning once again to the question of Thompson's FBI statement, the struggling lawyer raised the issue with the warden, then addressed the court with the request: "Will Your Honor order—"

Cutting him off in mid-sentence, Goodman put the matter to rest for good. "No I will not order anything. I will not order any confidential documents of the Department of Justice to be produced for your inspection. Proceed with your questioning."

Spagnoli unceremoniously ended his ineffective examination.

Vinkler's interrogation of Johnston was basically a series of unanswered questions. "Isn't it true, that as of May 4 of this year, at least forty percent of the inmates on Alcatraz were insane?"

Hennessy's objection based on relevance and materiality was sustained.

Vinkler's inquiries as to the availability of religious services and chaplain interviews drew similar objections and rulings. Questions regarding offenses that could result in an inmate being confined to D block, actions of the Alcatraz disciplinary board, comparisons of Alcatraz procedures with those of other prisons, and sanity problems affecting inmates were all blocked by successful objections. His patience exhausted, Goodman, directed, "Don't ask any more questions along that line."

Finally, Vinkler's effort to capitalize on a quotation from Johnston's recent book on penology fell short of the mark. Vinkler had anticipated an adverse evidentiary ruling, but, again, it was the question, not the answer, that he felt was important. "I think you expressed the opinion, Warden, in your book, 'Prison Life Is Different,' that you didn't blame a man for attempting to escape from prison. Isn't that correct?"

Despite the fact that Goodman sustained Hennessy's objection, Johnston felt compelled to respond, "Well I would like you to read the entire book and not just one part, so you get the full meaning."

As in his previous appearances during the trial, Johnston was a strong and effective government witness.

It was well into the afternoon before the warden's testimony was completed. With all the drama he could summon, Spagnoli announced, "We will call the defendant, Miran "Buddy" Thompson." The crowded courtroom was silent as the handsome convict strode confidently to the witness stand. He was enjoying his moment in the spotlight. Over the course of the trial, he had become aware of the reporters sitting together in the press section. After taking the oath and seating himself in the witness chair, he smiled broadly at the press corps. His story and perhaps his picture would be on the front pages of all the papers tomorrow, he thought, and he would have the opportunity to read about himself. Lost in this wave of ego was the gravity of his situation, and the fact that his life depended on the testimony he was about to give.

Spagnoli's first question invited Thompson to explain his criminal background. He eagerly explained that in Texas, he was running from the police, who were attempting to kill him, when he commandeered and drove a car across the state line. Fearing a stream of self-serving explanations, Hennessy objected. His objection was sustained. "I'm not interested in the previous convictions of this witness," Goodman ruled.

From the outset, Thompson's credibility was suspect. He and his attorneys could not settle on an explanation as to why he was laying-in on the afternoon of the riot. Initially, when Spagnoli asked if he had been ill and that was the reason he was excused from work, he responded in the affirmative. In the next breath, he testified that when he returned to his cell before the noon meal, he found a note from Coy inviting him to join the breakout so he sought the lay-in in order to join the escape attempt. On cross-examination, he stated that the note from Coy came after the noon meal. These inconsistencies followed Vinkler's failed effort to establish a domino game with Aeby as the reason for the lay-in. Finally at one point during cross examination, he stated that Herbert offered him the afternoon off to play dominos with Aeby, but he declined the offer.

Thompson admitted being present in Times Square during the capture of Weinhold, Simpson, Baker, and Sundstrom. He denied ever holding a firearm but admitted, "...somebody handed me a club, which I had for a while." His description of Sundstrom's capture was inconsistent with every other version. "I kinda liked Mr. Sundstrom, he never done me no harm. He's the first man who called my attention to this double sentence that they gave me on one of the charges there. So when Hubbard throw'd the rifle on him, I said, 'He's a pretty good guy, Hubbard, don't hurt him.' Cretzer then took the pistol and started to hit him and I said, 'No Cretzer, don't hurt that fellow, he's been a pretty good guy to me.' So he didn't hit Sundstrom, just told him to get into the cell.

"Then Coy said to go get the scaffold. So me and Carnes went down there in front of the library and was pulling on the scaffold and then the siren blowed, started to blow, and I said, 'Well it's getting too rough for me. I'm going to cut out.' So I ran off and Carnes was right behind me. When we got to the end of the cellblock I told Coy, 'Well I'm going to my cell, Coy. I don't want to be in on any shootin's.' Then I heard Coy say to Joe Carnes, 'Come on with me, old man,' or somethin' like that, and they took off towards the kitchen.

"I went up the stairs toward my cell and about the time I got in front of Jack Geary's cell, I heard a rifle shot. Then I asked Jack, 'What would you do if you was me? It's getting pretty tough down there.' And Jack said something like, 'Don't be a dammed fool Buddy, go to your cell before you get killed.' So I went to my cell. I slammed the door shut and I was in my cell for three or four minutes, maybe five or six minutes, when I heard shots down at the west end of the cell house. I heard somebody say, 'Oh take it easy, take it easy.' And then I heard Cretzer say, 'You guys didn't take it easy on me when you were beatin' the shit outta' me over in D block.'"

Thompson recalled seeing the clock in the library shortly after he got back to his cell and it was somewhere between 2:30 and 2:35. In answer to Spagnoli's questions, he vehemently denied urging Cretzer to kill the officers as the hostages had testified. He also heatedly denied the accusation that he aided and abetted in Miller's killing. He not only denied calling for Miller's death, but gratuitously added, "I would never help kill anyone." It was not a well reasoned answer from someone serving a life sentence for the murder of a police officer, and gave Hennessy the opportunity to revisit the defendant's criminal background during cross-examination.

Anxious to present evidence of mistreatment by prison authorities, Spagnoli questioned Thompson about the days immediately following the riot. Spagnoli hoped that this testimony would create some sympathy for his client as well as place the custodial force in a bad light.

Thompson testified how he was threatened and beaten following the riot. "Mr. Miller reached through the bars and grabbed me by the hair and beat me. He held me down with one hand and beat me with the other hand. Mr. Lageson said, 'Let me kill the son of a bitch. I want to get even with him anyhow. I want to fix him right now. Let me fix him up right now.' But Mr. Miller shoved him away and said, 'No, we'll save him for the courts. We can't kill him here, we'll kill him later.'" He then identified the shock of hair that Miller pulled from his head, which was admitted as Exhibit U.

"Then Mr. Miller told me that if I didn't identify everybody that was in on the break, everyone who participated in any way, he was going to kill me. He said he had a gun himself and if I didn't have everything wrote down in the next few minutes, he was going to kill me. He said he'd give me fifteen minutes to write down the names of everybody that was involved, then he left.

"Then about 12:30 in the afternoon on Saturday, Mr. Miller and Mr. Lageson and two or three other officers came back to my cell. They throw'd everything out, everything I owned, including the pictures of my family. They throw'd it all out into the water that was in the corridor. Then Lt. Johnson came to my cell with a rifle and yelled at me. 'I want to kill you, you son of a bitch. I hope you make a false move.' They took everything. All I had was my coveralls and the steel strap bunk to sleep on.

"When I didn't write down what he wanted me to, Mr. Miller said, 'You're gonna talk, you no-good bastard. You're gonna talk before this is all over with.' Then he came back again and threatened me and beat me and everything like they did. And I went all to pieces. I was a nervous wreck all that night. And that night two FBI agents took me, about eleven o'clock, and I was so nervous I couldn't hardly talk to them. And they kept telling me things they wanted me to say. They kept me there for about two hours and wrote out a statement and told me to sign it. I told them that I couldn't sign it and that I wanted to see a lawyer. Then one of them said, 'You will give us a statement before this is over with, or you will wish you did.'"

Thompson described how for the next three days he was deprived of food and then was interviewed again by the FBI. "Well yeah, I was sick by then. Dr. Roucek came in and saw me. And somebody brought me some stew that smelled like billy goat. He brought me some medicine and I drank it. Then he told me that the FBI agents were there and he wanted me to go up and talk to them. He told me that if I didn't, that I knew what Mr. Miller told me. So when I went up to these FBI agents they wrote down a statement they wanted me to sign. I wrote a few lines at the bottom, but

I don't even remember what I said. It was something about giving the statement freely and willingly and then I signed it."

"Did you know the contents of the statement that you signed?"

"No sir, Mr. Spagnoli, I didn't. I don't remember much about that. I was really a nervous wreck. I was scared to death. A man threatens your life, and I knew they had killed other men before over there. They'd shot other men and I knew they would kill me too. I never wrote out the statement and I never read it. I just did what they told me, wrote that little bit at the bottom and signed it."

Having done what he could to present his client to the jury in the best possible light, Spagnoli gestured with a wave to Hennessy and announced, "That is all. Take the witness."

Hennessy began his cross-examination by attacking Thompson's statement that he would never murder anyone. "Isn't it a fact that you were convicted of first degree murder in the state of Texas?" Hennessy challenged. When Spagnoli objected, Thompson interrupted with arrogant confidence, "That's alright, I can explain that."

"Yes, I was framed in that case. That is right, I was framed. Just like you're trying to do to me right now."

"You were convicted of murder in the first degree in Texas, isn't that correct?" Hennessy repeated.

"I was framed there, like you're trying to do here."

"You were convicted, weren't you," Hennessy accused, determined to make him admit his conviction.

"I don't know," Thompson snarled. "You've got the record there, what does it say? You can look at the record."

Thompson's hostility and rancor was glaringly inconsistent with the image Spagnoli had worked to build, of a frightened, nervous inmate, browbeaten into signing a statement. That portrait evaporated instantly under Hennessy's aggressive grilling. In its place was one of a hardened criminal and killer.

"And you are now serving a life sentence in the penitentiary at Alcatraz for kidnapping and murder?" Hennessy continued relentlessly.

"Well, it was supposed to be ninety-nine years." He responded venomously, "The police were trying to kill me. I got in a car with a girl that was going to Mexico and I asked her if I could go with her and she said yes. And when we got to the roadblock, I got out of the car before they could shoot at the car or that lady. And that is what I got life for."

Because Thompson had given three versions of the lay-in plus the contradictory domino testimony, Hennessy chose not to introduce his FBI statement. Although the statement was damning, as Thompson admitted knowing about the break several days in advance, Hennessy knew that Thompson would claim the statement was coerced. Hennessy would then be forced to defend the agents' actions, and call them as witnesses. This would unnecessarily complicate what was already gross inconsistency by the defense. Hennessy was happy just to accept the defense's own discrepancies.

Thompson's antagonistic attitude resurfaced when Hennessy questioned him about shooting the hostages. "Isn't it a fact that at that time and place you said, 'Yes, kill every one of them, we don't want any witnesses'?"

"Mr. Hennessy, like I told you, I was not there. I could not have said that. I was in my cell. I did not say that."

"Well didn't you accompany Cretzer to the next cell? Didn't Cretzer then fire into the cell where Captain Weinhold was with the other officers?"

Eyes narrowed and teeth clenched, Thompson sarcastically responded, "I might have a twin, like me. But it was not me. My twin may have been there, but not me."

Hennessy ended his cross-examination by accusing Thompson of using the rifle. "Didn't you have the rifle in your possession outside the cell in which Captain Weinhold was lying wounded?"

"No, I did not have a rifle."

"Captain Weinhold, therefore, was in error when he testified he saw you pass the cell with the rifle in your hand while he was lying wounded in the second cell?"

"I don't care what Captain Weinhold said, he never saw the rifle in my hand because I never had the rifle in my hand." The witness's soft image had been totally stripped away.

25

As each attorney arrived on that morning, the clerk advised him that the judge wished to meet with counsel in chambers prior to bringing in the jury. At five minutes to ten with all counsel gathered in chambers, Goodman announced, "Gentlemen, we have a problem with juror number one, Mr. Willis. As you know he is a self-employed architect practicing in Oakland. This morning he presented a note to the clerk, explaining that service on this jury has become an economic burden and continued service will work an extreme financial hardship on his family. I have discussed the situation with him and he advises that since he is self-employed and, now as a juror in this matter unable to work, he has received no income since the commencement of the trial, approximately a month ago. It would be my suggestion therefore, that unless one of you gentlemen have strong feelings to the contrary, we stipulate that Mr. Willis be excused and his place taken by the first alternate, Mr. Leland Butcher. We will still have one alternate juror and Mr. Zamloch has advised us that he estimates that his case will require no more than two days. I think that the case can be completed by the end of the week and surely we should be able to get by with one alternate for that period of time. Does anybody have any problem with that?"

Silence indicated the attorneys' acquiescence. As Goodman directed his clerk to have the bailiff bring in the jury, he added, "This really constitutes no significant change in jury composition as we are replacing one male professional with another. Mr. Butcher, as I recall, is an engineer. I will advise the jury of the situation." Turning to Zamloch he inquired, "Are you prepared to go forward with your case this morning, Mr. Zamloch?"

"Yes, Your Honor, and I am confident that we can complete Carnes's case before the end of the day tomorrow.

"Very well gentlemen, let's get to work."

"What do you think, Frank?" Deasy inquired as the prosecutors returned to the courtroom.

"It's fine with me," Hennessy remarked, "that guy Willis looked kind of squirrelly to me anyway. Besides, I like engineers. They're a little boring, but generally pretty hardnosed."

Once on the bench, Goodman addressed the jurors. "Circumstances have been presented to me which indicate that it would be improper for juror number one, Mr. Willis, to remain in the jury box. I have advised counsel on all sides of this case concerning the matter, and by stipulation Mr. Willis will be excused from further service on the jury. The first alternate is Mr. Butcher. He will assume Mr. Willis's place on the jury. You may be excused, Mr. Willis. Mr. Butcher, you may remain where you are in the box."

"When we finished Friday, Mr. Thompson was on the stand and Mr. Sullivan, you had a few questions, you wished to ask on cross-examination."

"Yes, Your Honor, that is correct." Sullivan's brief questioning was devoted to Thompson's observations of Shockley. "Well I saw Shockley in different places—I can't say I saw him in no certain place. He was just running up and down in front of the cells like he didn't know what he was doing. He just wrang his hands and was hollering, 'Let's get outta here, let's get outta here,' and that is about all I heard him saying."

When asked who was in charge, Thompson responded without equivocation. "Well, Cretzer was giving the orders. I would say he was giving even Marv Hubbard and Coy the orders as to what they were supposed to do. And, as to Shockley, he wasn't givin' no orders to nobody."

Zamloch had painstakingly prepared his case. Like Thompson, Carnes suggested a number of inmates who had volunteered to testify on his behalf. Unlike Spagnoli, however, Zamloch had meticulously followed each lead. He interviewed every inmate recommended, along with several others he found on his own. After several visits to Alcatraz and many hours of interviews, he settled on just eight witnesses, in addition to his client.

Like most good trial lawyers, Zamloch believed in keeping everything brief and simple, making it easy for the jury to follow his case. Every witness was called for a specific purpose, to prove one or more elements of the factual picture. Zamloch also believed that it was important to start his case with his most effective witness, and conclude with his client. Scheduled as his first witness was Theodore J. "Blackie" Audett. Audett would provide extremely helpful evidence, and was an affable, friendly individual, who would make a good impression on the jury. A handsome, dark-haired man, five feet, ten inches tall and forty-four years of age, he appeared candid, despite his extensive criminal record.

Born in Oregon in 1902 to farming parents, Audett's family moved to a homestead in Alberta, Canada when he was a child. His parents separated when he was ten and he lived alone or with relatives until he was fourteen. After convincing recruiters that he was seventeen, he joined the Canadian Army. He served heroically in France during World War I, suffering several wounds during combat and surviving two German poison gas attacks. After his discharge however, he craved the easy life, and became an alcohol runner. Audett's criminal career was launched.

Despite his congenial appearance, Audett was a hardened criminal with multiple convictions for robbery and escape. His prison background included four separate federal incarcerations, two each in McNeil Island and Leavenworth. He was also one of the few inmates to serve more than one term on Alcatraz, ultimately serving three separate incarcerations on the Rock. In 1946, however, he was experiencing good times. He was employed in the kitchen, where he enjoyed excellent working conditions. He had considerable free time to spend on recreational activities, and was within five months of discharge. Although he was a notorious escapist, he had less than a year to serve at the time of the riot, and had, therefore, rejected offers from Cretzer and Coy to join in the break.

After establishing Audett's background, Zamloch brought out that the inmate had finished his kitchen duties, and was on his way back to his cell shortly after 1:30 P.M. "When you stepped into the main cell house did you see any inmates?"

"I did. I saw Bernie Coy and Hubbard."

"Was Coy armed?"

"He was. And when I saw that I just turned around and ran right back into the kitchen. And as I came back into the kitchen, Mr. Burdett got up and started for the main cell house. When Mr. Burdett got about half way across the dining hall, Coy opened the door between the dining hall and the main cell house and waved for him to come. Burdett started to run, and just as he got to the door, Coy drawed the gun out from behind his back and pointed it at Mr. Burdett. After that I stayed in the kitchen."

"How long was it after you saw Mr. Burdett taken prisoner by Coy, till any inmates came into the kitchen?"

"In approximately five minutes, Coy carrying the rifle and Hubbard carrying a belt of ammunition came to the kitchen, and Coy asked me if there were any guards or stewards still in the kitchen. I told him no, and he and Hubbard left and went back to the cell house."

"What happened then?"

Audett explained how for the next few minutes he stood peering out from the safety of the kitchen into the cell house, and saw the parade of guards come down Broadway to be captured by the armed convicts. Following the capture of all the officers, he heard the escape siren. "After the alarm sounded, Coy, Hubbard, and Carnes came into the kitchen. Coy was still carrying the rifle and Hubbard had the cartridge belt slung over his shoulder."

"Did you have a conversation with any of the prisoners when they entered the kitchen?" inquired Zamloch.

"Yes. As Coy walked into the kitchen I heard him say to one of the other guys working in there, 'We got a rumble go'in out there. We can't make it.' Then Carnes asked me what we were having for supper." The young defendant's incongruous comment drew smiles from a number of the jurors. It also suggested that Carnes believed that the escape attempt had failed and he expected to have a regular prison dinner that night. As Audett spoke, Carnes sat stone-faced, his chin cupped in his hand, staring at the tabletop in front of him.

"Coy walked right on past me, past the officers' mess and into a small room with a window that looked down toward the dock. He smashed out one of the panes of glass and fired two shots through the window at the Dock Tower. Right after that, Carnes, who was standing near me, said something to Coy about the shooting. From where I was I couldn't hear just what he said, but it was something about his shooting."

"Did you observe Carnes go over to Hubbard and have a conversation with him?"

"Yes, I did, but I couldn't hear what they said either."

"What happened then?"

"Well, Coy went into the bakeshop, which is the room beyond the kitchen. He fired two more shots out one of the windows at the guard in the Hill Tower. He came out of the bakeshop and went over by the dish tank on the other side of the kitchen and fired two more shots out of that window at the Road Tower."

"Did you hear any other gunfire at that time?"

"Yes. Right after Coy shot out of the window by the dish tank, I heard a burst of gunfire in the cell house. In fact I heard two bursts; two short bursts of gunfire that sounded like they came from somewhere over by D block. And they were from a pistol, not a rifle."

"Where was Carnes when you heard those two short bursts of pistol fire?"

"He was standing between the kitchen and dining hall beside Hubbard."

"What happened next?" Zamloch prompted.

"Then the three of them left the kitchen and walked through the dining hall toward the cell house. As they did, Hubbard took the rifle from Coy."

"Let me interrupt you," interjected Zamloch. "As they were walking through the dining hall toward the cell house, was Carnes walking abreast of them or was he behind them?"

"Well, Coy and Hubbard were walking beside each other, Coy to Hubbard's left and Hubbard to Coy's right. By the time they got to the cell house door Carnes was walking behind Hubbard."

"What happened when they got to the cell house door?"

"Well, I seen the associate warden, Mr. Miller, coming down Broadway. He was about halfway down Broadway from the main gate. The three guys were talking, but I couldn't hear what they were saying. When they got to the door, Coy pulled the door open and Hubbard stepped out, threw the rifle to his shoulder, and fired at Mr. Miller. As he did, Carnes kept walking and shoved him, hit his arm. Carnes was only a couple of steps behind him when they got to the door. Hubbard dropped the gun from his shoulder, and turned around to face Carnes. Carnes backed away. Just what they said, I don't know. All I know is that Hubbard had the gun pointed into Carnes's face."

"What was the next thing you saw?"

"Well, Coy broke and ran into the cell house and Carnes and Hubbard did too. That was the last I saw of any of them and I stayed in the kitchen until Saturday night about eleven o'clock."

Hennessy's cross-examination merely gave Audett a chance to repeat his testimony and the prosecutor could not reduce his effectiveness. Unable to shake Audett's story or develop any inconsistencies, Hennessy attempted to lay a foundation for impeachment based on an earlier FBI statement. However, the few minor inconsistencies between Audett's testimony and his unsigned FBI statement were not significant enough to cast doubt on his credibility.

Zamloch's next witness was George Ward, a forty-four-year-old bank robber, whose gang had terrorized the Southwest banking community in the early 1930s. Ward was convicted in Oklahoma on three counts of bank robbery in 1934, and was sentenced to 45 years in prison. He was subsequently tried and convicted in federal court, and received a ninety-nine year sentence. Because of his lengthy sentences, he was viewed as an escape risk and transferred to Alcatraz. Ward would not complete his federal sentence until he was 131 years old nor be eligible for parole until age 120. At that time, he would still face the unserved Oklahoma sentence of 43 more years. Despite this bleak future, Ward was a likable inmate who had accepted his fate and lived comfortably within the prison rules and regulations.

Ward testified that on the day of the riot he had remained in his cell after dinner, as he was scheduled for visits to the barbershop and hospital. After the work crews cleared the cell house, he was released to the barbershop. Thereafter, he visited the hospital for treatment of a nagging skin rash. At approximately 2:00 P.M., he was released from the hospital and, along with inmate Peck Mahoney, descended the stairs to return to his cell. At the bottom of the stairs was a door that led into the dining hall. This door had a glass viewing panel, and anyone seeking passage through it needed to summon the cell house officer by ringing a buzzer that sounded in the cell house.

"What did you do when you reached this door?" asked Zamloch.

"Well, there is no guard stationed there all the time. So I rang the bell and sat down on the steps for a few minutes to wait till he came by."

"Who was the first person you saw walk by the door that afternoon?"

"The first person I saw was Blackie Audett. He came from the kitchen, through the mess hall and towards the door to the cellblock. But he didn't go into the cellblock. He opened the door, then turned around and went back into the kitchen. I yelled at him when I first saw him to tell the cell house officer I was waiting to be passed through, but he just looked into the cell house, shut the door, and ran back into the kitchen. I yelled at him again, 'Hey Blackie, let me outta here,' but he didn't pay no attention."

Ward stated that he next saw Burdett pass through the dining hall and open the door to the cell house. When the door opened, Ward observed Coy standing in the cell house with a rifle in his hands. Burdett then disappeared into the cell house behind the closing door.

Ward went on to describe his observations as he stood looking through the window. They were entirely consistent with those of Audett. He saw Coy and Hubbard go into the kitchen and in a minute or so return to the cell house. A few minutes later the siren sounded, and he saw Coy and Hubbard return to the kitchen, this time with Carnes. Coy carried the rifle and the other two were unarmed. He heard a series of rifle shots from the kitchen, after which the three inmates returned to the dining hall, heading for the cell house. When the trio was halfway across the dining hall, Ward heard two bursts of pistol fire, four or five shots in each burst. This sound came from within the cell house.

"When they got to the end of the mess hall, Coy walks up to the door and opens it. Then he stepped back and said to Hubbard, 'Let the son of a bitch have it.' Hubbard throw'd the rifle to his shoulder and fired. Just as he did, Carnes stepped up behind him and jostled his shoulder from behind, like this," and the witness lurched forward from his seat on the witness stand, demonstrating the movement made by Carnes.

"How many times did Hubbard fire?" the lawyer inquired.

"One shot, only one shot.

"Then Hubbard let the rifle down and turned around to Carnes, looking at Carnes. At that time Carnes backed up a little and said, 'I tripped, sorry, I tripped.' Coy was still holding the door and at that same instant he started to run back towards the kitchen. Hubbard and Carnes both started to run and I run up the hospital steps."

"Did you at any time come down those stairs to the dining hall again?"

"No sir."

"What happened to the other inmate who was with you?"

"Mahoney. Well he went up those stairs long before me. He was up there when I got up there. There's a little hallway up there and that's where we spent the next two days."

Although Ward had been interviewed by the FBI, they had never asked him about Carnes, and his testimony came as a complete surprise to the prosecution. Hennessy's cross-examination was brief and ineffective. Despite his extensive criminal background and monumental sentences, Ward was a convincing witness. His easy manner and candid style were well received by the jury. Zamloch made his testimony ever more forceful by keeping the examination brief and to the point. As a result Ward's testimony was clear and uninterrupted by prosecution objections.

Zamloch recalled Thomas Robinson, the college-educated kidnapper of Nashville socialite Alice Stoll. Robinson had been well prepared by Zamloch, and knew exactly how his testimony fit into Carnes's defense. "I was in cell 170 on the second tier, the first cell east of the cut-off on the north side of B block. Carnes occupied cell 146, that was on the flats and just a few cells to the west of and below me."

Robinson went on to explain that he was a cell house orderly, and as such would remain in his cell after dinner until approximately 2:30 P.M. At that time he would be let out to carry out his scheduled duties within the cell house. On May 2, however, he was never released to go to work. Instead, at some time around two o'clock that afternoon, he heard the escape siren sound. In clear, articulate language, the dapper convict described his observations.

"I would say, a few minutes following the blowing of the siren, there were several rifle shots. These did not come from the cell house. They came from the rear, someplace inside the building, but not in the main cell house, the west end of the building. Immediately following the rifle shots came two bursts of automatic pistol fire from the vicinity of D block in the main cell house." Based on his personal experience of having owned and frequently fired a .45, Robinson expressed the opinion that the two bursts he heard near D block were definitely from a .45 automatic pistol.

"Following the bursts of pistol fire, in less than a minute, I heard a single rifle shot. This rifle fire was inside the cell house and came from the west end of the cell house. I can't say just where the sound came from, but it was inside the cell house and near the west end."

"Following that single rifle shot, did you hear any more gunfire?"

"Yes. Right after the rifle shot, was one more pistol shot from the same general area as I had heard the two bursts of pistol fire. I would estimate that this final pistol shot was fired less than a minute after the single rifle shot."

Robinson then revealed that immediately after the final pistol shot, he was aware of a cell door below and to the west of his cell slide shut. "I also heard some inmates below me yell at Carnes. Then we all yelled at Carnes, several of us up in my tier, wanting to know what was happening and what was going on down there."

"Were you acquainted with Carnes at this time and familiar with his voice?" Zamloch led the witness.

"Yes, we were transferred from Leavenworth together and got to know each other. Also Carnes has a very soft voice that is easily recognizable. There is no question in my mind that it was Carnes's voice that I heard."

"What did you hear Carnes say at that time?"

"Well, Carnes stated that everything was all messed up and that several officers were hurt. He complained that the other fellows had lied to him. They had told him there would be no shooting or killing and as soon as he found out what was going on, he returned to his cell. He stated that he didn't want any part of the shooting or killing."

Robinson was also able to provide some testimony on the issue of post riot brutality. He testified that late Friday afternoon he observed the associate warden and several guards remove Carnes from his cell and, after stripping off his clothes, march him naked into the old library in A block. Giving credence to his other testimony, Robinson made no effort to fabricate any information regarding prison brutality.

Although not mentioned during his testimony, Robinson claimed to have evidence that one or more officers received advance warnings of the attempted breakout. He volunteered this knowledge to the FBI, but the investigating agents never followed up on the information. While rumors of all kinds circulated within the prison, it was unusual that the investigators took so little interest in Robinson's suggestions, particularly since he was not known as a purveyor of false information.

Handsome, young Ernest Lopez, who occupied a cell on the B block flats, five cells to the east of Carnes, was Zamloch's next witness. Lopez's initial federal offense was a relatively minor one, involving illegal dealings with gasoline ration stamps during World War II. Following his conviction, he attempted to escape, and in the process assaulted a federal officer. This resulted in the addition of ten years to his sentence. He was branded an escape risk and transferred to Alcatraz.

Lopez related a factual scenario almost identical to that set forth by Robinson. He heard cell doors rack open about 2:00 P.M., but paid no heed. His first awareness of anything unusual was the sound of the siren. Two or three minutes after the siren sounded, he heard the same series of gunshots testified to by Robinson. In addition, he heard a gas billy being activated after the single rifle shot at the west end of the cell house but before the single pistol shot from the vicinity of D block.

Within minutes after this final shot, he saw Carnes return to his cell. "Yes, I hollered at him," Lopez explained. "I asked him what was going on and he told me that everything was all messed up. He said that these so and sos had lied to him and that as soon as he saw what was going on he got away from them as quick as he could. He said some of the guards had been hurt and he didn't want any part of it."

Finally he confirmed Robinson's version of the events of May 3, when Carnes was removed from his cell, stripped, and taken naked to A block. He testified that he saw the young inmate with Associate Warden Miller, who struck him and referred to him as a "dirty Indian son of a bitch." They made him stand out in front of his cell with his hands up in the air and he had no clothes on. Then they took him over to A block. He still had his hands in the air and he didn't have no clothes on. That was the last time I ever seen him."

George Dillon was called as the next defense witness, and a lengthy delay occurred before the small, balding man was ushered into the courtroom through a side door. Considered a serious escape treat, he had been transported from the island in double shackles under triple guard. Several minutes were required to remove his various chains and manacles before he could be led to the witness stand. Regardless of the escape threat he presented, the unbending federal court policy prevailed and Dillon entered the courtroom free of physical restraints. During the delay, the jury waited patiently, unaware of the flurry of activity just outside the door.

Dillon's crimes included robbery, burglary, larceny, auto theft, several escapes, and assault. He had been bald since his youth, and maintained an extensive collection of toupees. While living in the Seattle area, he posed as a student, dating co-eds at the University of Washington and becoming an integral part of the student society. He gained information about students and their families, then burglarized the homes and businesses of those who had befriended him. He was finally apprehended and identified as the notorious Seattle cat burglar. After his conviction in 1944, he was imprisoned at McNeil Island. Because of repeated escape attempts, he was transferred to Alcatraz. Hostile and verbally aggressive, he was nonetheless a model prisoner, never attempting to escape from Alcatraz.

Dillon's testimony seemed candid and objective and was consistent with that of the two previous witnesses regarding the sequence of gunshots. Dillon also heard the gas billy explosion and recalled commenting to one of his neighbors, "Well, here comes the gas."

He then described seeing and hearing Carnes return to his cell. He stated that he, along with others, had called out to Carnes to find out what had been going on and paraphrased Carnes's responses. "Those guys are crazy. They took me out there and asked me if I wanted to 'go home' and told me they would be taking over things in the cell house. They said they could do everything without no injury to anyone and no shooting, and I fell for it. They told me that no one would be hurt. Now there's no chance on earth of getting outta here and they're going crazy, shooting everybody. They're crazy, and I sold out. When they started shooting people, I sold out and came back to my cell."

Unable to shake Dillon's testimony on cross-examination, Hennessy began questioning him about his prior convictions. Although he dealt with the questions satisfactorily for a time, Dillon eventually lost his composure and displayed a bitter hostility, partially tearing away his façade of objectivity. "I am not on trial here, and I do not see how that is pertinent," Dillon assailed Hennessy in anger.

"I am asking you the questions," Hennessy shot back coldly. "And you were convicted of robbery, were you not?"

"That is right," the hostile convict finally admitted, eyes burning and fists clenching the arms of the witness chair. Zamloch objected in an effort to protect his witness, but Hennessy, satisfied he had injured Dillon's credibility, dropped the line of inquiry and concluded his cross-examination.

The afternoon recess was a welcome respite. As the jury filed out, Zamloch looked over his notes and realized he had only three witnesses left to finish out the day. Carnes would take the stand in the morning, and his case would be complete. The attorney felt good about the defense. Everything had gone as he had planned. The only question was how the jury would react to what was before them. Engrossed in his notes and the day's remaining witnesses, Zamloch remained at the counsel table, passing up an opportunity for a cigarette break and hallway conversation with his fellow barristers.

Billy Bernard Bledsoe took the stand after the recess. The thirty-three-year-old Texas burglar was within nine months of completing his ten-year sentence, and had not been eager to appear as a witness. After several meetings and appeals to the inmate's "duty to do the right thing," Zamloch had convinced him to come to court and tell his story.

Bledsoe's version was a carbon copy of that given by Zamloch's other inmate witnesses. Occupying cell #168 on the second tier of B block in the cell immediately east of Tom Robinson, Bledsoe had been privy to all the same sounds and conversations. His descriptions of Carnes's comments dovetailed with those of the other witnesses and included Carnes regretfully wishing that he had never allowed himself to become involved in the attempted escape.

His case winding down, Zamloch called Kenneth G. Palmer, whose well fitting prison suit and white pocket handkerchief made him look more like a Montgomery Street broker than the Detroit auto worker turned bank robber that he was. Palmer commenced his twenty-year sentence in the federal prison at Atlanta, but after becoming a problem inmate was sent to Alcatraz. By May of 1946, his attitude had changed and, at the age of thirty-eight, he had settled into doing his time quietly.

On the day of the riot, Palmer was part of the regular work force. When the riot broke out he, along with the other outside inmates, was brought to the prison yard. After spending Thursday night and most of Friday in the yard, Palmer and the others were relocated to A block. He testified that sometime between 3:00 and 5:00 P.M. Friday, he observed Carnes being marched, naked, into an A block cell. "My cell was right in front of the stairs. I saw Mr. Miller and Carnes with his hands above his head. Carnes was naked."

When asked to describe what he observed, he stated, "Well, I heard a lot of swearing and cursing, and I heard Mr. Miller say, 'I'll knock your goddamn head off.' Then he said, 'I'll cut your goddamn head off, you Indian son of a bitch,' or something to that effect. Then I heard a lot of thumping. I didn't hear Carnes say anything. The only voice I recognized was Mr. Miller's. I heard a lot of grunting, like the sound of somebody being beat up, somebody getting hit a lot. Then I heard Mr. Miller say, 'I've got a knife. How does this feel to you, you Indian son of a bitch. I did hear him say that."

The final witness of the day, William Howard Dunn, corroborated Palmer's testimony regarding the beating of Carnes. He described how the naked Carnes was brought up the stairs in A block, pushed along and cursed at by the associate warden and two other officers. As the youngster was pushed into a cell, Dunn heard the associate warden threaten and beat the convict. "I'm gonna' show you what it's like to have a knife at your throat," he quoted Miller. Dunn went on to describe a great commotion, the sounds of blows being struck, and the sound of a body hitting the floor. He said the cells vibrated, as if somebody had hit the floor. "I heard the associate swearing and trying to get Carnes to confess. He kept saying, 'Didn't you kill that officer?' Carnes didn't say anything. Then they hit him again. In a few more minutes I heard Mr. Miller say, 'Can't you talk? I'll put this knife in your throat and show you how it feels to have a knife at your throat,' then I heard a body fall."

"Did you hear Carnes make any sounds?" Zamloch went on.

"Well, yes. It sounded like moaning to me. I couldn't say for sure whether it was moans or groans, but they were those kind of sounds coming from that cell."

26

Zamloch was tense as he made his way through the bustling crowds of Christmas shoppers. He barely noticed the festive Christmas decorations hanging from the lampposts and gracing the store windows, so lost was he in deep contemplation. His thoughts were consumed by the upcoming testimony of his teenage client, whose life was on the line today. All of his witnesses except Carnes had given their testimony, and it was finally the young Choctaw's turn. Zamloch expected that most of the court day would be devoted to Carnes's testimony.

He had done everything possible to prepare the youngster. Now it would all be up to Clarence, particularly during Hennessy's cross-examination. Zamloch believed that the humanitarian aspect of Carnes's defense was critical, and he hoped that Carnes's preoccupation with being a "tough con" would not prevent the young man from providing favorable testimony. The fact that he falsely reported all the hostages dead, combined with his efforts to save Lageson and Miller, might convince the jury to spare his life, provided his testimony was credible. Carnes's cross-examination would be the most frustrating portion of the trial for Zamloch, watching his client on the stand and not being able to help him. The young defendant would be entirely on his own. Although he was not a religious man, Zamloch realized he was saying a silent prayer that Carnes would do a good job.

In the courtroom, Zamloch appeared his usual cool, competent self. But his heart was pounding with nervous apprehension as he called Carnes to the stand. "How old are you, Clarence?" he began.

"Nineteen."

He then took Carnes through his early life, including the murder conviction when he was only sixteen. Overlooking his early boyhood misdeeds, Carnes testified that he had never been in any trouble up to that point. He went on to explain, candidly that the killing occurred during the course of a robbery, and that he was subsequently sentenced to life in prison. While at the Oklahoma State Reformatory he and two other young men ran away, commandeering an automobile and driver, then crossing the state line into Texas. After his capture, he pleaded *nolo contendere* to kidnap charges, and, although the owner of the automobile was uninjured, Carnes received a ninety-nine year sentence. After two months in Leavenworth he was transferred to Alcatraz, and, at the time of the riot, was on idle status by order of the prison doctor.

Visibly nervous at first, Carnes appeared to gain confidence with each question. He was suffering from a heavy cold and both the judge and his attorney had to periodically remind him to keep his voice up so the jurors could hear him.

Zamloch focused his questions on the events of May 2, and as the attorney had promised in his opening statement, Carnes's version of the facts varied only slightly from the versions of the custodial witnesses. Carnes testified that shortly after the noon meal Coy stopped by his cell with the electrifying news that a break was taking place that afternoon. "He came to my cell and he looked kinda nervous. He said to me, 'How much time are you doin', life?'

"Ninety-nine years," I said. "Then he laughed and said, 'Hell that's more than life. Well I'll tell ya, old man, there's gonna be something come off this evening and if you want to come, I'll rack open your door. If you wanna come out, you can come out. If you don't, just stay put.' Then he walked away."

Coy had told him stories of an old Spanish tunnel leading from the cell house to the dock that had been walled up in earlier years. Carnes wondered if that was to be the escape route. He lay on his bunk for some time, thinking about what his friend had just told him. Later in the afternoon, Coy again appeared outside Carnes's cell. This time he went to his small office directly across the corridor. "He was in his little office for a while, then he came to my cell and tossed a couple of notebooks on my bunk. 'Keep these for me, old man.' From the way he was acting, fixing up all the magazines, I thought the whole thing was off, but then he gave me a thumbs up signal, and I knew that everything was still going as planned. This time, when he came to my cell, he didn't appear nervous at all."

The young inmate stated he waited, not knowing what he should do, when heard the lock on his door click and realized that someone had just unlocked his cell. He slid the door open and stepped out of his cell. He looked up and down the corridor, but saw no one. He returned to his cell, grabbed the two notebooks Coy had given him and stuffed them in his pocket. "I walked out to the west end of B block, and just stood there. Then I heard someone trying to draw my attention, going 'psst, psst,' making a noise like that. First I thought it was coming from the tier on C block, then I glanced up and saw Hubbard standing on the outside of the gun gallery, with his feet on top of the sheet of steel at the bottom of the top tier of the gallery."

Carnes detailed how Hubbard directed him to pick up a homemade stiletto sitting on top of the basement stairway enclosure and instructed him to stand clear of the window in the door to the dining hall. As he assumed a position to keep a watch down Broadway, Carnes heard the hospital buzzer ring, and looked over at the door to see George Ward waiting to be passed into the cell house. About that same time, he observed Bristow coming down Broadway. "When I saw Mr. Bristow, he saw me. I knew that I couldn't go back to my cell now, as he would identify me as being involved in the break, so I decided I would stay with it.

"Bristow came on down Broadway, and when he got to the west end he looked around, looking for the officer, I guess, to let him through the door into the kitchen. He glanced at me, but he didn't pay much attention to me. I stood there for a moment, then I looked up at Hubbard. He was waving his hands at me and I couldn't tell whether he wanted me to take Bristow or let him through the dining hall door. I knew I had to do something, so I went over and took him by the coat lapel and showed him the stiletto. I said, 'I guess we better go over here.' I walked him over by the cell house officer's desk so we were out of sight of anyone coming down Broadway or looking out the window in the dining hall door."

"Did Bristow appear frightened?"

"Well, when we got under the gun cage, his face was calm, but I could feel his body shaking. It gave me courage."

Up to that point in his testimony, Carnes's manner had been stoic and unemotional, but when he described Bristow's obvious fear, he smiled slightly. This troubled Zamloch, for if the jury felt that Carnes had derived any pleasure from his victim's fear, the credibility of his humanitarian defense would suffer.

Carnes testified that he then saw Cretzer standing near the door to D block. Cretzer opened and closed the small viewing panel in the D block door, banging it twice quickly and making a loud noise. Then he directed Carnes to bring Bristow over to C block and place him in cell #404, which was used as the officers' toilet. "Just as I got there, the door to D block opened. Corwin looked out, and immediately closed the door. About that time there was a rumbling noise up in the gun cage. The door slammed and a real rumbling noise started."

When he arrived at cell #404 with Bristow, Carnes observed that Moyle and Egan, along with Officer Miller, were already confined to that cell. "We all stood there looking at the door in the gun cage and listening to the noise coming from the D block side. When it ended Cretzer said, 'We better get inside the cell, we don't know whose gonna come outta' that door,' so we all went in the cell. We were kinda peeking out to see what was happening."

"What did you see?" Zamloch asked.

"I saw Coy come out through the door with a rifle under his right arm. He motioned for somebody to come over, below the cage, then he disappeared back into D block. In a moment he reappeared, pulling Burch along. Burch was dazed and stumbling, but he was on his feet. Hubbard and Cretzer went over to the gallery and asked for the guns. Cretzer said, Gimme the pistol, Coy,' in kind of a whiny voice. Coy didn't pay any attention to them, cause he was busy with Burch. I stepped out of the cell and just stood there, watching Coy. He was dragging Burch along and Burch kept stumbling. Finally he hit Burch with his right hand. He hit him pretty hard and he just dropped, disappeared behind the steel shield."

Right after that, he saw Coy pass the guns down to Cretzer and Hubbard and the two, now armed, banged on the D block door, demanding entry. "Cretzer ran up to the door and lowered the shutter. He pointed the pistol at the glass and yelled to someone in D block, 'Open up, you son of a bitch.' Then Hubbard ran up with the rifle and pointed it at the glass and said, 'Open up, you bastard, or I'll blow your head off.' At that moment, the door opened and they went in."

Carnes testified that Hubbard was in D block for a short time, then came back under the gun gallery and received a number of clubs from Coy. "Hubbard was only in there—I couldn't say how long—just a short while and he came out. Coy handed him some clubs down from the gallery and he laid them all out on the cell house officer's desk. He got a bunch of keys too. Then Hubbard told me, 'Get you a club and stick around here.' So I got a club and stood guard outside of the end cell."

Thereafter, Carnes described how Lageson and Burdett entered the cell house, and were captured. "I think the next officer to come in was Mr. Lageson. It might have been Mr. Burdett, they came kinda at the same time and were taken by Coy and Hubbard. I don't know which one of them had the rifle, but they captured Lageson and Burdett and put them both in the end cell. Then I ran over to isolation to look. I had never been over there and didn't know what the place looked like. I had heard a lot about isolation, '…better stay outta isolation…' and all of that, so I went in there to have a look around. I was only in there for a minute or so and started back. When I was coming out, Cretzer was coming out with Corwin."

Carnes stated that he spent most of the time standing outside of the hostage cell holding a club. He recalled that at one point he was asked by Burdett to untie Miller. "I don't remember just when it happened, but while I was standing outside the end cell, Mr. Burdett asked me if he could untie Mr. Miller's hands and I said he could. Then he and Bristow untied Mr. Miller." Since this minor act of goodwill by Carnes resulted in the disappearance of key # 107, Zamloch considered it an important piece of his defense mosaic.

Carnes's testimony regarding Weinhold's capture was consistent with the captain's version. "Hubbard threw the rifle on him as he got to Times Square and Coy grabbed him by the arm. Then Hubbard said to me, 'Come'ere and give me a hand.' So I went over and we took him to Coy's cell. Coy took the captain's pants and jacket and his whistle. Then he told me, 'You stay here. Stay here with Weinhold.'"

"What did Captain Weinhold say to you and what did you say to him, as near as you can remember?" asked Zamloch.

"Well, I remember some questions, some remarks, but what I really remember is how calm he seemed. And then he said, 'What I would really like to know is how you guys got those guns.' I was standing right in front of the cell and I pointed up to where I had seen Hubbard and Coy. I told him that I thought Coy had a bar spreader and he got into the gun cage and took the guns.

"In a few minutes, Hubbard shouted, 'Bring that son of a bitch Weinhold over here,' so I told Weinhold to come out. I have this picture in my mind of seeing Sam Shockley hitting at Captain Weinhold, you know, hitting at him. The captain ducked and Sam missed him and fell down. I think Weinhold knocked him down, 'cause Sam got up yelling, and Cretzer had to calm him down."

Carnes's testimony turned to the capture of Baker and Lt. Simpson, and Goodman declared the morning recess. Maintaining his cool, emotionless appearance, Carnes stepped down from the witness stand and took his place at the counsel table. Zamloch sat beside him and put his arm around the young man's shoulder. "You're doing just fine, Clarence, just fine. Stay with it, just the way you're going and everything's going to be alright." It was the same kind of encouragement Zamloch had given clients on many occasions in the past. He didn't always believe what he said, but this time he did. Carnes was doing a good job and Zamloch was not concerned about his unemotional style. *After all*, he thought to himself, *to be where this kid is at age nineteen is not something to create a happy face. All I want is for the jury to believe him.*

Following the recess, Carnes testified that the two captive inmates became restless as the cell began to fill with guards. "Egan kept saying, 'Hey, get me and this other con the hell outta here,' and stuff like that. Finally Coy said, 'Okay come on out then,' and took them and put them in Cretzer's cell, just down the way."

Zamloch then had Carnes testify on behalf of his co-defendants. "Did you at any time ever see Thompson with a gun in his hands?"

"No Sir, never."

"Did you observe Shockley and how he was acting?"

"Yes."

"Will you tell the court and jury what he was doing and how he was acting?"

"Well Shockley was running around, and he talked to anyone who would talk to him. Nobody paid any attention to him. He was running up and down and talking, calling the officers in the cells sons of bitches, motherfuckers, every dirty name you could think of. All the time I saw him he was running around trying to talk to somebody. Finally, as Hubbard was going by, I grabbed his arm and said, 'Say, what's the matter with that guy?' referring to Shockley. And he said, 'Well, he's been in isolation and the hole too long, he's crazy.'"

As Zamloch turned to a new line of questioning, seeking to establish Carnes's state of mind during the riot, Goodman suddenly interrupted, criticizing him for moving too slowly. "We have been moving very slowly. Can't we move this thing along a little faster? This examination is awfully slow, counsel. It's taking an awfully long time to come down to the crux of the matter."

In fact, the examination was not slow, but merely thorough. Carnes had the right to relate his version of the events. While it may have seemed repetitive because many other witnesses had testified concerning the same events, these had been prosecution witnesses and witnesses called by the other defendants. Zamloch refused to be hurried. "May it please the court, that may be true, but I do not want to leave anything out here. I want to cover everything regarding this matter. I will try to speed it up, but I don't want to be rushed and leave something out."

Carnes then testified that when key #107 could not be found, he concluded that the escape was a failure and considered returning to his cell. "It occurred to me that I should return to my cell and I was considering doing that when Coy yelled at me to go get the scaffold. He yelled at Buddy too, so we both went and started pushing the scaffold toward the west end. We hadn't pushed it very far when the siren went off. We left the scaffold and ran back to the other end. That was the shortest way to my cell and I had it in my mind to return to my cell."

"When you arrived at the west end, what happened?"

"Coy was there, and he said, 'Come on with me, old man.' Although I was planning to go back to my cell, I thought for a minute. There had been stories of old Spanish tunnels and I thought that might be a way to get out of the cell house. Also, I was afraid that people would say I was a coward and yellow and all that if I went to my cell, so when Coy said for me to go with him, I did. I followed Coy and Hubbard into the kitchen."

Carnes's description of the activities that followed was entirely consistent with Blackie Audett's testimony. He described how Coy fired out of the kitchen widows at the Dock Tower, the Hill Tower, and finally, the Road Tower. "After he shot at the Dock Tower, Coy said, 'I got that son of a bitch,' and walked back towards me. I said to him, 'What was the good of that?,' and asked him to stop, but he didn't pay any attention to me. Then I went over to Hubbard and told him, 'What good is this going to do us? It won't get us out of here.' He just looked at me, but he didn't answer me. So I left the kitchen and went out into the dining hall, and Coy kept on shooting."

"While you were in the dining hall, did you hear any gunshots except for Coy firing in the kitchen?"

"Yes, I heard shooting back in the cell house. At first I thought it was coming from outside, but the shots were coming from inside the cell house. I couldn't tell how many shots there were 'cause Coy was still firing out of the kitchen."

"What happened then?"

"Well Coy and Hubbard came out of the kitchen and Coy was all happy saying how he shot the tower guards and killed them all and stuff like that.

He gave the gun to Hubbard as we were walking down the dining hall corridor between the tables, and then we saw the associate warden coming towards us down Broadway. When we got to the cell house door, Coy flung it open and said, 'There's Jughead, kill the son of a bitch.' Hubbard threw the rifle to his shoulder and aimed at Mr. Miller. I came up behind him and jostled his shoulder, so when he fired the shot went wild. Miller started to run toward the main gate and Hubbard swung around and pointed the rifle at me. I said, 'I tripped,' and I backed away. Then we saw the smoke coming out of the gas billy Miller had thrown and we thought it was the guards coming in with machine guns, so we all ran back toward the kitchen. We just ran a few steps when we realized it was just the gas billy so we went back into the cell house."

The jury listened intently as Carnes testified. "We went over to D block and Cretzer and Sam were standing against the wall. Hubbard said, 'Where's the screws?' and Cretzer said, 'There're all dead.' Then I noticed that Sam was barefooted. He came over and started yelling, 'There's a son of a bitch back in there that's still alive.' Cretzer came up and said, 'Yeah, kill the son of a bitch,' and he raised the pistol and started to shoot him. I said, 'Don't kill him. Lageson's a good screw; he never hurt nobody, never bothers anybody.' But Cretzer said, 'The son of a bitch will hang us if he gets a chance.' Then I said to Cretzer, 'The son of a bitch will hang you if you kill him.' But Cretzer took the pistol and aimed it at Lageson's head and pulled the trigger, but the gun was empty. He stepped out of my line of vision to reload, and when he did, I signaled to Lageson to duck. Then the gun went off and Lageson went down."

"After Cretzer fired at Lageson, what did you do?"

"Well, we all went to the west end of the block, and later Coy said, 'I might as well make damn sure that all those sons of bitches are dead.' I said, 'I'll go see.' I wheeled around and started for the cells, and no one followed me. I walked back and looked into the cells and I could see that all of them were still alive. They were still breathing. Somebody groaned. I don't know which one it was, but they was all still alive. So I went back to the west end and told Coy, 'Well, they're all dead, just like you left them. Then I told them, 'I'm going to my cell.' Coy said, 'All right, old man, sorry I got you into this thing. It's just one of those things. Sorry old man.' Just before I left I reached into my pocket and pulled out Coy's notebooks and handed them to him. 'Here's your notebooks,' I said. Then I went to my cell."

When asked about the comments he made to his fellow convicts after returning to his cell, Carnes's reply was vague and unresponsive. "The guys all started yellin' at me and askin' me what happened. I didn't want to talk to them. I answered some of their questions, but I didn't want to talk. Some of the questions I didn't answer. I talked to Lopez and I remember talking to Robinson and that's about all I can remember."

Carnes's testimony was interrupted at this point by the noon recess. Zamloch was so immersed in his client's testimony that he skipped lunch and had the marshals lock him in the holding cell with the defendants so he could continue to work with Carnes.

"It's going fine, Clarence, and you're doing a good job. I just want to tell you again what to expect from Hennessy and how to handle his questions. He's going to phrase his questions in such a way that no matter what you say it's gonna sound bad. Don't worry about it. Just tell your story the way you told it to me. Don't worry if it sounds bad, or if Hennessy tries to make you look bad. Just tell your story and don't let him push you around. Speak up and tell it your way. Don't lie or try to make yourself look good. Just tell your story."

Zamloch's examination during the afternoon session was brief. Although it shed no light on the primary issues in the case, Carnes, like his co-defendants before him, was permitted to testify to the abusive and brutal treatment he suffered at the hands of prison authorities following recapture of the cell house. He described how he was taken from his cell in B block, stripped naked, and forced to stand in the middle of the corridor while everything in his cell was ripped apart and thrown out. Thereafter, he was marched, still with no clothes on, to a cell in A block, where he was alternately beaten by Associate Warden Miller, other guards, and a lieutenant he could not identify. Miller threatened him with death, held a knife to his throat and kicked him repeatedly after knocking him to the floor. After being beaten and threatened, he was left cut and bleeding on the floor of the cell, still naked. Eventually, he was given a new set of coveralls and after a couple of more days, received some food. He remained in the A block cell for the next seventeen days, after which he was transferred to isolation where he was confined until the commencement of the trial.

On cross-examination, Hennessy's questions merely reinforced Carnes's direct testimony. Unable to successfully attack the young inmate on any other ground, Hennessy resorted to a review of his criminal background. It was an area where Carnes was truly vulnerable.

Over objection, Hennessy was allowed to question the youngster about the details of his escape from Granite State Reformatory, the kidnap of

Charlie Nance; and how he and his confederates tied up the victim and a passerby, leaving them on a lonely country road while they made their escape. Hennessy also brought out, as dramatically as he could, the fact that Carnes had murdered a service station attendant in the course of a hold-up and had clubbed a jailer in Oklahoma City as part of an escape attempt. All of these questions regarding his prior crimes were vociferously objected to by Zamloch, who correctly pointed out to the court that, while the prosecution was entitled to present evidence of a prior felony for purposes of impeachment, they were not permitted to develop the details of the individual crimes. Goodman, however, denied the objections, and allowed Hennessy to bring out all the highly prejudicial details, since Zamloch had opened the subject during his preliminary questioning of Carnes.

During redirect examination, Zamloch attempted to have Carnes explain to the jury that he fired the gun accidentally when the victim hurled a soft drink bottle at him. But like his fellow counsel before him, he encountered the evidence stonewall of Judge Goodman. Without any prosecution objection, the judge intervened, cutting Zamloch off and ruling that his questions were out of order.

Having quietly endured a dual standard of evidence admissibility throughout the trial, Zamloch finally erupted. "Your Honor, I may suggest this: When the defense offers evidence, such is the ruling of the court. When the prosecution offers the evidence, the ruling is to the contrary. Over my objection, Mr. Hennessy was allowed, not only to go behind these felony convictions, but also to go behind the circumstances and to show things that were not brought out, even on direct examination. I assumed that when the court permitted that, you would at least permit the defense equal latitude. There is nothing I can do now, but bow to this court's ruling." As he returned to his seat at the counsel table, Zamloch shook his head in baffled disillusionment. He had seen Sullivan and Spagnoli repeatedly blocked in their efforts to introduce favorable evidence, while at the same time, the court consistently ruled favorably for the prosecution. Now it was his turn. Hennessy continued to win the battles, *but at least*, thought Zamloch, *the outcome of the war is still in doubt.*

It had been a long day and Zamloch was exhausted. He knew he would sleep well. Argument would begin in the morning, but he would not address the jury until Thursday. Hennessy would consume a good portion of Wednesday, and Sullivan and Spagnoli would take up the time he didn't use.

Sullivan had some questions for Carnes, but the judge soon cut him off. He was able to establish, however, that Shockley appeared to be a man out of control. "Well nobody seemed to pay any attention to him," Carnes explained. "He was running around, yelling and trying to talk to people, but nobody paid him no mind. Toward the end, he was just standing there, leaning against the wall of D block with this really stupid look on his face. He didn't look to me like he really knew what was going on."

In response to Vinkler's questioning, Carnes provided additional support for the argument that Thompson returned to his cell immediately after the siren sounded. "We were pushing the scaffold and when the siren went off, me and Buddy ran down the corridor to the west end. Thompson took off and went up the stairs. I assume he went back to his cell."

At the conclusion of Vinkler's cross-examination, Zamloch rested his case.

Hennessy then rose and advised the court that he had a few short rebuttal witnesses, which he was prepared to call then or delay until the morning.

"Well, Counsel, I would prefer that we complete the evidence tonight so we can start argument in the morning. How long do you contemplate your rebuttal case will take?"

"I think we will require no more than thirty or forty minutes, Your Honor."

"I will give you thirty minutes. Proceed."

In rapid succession, Hennessy called FBI special agents John Polkinghorn, Philip Bowser, and Thomas Dowd. All three men were members of the investigation team that had interviewed various inmates following the riot. Since the testimony of witnesses Richard Myles and Percy Geary differed from their statements to the FBI, Hennessy sought to impeach them through the agents' testimony.

Both inmates told Polkinghorn immediately after the riot that they had not seen any inmates outside of their cells, but in trial both supported Thompson's story that he returned to his cell before any shooting occurred.

Agent Bowser was called to impeach Edwin Sharp. On the witness stand Sharp had stated that Shockley joined the others in his cell in D block within minutes of the sounding of the siren. He told Bowser during the investigation phase, that Shockley did not come to the cell until about thirty minutes after the series of shots from the cell house.

The testimony of Agent Dowd was totally ineffective. Hennessy called Dowd to impeach Audett, but the agent's testimony was not responsive, and upon Zamloch's objection most of it was either excluded or stricken.

As Hennessy announced with finality, "the government rests," several of the jurors looked at one another, wondering why Special Agent Dowd had been recalled at all.

At the conclusion of the government's case, Sullivan once again requested a jury view of the prison. Showing an uncharacteristic level of patience and concern, Goodman explained in detail his reasons for ruling against the young defense attorney. Noting that he had delayed his final decision until he had heard all of the evidence, he announced, "I am more convinced now than ever that the court should not grant this request. I'm saying that in no criticism of your motion, but I deny it on the ground that, in the discretion of the court, it appears to me that it would be an improper procedure in this case." He went on to explain that, although jury views are appropriate in some instances, in this case he believed that no useful purpose would be served. He stated that it would be difficult to restrict the jury's on-site activities, and virtually impossible to prevent extraneous matters from prejudicing the defendants. Stating that his ruling was intended to protect the defendants' interests, and suggesting that the jury view would actually be detrimental to Sullivan's client, Goodman finally put the issue to rest.

27

The anticipation of closing argument was in the air that morning as the attorneys took their places at the counsel table. The spectators, many of whom had been present throughout the entire trial, anxiously awaited the final words of the legal gladiators. The press corps, assembled in the spectator section, looked forward to some colorful statements with which to enliven their reports. The professional court watchers were prepared to compare and critique the attorneys' performances. The long suffering jury, waiting in the jury room, looked forward to the beginning of the end of their lengthy service and their return to a normal life.

Frank Hennessy sat reviewing his notes, exuding supreme confidence. He was generally satisfied with the way the case had gone, and felt certain he would convict Thompson and probably Carnes. Although he had been concerned about Dr. Alden's testimony and initially feared that Sullivan would establish a winning insanity defense, he now felt he might possibly convict the wild eyed-Shockley as well. He admitted to himself, however, that despite Goodman's many adverse rulings and abusive treatment of him, Sullivan had put on a strong case and he bemoaned the fact that he had no expert to counter Alden. The burden of proving Shockley's sanity was on the government and Hennessy harbored doubt as to whether he had carried that burden.

Final argument was Hennessy's favorite phase of a trial. While unemotional and calculating by nature, he was always able to convey emotional concern to the jury, as he skillfully incited their sense of right and justice. He felt added confidence in this case since Goodman's rulings had insured that the three defendants were on trial rather than Alcatraz.

He was also pleased with Goodman's decision not to permit the jury to return any verdicts other than murder or acquittal. During the conference on jury instructions with the judge the night before, the defense attorneys had argued that the jury should be permitted to consider a manslaughter verdict, but the judge had refused. "Gentlemen, this is not a manslaughter case," Goodman had stated firmly. "It's murder or nothing. The jury will get four forms of verdict for each defendant: first-degree murder, with or without capital punishment, second-degree murder, and acquittal. There will be no manslaughter issue submitted to the jury."

"Well, it went on a little longer than we expected," Hennessy commented to Deasy, "but we'll certainly wrap this thing up before Christmas."

"Not the best time of the year to be asking a jury to bring in three death verdicts," lamented the younger man.

"All in a day's work, Dan. All in a day's work."

Promptly at 10:00 A.M. the door to Goodman's chambers opened, and entering the courtroom in quick, measured strides, the judge ascended the bench. "Good morning, Ladies and Gentlemen. May the record show that the defendants are all present with their attorneys and the jury is in place. Ladies and Gentlemen, this is the time in the trial when the various attorneys will address you by way of summation of their case." He went on to explain the procedure of arguments of counsel, after which he nodded to Hennessy to commence his opening argument.

In his now familiar formal style and stentorian voice, Hennessy thanked the jury and carefully pointed out the gravity of their task. Playing to their egos, he stressed the importance of the jurors relying on their life experiences and common sense. "As I view you, Ladies and Gentlemen, I estimate conservatively that a collection of more than four hundred years of experience is present in this jury box, and I have the utmost faith and confidence in your ability to sort the wheat from the chaff as you perform your all-important role of meting out justice." Hennessy knew that Goodman would instruct the jury that they were not to consider conditions at Alcatraz or the conduct of the prison authorities in quelling the riot. Despite this, he anticipated an attempt by the defense to put the island prison on trial. So he stressed to the jury that neither Alcatraz conditions nor the conduct of prison personnel during the riot should be considered in arriving at their verdict. "You must decide this case on the evidence, and your verdict must be free of any feeling of sympathy, prejudice, or concern for matters beyond the precise issues of the guilt or innocence of the defendants."

Hennessy began with a discussion of the law of the case. He first tackled his most difficult task, convincing the jury they should convict the defendants of murder, although none of them did any shooting.

"It is important at the outset, Ladies and Gentlemen, that you be aware of and consider the law of this case. For although none of the defendants pulled the trigger that took the life of Office Miller, all three of these men are guilty of murder in the first-degree on two separate theories. In the first place, they are guilty because they aided and abetted Cretzer in taking that life. Secondly, they are guilty because they were all joint conspirators with Cretzer, and as such are just as guilty as he for any act he committed in furtherance of that conspiracy." He then went on to read and explain to the jury the precise instructions the court would give.

Hennessy's early comments were made dispassionately, but as he moved to a discussion of the credibility of witnesses, his tone became emotional. "This case is, in large part, about credibility. Even the attorneys for the defense will agree to that. In fact, they told you in their opening statements that the version of the convicts and the officers would differ and that it would be incumbent upon you to decide who was telling the truth. Let me assure you, Ladies and Gentlemen, that as the attorney for the prosecution I welcome this challenge and enthusiastically invite consideration of the entire question of the credibility of witnesses."

Hennessy explained that the court's instruction would assist the jury in determining which witnesses to believe. "The court will tell you that at the outset, as a witness takes the stand, he is presumed to tell the truth. This presumption may, however, be negated by the witness's conduct, manner of testimony, and a host of other factors. You may accept or reject the testimony of any given witness, based on the manner in which he testifies, the character of his testimony, and whether there is contradictory evidence. You may also consider the witness's motives and relationship with the case, including how the outcome of the case will affect him. You may consider a witness's intelligence and his demeanor on the stand. And you may consider, as an impeaching factor to a witness's testimony whether or not he has been convicted of a felony." As he mentioned impeachment by felony conviction, Hennessy paused for emphasis, allowing the jury to consider the fact that every inmate who testified for the defense carried a heavy portfolio of felony convictions. "And if you believe that a witness has willfully testified falsely in one aspect of his testimony, you may disregard all of that witness's testimony."

Hennessy believed that his strongest case was against Thompson. Thompson's principal theory of defense, his alibi, was weak. He and many of his witnesses had not performed well during the trial and neither had Spagnoli. Hennessy decided, therefore, that to the greatest extent possible, he would argue the case against the defendants as a group, emphasizing the role of Thompson. He recognized that each defendant was entitled to independent consideration and that each had presented a separate defense, but to the extent he could, he was determined to lump them together, hoping that his weaker cases against Shockley and Carnes would be bolstered by Thompson's anticipated conviction.

Hennessy launched a credibility attack on Thompson. "How was it that Thompson was in his cell that afternoon, when he should have been operating the tacking machine in the tailor shop?" Answering his own question, he explained that Thompson had been a part of the break from the beginning, and on several occasions earlier in the week had sought a lay-in from his supervisor, Haynes Herbert. Not having received Herbert's permission by Thursday morning, Thompson abandoned that course and, following the noon meal, reported to the hospital, faking an illness. He found an accommodating physician in Dr. Clark, and received an afternoon lay-in. "Clearly, he knew there was a break coming down and, by obtaining the lay-in, assured himself that he would be a part of it. That was why he was in his cell that afternoon rather than operating the tacking machine.

"But what does the defense say about why Thompson was in his cell that afternoon? Well unfortunately for their credibility these people can't seem to tell the same story twice, because during this trial we've heard four explanations of why Thompson was in his cell. First we were told that he became ill following dinner and obtained a lay-in from the doctor. Then we heard that when he returned from morning work detail, Thompson found Coy's note and this prompted him to seek the lay-in. Later he told us the note came after dinner. And of course, there is the preposterous 'domino theory,' where apparently Mr. Aeby forgot his lines, or maybe had a change of heart and told the truth. In any event, he did not support the defense argument. Finally, there is the pathetic suggestion that Mr. Herbert offered him the afternoon off to play dominos, but he declined the offer.

"This, Ladies and gentlemen, is all from the same man who testified under oath that he would never have used a weapon during the course of the escape to kill or injure any of the officers. A man who is serving a life term on Alcatraz for the murder of a Texas police officer. You simply cannot believe what these men say.

"It is admitted that the defendants were all part of the escape attempt. They claim they learned of the break and joined it that very afternoon. But is it logical that Coy, considering all of the planning and preparation that had to go into this escape attempt, would be gathering up participants at the last moment? Coy and Cretzer had been planning this break for months, perhaps years, and had hand picked each of their confederates well in advance of May 2nd. The defendants also claim they were not part of the conspiracy because they joined the escape on the assurance that no harm would come to anyone. They want you to believe that Coy invited them to participate in an escape from one of the most impenetrable prisons in the world using fire arms and other weapons, yet with the assurance that nobody would get hurt. What kind of fools do they think we are? Step one in this plan was to overpower Miller. Step two was to overpower Burch and obtain his guns and other weapons from the gun gallery. What were these gun and clubs for, if not to bring harm or death to custodial officers? How do you overpower guards without inflicting injury or death? All three of these men were part of the escape attempt and part of the conspiracy. They all carried weapons at one time or another. They all joined together to accomplish a criminal act and they are all guilty of the murder of William Miller."

Moving to the issue of aiding and abetting, Hennessy explained that the evidence on this aspect of the case proved two elements of the case. It not only established that the defendants aided and abetted, but also destroyed their claim of abandoning the conspiracy.

"Mr. Bristow told us he heard Shockley demand that Cretzer '…kill the sons of bitches' and specifically urge that he shoot Lageson when he saw that he was still alive. Officer Corwin quoted Shockley as ordering Cretzer to '…kill every one of the yellow-bellied bastards, so we won't have any testimony against us.' In addition, Lageson, Burdett, Simpson, and Baker all testified that Shockley was present at all times and calling for Cretzer to kill the hostages. Sundstrom described him as a 'vicious criminal' and 'as much of a leader as Cretzer or the others.'

"As to Thompson, we heard Lageson and Burdett quote him as calling for the deaths of the hostages to eliminate witnesses. Captain Weinhold saw him with the rifle after the hostages were shot, which destroys any alibi defense he might hope to prove. He was there with Cretzer through the whole thing, and demanded that he kill Lageson when Cretzer suggested Lageson should live.

"Carnes would have you folks believe that he wasn't present when Officer Miller was shot. By his own admission, he was present when Cretzer shot Lageson, and Lageson was shot just moments after Cretzer emptied his gun, first by shooting into cell 403 and then into 402. He was obviously present the entire time and was a part of the crime."

The prosecutor then ripped into Thompson's defenses. "We start with the fact that officers Corwin, Lageson, and Burdett all placed Thompson in front of the cells at the time of the shooting, with Lageson and Burdett hearing him urging Cretzer to kill the hostages and leave no witnesses. Additionally, after being mowed down in cold blood, Weinhold observed Thompson in front of the cell holding the rifle, obviously still a part of the conspiracy and escape attempt.

"But he claims he had abandoned the effort and returned to his cell. And how does he seek to prove that to you folks? Well, they brought over a lot of those 'lost men' from Alcatraz. On paper they pass as men, but they are reckless in everything they do or say. They are at war with society. Their testimony has added nothing to the trial of this case because they cannot be believed."

Briefly reviewing the testimony of each of them, Hennessy sought to discredit Thompson's inmate alibi witnesses. He stressed that some of them had given conflicting factual versions to the FBI investigators. He pointed out that all of them were subject to impeachment as convicted felons, one of whom had murdered his own father. And he urged that none of them were worthy of belief. "Why?" Hennessy asked the jury, "did defense counsel find it necessary to repeatedly ask the witnesses if they were telling the truth and make the point that the witnesses had been told to tell the truth? I'll tell you, Ladies and gentlemen. The defense doth protest too much. These men are not to believed and the defense knows it!"

Finally, unable to resist an all out attack on Spagnoli and his case, Hennessy commented on the disorganized testimony of what he referred to as the "know nothing witnesses." "These men: DeCloux, Sanders, Hilliard, and Davis knew nothing about the case. Their testimony was so worthless that the court admonished Thompson's lawyers that they could no longer subpoena witnesses until it was shown that the requested witness had something to contribute. It was an incredible order by the court, one I have never heard made before. A clear announcement that the court felt the witnesses were worthless, and a resounding indictment of the credibility of the defense witnesses."

Turning to Shockley's defense, Hennessy reminded the jury that as to the charges of conspiracy and aiding and abetting, Shockley had presented no defense. This, he urged, proved Shockley's involvement. When the cells in D block were opened approximately twenty prisoners were released, but only Shockley joined the escape. There was no question, Hennessy argued, that Shockley was part of the plan from the beginning and a participant from start to finish. He recalled for the jury that even Carnes had testified that Shockley struck both Sundstrom and Weinhold and called for Cretzer to shoot Lageson.

Hennessy showed nothing but scorn for Shockley's inability to recall the events of May 2nd. Using terms such as "convenient amnesia," "Alcatraz fog," and "Alcatraz blackout," Hennessy emotionally described the death of Miller as "...a foul, deliberate, premeditated and cowardly act, which the defendant says he doesn't remember. Ladies and Gentlemen, Shockley remembers everything that is important to his case. He could recall the details of his prior life, his jobs, his residences, and facts going back into the mid-thirties. Yet he could not remember the details of that spectacular event of just six months ago."

The prosecutor then swiftly and cogently laid out his view of the Shockley sanity issue. "Admittedly this in not the brightest guy in the world," Hennessy conceded, "but for a man of his intelligence and the type of person he is, this convicted kidnapper and bank robber has made the world his oyster. When he first got to Alcatraz, he worked for a while until he decided that was not what he wanted to do. So he quit his job and, in effect, retired. He retired to D block, where he didn't have to do anything. This was what he wanted. He didn't work, he had no responsibility. He had his meals served to him in his cell by the guards. He made occasional visits to the yard. He had what reading material interested him and he sat in his cell with a view of the bay, the San Francisco skyline, and the Golden Gate Bridge, living a very comfortable life at the taxpayers' expense. He was where he wanted to be, doing what he wanted to do. He was lazy, he was a criminal, and he was vicious. But believe me folks, he was not crazy.

"The question of Shockley's sanity was covered very simply and definitively by Dr. Alden. The doctor was appointed by the court to examine Mr. Shockley and render his report. Let me quote from the doctor's report, '...in my opinion, at the time of my examination on November 5, 1946, Sam

Richard Shockley was able to understand the nature and consequences of his actions, was capable of understanding the nature of the charges against him, was able to confer with his attorney, and was capable of preparing his defense.' That is the medical proof. And that is the end of this alleged insanity defense."

Stepping away from the lectern, he thrust his right hand into his jacket pocket. He then focused his remarks on the question of penalty, advising the jury of the four possible verdicts as to each defendant. "Ladies and Gentlemen, there is no question that the government has proven beyond any doubt that all three of these men are guilty of murder in the first degree."

Referring to Thompson, whom he described as a "felon with an abandoned and depraved heart, a deliberate and premeditated murderer," he stated that nowhere in the case were there any extenuating circumstances. "This man has lived outside the law his entire life. He killed a police officer. He has robbed, kidnapped and escaped from prison. He was intimately involved in the heinous crime for which he is presently on trial. So was Carnes and so was Shockley. Society owes these men nothing but even justice, and justice demands from you a verdict of guilty with no recommendation for leniency."

Following a brief and emotional description of Cretzer's brutality, which he delivered standing near the jury box, Hennessy returned to the lectern. Gripping it tightly with his large hands, he intoned, "The dead cry out for justice, but must do it through the prosecuting attorney. On behalf of the innocent, dead Officer Miller and his shattered family I cry out for justice in the form of guilty verdicts. I demand in the name of the Department of Justice that you do your duty and find each of these defendants guilty of murder in the first-degree and give each of them the maximum penalty. Since they are already serving life sentences, anything less would be no punishment at all. This case involves the security of the community. The prisoners on Alcatraz are desperate men and in this case a further life sentence would mean nothing. It would merely be giving the green light to other inmates to assault and kill guards. Guards who have undertaken the hazardous duty of watching these desperate men must be protected by decent law abiding citizens."

Hennessy concluded his argument with a quiet suggestion. "But if any of these defendants are entitled to your consideration, it would be the defendant Carnes because of his youth and demeanor on the witness stand. His behavior on the stand reflected utter frankness and I believe he was one of the better witnesses for the government. While he attempted to make himself out a hero, I'm not sure that was actually the case. Giving him the benefit of the doubt, it may be that he did assist in saving the life of Officer Lageson, or that was something he tried to do. But the ultimate disposition of this case will be for you and accordingly I now commend this matter to you for fair and just handling. God be with you as you exercise the judgment of this community."

As the jurors and spectators gathered up their personal belongings in preparation for the noon recess, Spagnoli moved swiftly toward the small band of newspapermen in the spectator section, again presenting himself for questions and comments.

"You gonna give 'em hell this afternoon, Ernie?" inquired Stanton Delaplane. Delaplane, a feature writer for the *Chronicle*, was making one of his rare appearances at the trial. He was preparing the lead story for the front page of the Saturday or Sunday edition, depending upon when the jury reached a verdict.

"Yeah, Stan, I'll have a few things to say. You want to be sure and be here. Quote me accurately, and for Christ's sake, spell my name right."

Sullivan chose to work at the counsel table during the noon recess. His lunch was a Baby Ruth candy bar and a Coke from Charlie Bright's newsstand in the lobby. As he sat with his notes spread out before him, the gravity of his mission weighed heavily on his mind. This was the end of the line for Sam Shockley. The evidence was in and he had one final opportunity to save his client's life. He was thoroughly convinced that Shockley had nothing to do with the planning of the escape and that the convict's involvement that afternoon was purely accidental. But, although he believed this with all his heart and soul, could he convince the jury?

He first undertook the chore of modifying his prepared argument in response to Hennessy's argument. Although there had been no major surprises in the U.S. attorney's presentation, he had made a number of points that Sullivan wanted to counter. Shockley's entire case turned on the insanity defense. Hennessy had not attacked Alden's testimony in response to the hypothetical questions, which both surprised and pleased Sullivan. The defense argument on the insanity issue would be critical. Sullivan felt that at least half of the jurors would initially lean toward sanity, and therefore conviction. This would make his argument even more important.

As he worked intensely, he lost track of time and nearly forgot to eat. He unwrapped the candy bar and bolted it down. Suddenly, he was aware of a stab of panic in his gut unlike anything he had ever experienced in a courtroom. It was the same feeling he had known during the European campaign just before he led his platoon into combat. As the leader of the platoon, his life hung in the balance every time they advanced. Now he was about to go into action again, but it was Sam Shockley's life hanging in the balance. As he had during the war, he felt nauseous.

The sensation vanished as he heard the bailiff enter the courtroom and unlock the doors to the corridor, permitting the jurors and spectators to enter. In a few minutes everyone was in place and Sullivan heard Goodman's firm voice directing, "You may proceed with your argument, Mr. Sullivan." The panic returned.

Sullivan appeared nervous and tentative as he began his argument. After thanking the jury for their kind attention and serious approach to the trial, he recalled for them the comments he made during his opening statement. He focused on the point that the real killer was not on trial and questioned why his client was. Vilifying Cretzer as a cold-blooded killer and the madman behind the plan, Sullivan reiterated his assertion that Cretzer had acted entirely on his own when he engaged in the frenzied shooting spree. Any plan that existed was one in which Sam Shockley played no role and of which he had no prior knowledge.

Speaking in a surprisingly objective and dispassionate manner, the serious young attorney explained that it was the government's burden to prove all of the elements necessary to establish the defendants' guilt. In the case of his client, it was also the obligation of the prosecution to prove that Sam Shockley was sane at the time Miller was killed. He then set about convincing the jury that the government had not met their burden of proof.

"Beginning with the conspiracy issue, let me explain to you how it was impossible for Sam Shockley to have been part of any alleged conspiracy and how the government has totally failed to carry its burden of proof. For more that three years, Sam was confined to D block, cut off from not only the outside world, but from the mainstream of life within the prison. He was never exposed to other prisoners except those who celled next to him in the isolation block. He ate his meals alone in his cell. On the rare occasions when he was allowed to go to the yard, he was alone and in the custody of an officer. There is no way he could have known that Coy was hatching an escape plan let alone become a part of it.

"Further evidence of Sam's non-involvement is seen in his participation in the D block riot of April 29, just three days before the attempted breakout. We know that Cretzer and Coy wanted Whitey Franklin in on the breakout, but he didn't know anything about the plan and joined in the earlier riot, breaking up his cell and ending up in solitary. Shockley did the same thing, but because there weren't enough solitary cells, he did his disciplinary time in a stripped isolation cell. Obviously neither of the men knew anything about Coy's plan. When Cretzer and Hubbard charged into D block, they were looking for Franklin, not Shockley. The only reason Shockley was out of his cell was because all the cells in the upper tiers were opened."

Sullivan further reasoned that it was folly to even consider that the ringleaders would have included Shockley in their plan. "Mr. Hennessy would have you believe that Sam was a part of this scheme, but he presented no evidence to support his claim and frankly the contention makes no sense. Sam was a hallucinating, mentally retarded moron, who didn't have the intellectual capacity to carry out such a complicated plan. It is unthinkable that men as careful as Coy and Cretzer would give such a life and death assignment to a lunatic like Sam. With his childish mentality he could never be trusted to keep plans secret, let alone carry them out. In addition, he would be totally unpredictable in the face of terrorizing gunfire, which the escapers knew they might face. Only proven gunmen and fearless escapers were fit for this role. Shockley did not measure up."

Moving cautiously so as not to unnecessarily implicate the other defendants, Sullivan described for the jury how everyone except Shockley played a role in the escape attempt. "Carnes was there from the beginning and captured Bristow. Thereafter, he stood guard over Weinhold and later the other hostages. He gave permission for Miller's hands to be untied and both he and Thompson were involved in moving the scaffold. Thompson took part in the capturing of the hostages and was involved in trying to open the door to the yard. But Sam had no role and no duties. He was simply there! He was running around, yelling and getting in the way of the true participants. There is no evidence he ever did anything more than act as a cheerleader."

Reminding the jury of Shockley's conduct upon being released from his cell, Sullivan emphasized that it was not the behavior of an escapist, but the rantings of a madman. "The first thing he did was run into the officers' toilet in D block and destroy the sink and toilet. 'I'm still smashing stuff up,' he screamed wildly, under the evident belief that the April 29 riot and destruction of property was still underway. If he was part of an escape plan, he would not have wasted either the time or the energy to stop and destroy toilet fixtures. This was most certainly not the conduct of a conspirator in one of American penal history's most well thought out and planned escapes. It was the act of a crazed, mentally deficient convict, who had suddenly and unexpectedly experienced freedom after years of solitary confinement."

On the issue of aiding and abetting, Sullivan argued that his client didn't have the intellect to form the necessary intent. "Since the medical file and the testimony of Dr. Alden establish beyond any doubt that Shockley had the mind of an eight-year-old, how could he form the intent necessary to aid or abet? You know, Ladies and Gentlemen, in today's society we don't prosecute children for murder. This is because the law recognizes that until the age of about fourteen, a child does not have the mental capacity to form the necessary intent, premeditation, malice, and other mental elements that constitute the crime. How then, can Sam Shockley, who admittedly has a mental age of eight, be said to have had the necessary intellectual capacity to be found guilty of murder? His chronological age is meaningless. It is mental age that is important and Sam does not have sufficient mental age or intellect to be guilty of aiding or abetting, of being part of a conspiracy, or of committing any of the acts necessary to constitute murder.

"The only evidence of aiding and abetting by Sam was the testimony of the hostages that he called for Cretzer to shoot them. Assuming for purposes of the argument that Sam said the things he's accused of saying, this still does not establish his guilt. The uncontroverted testimony of Dr. Alden was to the effect that at that time and place Sam didn't know right from wrong and didn't know what he was saying."

By this point in his argument, Sullivan had lost all trace of nervousness and was totally at ease. Having dealt with the prosecution's case and laid the necessary factual foundation, he was ready for the second phase of his argument.

"Now that I've explained to you how the prosecution has failed to carry its burden of proof," Sullivan went on, "let me tell you what this case is all about. Let me tell you why, after you consider all the circumstances, the only conclusion you can come to is that Sam is not guilty of murder. It is a sad, almost pathetic story of the unfortunate son of poor sharecroppers to whom fate dealt an unfair hand. Sam began life on an Oklahoma farm as a normal boy of low intelligence. He was the youngest of six children, part of a hard working but poverty stricken family. When but a child of five, his mother died, leaving his father to work the small farm and raise the six children.

"At the ages of seventeen and eighteen he suffered two serious beatings involving skull and brain damage, from which he never recovered. About this same time he began to develop the symptoms of the dreadful mental disorder that now afflicts him, schizophrenia. You will recall that Dr. Alden described schizophrenia as one of the most serious mental diseases known to man. All of these factors can probably be tied together, his mental illness, his poverty, his diminished mental capacity, and the fact that he received no treatment. With life stacked against him, Sam turned to crime, and things only got worse. His effort at bank robbery failed, resulting in his capture, conviction and imprisonment at the federal prison at Leavenworth, Kansas.

"And what did the authorities at Leavenworth do with this pitiful, sick man? Did they treat him? Did they try to help him? Did they send him to the mental facility at Springfield for evaluation and treatment? Did they do anything for this man? No, Ladies and Gentlemen, they sent him to Alcatraz. Almost immediately they sent him to Alcatraz. He arrived at Leavenworth in May of 1938 and by September of that year he was number 462 at Alcatraz Island Prison.

"Why was he sent to Alcatraz and not Springfield, where a complete mental hospital and rehabilitation facility was available? Sam Shockley was not Al Capone or Machine Gun Kelly, the type of inmate for whom Alcatraz was designed. It was the worst thing that could have been done to Sam. Alcatraz was not designed for mentally ill prisoners. On the contrary, Alcatraz was designed to drive men into a state of submission, which at times meant driving them insane.

"Keep in mind, Ladies and Gentlemen," Sullivan reminded the jury, "that the nature of this man's disease was progressive, and as time went on his condition was deteriorating. So, with his transfer to Alcatraz in 1938, what was done to help this man, who had been diagnosed as mentally ill and in need of immediate and extensive treatment? Well believe it or not, nothing was done. When he misbehaved, no matter how minor the infraction, they, 'threw him in the hole.' Repeatedly, he was incarcerated in the dungeon for periods of up to eighteen days at a time. During these times, he lived in total darkness, without hygienic materials such as soap, toothbrush, toothpaste, towel or wash cloth, in a cell containing nothing but a sink, toilet and bunk. He was limited to a restricted diet. At night he was given a thin mattress and two blankets for a bed. The rest of the time he sat, lay, or stood on the cold concrete floor or his steel bunk.

"And what happened to him at Alcatraz?" Sullivan inquired. "The results were not surprising. His condition continued to worsen, and within three years his IQ had dropped from 68 to 54, indicating the mental capacity of an eight-year-old. In time his mental and emotional condition degenerated to such an extent that he could not cope with normal life on Alcatraz.

"He got into fights and other trouble. He refused to work, destroyed property, and was mentally out of control. He was not a good worker. He bumped around from job to job until he finally refused to work because of his deranged belief that the prison administration was persecuting him by preventing him from working in the kitchen. He developed a reputation as a crazy man and was referred to by guards and prisoners alike as 'Crazy Sam.' You heard the testimony of, among others, Whitey Franklin, who has known him for a long period of time and described him simply as 'crazy.'

"In his psychotic state, he rejected all other jobs to which he was assigned and as a result was permanently confined in isolation. Removed from prison society, he virtually became invisible. He was confined to his isolation cell for over three years, leaving that tiny cubicle for no more than an hour or so every couple of weeks. With nothing to occupy his time, he slipped deeper and deeper into his own little world of madness. Having left school at the age of twelve, and with the mental capacity of an eight year old, there was little in the prison library simple enough for him to read. Consider the tedious, tormented existence to which this man was subjected. He couldn't read; he couldn't carry on a conversation. He began to hear voices coming from the walls, the sink and the toilet. He experienced hallucinations. He imagined bizarre events such as being born in a different century and on another planet. Believing there were minerals and light rays in his food and that people were trying to kill him, he showed the classic signs of paranoia common to schizophrenics. Mr. Hennessy would have you believe that Sam was living like a king, with his food being served to him in his cell and a beautiful view of the bay. Actually, Sam was living like an animal and it was taking a terrible toll on his pathetic life and what little mental capacity he retained.

"We know from the testimony of inmates Kuykendall and Gant that periodically Sam was hospitalized for psychiatric treatment and medication, and that during some of these periods he was restrained in the '...bug cage, where they put the crazy people.'

"No one ever seemed to care about Sam. No one ever seemed to recognize his needs. They just warehoused him. It was just Sam and the voices and the hallucinations.

"Not only would the authorities not help Sam with his enormous mental and psychiatric problems, they wouldn't even let Sam help himself. You heard the testimony of Henri Young, who, because of the harsh and brutal conditions on Alcatraz, had himself gone insane. But Young managed to accomplish a self-cure, and recognizing Sam's problem, offered to help him.

"Sam knew he had mental problems and he welcomed Young's help. Both men were confined to D block. But the authorities wouldn't cooperate. Everyone knew that Sam was crazy and needed help, but Alcatraz kept any help from him. The Bureau of Prisons kept any help from him."

Suddenly, moving from the lectern, Sullivan charged to the counsel table and pulled the stunned Shockley to his feet. Leading, almost dragging him, to the jury box he stood the confused convict directly in front of juror #12, Della McVittie. "Look into his eyes, Ladies and Gentlemen," Sullivan commanded. "These are the eyes of a madman. These are not the eyes of a normal human being, but the eyes of an insane man." Sullivan began pushing the thin, pale-faced defendant down the length of the jury box, pausing in front of each fascinated juror inviting them to "…look into my client's eyes."

Astonished by the exhibition, yet not sure an objection would be effective, Hennessy allowed the drama to play out as each juror attempted to peer into Shockley's eyes.

The startled Goodman maintained a quiet vigil on the bench. Hearing no objection from the prosecution and not sure himself of the propriety of Sullivan's conduct, he chose not to interfere, and allowed the performance to continue. For several minutes no one spoke as Shockley was guided by his attorney slowly along the front row of jurors. Those in the back row leaned forward, craning their necks for a closer look. Jurors Flammer, Beine, and Varney all left their chairs and moved forward, fascinated by the demonstration. Sullivan finally led his bewildered client back to his seat, and without speaking, returned to the lectern.

"So this was Sam Shockley on May 2. A feeble-minded moron, hallucinating, hearing voices, paranoid, potentially assaultive, potentially dangerous to himself and others, unstable, suffering from one of the most serious mental diseases known to man. And we know from Dr. Alden that his condition was not fabricated, but legitimate and deteriorating. He was a virtual Humpty-Dumpty sitting on the wall, an egg ready to crack. Despite all of the warnings and all the opportunities to do something for him, the government and Alcatraz wouldn't help him.

"With Sam in this Humpty-Dumpty, eggshell condition, what happened to him as a result of being let out of his cell during the escape attempt? The testimony on this subject came from Dr. Alden, the only medical witness to appear in this trial. And his opinions were based on facts not available to him when he examined Sam in November, but of which I advised him by way of hypothetical questions. And you should note," Sullivan confidently reminded the jury, "that during the testimony of Dr. Alden, Mr. Hennessy agreed that the doctor was a highly qualified psychiatrist. Also, you will recall, Dr. Alden was appointed by the court to examine the defendant and report to you and the court regarding his findings.

"What did Dr. Alden tell us Sam's mental condition was on May 2? He told us that Sam did not know what he was doing. It was his opinion that Sam was unable to comprehend the nature and consequences of his acts, that he was unable to distinguish right from wrong, and that he was, quite likely, legally insane. I am summarizing the doctor's testimony for brevity, but you may have the entire transcript on this point reread if there is any question in your minds. And on this point Ladies and Gentlemen, keep in mind that it is the government's burden to prove that Sam was sane. It is not our burden to prove him insane. But, by the testimony of Dr. Alden, we have done just that.

"Sam blacked out. He has no recollection of events that took place. His mind was a blur. Those who saw him described him as a madman. Remember what Carnes said about him. He told you that the first time he had ever seen Sam was during the break when he saw him running around, cursing, swearing, and shouting obscenities at the guards. He was also trying to talk to the various participants in the escape but was ignored by everyone. Bewildered by what he saw, Carnes asked Hubbard, 'What's the matter with that guy?' His conduct was so bizarre that it did not fit the situation. Hubbard's response, you'll recall, was 'he's crazy, he's been too long in the hole. He's been too long in isolation.'

"Crazy Sam was just that, a madman suddenly released from bondage with no concept of what he was doing. He was totally and legally insane during the events that took place that afternoon in May, and Dr. Alden agrees with this evaluation."

Again temporarily leaving the lectern and moving across the room to stand behind his client, Sullivan moved on to the final phase of his argument. "The tragedy of Sam Shockley does not end there, Ladies and Gentlemen. Sam is now the target of the institution that is responsible for this catastrophic event. Because of the inhuman and unbearable conditions in which the prisoners found themselves, Coy, Cretzer, and Hubbard spent months, perhaps years planning their escape. Because these men were so desperate to get off that Rock, they were willing to face anything, even death, to make good their escape.

"With much clever planning and execution, they got their plan underway. But before the riot got out of control, the guard on duty in D block, Cecil Corwin had the opportunity to put a stop to the entire affair. He knew someone was attacking Burch in the gun gallery and was aware that there were convicts loose in the main cell house. But he froze and did nothing to alert his fellow officers. Because he was poorly trained, because he panicked and became transfixed with fear, he didn't follow the prescribed procedure and turn in the alarm. Although there was ample time and nothing to prevent him from picking up the phone and calling the armory, he didn't take this simple step. As a result the riot got out of hand and a bad situation became a catastrophe.

"Corwin was not alone in his ineptitude. In the administration offices confusion reigned. When trouble was suspected, Weinhold, Simpson, Baker, and Sundstrom ran blindly into the cell house and were captured. When they didn't return and Fish was unable to reach anyone by telephone, further confusion developed. But at no time, until after nine hostages had been captured, did anyone have the foresight to man the east gun gallery. The entire affair could have been brought to a halt by merely manning the two levels of the east gun gallery with armed guards who could have laid down a barrage of gunfire to bring the entire riot to a halt. But this was not done until after the arrival of Associate Warden Miller. By then, all of the damage had been done.

"But Ladies and Gentlemen, the worst is yet to come." Sullivan's tone was angry as he returned to the lectern. "And that I will describe as the fatal delay.

"When Associate Warden Miller finally became involved in the conflict and it was known that the convicts were loose in the cell house with weapons, it was still very early in the course of these events and there was plenty of time to bring the hostilities to a swift conclusion. The simplest analysis would have told any officer that the convicts had only the two guns from the west gun gallery, a rifle, a pistol, and seventy-one rounds of ammunition. It could have been no other way. Every other gun and bullet on the island was accounted for. There were no other firearms in the cell house and there could not have been any other guns in the cell house.

"In contrast, the Alcatraz arsenal was hundreds of times greater. The armory contained rifles, pistols, machine guns, riot guns, shotguns, gas guns, and every manner of weapon known to the prison system. But with all these weapons, with dozens of well-trained, heavily armed custodial officers, no attempt was made to rescue the hostages for almost ten hours. For whatever reason, the prison authorities chose to do nothing by way of rescuing the hostages.

"And now to the real tragedy of this case." Sullivan paused and made deliberate eye contact with the jurors. "We learned it from the autopsy surgeon, Dr. Jeanne Miller, who, as you will recall, was one of the very first witnesses called by the prosecution. When we asked her for her opinion as to Miller's cause of death, her response was '…hemorrhaging from the lungs into the pleural cavity and the resulting shock.' In other words, Officer Miller bled to death as a result of his wound, his blood filling the lung cavity, snuffing out his oxygen supply, sending him into shock and to his death. Had he been rescued and given timely medical care, Officer Miller may not have died."

With this statement, Hennessy exploded to his feet, objecting to Sullivan's argument. Goodman reacted almost as quickly in sustaining the objection and ordering that his argument was out of order. But Sullivan had rung a bell that could never be stilled. He had placed the blame for Miller's death squarely on the Alcatraz prison administration for their inept handling of the riot and their failure to effect a timely rescue of the hostages.

Undaunted, Sullivan continued his emotional argument. The courtroom observers were silent and the jury hung on his every word. Hennessy, waiting for the next bomb to explode, sat attentively on the edge of his chair.

"Now these same prison authorities want all these men dead to cover up their own blundering. They made no effort to capture Coy, Cretzer, and Hubbard, as you could tell from the autopsy testimony of Dr. Kerhules. Instead of trying to capture these men, they simply blew their heads off. They silenced any possible criticism these men could have provided.

"The authorities mercilessly bombarded D block throughout the night of May 2 and the following day under the claimed belief that inmates in D block had been involved in the escape attempt. Inmates from D block had wandered into the main cell house after Cretzer had opened their cells.

Claiming that some of these D block inmates had been involved in the riot, the authorities, out of revenge, shelled D block for thirty-six hours in an effort to kill or maim the participants.

"Now, since their brutal bombardment of the prison failed, they are after the lives of Shockley, Carnes, and Thompson to make their job complete. You folks are the last line of defense against further inhumane treatment of these men—these men here in court and the men still on Alcatraz.

"The prosecution tried to argue that Miller's death was somehow due to Sam's statements. That is preposterous. Cretzer paid no attention to anyone, let alone Sam Shockley. Nobody ever paid attention to Crazy Sam and that is the true tragedy of this case. Sam is as much a victim of these events as any of the hostages. In fact, he may be more of a victim, since all the other persons involved in this tragic drama were at least of normal intelligence. Sam never stood a chance.

"Sam may or may not have been there when these shots were fired. There is evidence on both sides of this issue, and it is for you to decide. But even if he was there, and even if he said the things he is accused of saying, what he said was irrelevant. It was as meaningless as the call to 'Kill the umpire!' voiced by a rabid baseball fan at Seal's Stadium. What Sam said was meaningless."

Sullivan snatched the .45 automatic pistol from among the trial exhibits, and waved it over his head. "What did the talking that day was this, this deadly killing machine in the hands of Joe Cretzer. That is what did the killing that day, not Sam Shockley's imbecilic words." Every eye in the courtroom was fixed upon him and Sullivan knew his argument was effective.

"This horrible institution known as Alcatraz is what killed Officer Miller, through the conduct of Cretzer and the misconduct of the prison administration. In 1938, Alcatraz received a forsaken piece of human flotsam in the form of Sam Shockley. They mistreated him and failed to deal with his obvious mental disorder. They exacerbated his illness until he was hallucinating and became known by all as a crazy man. Then the riot broke out, led by desperate men who were prepared to face death by gunfire rather than endure a living death as Alcatraz prisoners. Because of prison ineptitude, the riot got out of hand. Sam Shockley was gratuitously released from his cell and ended up an observer, a cheerleader, although never a participant. Now they seek to hang their own failures on Sam and take the life of yet another Alcatraz victim. This is a gross miscarriage of justice and a disgrace to the law.

"Alcatraz is the black sheep of the federal prison system. It drives men crazy and should be wiped off the face of the earth. I viewed concentration camps in Europe during the War that weren't as bad as Alcatraz." Another Hennessy objection was sustained and Sullivan backed away from his attack on Alcatraz, bringing his argument to a close.

"I've done what I can, Ladies and Gentlemen. I've fought the good fight for Sam. The world is against Sam. The prison system is against Sam. The courts are against Sam. Society is against Sam. Here is a man who never really had a chance in life. And now, you members of this jury are his last chance. You are his last hope."

As they had divided the preparation and presentation of the case, Spagnoli and Vinkler divided the argument. Spagnoli had developed the alibi phase of the case, and Vinkler the brutality issues. Spagnoli planned to open the argument and cover the alibi defense. Vinkler would follow and argue the brutality defense to the extent Goodman would permit. The two attorneys had serious questions as to how far Vinkler would be permitted to go with these issues, in view of the judge's ruling forbidding the jury to consider prison discipline, procedures, or conditions. Since Vinkler's assignment was the more difficult one, he would close. His subject was also more emotional, and therefore a better closing subject. Considering the size of Spagnoli's ego, allowing Vinkler to close was an act of supreme generosity.

Clad in the navy blue three-piece suit he reserved for weddings, funerals and jury arguments, Spagnoli appeared trim and athletic despite his sixty-one years as he stationed himself behind the lectern. With only a half-dozen index cards to assist him, the gray-haired barrister appeared confident and at ease as he faced the jury. With little by way of introduction, he got right to the point.

"Ladies and Gentlemen, I'm going to talk to you about what the law calls an alibi defense. What that means in this case, as you all know from the evidence that you've heard, is that my client Buddy Thompson wasn't there when Officer Miller got shot. He wasn't present when this crime was committed, but was back in his cell having discarded any thought of escaping from Alcatraz. It's as simple as that. That's what an alibi is all about. He wasn't there and therefore he can't be guilty."

Spagnoli launched into a sarcastic personal attack on his prosecution adversary. "Mr. Hennessy argued to you for about two hours and he's got the right to come back—who knows, maybe for another two hours—to argue to you some more tomorrow. And he talked to you all about the law, and instructions, and legal theories, legal definitions, and conspiracy, and aiding and abetting. You must admit, Mr. Hennessy did a lot of talking. Mr. Hennessy is a great talker and that is what he knows best.

"The prosecution has made a big deal out of this case. They've taken a simple set of facts and blown them completely out of proportion. We were in trial for a month on this case, when at the outset you were told that it would be completed in two weeks. The government called over thirty witnesses, presented dozens of exhibits, and took nearly three weeks to put on their case. It was a major production and total overkill. The same kind of overkill that the Alcatraz prison authorities engaged in during this so-called riot. And then after all those witnesses and exhibits, the prosecutor went on for better than two hours, continuing to make this case something that it isn't."

Spagnoli described Hennessy as a prominent political figure, who desired to make headlines at the defendants' expense. He warned the jury not to be misled by Mr. Hennessy's trained "radio announcer voice" and the theatrical approach that covered his true agenda. "It is Mr. Hennessy's goal to shift the blame from the real killer, who is dead and cannot be prosecuted, to these defendants. At the same time, he seeks to cover up the negligent, inept handling of the entire affair by the prison authorities."

Spagnoli contrasted himself with Hennessy. "Unlike the politically well-placed Mr. Hennessy, I am not your big city lawyer. I was born in Jackson, California, up in the hills and I'm 'plain folks' just like you. I call things like I see them and that's what I want to do with you folks here today. Mr. Vinkler and I aren't going to take a lot of time arguing this case to you, because we think we can do it in short order."

Stressing that the facts were straightforward, Spagnoli offered the jury a brief summary of the case. "Buddy Thompson was invited to join in the escape just as it was about to begin. It looked safe enough to him, particularly when Coy assured him that the plan was such that nobody would get hurt. Soon after the plan got underway, however, it failed when the inmate leaders could not find the critical key, #107. Realizing that the escape was a failure, Buddy immediately withdrew and returned to his cell. Cretzer, driven mad by years of isolated confinement and brutal torture, became irrational at the thought of failure, and mercilessly gunned down the hostages in the two cells. This conduct was not part of the escape, was never contemplated by the others and was the act of a madman."

Repeating that Thompson was not present when this shooting took place,

Spagnoli contended that Cretzer was acting totally on his own. "The break was over and the three defendants returned to their cells, while the other three determined to fight to the death rather than continue their life of hell on the island prison.

"And there are many," he proclaimed, "who believe that Cretzer, Coy, and Hubbard are better off now; dead rather than incarcerated in the hell hole that is known as Alcatraz."

In defense of Thompson's credibility, Spagnoli characterized his client's testimony as clear and consistent. He maintained that there was no evidence to suggest that Thompson had advance knowledge of the escape or was involved in planning the break. Discussing the lay-in, Spagnoli explained the sequence of events. "Earlier in the week Thompson had discussed with Herbert the possibility of laying-in Thursday to play dominoes with his friend Aubrey Aeby. But as it developed, the game fell through and Thompson did not pursue the matter on Thursday, the day of the break. Instead, following the noon meal he became ill and sought a medical lay-in, which he was granted. And we all know, if Thompson had not really been ill he would never have been granted a lay-in by the prison doctor. That was just not the Alcatraz way.

"Having obtained a legitimate medical excuse to be in his cell, Thompson was relaxing on his bunk when Coy passed by and tossed him the note, inviting him to join the break within the hour. There was nothing inconsistent in Thompson's testimony as to how he came to be a part of the break. He was certainly not a leader, but simply went along with Coy. He joined what he believed to be an attempt to escape, not a killing fest.

"Later on he heard the ruckus in the gun gallery and saw Cretzer and Hubbard armed with guns. The break was underway and when Hubbard asked him if he wanted to be let out of his cell, Buddy Thompson became a part of it."

Spagnoli reviewed the evidence, detailing for the jury how Thompson was present during the capture of Weinhold, Simpson, Baker, and Sundstrom. "You'll recall Mr. Thompson's testimony of how he intervened on behalf of Sundstrom, first when Cretzer seemed about to strike the officer and subsequently, when Hubbard threatened to hit him. Sundstrom had helped Mr. Thompson in filing legal papers and he liked and respected the officer. This was clear evidence," Spagnoli explained to the jury, "that Buddy was concerned only with escaping from prison, not with inflicting harm or injury on any of the officers.

"As problems developed over the missing key #107, Coy directed Buddy and Carnes to move the scaffold. What Coy had in mind for the scaffold will remain one of the mysteries he took with him to the grave. For as the two men struggled to move the large device toward the west end, the escape siren sounded. This not only signaled to the outside world that an escape was in progress, but announced to those involved that the break was over.

"At that point," Spagnoli analyzed, "the decision became clear and you will probably recall the testimony of Lt. Simpson. He said he heard voices that he could not identify stating, '...Well it's all up to us now. We'll have to go the hard way.' The break was over. They could return to their cells and take whatever punishment they had coming, or they could stay and fight to the death.

"You'll remember also the testimony of Buddy Thompson on this subject when he told you that as far as he was concerned it was '...getting too rough for me,' and he concluded that the leaders of he group '...were going crazy.' Whatever the plans were up to that time, they had ended. Three men quit and three men stayed. That was the end of the break as Carnes, Shockley, and Thompson knew it.

"What we've got to do," Spagnoli explained, "is examine the evidence showing that Buddy returned to his cell and compare it with the prosecution evidence that he was still present. In addition to Buddy himself, we called six witnesses, all of whom were in the vicinity of the events that took place that afternoon. All of them supported Mr. Thompson's testimony that he was back in his cell when Cretzer went crazy and began shooting the officers."

He went on to summarize the testimony of Geary, Myles, Hamilton, Peabody, Cook, and Baker, pointing out how they established Thompson's alibi. The sum of their testimony was that they had seen him return to his cell and could place him in his cell before Cretzer's shooting rampage.

"So there are six witnesses, Ladies and Gentlemen, placing Mr. Thompson in his cell before the shooting took place. There is no conflict or inconsistency in what these men have to say. They were all objective spectators, safe in their cells or the library, not involved in the affair that was taking place, and simply watching the events unfold. There was nothing to cloud their powers of observation, nothing to interfere with their ability to perceive. They had nothing to do but watch and listen,

Despite the cross-examination by Mr. Hennessy, their stories remained completely consistent.

"On the other hand," Spagnoli cautioned, "the evidence presented by the prosecution was flawed and inconsistent. Think of the situation confronting the eight hostages as they stared down the muzzle of that monstrous .45 automatic pistol wielded by Cretzer. These men were all facing death. Five of them were shot and three almost died. Five hostages didn't see Mr. Thompson there when the shooting took place. In fact, more of them didn't see him than did. Everyone saw Cretzer and everyone saw Crazy Sam. So why didn't they see Buddy?

"The obvious explanation is that because of those terrifying, nerve-racking conditions, the observations of the officers cannot be relied upon. Captain Weinhold, for example, does not recall seeing Mr. Thompson there when he was shot. However, at some later time after regaining consciousness, he claims to have seen Buddy in front of the cell. I suggest to you that this was the hallucination of a badly wounded man. Both Corwin and Lageson were shot, and their recollections must similarly be discounted.

"Keep in mind also," Spagnoli admonished the jury, "that there are three inmates on Alcatraz by the name of Thompson. It is well within the realm of possibility that this could be a factor in the confusing identification process.

"I do not suggest here that the hostages are saying anything except what they think they saw. There is, however, an issue of witness bias and Mr. Vinkler will discuss that with you later. My point, however, concerns the opportunity the various witnesses had to observe. While the defense witnesses were safe and secure with nothing to do but observe the events in progress, the prosecution witnesses made their observations under life-threatening stress. Whereas the inmate witnesses presented unanimity in their testimony, the officers were inconsistent with more of them not seeing Buddy than saying he was there.

"From the beginning, Buddy's only interest was to escape from the horrible confinement of Alcatraz. He had no desire for any injury to come to the officers. This would gain him nothing except perhaps a longer sentence at the dreaded prison from which he sought to escape. He had joined the escape attempt under the impression that no death or injury would come to anyone. The escape attempt of which he was a part had long since ended and he was back in his cell when Coy, Cretzer, and Hubbard designed a whole new plan of action. The new plan contemplated a fight to the death and taking whatever hostages and other officers with them that they could. Mr. Thompson never was, nor would he ever be, a part of such a plan. The fact that he is still alive is positive proof that he was never a part of this revised strategy and that he deserves to be acquitted.

～

Vinkler had spent days considering ways to make the brutality argument and withstand the prosecution objections. After reviewing the testimony of DeCloux, Sanders, Hilliard, and others, he was forced to conclude that none of them had contributed anything relevant on the issue of prison brutality. He decided, therefore, to attack the credibility of the Alcatraz guards and administrators on the ground of bias. He would attempt to weave in examples of the officers' brutal treatment of the inmates as evidence of their hatred and bias towards them. It was the only way Vinkler felt he could inject the brutality issue into the argument without being blocked by Hennessy.

His approach was complicated by the fact that, during his portion of the argument Spagnoli had not attacked the credibility of the Alcatraz officials, but had merely questioned their ability to observe. Vinkler would have to confront the custodial personnel head-on, accuse the hostages of bias, and hope for the best. It was the most difficult assignment faced by any of the attorneys in the case and one of the most difficult arguments he had ever had to make.

Before he tackled these issues, however, he addressed a subject that had not been emphasized by any of the defense attorneys. That was the fact that the east gun gallery was manned about the same time the associate warden entered the cell house at which point the entire cell house came under constant surveillance.

"I want to urge that you consider the testimony of two rather brief, but important witnesses," he began. "You will recall that inmate Hollingsworth, whose cell is near the east end of the cell house, testified that approximately five minutes after hearing the siren, he heard the doors in the east gun gallery being opened and closed. This indicated that the east gun gallery was being manned. We also heard the testimony of officer Mullane, who was sent into the east gallery within a few minutes of hearing the siren. In fact he stated that it was just as Associate Warden Miller emerged from the cell house that he assumed his post in the gallery.

"We know, therefore, that within minutes after the siren sounded, the east gun gallery was manned, and we know that there were ultimately four officers stationed there. These men had unobstructed views of the cell house and were able to look down all three corridors. None of these men ever saw Mr. Thompson outside of his cell, because he was back in his cell within minutes of the siren sounding.

"We must find an explanation, Ladies and Gentlemen, as to why two groups of people can witness the same act or series of acts, and arrive at two diametrically opposed views of what took place. How do we explain this? Six convicts, safe and sound in their cells and the library observing the unfolding drama state with unanimity that Buddy Thompson was in his cell before Cretzer began shooting into the hostage cells. At the same time, five of eight hostages do not see Mr. Thompson standing beside Cretzer as he performed his murderous deeds but three do.

"This, in my opinion, is the central and foremost issue in this case. For if Buddy is standing with Cretzer urging him to kill the officers it is one thing. On the other hand, if he is locked in his cell, having totally given up all thought of escape from Alcatraz when Officer Miller was shot, your vote must be for acquittal. Viewing this case at its purest and simplest, that is the issue you must decide.

"Mr. Spagnoli suggested one possible explanation for the disparity, which is eminently cogent and which he developed with you in detail. That was the opportunity of the various witnesses to observe the events. I will not repeat these arguments, except to state Mr. Spagnoli's conclusion. While the inmates were mere spectators with unlimited and unimpaired opportunity to see and hear all the events, the guards' observations were made under threat of death and in the face of terror that few men have ever experienced. Given these facts, it seems logical that the six prisoner witnesses are far more believable than the three out of eight officer hostages. Since five of the hostages did not see Thompson, the testimony of the three who claim he was there is immediately called into question.

"Mr. Hennessy argued to you that the inmates could not be believed because they're all criminals. But Ladies and Gentlemen, this defies all logic. Why would these men lie and put themselves in a position to receive more abuse than they are already experiencing at Alcatraz? God knows their lives are bad enough as it is. Why would they want to make things worse? Myles and Audett are within months of discharge from Alcatraz. Why would they or any of the others take a foolish gamble with their future by coming before you and swearing falsely? They wouldn't. It's as simple as that.

"Some of the witnesses, such as Baker and Cook, hold comfortable and desirable prison jobs, which would surely be taken from them if they came to court and perjured themselves. Yes, these men are criminals. But that, in and of itself, does not mean that their testimony cannot be believed. Each of these men has told the same story, that Mr. Thompson broke off his involvement in the escape when the siren sounded and was in his cell when the shots were fired.

"The hostage witnesses, on the other hand, are confused. Under the circumstances to which they were exposed, their observations are unreliable. Five of them don't place Mr. Thompson at the site of the shooting. Three think he was here. Their testimony must be viewed with considerable question.

"I am going to add yet another element to this question of credibility. This is something that Judge Goodman will point out to you in his instructions. In determining whether or not to accept the testimony of a witness and deciding what degree of credibility you assign to the testimony of any given witness, you may consider the connection or relationship that witness bears to the government. You may also consider the circumstances under which the witness has testified, and his demeanor or manner on the stand. In other words, you may examine the witness's testimony for bias or prejudice. If you conclude that some or all of the government witnesses who testified as to Mr. Thompson's whereabouts when Miller was shot were motivated by feelings of bias and prejudice against Mr. Thompson, you may view their testimony as tainted and disregard it.

"You heard the evidence, not only from Buddy himself, but from other prisoners who saw and heard the beatings, kicking, and threats to which Mr. Thompson was subjected. Associate Warden Miller at one point threatened to kill him if he did not confess to involvement in the riot. On another occasion he was beaten and the associate warden ripped a handful of his hair from his scalp. He was denied food, was placed in an isolated cell without adequate clothing or bedding and, as I said earlier, was threatened with death. Witnesses told you how Lageson approached Mr. Thompson with a blackjack prepared to do him bodily harm and had to be restrained. This clearly shows bias on the part of that witness, who incidentally is one of the three who testified that Thompson was present at the time of the shooting."

By arguing the issue of bias, Vinkler had successfully opened the subject of prison brutality without objection from Hennessy. Believing he had nothing to lose by expanding his argument, he slipped into a general discussion of the harsh conditions on the island. He graphically detailed the limited privileges available to the prisoners, the constant surveillance, limited visitation rights, lack of newspapers and radios, and other harsh rules that, if violated, could place the offending inmate in solitary confinement for lengthy periods of time. He went on to quote from Warden Johnston's book, *Prison Life Is Different*. "Remember the words written by Warden Johnston, that, "...he didn't blame a man for trying to escape from prison." By the time Vinkler finished reminding the jury of Johnston's testimony that during his years as warden many of the prisoners had gone insane, Hennessy realized that Vinkler was deep into an attack on prison conditions. His initial instinct was to object, but he thought better of it and permitted the attorney to continue. Hennessy feared that, given Vinkler's clever handling of the issue, an objection might be overruled, and accomplish little more than irritate the jury. *After all*, he thought to himself, *what more can they say about Alcatraz that hasn't already been said?*

Vinkler reminded the jury of the testimony of the men in D block of the withering barrage of gunfire throughout Thursday night and most of Friday. "Despite the fact that prison authorities knew none of the rioters were in isolation, thousands of rounds of pistol, rifle, grenade, mortar, and naval gunfire were poured into D block. Robert Stroud told you that he counted seventy-nine bullet holes in the walls of his cell alone, and estimated that more than four hundred rounds hit the wall in the general vicinity of his cell. Miller's rescue team had locked the door to D block, and the guards knew that Coy, Cretzer, and Hubbard were holed up in the C block utility corridor. Nevertheless, the senseless and merciless shelling of D block continued. It was the order of one of the lieutenants in charge to '...kill anybody that moves.' It was a simple matter of revenge and a demonstration of the enormous hatred the officers felt toward the inmates."

Vinkler then touched briefly on the brutal bombardment of C block by the Marines. "Think about it Ladies and Gentlemen, the prison authorities literally blew the prison apart to kill three men, who between them had but two guns and seventy-one bullets. They were all shot in the head, uncontroverted evidence that the intent was to kill, not capture.

"Finally, in an effort to wring confessions from the defendants, the FBI in concert with prison authorities, used unconstitutional and illegal interrogation methods. Showing complete disregard for the human rights and dignity of the defendants, they brutalized them, placed them in isolated cells without adequate food, threatened them, and exhibited the hatred, prejudice and bias that has been demonstrated during this trial through the testimony of the government witnesses. The Alcatraz brutality evidence is an important element in this case. There is overwhelming proof of brutality before, during and after the events that are the subject of this trial, and we want you to consider such evidence in your deliberations. Mr. Hennessy will tell you that you are to ignore this evidence as it is not an issue in the case. But I implore you to listen carefully to the court's instructions on this point. The judge will tell you that while this evidence may not be considered as evidence of guilt or innocence of the defendants, it may be considered when you deal with the question of credibility, particularly the credibility of the government witnesses. You cannot believe both the government and defense witnesses on the issue of whether Thompson was present when the shooting took place. And in making that decision you must consider the bias, the opportunity to observe, and the ability to observe of the government witnesses. To the extent that the conduct of the authorities affects the officers' bias, you must consider such conduct. For if a witness so despises a person that he will beat him, kick him, pull his hair out of this head, threaten to kill him, shoot at him, and try to kill him, can you really believe what that witness says about that individual? We have presented this evidence for a specific purpose, namely to place the testimony of the officers in its proper light. Their conduct not only demonstrates their hatred and malice toward the prisoners on Alcatraz generally, and these defendants in particular, but speaks volumes about how far they will go in testifying against these defendants.

"Alcatraz has been compared to the German concentration camps, and though I've never seen one, I believe the comparison is accurate. It is a horrible place that over the years has produced horrible things. The only good thing that can come out of this case is the abolition of places like Alcatraz."

His argument finished, Vinkler returned to the counsel table, making eye contact with Sullivan as he did. Sullivan was tired and the weariness showed on his face. It had been a difficult trial, but finally, everything was behind him. *Tonight will be a good night for a couple of drinks or maybe even more, at the Bar Association lounge,* Sullivan thought as he packed up his files. He was about to complete his first capital case and he felt good about the way it had gone. He was also happy with how his argument had gone. Although he felt strongly that Sam deserved an acquittal, he was positive that the worst the jury would give him was first-degree without capital punishment. From this point on however, there was nothing to do but wait.

28

As he had with every phase of his case, Zamloch prepared his argument with meticulous care. He viewed the greatest strengths of his case to be Carnes's youth, the humanitarian acts he performed during the riot and the fact that his testimony, unlike that of the other defendants, was generally in accord with the hostages.

There were also aspects of the case that troubled the attorney. Carnes was the second inmate to arm himself, and committed one of the early acts of violence when he captured Bristow. Despite his contention that he joined the escape at the last minute, his acts were easily susceptible to the interpretation that he was in on the planning from the beginning and knew much more about the escape than he admitted. Additionally, although he testified that he abandoned the break when he heard the siren, he then joined Coy and Hubbard as Coy gunned down three tower guards from the kitchen windows. These facts all conflicted with Zamloch's image of Carnes as a misguided, unsophisticated teenager.

Zamloch's challenge in his argument was the same as when he undertook the defense of the case, to save Clarence's life. Given the fact that his client was already serving ninety-nine years with a subsequent life sentence awaiting him, the question of conviction or acquittal paled in the face of the death penalty. Although the jury would be instructed not to base their verdict on feelings of sympathy or prejudice, Zamloch was determined to do everything he could to engender both sympathy for his teenage client and prejudice toward the prison administration.

On the death penalty issue, Hennessy had given Zamloch an unexpected opportunity. In contrasting the degree of guilt of the defendants, he had opened the door for Zamloch by suggesting to the jury that if any of the defendants deserved special consideration, it was Carnes. That statement hit Zamloch like a bolt of lightning, and he was determined to use it to the fullest possible extent. As the young defense attorney moved toward the lectern, he instinctively threw back his shoulders and stood erect, using all of his 5'4" height.

By way of introduction, Zamloch reviewed Carnes's criminal background, pointing out how fate had been terribly unkind to the young Oklahoma lad. "Because of a couple of mistakes, admittedly serious ones, made when he was barely out of childhood, Clarence found himself on Alcatraz by the time he was only eighteen-years-old. A murder conviction resulting from what was basically an accident had brought him a life sentence in Oklahoma. Then running away from the reformatory, which involved commandeering a truck and its driver, resulted in a ninety-nine year kidnapping sentence in the federal prison. So at his young age, Clarence faced a life of hopelessness and disillusionment, incarcerated in the harshest and most brutal prison in the nation.

"Soon after he arrived on Alcatraz, Clarence met Bernie Coy, who liked and felt sorry for him. As he moved about the cell house delivering books and magazines, Coy spent time talking with the impressionable young man. He had few close friends within the prison, and Clarence developed a respect and admiration for Coy, a man forty-six years of age, wise in the ways of prison life and a father figure to the boy."

Zamloch's easy manner permitted him to establish a quick and comfortable rapport with the jury. His well-ordered, friendly delivery was in contrast to Sullivan's excitable style; Hennessy's bombastic rhetoric; and Spagnoli's earthy, disorganized rambling. He maintained a large stack of notes on the lectern before him, but never referred to them. As he spoke, he stood in front of or beside the lectern as if to compensate for his stature.

Zamloch reminded the jurors how quickly events had moved, sweeping Carnes along and into the escape. "Coy came to Clarence's cell and told him there was a break planned for that very afternoon, and that he could come along. He told Clarence it was a sure thing, it couldn't fail, and nobody would get hurt. 'When everything's ready,' he told Clarence, 'I'll open your cell and if you want to go just step out.' Within a couple of hours, as he lay on his bunk thinking about the incredible news he had just received, Clarence's cell door opened. Things were happening so fast that the youngster was almost overcome by confusion and apprehension."

Zamloch emphasized the young man's fear and indecision. "While excited by the prospect of a breakout, Carnes knew nothing of the plans and initially had doubts and fears as to whether he should get involved. When he arrived at Times Square he looked around, but saw no one. Perplexed and wondering if he was doing the right thing, he was signaled to by Hubbard who was hanging on the outside of the top tier of the gun gallery. At Hubbard's direction he picked up the homemade shiv, though he still didn't know what he was supposed to be doing and did not know for sure if there even was a break. The Chief Steward Bristow arrived, and, as Clarence testified, once Bristow had seen him out of his cell, he assumed he'd be considered a part of whatever was going on. The decision as to whether or not to join was made for him. At that moment, whether he really wanted to or not, he became involved. Clarence told you that at that time his feelings were a combination of fear, surprise, and confusion, but he felt it was too late to turn back."

Zamloch described Carnes's subsequent involvement, pointing out how he was nothing but an observer. "He observed the activity in the gun gallery as Coy overpowered Burch and obtained the guns. He watched as Hubbard and Cretzer stormed D block, captured Corwin and tried to free Whitey Franklin, and he was present when Lageson and Burdett were captured by Coy, Cretzer, and Hubbard. Clarence was simply an interested spectator, along for the ride, hoping to escape from Alcatraz. After Hubbard received the weapons from Coy, he handed Clarence a club and told him to stand guard outside cell #404. While doing so, his only affirmative act was to grant Burdett's request to untie Miller's hands. In performing this act of kindness," Zamloch pointed out, "Clarence unwittingly facilitated the hiding of key #107 by Burdett, an act which ultimately foiled the entire escape.

"At no time during the trial," Zamloch observed, "did any of the officers testify that Clarence was a ringleader or active participant. He was there, doing what he was told. He was nothing more than a follower, a tagalong, an invited guest. He was never aggressive or assertive. He was there ready to go if the door was opened. Beyond that, he was a follower.

"When it became evident that the critical key #107 could not be located, Clarence decided that the escape was a failure. He considered abandoning the effort and returning to his cell. But at that very moment his friend and leader Bernie Coy directed him to move the scaffold from the library to the west end of the cell house. Again Clarence did as he was told. You will recall that he told you he didn't know what Coy had in mind.

He assumed that since they had not found key #107, the scaffold would somehow help get them out of the cell house.

"When the siren sounded, Clarence knew that the escape was over. Immediately he abandoned the scaffold. He ran to the west end of the cell house, intending to return to his cell. The scene was now one of total chaos. Cretzer was storming back and forth in front of the hostage cells, menacingly waving the .45 automatic. 'They fucked us on the key,' Cretzer complained, 'Frisco's as far as ever. We might as well go the hard way.'

"Imagine the fear and confusion that must have gripped young Clarence at that time. Only minutes earlier he had joined an escape that his wise friend assured him was a sure thing, with everything planned perfectly so nobody would get hurt. Suddenly there was confusion and chaos everywhere, the alarm was sounding and the critical key was missing. Before the youngster could sort out the facts for himself, Coy again intervened. 'Come on with me, old man, come on with me.' His was a reassuring voice in a time of crisis, and once again, young Clarence did as he was told.

"Why didn't he return to his cell? Clarence was not motivated by logic. His was the conduct of a confused young man, lacking in sophistication and experience. Under these circumstances, Coy represented stability and guidance. He was the mastermind of the plan. The specter of the old Spanish tunnels loomed in Clarence's mind. Maybe that was where Coy was taking him. Despite the confusion, Clarence wanted the escape to work. The only possibility of success was with Coy, the father figure.

"In addition, young Carnes had a childish fear of being branded a coward. He didn't want to be the first to quit. Even if the escape was a failure, it was important that he remain involved long enough to be identified as a participant. Participation would be a badge of honor and a status symbol.

"But everything changed for Clarence Carnes," Zamloch declared somberly, "after he followed Coy and Hubbard into the kitchen. Having been assured by Coy that nobody would get hurt, imagine the shock that this young man experienced when he observed Coy smash out kitchen windows and cut down the guards in the Dock, Hill, and Road Towers. He stared in disbelief as Coy fired first at the Dock Tower and officer Jim Commerford crumpled in a heap on the steel deck of the tower. Stepping back from the window, Coy bragged to nobody in particular, 'I got the son of a bitch.' Then Coy fired two shots at Officer Elmus Besk on the Hill Tower catwalk, tearing through both of his legs, spinning him around and knocking him to the deck. Think of what went through this boy's mind as he stood helplessly watching his friend, whom he so admired, turn into a senseless cold-blooded killer.

"He protested, asking Coy, '...what good will shooting do? It won't get us outta here.' Ignored by Coy, he turned to Hubbard and asked again, '...what is the good of this?' Audett, who by this time feared for his own safety, observed his protestations to both men. When he saw Coy shoot Officer Irv Levinson in the Road Tower, Clarence stumbled numbly into the dining room and sat at one of the tables with his head in his hands, frightened and confused.

"His savage mission completed, Coy, with Hubbard at his side, walked out of the kitchen and through the dining room, to the cell house. He handed the rifle to Hubbard as Carnes fell in step behind them, like a dog following its master. As they reached the cell house door, they saw Associate Warden Miller running toward them. Throwing the door wide open, Coy urged Hubbard to '...kill the son of a bitch, and Hubbard raised the rifle to his shoulder.

"It was all too much for Clarence, Ladies and Gentlemen. Miller was an easy target, only ten or fifteen paces away. In seconds he would be dead. But something in the youngster's mind told him not to let this happen. He took another couple of steps and as Hubbard carefully squeezed the trigger, Clarence bumped him from behind. The jolt knocked the rifle barrel off line and sent the bullet harmlessly up into the prison ceiling.

"As Miller turned and raced from the cell house, Hubbard spun around and pointed the gun at Clarence's chest. At that point the young inmate believed the next bullet would be for him. He stammered an apology to Hubbard, claiming he had stumbled. Fortunately for the youngster, Hubbard hesitated just long enough for his fury to cool and he pulled the gun back from Clarence's chest. In the confusion, Miller scampered down Broadway, throwing his activated gas billy over his shoulder. He reached the east end of the cell house before Hubbard could compose himself and fire another round. There is no question, Ladies and Gentlemen, that Clarence Carnes saved the life of Associate Warden Miller. Yet this man came before you as part of the prosecution's case and testified in an attempt to take the life of the young man who saved his. The irony is beyond belief. Mr. Hennessy talked to you about justice. Consider the justice Associate Warden Miller seeks to apply to Clarence, the man who saved his life."

His anger building, Zamloch launched into a personal attack on Miller, eventually drawing an objection from Hennessy. Hammering away on the theme that Carnes, at great personal risk to himself, intervened to save Miller's life, Zamloch branded Miller's testimony as "...a pack of lies." "Ladies and Gentlemen, I've seen witnesses arrested at the courtroom door for lessor examples of perjury than we heard during this trial from Associate Warden Miller. Small wonder that this man the inmates call 'Jughead' is so feared and despised. He sat on that witness stand and lied to you through his teeth, without so much as a pang of conscience."

Zamloch was careful to point out that the defense version was not based solely on Carnes's testimony. He reminded the jury that two unimpeached witnesses, George Ward and Blackie Audett, observed the entire episode and their testimony corroborated Carnes. "Both Audett and Ward placed him in the kitchen when Cretzer was shooting into the hostage cells. In fact, Ward actually heard the gunfire in the cell house while he saw Clarence in the kitchen and dining room area. In addition, the witnesses Robinson, Lopez, Dillon, Bledsoe, Baker, Myles, and Cook all heard the same pattern of gunfire that was consistent with Clarence's factual account. This testimony forcefully supports our position that Clarence was in the kitchen and not in front of the cells when Cretzer shot Miller. While the inmate testimony was unequivocal on this point, the hostage evidence was vague, inconsistent, and confused. This is not surprising when you consider that the officers were under life-threatening fear, and not in a position to make the same objective observations as the inmates."

Continuing to focus on Carnes's humanitarian conduct, Zamloch reviewed the facts surrounding the shooting of Lageson. He recalled how Shockley spotted Lageson sitting in the back of the cell alive and unhurt. "Screaming to Cretzer, Shockley demanded, '...kill the son of a bitch.' But wanting no more bloodshed, Clarence intervened on behalf of the officer, urging Cretzer, '...he's a good guy. Don't shoot him.' Ignoring the plea, Cretzer leveled the pistol at the officer and fired, but the gun was empty and the hammer only clicked. Cretzer rammed home a fresh clip of seven bullets and again aimed the gun at Lageson. Clarence moved behind Cretzer, out of the view of the other inmates and signaled for Lageson to duck. Apparently heeding Clarence's advice, Lageson lurched forward as Cretzer fired and the bullet merely grazed his left cheek. The youngster had now save two lives, but he wasn't done."

He went on to describe Carnes's final act of mercy. "Coy indicated he was going to check the hostages to be sure they were all dead, but Clarence volunteered for the mission. Arriving at the front of the cells, he studied the bodies of the nine officers, and observed they were all still alive, although several were wounded. He heard one of them groan. He did not enter either cell, but returned to the west end and announced '...they're all laying the same way you left them. They're all dead.' In fact, Ladies and Gentlemen, at that moment, all the hostages, including William Miller, were still alive.

"Clarence was a hero, not a killer. He saved ten lives that day, although one of the men died later despite his efforts. Bill Miller died, not because of any conduct by Clarence, but as a result of the delay by prison authorities in getting him treatment. An earlier rescue would have saved his life. If Clarence Carnes had not been involved in the escape attempt every one of those officers would have been killed."

Zamloch repeatedly asked the jury to examine the testimony of Associate Warden Miller and compare it to the other evidence in the case. He reminded them of Miller's savage brutality against Carnes and Thompson following the riot. Numerous convicts heard Miller beating Carnes and threatening him with further beatings and death if he didn't confess and reveal the names of all the participants. He had also beaten Thompson and ripped a handful of hair from his scalp while banging the inmate's head against the bars of his cell.

"While the evidence of his vicious conduct is overwhelming, the black-hearted beast sat up there on the stand and categorically denied every allegation, stating under oath that he had never struck a prisoner in his life. Do you believe that testimony, Ladies and Gentlemen? I certainly don't. How did Thompson's hair get here? What was it that all those inmate witnesses saw and heard? How can we just ignore their testimony?" The small man's voice reverberated throughout the courtroom. He held aloft the shock of Thompson's hair as he berated the associate warden.

"As I promised during my opening statement, Carnes' defense is not based on the brutality that took place on Alcatraz. We bring this evidence to your attention only to show you that Miller is a liar. He lied on the witness stand regarding his brutality and he lied when he told you who shot at him and how many shots were fired. The evidence is clear, Ladies and Gentlemen, as to what took place. Nearly a dozen witnesses heard the same thing. One shot at Miller, not two or three as he would have you believe.

"This is an evil man, whose life was saved by my client. To show his gratitude, he delivered a bloody beating to young Clarence, then destroyed his cell and personal effects. He kept him naked for several hours, placed him in a cold, stripped cell for more than two weeks, and deprived him of a regular diet. After all that he comes before you and lies on the witness stand. Now you can see just how far men in public life will go to accomplish their goal. Miller's goal is to end the life of this unfortunate nineteen-year-old boy, who had the bad luck to be misled by older, more experienced men whom he mistakenly trusted. He wants Clarence dead, just as he wanted Coy, Cretzer, and Hubbard dead. But you, Ladies and Gentlemen of the jury, can prevent this greatest of all injustices and save the life of this confused young man."

As his level of emotion and indignation escalated, Zamloch attacked the federal government and the case presented against the defendants. "This whole trial has been an attempt by the Justice Department to clean its skirts and whitewash its record. The Department has to explain how a handful of convicts, who fired no more than fifty shots, could hold the cell house for three days against the overwhelming forces of the Bureau of Prisons and the United States military.

"The government has to explain their own bumbling and failures. You had three convicts with two guns and a handful of bullets. That's all there was. But because they didn't know what they were doing, the authorities brought in the Marines. They brought in guards from prisons around the country. They had the Coast Guard and Navy shell the cell house. They destroyed the inside of the cell house, and they blew the heads off the real conspirators, Coy, Cretzer, and Hubbard.

"This trial has been an attempt to expand the entire episode and the number of participants to make it appear a huge riot, to justify the overkill and deadly bombardment of rifles, pistols, machine guns, grenades, mortars, and even Naval gunfire. The government is seeking to cover up their acts of revenge and their murderous assault on innocent prisoners. What they did was motivated by ignorance, incompetence, and revenge. It was done to kill and injure prisoners as a warning to those who might be inclined to attempt escape in the future. And it was an act of revenge; a payback for Cretzer's maniacal shooting spree. Now in the aftermath of their inexcusable wrongdoing, they seek to implicate as many people as then can. It's all a matter of justification. Justification for their shocking performance.

"Compare this savage, homicidal conduct of the officers to the actions of the defendant, Clarence Carnes. Yes, he joined the plan to escape as it began to unfold. But when he saw it was failing he abandoned it, just as quickly as he had joined. He attempted to dissuade Coy from shooing at the tower guards, pleading with both Coy and Hubbard to lay down their arms. There is no question that he saved the life of Associate Warden. It is undisputed, even admitted by Mr. Hennessy in his argument, that Clarence saved the life of Mr. Lageson. This fact was even corroborated by Lageson, who made a point of returning to the witness stand to clear up any confusion and acknowledge Clarence's act. Later, Clarence lied to the others to save the lives of all the hostages. Finally, after all these acts of extraordinary bravery, courage and humanitarianism, he returned to his cell.

"Then Hennessy, used the very men whose lives Clarence saved to build a case of murder against him. But these unjust charges against Clarence became too much for Hennessy, and the injustice stuck in his throat as he called for this boy's death. Even Hennessy, the hard-boiled prosecutor, was moved by the facts of this case and the potential injustice being visited upon this youngster. He admitted to you from this very rostrum: 'He probably did assist in the saving of Lageson's life, or at least he tried to.' And then he went on and suggested to you, '...that if any of the defendants in this case were entitled to special consideration, it would be Carnes, because of his youth and demeanor on the stand.' He described him as testifying '...with utter frankness,' and depicted him as '...one of the better witnesses for the government.'

"And to those factors cited by the prosecutor, I add the fact that young Clarence Carnes saved the lives of all the hostage witnesses who have testified against him. Without Mr. Carnes, none of these hostages would be alive today, and the government would have no case. I urge you, Ladies and Gentlemen, to heed the words of the prosecutor and grant the consideration that he suggested. Save the life of this unfortunate young man with a verdict of not guilty.

"If Clarence Carnes hadn't participated in that filling station robbery back when he was just sixteen-years-old, and if the victim hadn't thrown that pop bottle at him causing his gun to fire accidentally, he would now be a simple shepherd boy on the wide plains of Oklahoma. Instead, this poor Choctaw lad, who never really had a chance in life, is here before you seeking your mercy. He saved ten lives during that ill-fated escape attempt and now the government seeks to take his. Is that justice? I say to you that it is not.

"This, Ladies and Gentlemen, is the most important event of your lives, for you have control over the life or death of these three men, one of whom is only nineteen years of age. You are the sole bulwark between Clarence Carnes and injustice. If you convict Clarence, Warden Johnston will congratulate you. The prosecution will say you've done your duty and Clarence Carnes, a nineteen-year-old boy from Oklahoma will die. That would be wrong, and I implore you to save his life with a verdict of not guilty. It is not that you will be setting Clarence free, for he still must serve his lengthy terms. But you will be saving the life of a boy who may yet be able to do some good in this world, and contribute usefully to society, even if it be a prison society. I urge you to accept the alternative that was given to you by Mr. Hennessy and save his life. He does not deserve to die."

His argument complete, Zamloch paused and remained at the lectern. Every eye in the courtroom remained fixed on the small man, his impassioned words still ringing in their ears. The silence of the occasion was abruptly broken by Judge Goodman's announcement that court would recess until 2:00 P.M., at which time the prosecution would complete their argument and the case would be adjourned for the day.

At the commencement of the afternoon session, Hennessy stunned the defense attorneys by announcing that Dan Deasy would deliver the prosecution's closing argument. This was a highly unusual move, even for the unpredictable U.S. Attorney. Considered by most trial lawyers to be one of their mightiest trial weapons, the final argument to the jury was made by the party with the burden of proof. In a criminal case the prosecution had the final argument. To have the last word to the jury, which could not be answered by your adversary, was a tremendous advantage and it was a shock that Hennessy would permit his associate to make this crucial argument. Hennessy had questioned all but one of the witnesses, and had delivered the opening statement as well as the opening argument. It seemed to Zamloch that his adversary was diminishing the tactical advantage of closing argument. Hennessy appeared to be making a tacit statement to the jury that this phase of the case was so unimportant that he could pass it off to his associate. The defense attorney welcomed the choice by Hennessy, but did not understand it. Zamloch was a firebrand, and always coveted the opportunity to be the last attorney the jury heard. He would never have relinquished this right to a co-counsel. Although he couldn't imagine what it might be, he wondered if the wily prosecutor had something up his sleeve.

Deasy had established no rapport with the jury during the trial, having examined only one minor witness. He awkwardly made his way to the lectern to commence his phase of the argument. Although he had tried numerous cases, including several homicides, and had delivered scores of jury arguments, Deasy seemed wooden and ill at ease as he began his presentation. Having played so minor a role in the trial, Deasy was obviously uncomfortable now in so visible a position. The inquiring looks from many of the jurors added to his discomfort, which he could not hide from the searching gazes of the courtroom observers.

The prosecution's closing argument is rebuttal to the defense and is limited to the points raised in argument by the defense. All three defense attorneys had argued for verdicts of not guilty, and in so doing placed all matters relating to the defendants' guilt in issue. This gave the prosecution carte blanch to reargue the entire case. A properly prepared argument could have done this, while at the same time answering specific defense points. Since he had not given the opening argument, Deasy could easily reargue the case without repeating himself. He chose instead to put forth a series of responses to the various defense attorneys and their arguments. He attempted to inject emotion into his presentation, but it paled in comparison to the other lawyers' arguments.

Following a brief introduction, almost an apology for the fact that he, rather than Hennessy was giving the final argument, he directed his attention to Dr. Alden's admission that his one-hour examination of Shockley was not entirely satisfactory, and that he would have preferred more time with the defendant. "During his examination of November 5, the doctor formed no opinion as to whether or not Shockley was sane on the 2nd of May. But he did conclude that as of November 5, Shockley was able to understand the nature and consequences of his acts, was capable of understanding the nature of the charges against him, and was fully able to confer with his lawyer in the preparation of his defense.

"Keep in mind, Ladies and Gentlemen, Dr. Alden found Sam Shockley to be sane. At no time had Dr. Alden or any other medical practitioner made the diagnosis that Sam Shockley is insane. The most that Dr. Alden said was, that based on information set forth in the hypothetical questions of Mr. Sullivan, it was possible that on May 2 Shockley may not have known the full nature and extent of his actions. The doctor didn't say he was insane, but said that it was a possibility. In addition, keep in mind, that what he was given by Mr. Sullivan were assumed facts, which may or may not have been true."

Although Deasy's portrayal of Alden's testimony was not false, it was a distortion. He neglected to tell the jury that Alden had stated it was probable that Shockley did not comprehend the nature and consequences of his actions at the time of the riot on May 2. Deasy's version of the doctor's testimony was the last word the jury heard on the subject of insanity. Tormented by what he viewed as a miscasting, if not a misstatement of the evidence, Sullivan chose to endure it in silence rather than risk making an objection and having it overruled.

Deasy stressed how speculative the insanity argument was, and that the jury need not accept it. "What Dr. Alden said about whether Shockley was sane on May 2 was only his opinion based on a single examination and his review of medical records. It was just an opinion and not something you are required to accept. You must also consider the evidence that supports a finding of sanity such as the details of his interview with the doctor. He was willing to discuss subjects helpful to his defense, such as his family background, his symptoms and his alleged mental difficulties. But when asked to relate the facts of May 2, he very carefully pointed out that, '…I don't care to go into that, as I have this indictment against me and what I say may be used against me.'

"He was absolutely correct," Deasy assured the jury. "If he had said anything to the doctor that was damaging to his case, it would have been used against him. He was sane enough to know that and declined to discuss the escape and the events of May 2 with the doctor. This, Ladies and Gentlemen, is hardly the raving of a madman as Mr. Sullivan would have you believe, but rather the statements and reasoning of a sane man. And that is what Shockley is, perfectly sane.

Deasy next addressed the claim that Shockley returned to his cell in D block before any shooting in the cell house occurred. With absolute contempt for the defense argument, he reminded the jury that all the hostages had testified that Shockley was present when Cretzer did the shooting. "Every one of the officers who survived testified that Shockley was present at all times up to and including Cretzer's shooting spree. But more than that, Ladies and Gentlemen, they also heard him repeatedly urge Cretzer to kill the hostages, shouting '…kill the yellow bellied sons of bitches.' Admittedly, in any factual situation there will be variations in the testimony of witnesses observing the same event, and that is to be expected. In this case, eight men could not be expected to describe all the events that took place without some variation. Yet there was total agreement among all the hostages that Shockley was there the entire time, urging Cretzer to kill all the officers. The evidence is overwhelming and capable of only one interpretation.

"In contrast to the solid and unanimous testimony of the hostages was the pitiful case advanced by Shockley to support his contention that he was in his cell in D block when the shooting took place. Although Mr. Sullivan called four witnesses on the issue, you need go no further than the testimony of one of them, Howard Butler, for proof that Shockley was not in his cell until long after the shooting had taken place." Quoting from Butler's testimony, Deasy related how the inmate described Shockley returning to his cell about fifteen to twenty minutes after the siren had sounded, which would have been ten or fifteen minutes after the shooting took place. "It was clear from Butler's version," Deasy explained, "that Shockley was present during the shooting. This, coupled with the testimony of the hostages, established without doubt that he aided and abetted in the death of Miller."

Deasy referred to the testimony of inmate Jack Pepper, who remembered seeing "Shockley remove money from his pocket that had been previously taken from Sundstrom, tear it up and flush it down the toilet. "This," Deasy told the jury, "would have been used on the mainland had they gotten away. Why was this money in Shockley's possession? Because Shockley was an integral part of the plan from the outset, and his having that money demonstrated how deeply involved in the details and execution of the plot he was. It also indicated that he was sane enough to dispose of the incriminating evidence, which he did quietly and without explanation to the other prisoners in the cell."

Finally, Deasy recalled for the jury how during cross-examination Shockley had answered all Hennessy's questions about his social history, his early life, the jobs he held, the places he lived, and other personal details, many of which went back several years. He had been able to recall details of the April 29 uprising in D block, and the fact that on May 2 he was still being punished for his involvement in that fracas. Yet when asked for details of the events that occurred on May 2, his answer to more than fifty questions was 'I don't know.'

"When he was interviewed by Dr. Alden this past November, Shockley did not claim any loss of memory and spoke freely until the questioning turned to the events of May 2. At that time he told the doctor that he didn't want to talk about the break, in view of the pending indictment and trial.

He didn't say he couldn't remember. It was clear that he was protecting himself because he knew that anything he said would be used against him and it was obvious that he feared that he might make a damaging admission. Let me assure you, Ladies and Gentlemen, that 'Not So Crazy Sam' was exercising perfectly sound and sane judgement when he refused to discuss the events for which he was about to go on trial. The claimed loss of memory, folks, didn't surface until the time of trial, when it became one of Shockley's main lines of defense.

"There's nothing wrong with this man's memory and there's nothing wrong with his sanity. He chose to take this approach in answering Mr. Hennessy's questions to avoid incriminating himself, just as he chose not to discuss the case with Dr. Alden. That's Shockley's defense tactic in this case: claim no memory of the events and hope that the speculative testimony of Dr. Alden will be enough to establish insanity. It's a clever plan, but I am confident you folks will see through it and come to a just verdict of guilty."

During Deasy's argument, Shockley sat staring straight ahead as if in a stupor, occasionally writing on a yellow pad. Periodically he would concentrate his gaze on Deasy, then, as if looking for guidance, would stare for several minutes at the judge. He rarely spoke to Sullivan, but when he did it was with deference and respect, usually asking a question about the proceedings.

While at the outset it appeared that Deasy's plan was to discuss each of the defendants individually, his presentation soon became muddled, and he began dealing with the Thompson and Carnes cases simultaneously. He started with an attack on Thompson's contention that he became involved in the escape attempt only after being assured by Coy that no one would get hurt. Recognizing that Carnes had also advanced this argument, he expanded his discussion to include both defendants. "They were both convicted killers, and it is preposterous to assume that either of them would refrain from joining the escape unless assured that no harm would come to any of the officers. What were the guns for? What were the clubs for? What was the knife for? What was the shiv for? What did they expect would happen if some guards tried to stop them? Would they negotiate their way off the island? No, Ladies and Gentlemen, they would do whatever had to be done to get away, including killing anyone that got in their way. All six of those convicts were in prison for crimes committed with guns. Three of them were convicted murderers. If necessary, all six would have killed without hesitation."

Turning to Thompson's alibi, Deasy stated that it really wasn't important where Thompson was when Miller was shot, because he was guilty whether present or not. "The court will instruct you," he promised, "that the defendants need not be present when the crime was committed, because if they were part of the conspiracy and the crime was in furtherance of the conspiracy, they are all guilty."

Addressing Spagnoli's suggestion that because of fear and anxiety the hostage witnesses had been confused in their identification of Thompson, Deasy sneered. "Let me suggest to you, Ladies and Gentlemen, that if Joe Cretzer was pointing a loaded .45 automatic at you, while Thompson and Shockley stood beside him demanding that he kill you, that picture would be burned in your memory forever. It would not be something you would soon forget and certainly not something about which you would have the slightest bit of confusion. Well that's what happened to these men, and they will never forget that sight, that vision, as long as they live. They were not confused in any way when they described for you what they saw and what they heard. And what they heard was Thompson and Shockley calling for their deaths. What they saw was the deadly eruption of that .45.

"The suggestion made by the defense of misidentification is ludicrous. All these prisoners were well known to the hostages, who saw them on virtually a daily basis and had for months and years. Mistaken identity is not a realistic possibility. Besides, one of the prime observers was Officer Lageson, who in addition to observing the events of the afternoon, had the calmness and presence of mind to write the names of all the perpetrators on the wall of the death cell and eliminate completely any question about identity.

"Mr. Spagnoli and Mr. Vinkler called the credibility of the officers into question during the course of the trial. Mr. Vinkler told you in his opening statement that there would be a conflict between testimony of the guards and the convicts and that you would have to choose between the two groups." Deasy announced to the jury that it was now time to make that comparison and believe the testimony of one group or the other.

"Thompson's witnesses are thieves and killers; men at war with society, who between them are serving hundreds of years for serious violations of the law. They are the worst criminals in the United States. Not only are they hardened criminals with multiple felony convictions, but are such sociopaths as to be unmanageable in all the federal prisons of the United States except Alcatraz. These are the worst possible examples of humanity. And yet these are the men whom the defendants rely upon in this case. In contrast the officers are fine men doing their jobs, who found themselves facing the murderous attack of escaping killers and thieves. They have not committed any crime or wrongdoing, but have come here to describe for you what happened. As is to be expected, their versions of the facts varied slightly, unlike the convict witnesses whose stories were suspiciously similar."

Shifting to a discussion of the conspiracy issue, Deasy told the jury that this theory alone could support a conviction of all three defendants. "The entire case against the defendants can be explained on the basis of conspiracy. There is no doubt that these men joined in the escape and therefore joined in the conspiracy to escape. This is undisputed. Even if they joined after the conspiracy was underway, the defendants are all still part of the conspiracy."

Deasy then enumerated for the jury exactly what each of the defendants had done as part of the conspiracy. "Shockley was involved in the capture of several of the officers, was seen to be carrying a weapon, struck two of the officers, and urged the killing of the hostages. Thompson was also involved in the capture of several of the officers, at one point carried the rifle, urged the killing of the hostages and, along with Carnes, attempted to move the scaffold into position. Carnes used both a club and a shiv as weapons in guarding and apprehending officers, single-handedly captured Bristow, stood guard over the hostage cells and, along with Thompson, helped move the scaffold in response to Coy's directions.

"The only remaining question is whether or not Cretzer's killing of Miller was in furtherance of the conspiratorial plan. It most certainly was. Cretzer killed Miller as part of an effort to leave no witnesses who could testify against the conspirators. Cretzer announced this intention when he shot Lageson. There is no question that a conspiracy existed. There is no question that all three defendants were a part of it. And there is no question that the shooting was done to eliminate witnesses after the escape had failed. These defendants were a part of the whole affair and cannot now divorce themselves from it. Their guilt is patent, and you must find them guilty."

In conclusion, Deasy directed his full attention to Clarence Carnes. Reminding the jury that everything he had previously argued regarding aiding and abetting and conspiracy applied to Carnes. He ferociously attacked the young defendant's story that he had given up the escape when he realized that it was a failure. "Four of the hostages, Lageson,

Bristow, Simpson, and Burdett, all testified without question that Carnes was part of the group of inmates present when Cretzer fired into the cells. Although no officer quoted Carnes as calling for the hostages' death or urging Cretzer to fire, his presence as part of the escape conspiracy and his acquiescence in Cretzer's act of murder made him as guilty as if he had pulled the trigger himself. In the face of the testimony of these four hostages, Carnes's assertion that he was with Coy in the kitchen at the time Miller was shot is not worthy of belief.

"But, even accepting Carnes's version, that factual scenario still makes him a member of the conspiracy and guilty as a co-conspirator. While Miller and the others in the hostage cells were being gunned down, Coy was shooting three tower officers, wounding one and spraying the others with bullet fragments and shards of glass. The shooting sprees of both these convicts were a part of the conspiracy and Carnes was a member of that conspiracy.

"Carnes was the first convict of the six to arm himself. Even before Coy had overpowered Burch, Carnes had armed himself with the shiv and captured Bristow. It was Carnes, therefore, that took the first armed act, solid evidence that he was a part of the conspiracy from the very outset."

Having belabored the theories of conspiracy and aiding and abetting until even he recognized that he was becoming repetitious, Deasy brought his argument to a close with the demand that the jury find the defendants guilty and impose the death penalty on all three of them. Ignoring Hennessy's earlier suggestion that special circumstance might apply to Carnes, he insisted that the government had proven the defendants' guilt beyond any doubt and to a moral certainty. "Anything less than the death sentence for these hardened killers, thieves and kidnappers would be no punishment at all. Justice demands a verdict of guilty with the death penalty, and the Government implores you to return that verdict as to all three."

The prosecutor's words were like a knife thrust into Zamloch's heart. He couldn't believe what he heard. "That son of a bitch," he whispered to himself, "that's why he gave the closing to Deasy. He's going for the death penalty and after his opening he couldn't ask the jury for it himself." Zamloch felt betrayed. Hennessy had let down his guard during his opening and invited the jury to exercise leniency toward Carnes. Obviously, he later had second thoughts and decided to push for the death penalty for all three. Knowing he couldn't do so effectively in view of what he had said in the opening argument, he turned the entire closing statement over to his associate. Deasy, unfettered by Hennessy's remarks, ignored the suggestion for special consideration and demanded the death penalty for all of them. Zamloch had felt quite comfortable being able to point out to the jury that the prosecutor had tacitly approved something less than the death penalty for Carnes. Now that suggestion was gone and he had the feeling Deasy had pulled the rug out from under him. *It was a shitty trick*, he thought to himself. But it was certainly within the purview of the prosecution and there was nothing he could do about it.

Deasy completed his argument well before four o'clock, and court adjourned early. The attorneys, more relaxed and cordial than at any time during the trial, engaged in friendly banter as they gathered up their notes and files for the last time. An air of conviviality replaced the somber climate that had existed for most of the month-long trial. Tomorrow would be the judge's instructions to the jury, followed by the agonizing wait for the verdict. Very little lawyer involvement remained, except for answering any questions the jury might ask. It would soon be the jury's turn to take control of the case as it performed its grim task in the quiet secrecy of the jury room.

Spectators, formerly strangers, now engaged in animated speculation as to the outcome of the case. Even the court attaches, greatly relieved that the high security trial was almost over, joined in the conversations, more relaxed than they had been for weeks. Considerable differences of opinion existed among the observers as to the Thompson and Carnes cases, but there was general agreement that "Shockley was crazy" and the jury's verdict would somehow reflect this.

Two new faces in the audience were those of Meyer Rosenberg and Fred Flynn, notorious San Francisco bookies. Ready to turn any situation into a business venture, the two moved quietly among the groups of spectators quoting odds and inviting bets. Both quoted 100 to 1 odds for Carnes's acquittal, with Rosenberg offering 5 to 1 that there would be a murder conviction of Thompson and Shockley within four hours.

Eager for the comfort and relaxation of his Los Altos residence, Hennessy headed directly for the Southern Pacific train station and his hour-long ride home, leaving Deasy to return to the office to tie up loose ends.

Vinkler hurried to the Emporium department store a few blocks away on Market Street, where he picked up gifts for his two young daughters as a peace offering for the disruption the trial had caused in his normally placid home life. A dedicated husband and father, Vinkler always found time to spend with his family regardless of the demands of his practice. Unfortunately, over the past month, these demands had been so great that he had not been able to spend much time at home. This was not his only regret. He was deeply disappointed by his inability to focus the Thompson defense on the conditions and brutality at Alcatraz. Although he had tried repeatedly to get such evidence before the jury, he had been blocked time and again by the resolute Goodman.

Sullivan and Zamloch, both busy young trial lawyers, headed for their offices, eager to get to the backlog of legal work awaiting their attention. Both would have welcomed an evening of relaxation, but chose instead to begin reviewing and responding to correspondence that had piled up during the past month. Zamloch was still smarting over the prosecution's flip-flop on the death penalty. More that anything he was angered that he hadn't seen it coming, although he knew that there was nothing he could have done to prevent it.

Spagnoli joined *Examiner* reporters Clint Mosher and Dick Pollard, and headed for the News Room, a favorite San Francisco newspaper haunt. Many bourbon and waters later, he hailed a cab at 5th and Mission and headed for home.

29

The day brought more gray, cold weather. Rain was in the forecast and many of the jurors arrived carrying umbrellas. The crowd of spectators was markedly reduced, limited to the regular court watchers, a few employees from the building, and the two bookies.

Goodman, like many judges, enjoyed instructing juries. It was the time when the judge became the center of attention without having to share the limelight with the attorneys. Goodman approached the task in a professorial, yet fatherly manner. Although he read the instructions, he knew them so well that he seemed to be making an extemporaneous presentation. He had a standard set of criminal instructions, which he modified only slightly from case to case. Since every trial was different and the attorneys would always make unique instruction requests, no two sets of instructions were ever the same.

The attorneys looked upon jury instructions as a necessary but boring part of the trial. They knew exactly what was coming since the instructions had all previously been discussed and debated with the judge. Since no objections could be raised at this stage, there was only limited motivation for the attorneys to pay close attention. Instructions were dry, uninteresting statements of the applicable principles of law that the jury had to follow during their deliberations. They included definitions, elements of the crimes, factors to be considered during deliberations, and suggestions as to how the jurors should approach their task. Instructions were complex and technical, and there existed a sharp dichotomy among lawyers as to how much of them the juries understood.

Many litigators felt that the most effective tactical use of instructions was to educate the jury during argument as to the critical instructions. Successful trial lawyers would therefore read, paraphrase, and explain to the jury the few instructions they considered important. Use of the precise language of the instruction was key, so that when the jury heard the specific instruction coming from the judge, their attention would be drawn to it.

Both Hennessy and Sullivan had followed that practice during their arguments. Hennessy concentrated extensively on the definitions of both conspiracy and aiding and abetting, explaining how the Government's evidence fit into the definitions and how the elements of the crime had been established. He also focused on the questions of the alleged brutality, excessive force used in quelling the riot, and allegations of harsh living conditions, all the time cautioning the jury that Goodman would direct them to ignore this evidence in arriving at their verdicts. Sullivan had repeatedly read and paraphrased the insanity instructions, comparing the language to the testimony of Dr. Alden.

In contrast, Spagnoli paid so little attention to instructions that he not only failed to discuss them during his argument, but had not even submitted proposed instructions for Goodman's consideration. Instead, he relied on the other defense attorneys to propose favorable instructions and the judge to frame appropriate statements of the law.

One barometer of how effectively a trial attorney had educated the jury as to a critical instruction was if the reading of the instruction prompted any reaction. Sullivan felt a jolt of excitement when two of the female jurors in the front row made eye contact with him during Goodman's reading of the insanity instruction.

Goodman's instructions were standard and uneventful. True to his word, however, he took time to make it clear to the jury that Alcatraz conditions and procedures were not to be considered by them in determining the guilt or innocence of the defendants. This instruction carried great meaning for those members of the press who had also covered the Henri Young case. There was an exchange of silent, knowing glances among the reporters, who were both interested and amused by Goodman's firm denunciation of the Alcatraz brutality issue. It was obvious that the judge was doing what he could to prevent a rerun of the Henri Young debacle.

"In that connection," Goodman read with deliberate emphasis, "I deem it important to point out certain matters with which the jury is not to be concerned in determining this case. The jury is not to be concerned with the manner in which the discipline of the inmates of Alcatraz is maintained by the custodial officers. Whether discipline was too severe or proper is not an issue in this case and you shall disregard such matters as extraneous to the question that you have to decide, namely the guilt or innocence of the defendants. Likewise, whether the officers were brave or cautious or inefficient during the events of the attempted jailbreak is incompetent and immaterial. How much or how little force the custodial officers used in suppressing the escape attempt, is not a matter for your consideration. What kinds of prisons the United States maintains, the manner of their maintenance, or the type of inmate selected for imprisonment at different prisons are matters entrusted to the Department of Justice. Such issues are also extraneous to the matters to be decided by you."

Following the reading of the instructions, Goodman inquired of the attorneys as to whether any of them wished to note exceptions. Hennessy, satisfied with the instructions, declined, while all three defense attorneys, outside the presence of the jury, stated various objections and exceptions to the judge's version of the law of the case.

With the jury sequestered in the jury room, Hennessy and Deasy retreated to their offices on the floor above, while the defense attorneys took up their vigil in the courtroom. Their offices were all several blocks away, and none of them were allowed the luxury of returning to their chambers. The attorneys were required to remain in the building or keep the bailiff advised of their whereabouts.

As usual, Spagnoli joined the knot of newspapermen enjoying cigarettes in the corridor. "Boy, Ernie," quipped the heavy-set, red-faced *Examiner* reporter, who had sat through the entire trial, "Goodman really stuck it to you guys and your anti-Alcatraz argument. I couldn't believe it. It's pretty obvious that he doesn't want a repeat of that Henri Young mess. I guess Mike Roche took a lot of shit for the way he handled that case and Goodman made sure he wasn't going down that same road."

"Yeah," Spagnoli dejectedly admitted, "I was never satisfied that was a good argument in our case anyway, but Vinkler thought it would work, so I let him run with it. He got a little mileage out of it in argument; but you're right, Goodman shut us down."

The newsmen headed for one of the many Mission Street bars and a liquid lunch, after advising the clerk where he should call them in the unlikely event there was a verdict in the next couple of hours. It was highly unlikely that the jury would arrive at a verdict before the noon meal. The thirsty members of the press were well aware of this and knew they had at least three hours before the jury would return from lunch. Yielding to their invitation to join them, Spagnoli left Vinkler with the courtroom watch and instructed him to call immediately if anything required his presence. Spagnoli then hurried down the hall to join the retreating reporters.

Within their first hour of deliberation, the jury sent a communication to the court requesting a complete copy of the trial transcript. The note was signed by juror number five, Donald MacLean, who had been chosen foreman. MacLean was the executive vice-president of a large corporation and resided in the affluent suburb of San Mateo. Given his executive employment, and professional bearing, the attorneys were not surprised at his selection as foreman.

The judge and attorneys quickly agreed that the jury could not receive the transcript and hastily prepared a response, which the bailiff delivered to the foreman. The judge's note advised them that since the transcript was not an exhibit it was not proper to provide them with a copy. If they wished any portion of the testimony reread, the panel could return to the courtroom for that purpose.

At 12:15, in the company of the two marshals and a matron, the panel was taken to lunch at the nearby Whitcomb Hotel, returning at 2:00. At 3:50, the jury sent the following written communication to the judge: "Is it permitted that the jury may have a copy of the judge's instructions to the jury, also the wording of the indictment? If not, the jury wishes to have read in court the part of the instructions relating to the various laws relating to murder and conspiracy and the indictment." Fifteen minutes later the jury was back in the box and court was in session.

Foreman MacLean also requested that the direct examination of Captain Weinhold be reread. Goodman read back the full text of the indictment, then reread the instructions on murder and conspiracy. When one of the jurors spontaneously called out, "aiding and abetting," Goodman went on to read that instruction as well.

"You say you wish to have the direct examination of Captain Weinhold read?" Goodman inquired of the foreman.

"We wish particularly to hear that testimony of Captain Weinhold in which he described those who were before his cell at the time, or just preceeding the time he was shot," MacLean responded.

Goodman read back the witness's testimony without emphasis or inflection. Weinhold's testimony placed Cretzer and Shockley in front of the cell at the time of the shooting. After the shooting he saw Cretzer, Shockley, and Thompson in front of the cell, the latter holding the rifle. By 4:30, the jury was ready to return to their deliberations.

The jury's request was not a good sign for the defense. They had requested only the direct examination, and when Vinkler suggested that Goodman read the cross-examination as well, the judge refused. The testimony was extremely damaging to Shockley. Sullivan winced as he heard Weinhold's words read to the jury at so critical a point in the deliberations, for Shockley's statements did not sound like the ravings of an insane man. Sullivan wondered exactly what the jury was looking for and how they had received the testimony. *They're obviously concerned with the issue of actual presence during the shooting and how that fits as an element of the crime*, he thought to himself. He reminded himself again that nothing mattered except their finding of insanity, and that there was plenty of evidence that Sam was crazy.

The mood at the Thompson corner of the table was gloomy. Although Weinhold did not place Thompson with Cretzer during the shooting spree, he placed him in front of the cell holding a rifle moments after the gunfire. Weinhold's version exploded Thompson's alibi defense. On the other hand, Spagnoli and Vinkler took solace in the fact that Weinhold had admitted losing consciousness for some period of time, which could cause the jury to question the reliability of his observations.

Sullivan contemplated the fact that the jury had not requested any instructions on insanity. Realizing that it was possible that they had already made a finding of sanity or insanity, were still deliberating without any question, or had not as yet even reached the issue, he experienced a silent flush of embarrassment for even having considered it. *I'm becoming as paranoid as Sam*, he thought, and quickly put the question out of his mind.

Sullivan had tried, without success, to read the eyes and faces of the jurors. They gave no indication of hostility among themselves, suggesting that the deliberations were going smoothly and that no polarization existed within the group. A careful study of the entire panel provided no clue as to their thinking. Shockley, who along with the other two defendants had been brought up from the holding cell, maintained his customary blank stare throughout the entire proceeding. It appeared to Sullivan that he didn't comprehend what was going on and the attorney made no effort to explain the situation.

Thompson, shrewd and street wise, clearly understood the gravity of the situation. As the captain's testimony was read, he turned to Spagnoli and whispered, "Weinhold lied. He's a no good son of a bitch. Cretzer should've killed him." Placing his right index finger vertically across his lips, Spagnoli motioned to his client to remain silent until the jury was out of the room. Thompson did so, but glared icily at the panel.

Deliberations continued without interruption until 6:30 that evening. On Goodman's orders, the bailiffs accompanied the jurors to the Whitcomb Hotel dining room for dinner. Shortly after 8:00, they were back in the jury room to resume their deliberations.

In the courtroom, tension mounted. Sullivan paced back and forth in the deserted corridor, making small talk with the janitors as they mopped the marble floor. Hennessy made two brief visits to the courtroom during the evening, but he and Deasy remained in their offices most of the time. Zamloch half-heartedly attempted to review a new file just referred to him. It was a simple criminal matter, but the tension of the situation impaired his concentration, and he finally joined Sullivan and the janitors in the corridor.

At 9:45, Goodman sent a note to the jury suggesting that they be sequestered at the Whitcomb until morning. The court day to that point had been more than twelve hours, and the judge felt the jury had worked long enough. In response, the foreman sent back a note asking that they be given another thirty minutes of deliberation and the judge acceded. Shortly after 10:00, however, MacLean knocked on the jury room door and requested that the jury be permitted to retire. Arrangements had previously been made, and the marshals escorted the panel to the hotel for the evening. It was the first sequestered jury in San Francisco since the end of World War II. During the war, hotel space had been so limited that it was not possible to sequester juries.

Having waited hours for nothing more newsworthy than idle conversation with Spagnoli, the dwindling band of newsmen headed for the prisoner's entrance of the marshal's office, hoping to pick up some quotes from the defendants as they boarded the van for the county jail. Shockley happily shouted to the waiting reporters, "They won't convict me, I'm crazy." Thompson, ever the tough guy, passed his comment to the press through a deputy marshal. "Tell 'em I want to go the whole route, gas chamber or acquittal." It had been a long, tense day and the attorneys all slipped quietly from the now deserted building into the chill December night.

30

By 9:00, the jury had eaten breakfast and was back in the jury room. At 11:50, they sent a note to the judge. "Is it a correct statement of the law that it is not necessary that one who aids and abets in the commission of a crime shall be doing the acts constituting aiding and abetting at the precise time when the crime is committed in order to sustain his conviction as a principal?" Sharing the note with all counsel, Goodman indicated his course of action and had the jury returned to the courtroom.

Reading the jury's note back to them to confirm their request, Goodman went on to answer their inquiry. "The answer of the court to your question is no. The court has already instructed you that it is not necessary that one who aids and abets the commission of a crime shall be present at the time the crime is committed." After the judge finished his answer there was considerable nodding and whispering among the jurors.

As the judge addressed the jurors, the defense attorneys speculated as to the significance of the inquiry as to their clients. Sullivan concluded that it had nothing to do with Shockley, since his presence had been pretty well established. Vinkler worried that they were considering finding Thompson guilty even if they believed he was back in his cell when Miller was shot. This line of reasoning would be devastating for Thompson. Zamloch wondered if the jury could be thinking about Carnes, who similarly claimed that he was not present at the time of the shooting. Were they concerned about his claim that he was in the kitchen at the time of the shooting? Were they satisfied that he was in the kitchen, yet inclined to find aiding and abetting nevertheless?

The jury also asked to hear the testimony of Lieutenant Simpson commencing with when he was placed in cell 402. After scouring the record for all of Simpson's testimony dealing with the time period requested, Goodman again read to the jury. It was unusual for the judge to read back testimony, as this was usually done by the court reporter. While probably ego-driven, Goodman explained his reading of the testimony as a means of insuring total accuracy and objectivity in the reading of the transcript.

The jury's request to hear the Simpson evidence seemed particularly harmful to Shockley and Thompson. In his testimony Simpson had stated that Shockley, Thompson, Cretzer, Coy, and Carnes were all present when he was captured. Thompson carried the rifle and kept jabbing it into his back. He described how Shockley struck Sundstrom as the officer was placed in cell 402, then how he strutted back and forth in front of the cell carrying either a wrench or a club. He recounted Shockley's demands for the hostages' deaths immediately after the siren sounded, and testified that both Shockley and Carnes were present outside the cell when he was shot the second time.

The reading of Simpson's testimony went on for several minutes, a very unpleasant time for Spagnoli and Vinkler. Sullivan on the other hand, remained supremely optimistic. There was little dispute as to Shockley's conduct. Sullivan knew his case turned on the question of sanity, and it seemed evident from the jury's lack of questions that the sanity issue was not causing them any confusion. He firmly believed they would find Shockley insane and would never bring back a death penalty verdict. He knew it was dangerous to have such positive opinions, but he couldn't envision this jury ordering Shockley's death. By 12:30, Goodman had read all the requested testimony, and the jury indicated their satisfaction.

Ten minutes after leaving the courtroom, the jury announced that they had a verdict. Hennessy and Deasy, already back in their offices, were summoned by the clerk. The defense attorneys sat in tense silence. The courtroom was unusually quiet. As the defendants were led back into the courtroom, all three fidgeted nervously and took their seats without speaking.

The jury filed in and took their seats. The lawyers studied their faces for a clue as to their decision. None gave the slightest signal of what was in the bundle of verdict forms carried by Foreman MacLean.

With the jury seated, Goodman emerged from his chambers and took his place on the bench. He looked down on the near empty courtroom, and saw less than a dozen observers plus the ever-present cadre of reporters. "Mr. Foreman, has the jury agreed on a verdict?" he asked MacLean.

"Yes sir, Your Honor, we have."

"You may hand the verdicts to the marshal."

With that, the bailiff retrieved the verdict forms, which he delivered to the judge. The judge reviewed the signed verdicts, and handed them to the clerk, who had quietly stationed himself in front of the bench. "Read the verdicts, Mr. Clerk."

"Ladies and Gentlemen," proclaimed the clerk, "hearken to your verdicts as they shall stand recorded:

'We, the jury, find Sam Richard Shockley, the defendant at the bar, guilty of murder in the first degree. Signed, Donald MacLean, Foreman.'

"Just a moment," a stunned Goodman interrupted, "is that the verdict of the jury?"

"That is the unanimous verdict, Your Honor," MacLean responded.

"Very well, Mr. Clerk, you may poll the jury." With that, as everyone in the courtroom sat in anticipation of the fate of the other two defendants, the clerk laboriously polled the entire panel, asking each juror in turn whether his or her verdict was as read. Each of the twelve responded in the affirmative, after which the clerk read again:

"We the jury find Miran Edgar Thompson, the defendant at the bar, guilty of murder in the first degree. Signed, Donald MacLean, Foreman."

Again the judge directed the clerk to poll the jury and the procedure was repeated.

Finally, the clerk read:

"We the jury find Clarence Victor Carnes, the defendant at the bar, guilty of murder in the first degree, without capital punishment. Signed, Donald MacLean, Foreman."

Following the final polling of the jury, Goodman directed, 'Mr. Clerk, you may record the verdicts."

Sullivan was in a state of shock. He had been certain from the day of Alden's testimony that Shockley would be found insane. The verdict was incomprehensible. He looked over at Sam. The convict stared straight ahead, his expressionless face pale and ghostly. As always, he looked as though he didn't understand what was happening. Sullivan knew, however, that the pathetic soul did understand that he had just been sentenced to death. It would have been easier for Sullivan if Shockley hadn't displayed such a pitiful, childlike nature. Because of Sam's mental retardation, Sullivan felt the need to somehow accept the verdict for him and shelter him from the harsh world that had just pronounced his death sentence. Shockley's criminal past seemed unimportant now. All Sullivan could see before him was a man whose stunted mind was totally incapable of forming any murderous intent when he tagged along on May 2. For being in the wrong place at the wrong time and not knowing how to deal with it, he would pay with his life. Sullivan reluctantly turned to look into the stunned faces of Pat Shockley and his family on this final tragic day of their vigil.

Sullivan had seen friends and acquaintances die on the battlefields of Europe, but this experience was much harder for him to bear. Shockley was insane on May 2. He didn't know right from wrong, and the testimony of Dr. Alden had proven that. Yet, in the face of clear proof of the man's insanity, the jury had decreed that he die. The unfairness of it shattered the young lawyer. He felt a sharp pain in his abdomen, as though someone had driven a spike through his body. He swallowed hard and struggled to look professional.

"Don't worry, Sam, we'll take this up on appeal. It's a wrong result and I'll do everything I can to reverse it."

"Sure, Mr. Sullivan, sure. I know you will, Mr. Sullivan. What happens now?"

The question ripped at Sullivan's insides and his voice cracked with emotion as he responded. "Well, you and Buddy will probably be taken to San Quentin in the next day or two, and Carnes will go back to Alcatraz." Shockley said nothing more, and simply nodded affirmatively. Sullivan had intentionally not mentioned that it was Death Row at San Quentin to which Sam would be transferred.

Sullivan's thoughts were interrupted by Goodman addressing the jury. "The court wishes to extend thanks for your long and dedicated service during the trial. I know you are anxious to get to your homes and businesses and I won't detain you." As he struggled with his disappointment, Sullivan studied the judge's face. Obviously he was surprised, but it appeared to Sullivan that he was satisfied with the verdicts.

Goodman excused the jury, and the reporters scampered after them hoping for interviews they could use in the late afternoon and early morning editions. As the last juror exited, Goodman shocked the defense attorneys by looking directly at Sullivan and asking, "Now, as counsel for defendant Shockley, do you have any reason to present why judgment should not be pronounced in this case?"

A stunned Sullivan rose and announced to the court that it was his intention to move for a new trial and also to pursue an appeal. In order to do this, he intended to request the court to appoint another attorney to assist him and request that these matters be set for further argument on the following Tuesday. "Well, I see no reason why you cannot state your grounds for a new trial right now," the judge demanded, forcing the young defense lawyer to immediately frame his motion for a new trial. It was an incredible demand in a case of this complexity to require the defense to present a motion for new trial on the spur of the moment without any preparation. The trial had lasted more than a month. Seventy-four witnesses had testified and more than ninety exhibits had been placed in evidence. The trial transcript exceeded two thousand pages. A proper motion for new trial required review and analysis of all the testimony and exhibits for possible judicial error as well as extensive legal research. To be forced to make an oral motion under such circumstances was grossly unfair, and Sullivan could not believe it was happening.

Realizing that he had no choice, Sullivan related the various instances of prejudicial misconduct that came to mind. He argued that the court erred in not permitting his inmate witnesses to testify as to Shockley's sanity, and urged that by not presenting any evidence in response to Shockley's insanity evidence, the government woefully failed to carry its burden of proof that he was sane. He set forth how the defense had presented a prima facia case through Dr. Alden's testimony, demonstrating that at the time of the events in question Shockley did not know right from wrong and could not appreciate the consequences of his acts. In response, the government had presented no evidence to overcome the presumption of insanity that had unequivocally been established. In the absence of any contrary evidence from the government, the verdict could not stand.

Sullivan also complained of the judge's refusal to permit a jury inspection of the west end of the cell house and D block, arguing that the photographs and diagrams of the area were inadequate and that the jury was therefore denied critical information. He also noted numerous evidence rulings with which he took issue, pleading that he had not had time to review the entire transcript to identify all such erroneous rulings and other acts of judicial misconduct.

"And to what do you refer when you make the allegation of judicial misconduct?" Goodman demanded caustically.

Sullivan replied that he had reference to the many adverse comments made by Goodman during the trial relating to his competence as a trial attorney, his inexperience, and his handling of the case, all of which, Sullivan believed, caused the jury to draw unfavorable inferences.

Sullivan went on arguing point after point, presenting an impressive list of errors and a cogent argument for a new trial. Unfortunately, his arguments fell on deaf ears. At the conclusion of Sullivan's presentation and without even requesting comment from the prosecutor, Goodman ruled without hesitation, "Well, I think all of the matters to which you have referred counsel, have already been considered during the course of the trial. I don't believe there are any grounds for the court granting a new trial. It would simply be a repetitious reconsideration of the rulings of the court during the trial. I considered all the matters that came before me or I would not have ruled the way I did. I will deny the motion for a new trial."

Turning to Spagnoli, the judge made a similar request, seeking a response as to why judgment against his client should not immediately be pronounced. Spagnoli, like Sullivan, pleaded for additional time within which to file a formal motion, complaining that he was not prepared to go forward with an oral request for a new trial. He added that the verdict was totally unexpected by the defense and that he had given no consideration to a motion for new trial. "To force a motion at this time would be highly prejudicial to the interest of both these defendants, Your Honor; I cannot believe this is happening." Faced with no alternative but to proceed, Spagnoli and Vinkler made the best argument they could under the circumstances.

Unmoved by the points made by the aging defense lawyer or those put forth by Vinkler, Goodman denied the motion. "I do not feel there is any ground for deferring the pronouncement of judgment after the verdict of the jury in a case that has been as long and as thoroughly considered as this one," he snapped, visibly annoyed.

Although he realized that it was a lost cause, Spagnoli would not be stilled. He protested that in his view, the court had erred by instructing the jury that they could consider Thompson's entire criminal record in evaluating his credibility rather than, as the law provided, merely considering the fact that he was a convicted felon. He cited failure to provide a verdict form for the lessor-included offense of manslaughter, as well as improper instruction to the jury on the definition of aiding and abetting. He referred to a number of other errors and exceptions, urging that the court provide the defense additional time to make a formal motion.

Brushing Spagnoli's objections aside, Goodman turned to Vinkler with the impatient demand, "Do you wish to say anything more?"

Despite the judge's clear implication that he didn't want to hear any more argument, Vinkler raised the issue of the jury having been separated during the course of their deliberation, when one of the jurors was separated from the rest of the panel.

Goodman brusquely interrupted the attorney, demanding to know who was separated. When Vinkler began to provide the details of the situation, Goodman angrily cut him off and lashed out, remonstrating, "I know what you refer to. Juror #3, Mr. Elinsky, was the man who lost both legs in World War I. He was unable to walk to the Whitcomb Hotel, one block from here. As a result the court directed that an officer of the court take him there in an automobile so he could go to the hotel and sleep last night. In the opinion of the court that was not separation of the jury. There is no merit to that point." Goodman flatly refused to consider Vinkler's request for additional time and again denied the motion.

Goodman was clearly defensive about being called to task for his conduct of the previous evening. Elinsky had been pushed to and from the Whitcomb in his wheelchair for lunch and dinner, but Goodman had inexplicably altered the procedure at the evening recess. Without consulting or advising the attorneys, he directed a deputy marshal to drive Elinsky, thereby separating him from the rest of the panel, all of whom walked to the hotel. While probably an innocent mistake, and perhaps not even prejudicial error, it was contrary to law. Given the magnitude of the sentences, and the fact that the juror was alone with a federal law enforcement officer out of the presence of the other jurors, Goodman should have at least permitted the attorneys to explore the incident. Instead, he reacted with hostility, criticizing Vinkler for even raising the issue. Staggered by the judge's reaction, Vinkler backed down.

Sullivan sought to make a motion to set aside the verdict for lack of evidence that Shockley was sane, but Goodman cut him off abruptly, rejecting his claim and denying the motion.

Goodman's rulings were precipitous, almost reckless. He had clearly decided before the motions were made that no new trial would be granted in the event of a conviction, and he made no effort whatsoever to conceal his annoyance with the defense attorneys.

With his denials on the record, Goodman stated without emotion that pronouncement of judgment in the case, "…is no pleasant task. The matter of judgment is a mere formality, for the jury has already decided the case. I find no conflict with the decision of the jury in this case. Even though counsel had some brushes with the court in the matter, they have unquestionably given a sincere, earnest, and aggressive defense of each defendant."

He then decreed: "It is ordered that Sam Richard Shockley be committed to the custody of the United States Marshal and by him to be caused to be put to death in accordance with the law of the state of California.

"In the case of the defendant Miran Edgar Thompson, the judgment of the court is that he be put into the custody of the United States Marshal, to be by him caused to be put to death in the manner prescribed by the law of the State of California.

"In the case of the defendant Clarence Victor Carnes, the judgment of the court is that he be sentenced to life imprisonment, and that he be imprisoned for the remainder of his life."

These final details complete, Goodman announced that court was adjourned, ringing down the curtain on the trial phase of *The United States of America vs. Sam Richard Shockley, Miran Edgar Thompson and Clarence Victor Carnes.*

Carnes sat dejectedly, fidgeting with his fingers in his lap. He appeared to be more distressed by the verdict than either of his co-defendants. As the courtroom emptied, and the marshals readied his chains and manacles for the trip back to Alcatraz, he turned to Zamloch and spoke in a quiet voice. "I don't know how you did it, Mr. Zamloch, but you saved my life. And I thank you for that. But, you know, they're gonna kill Sam, and he's crazy. It don't make no sense. It's really lousy. Sam would have been up for parole in about eight years, and now he's gonna' die."

Zamloch was moved by the young convict's pity for Crazy Sam. He too, felt a nagging compassion for the condemned inmate and the young war hero who had so valiantly defended him. Although an appeal lay ahead, Zamloch held out little hope for Shockley's future.

The marshal assigned to Thompson began clamping on his manacles, and found himself avoiding the outlaw's gaze. Breaking the silent tension, the handsome killer forced a smile and announced, "Hell, I'm not afraid to die. If I was I would never have been in this racket. Besides, it's just as well. I'd rather have it this way than go back to that fuckin' Rock for the rest of my life."

Several reporters, their juror interviews completed, returned to the courtroom scouting additional information. Their efforts to interview the defendants were futile, as the marshals refused to permit any contact. The newsmen had to settle for brief interviews with a few Alcatraz guards. "Carnes is in the clink for the rest of his life now for sure," remarked one of the custodial officers. "By count he's gonna be eighty years old before he's eligible for parole."

"Yeah," another officer volunteered, "that old convict joke really applies to Carnes. They describe the Alcatraz prison launch as the fastest boat in the world. It can take you so far in ten minutes that it will take you twenty years to get back. It'll be a helluva' lot longer than that in Carnes's case."

The reporters' jury interviews had revealed some unexpected information. There were a total of six ballots taken during the deliberation. Contrary to the expectations of the press and courtroom observers, the jury came to an early conclusion that Shockley was both sane and an active participant in the bloody affair. Thompson, however, presented a more difficult problem, and they discussed the case against him during much of Friday and all Saturday morning. The jury placed considerable emphasis on the testimony of Lageson and his handwritten list of the participants, as well as the testimony of Weinhold. They were particularly impressed by the fact that the captain placed Thompson in front of the cell with a rifle immediately after the shooting. The fact that Weinhold was in and out of consciousness after being wounded did not diminish his credibility.

According to the jurors, Carnes was treated compassionately because of his age and the kindness he had extended to Miller in allowing his hands to be untied. Hennessy's suggestion of "special consideration" for the young inmate was also a factor in the minds of many of them.

At the defense end of the counsel table, the major shock was the jury's treatment of Shockley's insanity defense. The defense attorneys had conflicting views on many of the issues, but there was complete agreement that, under the law of the case, Crazy Sam was insane. Even Hennessy expressed surprise at the verdict. The hard-nosed prosecutor repeatedly commented, "I can't believe the Shockley verdict." The case also carried the distinction of being the first and only time that an inmate had received the death sentence for a crime committed on the Rock.

As the marshals and custodial officers locked the manacles and leg irons on the defendants, young Carnes looked sadly into the eyes of his fellow inmates. He was heading back to Alcatraz, but Shockley and Thompson would be taken to the city prison for transportation to San Quentin's Death Row. "Good luck to you guys, okay? he stated softly. "Hang in there, Injun Joe," Thompson replied confidently. "We'll see you later."

Shockley stood numbly silent, staring straight ahead.

EPILOGUE

Post-Trial Proceedings

The first post-trial matter dealt with by Judge Goodman was his contempt ruling as to Sullivan. During a subdued hearing a few days after the trial, Goodman delivered a mild admonition to the young lawyer and fined him $25.00.

Within three days of the jury verdict, Sullivan filed a Notice of Appeal seeking relief from the Ninth Circuit Court of Appeal. Less than a week later Spagnoli and Vinkler filed a similar notice on behalf of Thompson. On August 9, 1947 the brief on behalf of Shockley, prepared jointly by trial counsel William Sullivan and associate counsel James E. "Ned" Burns was filed. It took Spagnoli and Vinkler an additional two months to file their opening brief.

As he had been during the trial, Thompson was a contentious client. He insisted on participating actively in the appellate proceedings, frequently demanding that his attorneys follow his recommendations regarding tactics and legal arguments. Spagnoli knew that the likelihood of overturning the verdict on appeal was slim, and was not as solicitous of Thompson's input as he had been during the trial. Friction developed between the two men and Thompson decided he was not being properly represented. His dissatisfaction soon turned into indignation and he began complaining bitterly about Spagnoli's representation. One of those to whom he complained was his mother, who resided in Texas and with whom he corresponded on a regular basis. Concerned, she scraped together what funds she could and made them available to her son.

The Appeal

On September 25, 1947, Thompson wrote to the court complaining that his attorney was not giving the case adequate attention. This complaint apparently stemmed from the fact that Spagnoli had obtained several extensions of time within which to file the opening brief. Upon receipt of Thompson's letter the court directed that Spagnoli file his opening brief without further delay. This was accomplished on October 11, 1947.

On October 9, 1947, it was suspected that Shockley and Thompson, along with inmate Erwin A. Walker were planning an escape from San Quentin's Death Row. A search of Shockley's and Thompson's cells was negative, but various contraband material was found in Walker's cell. In addition to a homemade wrench that fit the bolts on the cell door perfectly, a number of homemade keys, one of which fit the cell door, were discovered. The contraband was confiscated and the matter closed. No disciplinary action was taken as to any of the inmates involved.

The opening brief revealed the struggle Spagnoli and Vinkler faced in shaping an appellate argument adequate to overturn the jury's verdict. They enumerated fifteen specific claims of error by the trial judge, most of which had little merit. At the end of the brief the attorneys included an additional fifteen points raised by Thompson himself, which had even less merit.

The defense focused on Goodman's instructions to the jury regarding credibility of witnesses. Spagnoli and Vinkler argued that the instructions created the impression that greater weight should be given to the government's witnesses than to those called by the defense, since the jury was told they could consider a witness's criminal record in evaluating his testimony. In fact, the law permitted impeachment by showing conviction of a felony, and unfortunately for Thompson, all his witnesses were convicted felons. The instruction was unfavorable to the defense case, but proper.

The brief also cited several examples of alleged misconduct by the prosecuting attorney and prejudicial remarks by the judge. Most of these were highly technical and would not constitute prejudicial error such that an appellate court would reverse the court below. The most critical argument was the claimed error in admitting evidence regarding the death of Stites. Pointing out to the justices that this evidence was not only irrelevant but highly prejudicial, Spagnoli and Vinkler restated the unsuccessful arguments they made at the trial.

The situation between Thompson and his attorneys continued to deteriorate, and on the day before Spagnoli and Vinkler filed their reply brief, Thompson made an in *Pro Persona* motion to the Ninth Circuit to discharge them as his attorneys. The appellate court took no immediate action on the motion, but changes in Thompson's representation were already underway. At the request of Thompson's mother, Melvin Belli, a prominent, young San Francisco trial lawyer agreed to enter the case. On December 29, 1947 with assistance from Van H. Pinney, an attorney skilled in appellate work, Belli filed an *Amicus Curiae* brief on Thompson's behalf. Soon thereafter, Thompson notified the court by letter that Spagnoli and Vinkler were discharged and Melvin M. Belli was his new counsel.

In the amicus brief Belli set forth three types of error committed by the trial judge, each of which deprived the defendants of a fair trial. By far the most egregious misconduct, he alleged, was the lack of due process occasioned by Goodman's outspoken bias and hostility. Secondly, Belli alleged error in Goodman's refusal to receive affidavits as to jury misconduct and on the issue of a new trial. Finally, he asserted a series of errors in the instructions to the jury.

Belli cited thirteen occasions when Goodman cut short the defense attorneys or admonished them to speed up the trial, thereby interfering with their ability to provide a proper defense. He cited frequent instances of Goodman complaining that the defense attorneys were "…consuming too much time," and alleged that he repeatedly refused to allow defense counsel to argue points of law or cite authorities in the interest of expediency. Belli argued that despite the fact that the defendants were on trial for their lives, Goodman was preoccupied with moving the case along rather than assuring that the defendants received a fair trial.

Belli also argued that at times Goodman had literally become an advocate for the prosecution. On these occasions, the judge made his own objections and then ruled against the defense, even though the prosecution had not objected. Belli pointed out instances where Goodman sustained prosecution objections although Hennessy failed to state grounds for the objection.

Belli and Pinney enumerated fifteen examples of improper comments by the court. Goodman repeatedly castigated the defense attorneys, but never once admonished the prosecution. The defense attorneys were repeatedly embarrassed by stinging comments from the bench, yet no such remarks were ever directed at the prosecutors. Belli noted several instances where the prosecution baited the defense attorneys into making argumentative statements, and Goodman chastised only the defense.

In all, Belli documented thirty-four examples of error by Goodman. Quoting from a leading appellate case he urged, "The trial judge should be so impartial in the trial of a criminal case that by no word or act of his may the jury be able to detect his personal convictions as to the guilt or innocence of the accused." Belli argued that repeated misconduct of the trial judge could only infect the jury with antagonism and prejudice toward the defendants.

The second main argument raised in Belli's brief dealt with Goodman's refusal to allow the defense attorneys time to investigate jury misconduct or adequately prepare motions for a new trial. Belli argued whether or not any impropriety actually occurred between Juror Elinsky and the marshal when Elinsky was separated from the rest of the panel, the fact that the judge denied the defense attorneys an opportunity to investigate, and sternly admonished Vinkler for even raising the question, constituted prejudicial error.

Belli further contended that it was inconceivable in a capital case of such magnitude for the judge to deny the defense attorneys time to prepare a formal motion for a new trial. Goodman expressed his intention to enter judgment immediately upon discharge of the jury. When counsel for Thompson and Shockley indicated an intention to move for a new trial, Goodman forced them to make the motion immediately with no preparation. He then denied both motions after no deliberation or any opposition from the prosecution.

The Shockley appeal raised a number of legal issues, but Sullivan and Burns concentrated on two major points. They first argued that the trial court's failure to grant the Motion to Sever, which required Shockley to be tried with the other two defendants, deprived him of a fair trial. Secondly, they contended that the government had not sustained its burden of proof that Shockley was sane in view of the convincing insanity evidence presented by the defense.

Shockley's brief urged that Burns had been Shockley's attorney from the outset, and it was only because of a potential conflict that Sullivan was brought into the case. He attempted to do his best, but Sullivan's inexperience resulted in repeated remonstrations and criticism by Goodman in front of the jury. Ultimately the judge held him in contempt. The brief alleged that as a result of being denied a separate trial, Shockley was not only denied the attorney of his choice, but was given an attorney who made numerous mistakes during the trial and was highly criticized by the judge. Burns and Sullivan cited thirteen occasions where Sullivan was reprimanded, admonished or embarrassed by Goodman in the presence of the jury. They argued that the issue was not the competence or conduct of the attorney, but whether the defendant received a fair trial.

Shockley's brief also argued that prejudice was demonstrated by the fact that the same jury gave Carnes a life term and Shockley the death penalty. Carnes had been in on the escape from the start and was the first inmate to wield a weapon. The evidence was uncontradicted that Carnes was far more involved in the details of the break than Shockley, but since his attorney was not the target of judicial abuse, the jury was more lenient with him.

Burns and Sullivan also made a strong argument as to the government's failure to prove Shockley's sanity. It was the government's burden to prove the defendant's sanity beyond a reasonable doubt, and the defense contended that the evidence of insanity was overwhelming. Dr. Alden, a highly respected psychiatrist, testified that in his opinion "…it was not only possible but probable that Shockley's judgment was so distorted at the time of the escape that he was unable to comprehend the nature and consequences of his actions." Alden further testified that "…under the circumstances that existed it was quite possible that the defendant did not know right from wrong." Dr. Alden's testimony was unchallenged and established that Shockley met the legal test for insanity.

The defense also argued that the judge's conduct was prejudicial. Goodman permitted the government to present testimony from hostage witnesses that Shockley appeared normal and sane, but denied Sullivan the opportunity to present inmate testimony as to Shockley's insanity. Goodman ruled that, with the exception of Franklin, none of the inmate witnesses, despite their close association with Shockley, had established an intimate enough relationship with him to express an opinion as to his sanity.

The Shockley case also benefited from Belli's amicus brief. Belli concluded that Goodman had committed so much error in his repeated attacks on Sullivan that a fair trial for Thompson was impossible. He argued that the judge imbued the jury with a sense of guilt as to the "depraved defendants." He further urged, "Time and again the learned trial judge indicated that the trial had 'already taken too long.' The lives of three men were being forfeited, yet the judge so repeatedly showed his impatience that it became infectious and even one of the jurors expressed himself as wanting to be done with the case as soon as possible."

The Government's response brief quoted extensively from the trial transcript, citing the hostage testimony supporting the charges of aiding and abetting and conspiracy. Hennessy and Deasy argued that conviction was a factual matter, and that the jury had considered the evidence and concluded there was sufficient evidence to convict.

On the sanity issue, once again, the government relied on the hostage testimony. The prosecutors advanced the incredible argument that: "Reading the entire testimony it is apparent that he (Dr. Alden) did not express any opinion as to the sanity of Shockley on May 2, 1946 at the time of the slaying of guard Miller." This statement appears in Hennessy's brief despite the fact that on a number of occasions Alden expressed the opinion that Shockley did not know the nature and consequences of his acts on the day of the escape attempt.

THE APPELLATE COURT OPINION

On March 10, 1948 Justice Bone, circuit judge of the Ninth Circuit Court of Appeal, wrote the court's opinion with Justices Garrecht and Healy concurring. The opinion began with a summary of the facts, which did not coincide with the facts developed during the trial. As feared by the defense, the justices concluded that Stites was killed by Cretzer. In their factual statement, the justices announced, "During this escape attempt two guards and three inmates were killed and thirteen guards were wounded. Both guards were killed by Cretzer..."

Describing Judge Goodman as "an able and experienced jurist," Justice Bone placed the blame for the trial judge's remarks on the defense attorneys, noting that: "The energetic and aggressive defense lawyers did not yield gracefully to his (Goodman's) rulings. Upon these occasions they couched their protests in exceedingly pungent, vigorous, and even profane speech...the replies of the judge in attempting to answer these protests formed the basis for appellants' contention that they prejudiced the defense in the minds of the jury." The justices concluded that the comments between Goodman and the defense attorneys did not mislead or prejudice the jurors. Announcing their faith in the federal jury system, the justices went on to state, "We cannot abandon our faith in the capacity and desire of a federal jury to avoid being mired in irrelevancies, and the record does not reveal that the jurors in the case lost or discarded their innate sense of fair play and were inspired to render a verdict not based entirely on the evidence."

As to the sufficiency of the evidence, the court quoted liberally from the testimony of the hostages who observed Shockley and Thompson standing in front of the cells urging Crtezer to kill the hostages. Inexplicably, the court again referred to the death of Harold Stites, stating unequivocally that he was shot and killed by Cretzer. After a review of the hostage testimony, the justices concluded that: "The record convinces us that the evidence introduced to prove the facts outlined above was properly admitted and that it fully supported the verdict...that at the time of the shooting both defendants actively engaged in the execution of the common purpose and design of the conspiracy and did actively aid and abet inmate Cretzer in his act of shooting guard Miller and they did urge and counsel Cretzer to commit this offense."

In response to the defense argument that various parts of the trial court's instructions were erroneous, the justices refused to consider the issue because defense counsel had not registered their objections at the time the instructions were read. This was a highly technical ruling since the attorneys had stated their objections during a conference with the judge prior to the instructions being read to the jury. Since two lives depended on the outcome of the appeal, it was also a particularly harsh ruling. Because errors in the instructions constituted the major argument on behalf of Thompson, the court's ruling eliminated the bulk of his appellate argument.

The court dismissed the jury separation issue with almost no explanation. Stating there was nothing in the record to indicate that Elinsky's separation from the rest of the panel affected the verdict, the justices concluded that even if it was error, there was no showing of prejudice. Not mentioned by the court was the fact that as a result of the trial court's ruling the defendants were prevented from establishing prejudice.

By far the most puzzling aspect of the opinion was the manner in which the justices addressed Shockley's insanity defense. The appellate court resolved this critical issue in only three sentences and a footnote. The justices acknowledged that the defense had been raised, but never mentioned that the burden of proof was with the prosecution. The opinion did not discuss any of the facts relating to the insanity issue. The justices simply announced that the trial court submitted the question to the jury and the jury concluded that Shockley was sane. The court's explanation was set forth in a footnote. The justices noted, "Prior to the trial the court ordered examination of Shockley had taken place. At the time of the examination the doctor had found Shockley able to understand the nature and consequences of his action and capable of understanding the nature of the charges against him." The court then added the incredible comment, "The physician expressed no opinion in this report (or in his subsequent testimony at the trial) as to the sanity of Shockley on May 2, 1946."

~

Defense counsel immediately filed a Motion for Reconsideration on behalf of each defendant. These were denied. On June 14, 1948, the United States Supreme Court denied a petition for *Certiorari* without opinion or comment. This exhausted the defendants' judicial remedies, and Judge Goodman set the executions for September 24, 1948. On August 24, pursuant to motions filed on behalf of both men, Goodman stayed the executions until December 3 to permit more time for clemency pleas to be made to President Harry Truman.

Following the August 24 hearing, Shockley was being returned to San Quentin when the automobile in which he was riding was involved in a serious accident. The vehicle, driven by Deputy United States Marshal Emil Canepa, blew a tire while traveling at high speed just north of the Golden Gate Bridge. The automobile went into a spin and narrowly missed going over an embankment, which would probably have resulted in serious injury or death to the occupants.

When President Truman denied his bid for executive clemency, Shockley accepted his fate and rejected any further efforts to stay the execution. Thompson, representing himself, continued to prepare and file briefs and petitions seeking to stay his execution and obtain further review. On November 6, 1948 he presented a petition endorsed by 2745 individuals to President Truman. He then filed a lengthy petition seeking a stay. By this time the two defendants had developed a deep hatred for one another and, although they occupied adjoining death row cells, never spoke.

THE EXECUTION

At seven o'clock on the evening of Thursday December 2, 1948 Shockley ate a large chicken dinner and retired for the night. He slept soundly, and woke at 7:30 on the morning of his execution. He rejected all offers of spiritual aid with the terse comment, "Don't bother me—and that includes the chaplain."

At 5:00 Thursday evening, Thompson dispatched a garbled telegram to the U.S. Supreme Court begging for a further stay of execution. He then called for Mrs. Bessie Clayton of the San Francisco Four Square Gospel Church, who visited with him in his cell for three and a half hours. She departed at 10:00, after which Thompson worked all night on legal papers he intended to file when the Supreme Court granted his stay. He ate four light meals during the night. As he was taken from his cell just before

10:00 A.M. Friday for the fifteen-foot walk to the gas chamber, Thompson asked Deputy U.S. Marshal John Roseen if the court had acted on his telegram. Advised that there had been no reply, he pleaded for a delay until the court's answer was received. This request was denied. In fact, the court had already rejected Thompson's final plea.

In the gas chamber the men were strapped in the two chairs back to back. They were dressed alike, in dark trousers and white shirts open at the neck. Shockley appeared pale and emaciated, twenty-five pounds lighter than at the trial. He kept his head bowed, never lifting his eyes. Neither man spoke. As the door to the chamber closed, Thompson spoke to Shockley, but Shockley did not react. Thompson forced a wan smile.

Among the official witnesses to the executions were three Alcatraz officers: Robert Baker, Frank Johnson, and Joe Steere. As the two men in the gas chamber took their first breath of the deadly cyanide gas, their heads slumped forward on their chests. When it was announced that both men were dead, Baker remarked, "That makes it five to two. It's a little more even now."

THE LATER YEARS

CLARENCE V. CARNES

Carnes was returned to Alcatraz and placed in isolation where he remained for more than six years. He was assigned a cell next to Robert Stroud with whom he became friends. Stroud was an excellent chess player and the two played every day. Each man maintained a board and two complete chess sets and called out the moves and positions of the various pieces. By the time he returned to the general prison population, Carnes was an accomplished chess player and reigned as prison champion for more than ten years.

In January of 1963, just four months before Alcatraz was closed, Carnes was transferred to the Medical Center in Springfield, Missouri for gallbladder surgery. He was thirty-six years of age and had served twenty years in prison, seventeen and a half of those years on Alcatraz.

Following his surgery, Carnes was transferred to Leavenworth. There, he worked at various clerical jobs and comported himself as a model prisoner. He earned a high school equivalency certificate, and completed numerous college courses.

In 1974, Carnes was paroled to the custody of his sister in Kansas City, Missouri. He had weathered some of the toughest prisons in America, but the aging Choctaw could not survive "on the outside." He found the free life lonely, frightening, and overwhelming. Unable to cope with his new status, Carnes intentionally violated his parole in 1976 so he could return to prison. He served an additional eighteen months in Leavenworth, and was paroled again in 1978.

In 1979, Carnes's autobiography was purchased by a Hollywood production company and developed into a two-part television movie. Carnes was hired as a consultant, and was paid $20,000. He spent several months on Hollywood sound stages and on location at Alcatraz. The movie, *Alcatraz—The Whole Shocking Story* aired in 1980.

By that time Carnes's $20,000 had been dissipated on high living, alcohol, and unpaid loans to "friends." His health began to fail and he slipped into the oblivion of life on the Kansas City streets. He lived in halfway houses, vacant buildings and on the street until his alcohol-ravaged body gave out. Suffering from diabetes and numerous other medical disorders, he was again confined in the medical facility in Springfield. An entry in his file made February 2, 1987 summarized his status:

"Carnes remains very much an institutionalized individual. He suffers from alcoholism, diabetes, and loneliness. He has most recently stated that he wants to die in a federal penal institution rather than an old folks home. Carnes states he will refuse any release from parole. He has little else but the federal system to live in and for. Carnes has great difficulty adjusting to community living. Carnes is no threat to anyone but himself. I believe he is as stable as he ever will be. Prison is home.

Clarence Carnes died of AIDS at the U.S. Medical Center for Federal Prisoners, Springfield, Missouri, in 1988 at the age of 61.

ERNEST B. LAGESON

Ernest Lageson continued as an Alcatraz custodial officer until January 1948, when he resigned to resume his career as an educator. He accepted employment as a high school biology and history teacher in Pittsburg, California.

Back in education, Lageson was able to do what he could not do at Alcatraz, have a meaningful positive impact on the lives of his students. He was one of the most respected teachers in the school and his "velvet-fisted" discipline altered the lives of several young men, who without his counsel and guidance may well have ended up like the Thompsons and Carneses with whom he had dealt on Alcatraz.

In 1952, Lageson became assistant principal and dean of boys at Pittsburg Jr. High School. He died of cancer in the summer of 1953 at the age of 42.

ROBERT BAKER

Following his recovery, Baker returned to Alcatraz and worked until his retirement. He continued to reside north of San Francisco in Marin County, and upon retirement developed an interest in the wine industry. He accepted employment with the Almaden Winery in St. Helena, California where he worked until his death.

PHILLIP R. BERGEN

In time, Bergen was appointed captain of the guards, a post he held for several years. He left the island after serving there for sixteen years. He subsequently served as correctional inspector, Federal Bureau of Prisons, and as associate warden at the Federal Correctional Institution at La Tuna, Texas. Now in his nineties, he is retired and resides in Arizona.

ROBERT C. BRISTOW

Following his retirement from Alcatraz, Bristow accepted employment as a custodian in the Sacramento School District and he and his wife, Irene, lived in the Sacramento area until their deaths.

BERT A. BURCH

Upon his retirement from Alcatraz, Burch moved to Arizona where he lived with his son Dean until his death.

JOSEPH V. BURDETT

Burdett retired from Alcatraz and moved to a retirement community near Davis, California, where he lived until his death. Also residing there was Frank Johnson, who was on duty in the Main Tower when the riot began and was involved in the re-capture of the west gun gallery.

CECIL D. CORWIN

Following a lengthy period of convalescence and rehabilitation, Corwin returned to duty. Several years later he was investigated for allegedly carrying unauthorized letters out of the prison for inmates. Soon after the investigation began, Corwin retired and the matter was dropped. He and his wife moved to Stockton, California and later to Long Beach, California where he resided until his death.

CLIFFORD G. FISH

Fish continued on at Alcatraz as the armory officer until his retirement. He presently lives in Northern California.

EDWARD J. MILLER

E.J. "Jughead" Miller retired in 1947. He and his wife returned to Leavenworth, Kansas where he had begun his career in the Federal Prison Service thirty years earlier. Failing health overtook him. He struggled with diabetes and a serious heart condition. He died soon after retiring.

JOSEPH H. SIMPSON

Because of his wounds, Simpson never returned to active duty, and received a medical retirement. He and is wife moved to Leavenworth, Kansas, where they lived until their deaths.

CARL W. SUNDSTROM

Sundstrom resumed his duties as prison records clerk and held that post until his retirement. He continued to live in San Francisco and maintained contact with his many friends on the island. He suffered a fatal stroke after several years in retirement.

JAMES A. JOHNSTON

Warden Johnston retired in April 1948 at the age of 74, while the appeals of Shockley and Thompson were still pending. He was then appointed by President Harry Truman to the United States Board of Parole, where he served for several years as one of the board's most distinguished and effective parole judges. Johnston died in San Francisco at the age of 84.

Captain Henry W. Weinhold

The injuries suffered by Captain Weinhold prevented his return to work and he received a medical retirement from the Bureau of Prisons. He moved to San Diego with his wife to be near their daughter. He suffered a fatal heart attack in 1967.

Louis E. Goodman

Judge Goodman served with distinction on the Federal District Court until his death in September 1961. He presided over several noteworthy cases including the Tule Lake Japanese citizenship hearings, The German Bund denaturalization cases, and the Harry Bridges denaturalization case. At the time of his death, Judge Goodman was the Chief Judge of the United States District Court, Southern Division, Northern District of California.

Frank J. Hennessy

Hennessy continued to serve as United States Attorney for the Northern District of California until his retirement in 1951. He was periodically mentioned as a candidate for a federal judgeship, but he did not enjoy the same personal relationship with President Truman that he had with Roosevelt, and he was never appointed. Hennessy died in 1957 at the age of 77.

James E. "Ned" Burns

Ned Burns enjoyed a long and distinguished career as one of the top federal court trial lawyers in the country, specializing in defense of white-collar crime. He gained his greatest fame representing defendants in the 1952 Internal Revenue Service scandals. He also represented many prominent criminal defendants, including Sebastino Nani of the Waxy Gordan narcotics ring and prominent San Francisco attorney Vincent Hallinan and his wife Vivian in federal tax evasion charges. He taught classes at the University of San Francisco Law School and gave so freely of his time that he was known in the profession as the "Friend of the Indigents."

Burns died in 1964 at the height of his career following a long battle with cancer. He was 51.

ERNEST SPAGNOLI

Spagnoli continued to practice at a declining rate into the early 1950s. Following the death of Clare, his wife of more than twenty-five years, he lived with his sister, Roma DeRoza in San Francisco until his death in 1972 at age 85.

WILLIAM A. SULLIVAN

In 1948, Sullivan married Kay Broad, the sister of his friend, attorney John Broad. Together they had six children. In the early 1950s Sullivan moved his family and practice to San Mateo, a suburb south of San Francisco. Here he maintained a successful general practice and was active in community affairs for more than thirty years.

Sullivan died in March of 1986. His widow, Kay Sullivan, resides in Issaquah, Washington.

AARON VINKLER

Vinkler continued to successfully pursue his law practice and synagogue activities until his death in July of 1963. His widow still resides in San Francisco. His daughters Hermine and Lois died in 1999 and 2000, respectively.

ARCHER ZAMLOCH

Zamloch's career flourished following the Alcatraz trial until June of 1950, when he was indicted by federal authorities on charges of conspiracy to obstruct justice and bribery of a witness. The charges arose out of a narcotics case in which Zamloch acted as defense attorney for the accused. In the highly publicized trial that followed, he was prosecuted by Deputy U.S. Attorney Joseph Karesh and defended by his law partner James Martin MacInnis. Following a two-week trial he was convicted and sentenced to federal prison. In July of 1952 he was disbarred.

On January 5, 1960 the California Supreme Court reinstated Zamloch to the practice of law. He returned to his profession in Southern California and enjoyed a highly successful civil law practice until his retirement. Now 85 years old, he resides in Southern California.

DR. JOHN ALDEN

Dr. Alden continued to practice psychiatry in his San Francisco office until he was in his nineties. He died in 1998 from injuries he received in an automobile accident.

ALCATRAZ CLOSES

On March 21, 1963 all of the inmates were removed from Alcatraz, and on May 15, 1963, seventeen years after the bloody outbreak of 1946, Alcatraz Island prison was officially closed. Many of the inmates were transferred to the new federal maximum security in Marion, Illinois. Today Alcatraz is part of the United States Department of the Interior, National Park Service. It is a property within the Golden Gate National Recreation Area and is operated as a national park and museum. Approximately one and a half million visitors a year tour the island and its remaining structures. During the twenty-eight years Alcatraz functioned as a federal prison a total of thirty-four inmates took part in fourteen escape attempts. (Cretzer and Shockley each made two escape attempts, so technically there were thirty-six inmate attempts) Of this total, twenty-three were recaptured, seven were shot and killed, one drowned, and five disappeared without a trace in the frigid, swirling waters of the bay. No prisoner is ever known to have escaped from Alcatraz and lived.

ERNEST B. LAGESON received a BS degree in Business Administration from the University of California, Berkeley in 1954. He spent two years in the Navy and graduated from Boalt Hall School of Law, University of California, Berkeley in 1959. He began his career as a deputy district attorney in Contra Costa County. In 1961 he joined the San Francisco law firm of Bronson, Bronson, & McKinnon as a trial lawyer. Over the next twenty-five years he became a nationally known trial attorney. He was a member of such prestigious trial lawyer associations as the American College of Trial Lawyers, the American Board of Trial Advocates, and the International Association of Defense Counsel. In 1986 he served as President of the Defense Research Institute, a national trial lawyer organization. Lageson concluded his active legal career as a partner in the Walnut Creek law firm of Archer, McComas & Lageson, retiring in 1992. He and his wife, Jeanne, live in Kensington, CA. They have two grown children, Kristine Cardall and Ernest B. Lageson III, and five grandchildren. Mr. Lageson's first book, *Battle at Alcatraz*, was published in 1999. He has also written *The Other Alcatraz*, published in 2006, and *Guarding the Rock*, published in 2008.

lagesoneb@aol.com